of the Dawn

34

Story & Art by
Mizuho Kusanagi

Yona of the Dawn

Volume 34

CONTENTS

YON-HI.

I'VE EXECUTED ALL OF THE PRIESTS.

NOW NO ONE CAN LEARN YOUR SECRET...

...OR SNOOP AROUND OR TRY TO TAKE ADVANTAGE OF YOU.

I'LL MAKE SURE IL KEEPS QUIET.

Yona of the Dawn

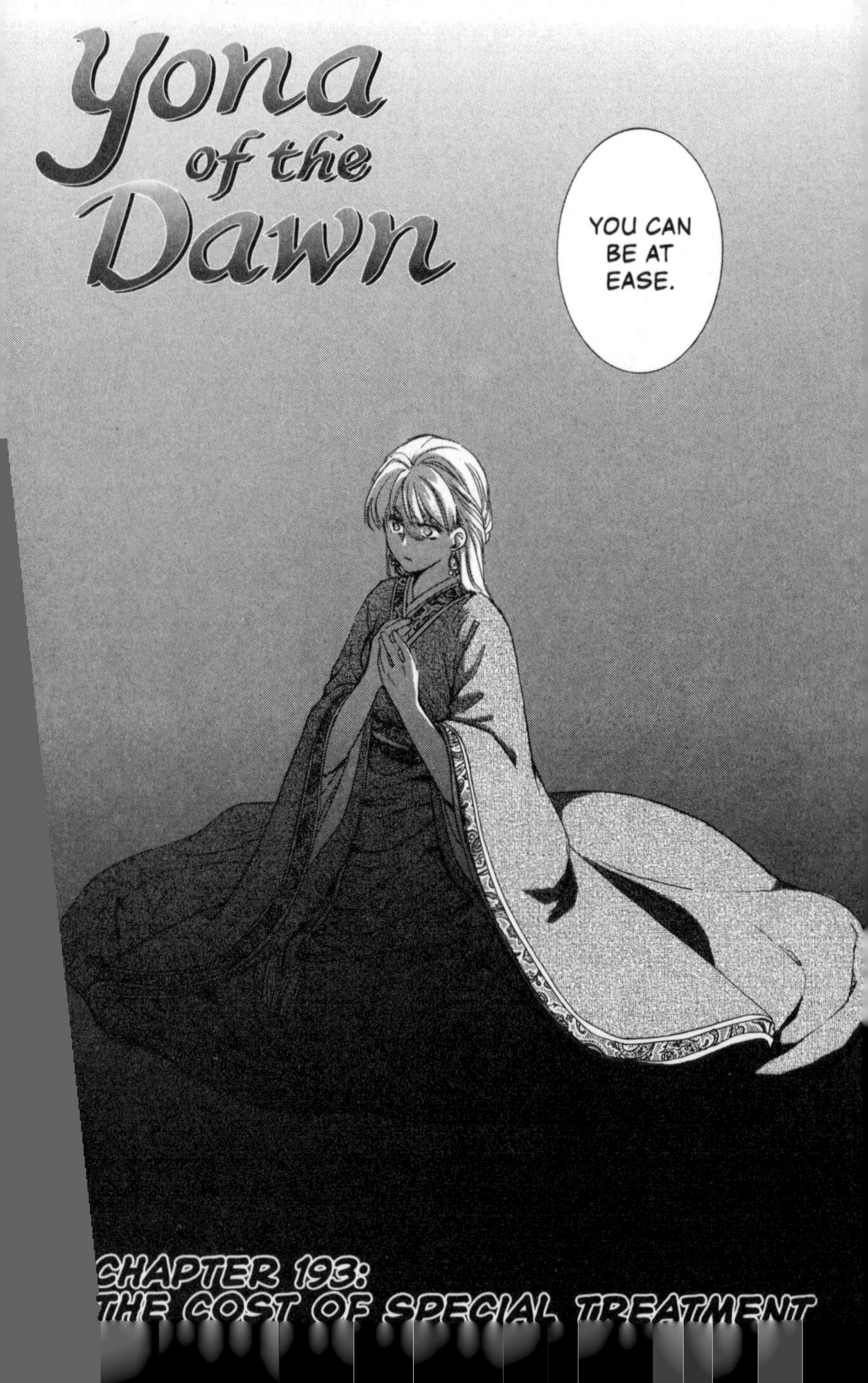
Yona of the Dawn
YOU CAN BE AT EASE.
CHAPTER 193:
THE COST OF SPECIAL TREATMENT

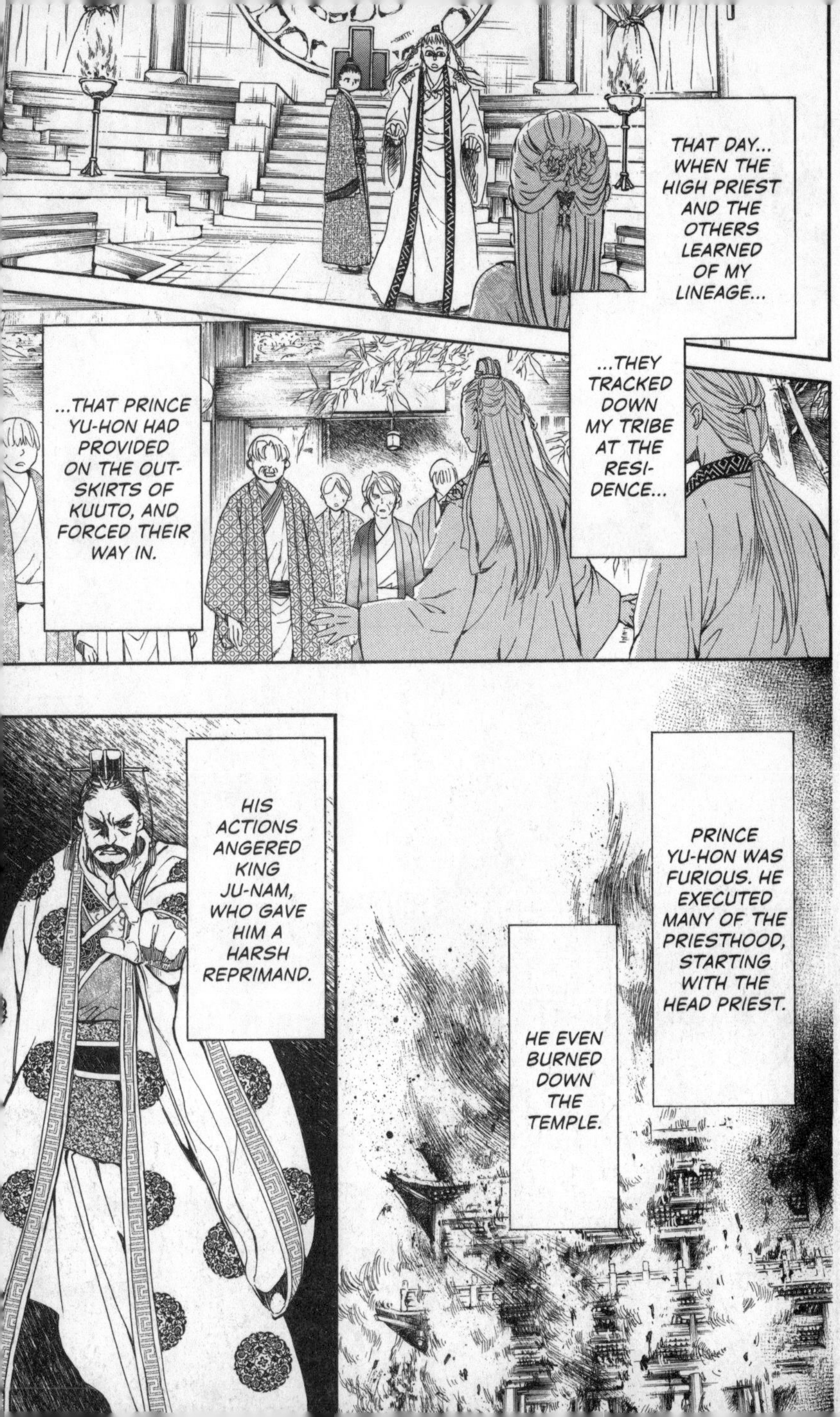
THAT DAY... WHEN THE HIGH PRIEST AND THE OTHERS LEARNED OF MY LINEAGE...
...THEY TRACKED DOWN MY TRIBE AT THE RESI-DENCE...
...THAT PRINCE YU-HON HAD PROVIDED ON THE OUT-SKIRTS OF KUUTO, AND FORCED THEIR WAY IN.
PRINCE YU-HON WAS FURIOUS. HE EXECUTED MANY OF THE PRIESTHOOD, STARTING WITH THE HEAD PRIEST.
HE EVEN BURNED DOWN THE TEMPLE.
HIS ACTIONS ANGERED KING JU-NAM, WHO GAVE HIM A HARSH REPRIMAND.

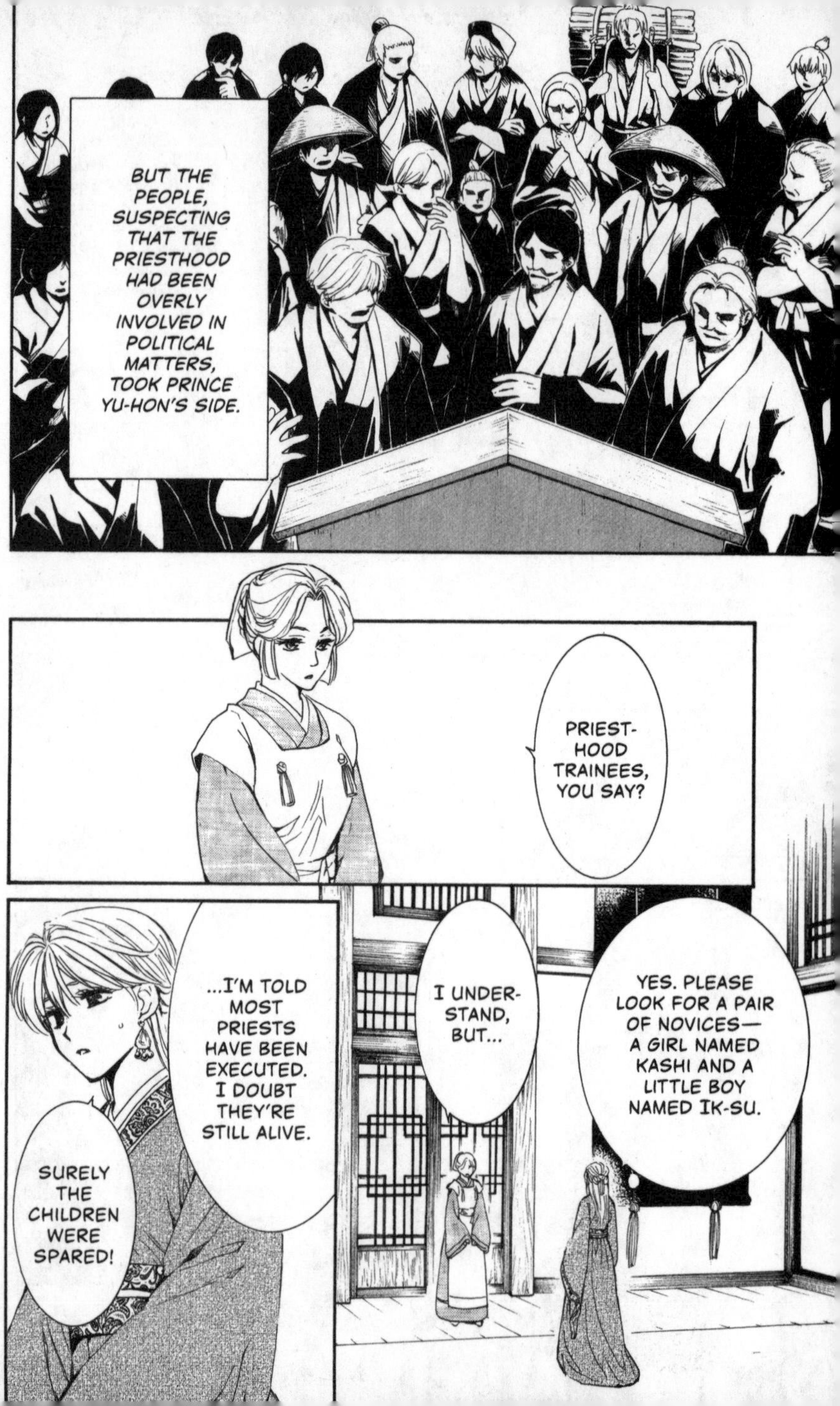
BUT THE PEOPLE, SUSPECTING THAT THE PRIESTHOOD HAD BEEN OVERLY INVOLVED IN POLITICAL MATTERS, TOOK PRINCE YU-HON'S SIDE.
PRIEST-HOOD TRAINEES, YOU SAY?
YES. PLEASE LOOK FOR A PAIR OF NOVICES— A GIRL NAMED KASHI AND A LITTLE BOY NAMED IK-SU.
I UNDER-STAND, BUT...
...I'M TOLD MOST PRIESTS HAVE BEEN EXECUTED. I DOUBT THEY'RE STILL ALIVE.
SURELY THE CHILDREN WERE SPARED!

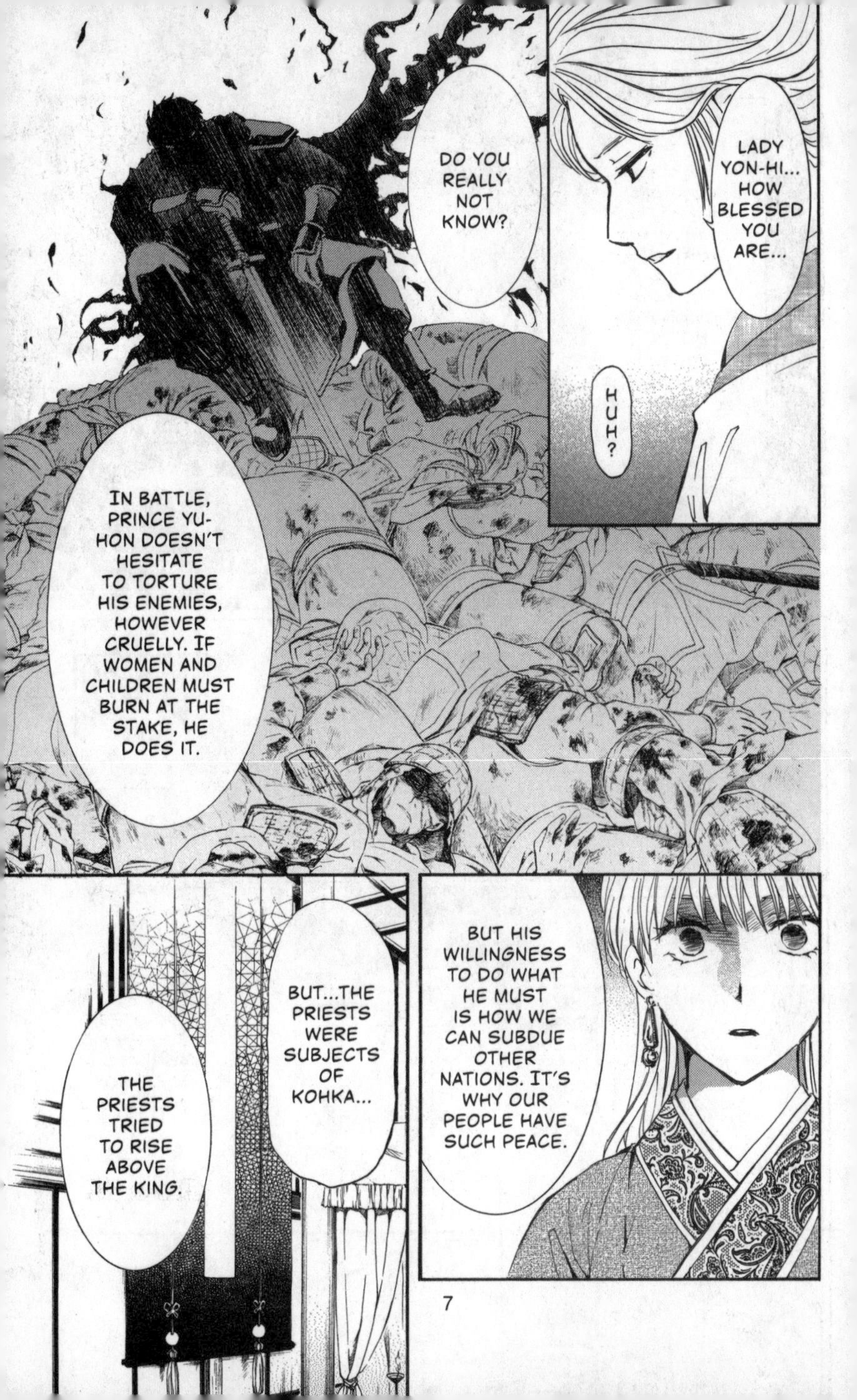
LADY YON-HI... HOW BLESSED YOU ARE...
HUH?
DO YOU REALLY NOT KNOW?
IN BATTLE, PRINCE YU-HON DOESN'T HESITATE TO TORTURE HIS ENEMIES, HOWEVER CRUELLY. IF WOMEN AND CHILDREN MUST BURN AT THE STAKE, HE DOES IT.
BUT HIS WILLINGNESS TO DO WHAT HE MUST IS HOW WE CAN SUBDUE OTHER NATIONS. IT'S WHY OUR PEOPLE HAVE SUCH PEACE.
BUT...THE PRIESTS WERE SUBJECTS OF KOHKA...
THE PRIESTS TRIED TO RISE ABOVE THE KING.

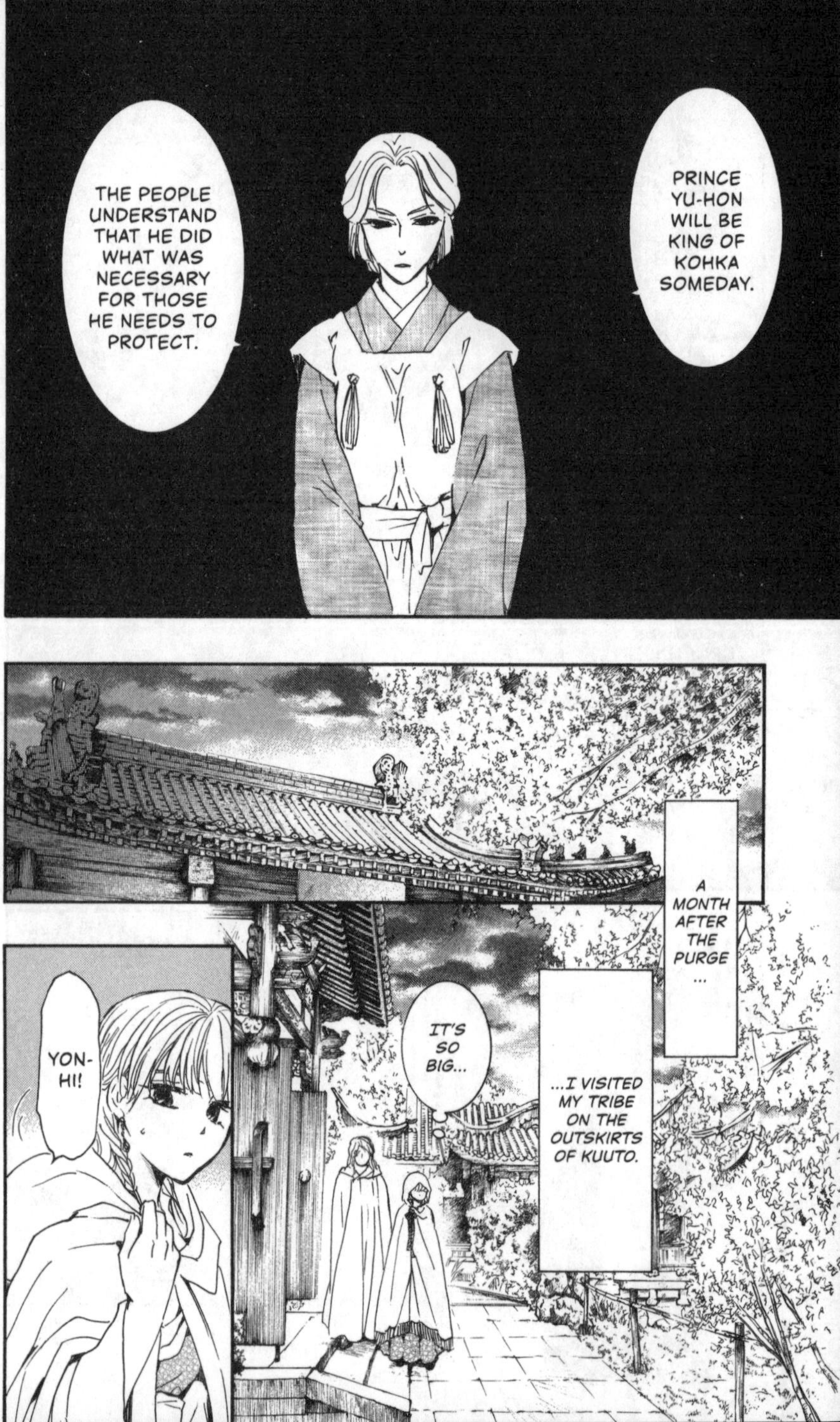
PRINCE YU-HON WILL BE KING OF KOHKA SOMEDAY.
THE PEOPLE UNDERSTAND THAT HE DID WHAT WAS NECESSARY FOR THOSE HE NEEDS TO PROTECT.
A MONTH AFTER THE PURGE ...
...I VISITED MY TRIBE ON THE OUTSKIRTS OF KUUTO.
IT'S SO BIG...
YON-HI!

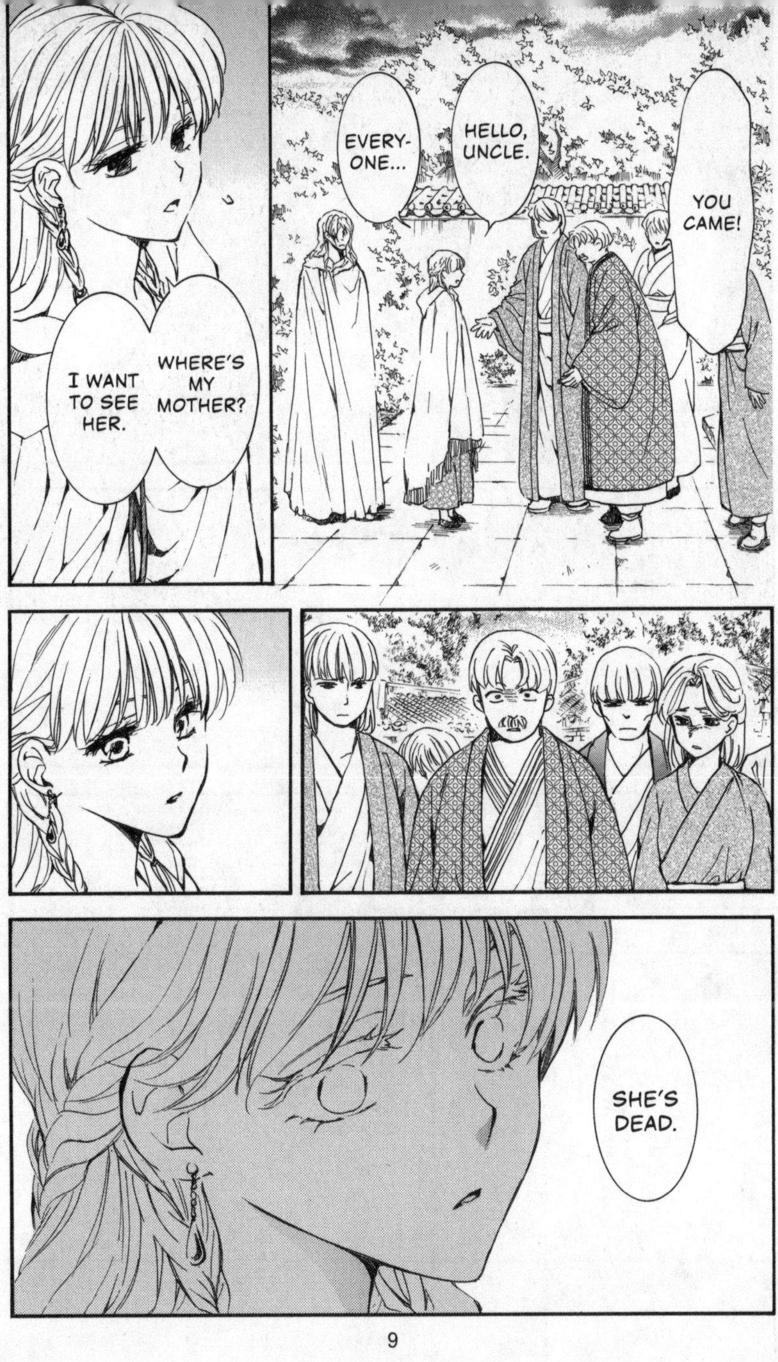
YOU CAME!
HELLO, UNCLE.
EVERY-ONE...
WHERE'S MY MOTHER?
I WANT TO SEE HER.
SHE'S DEAD.

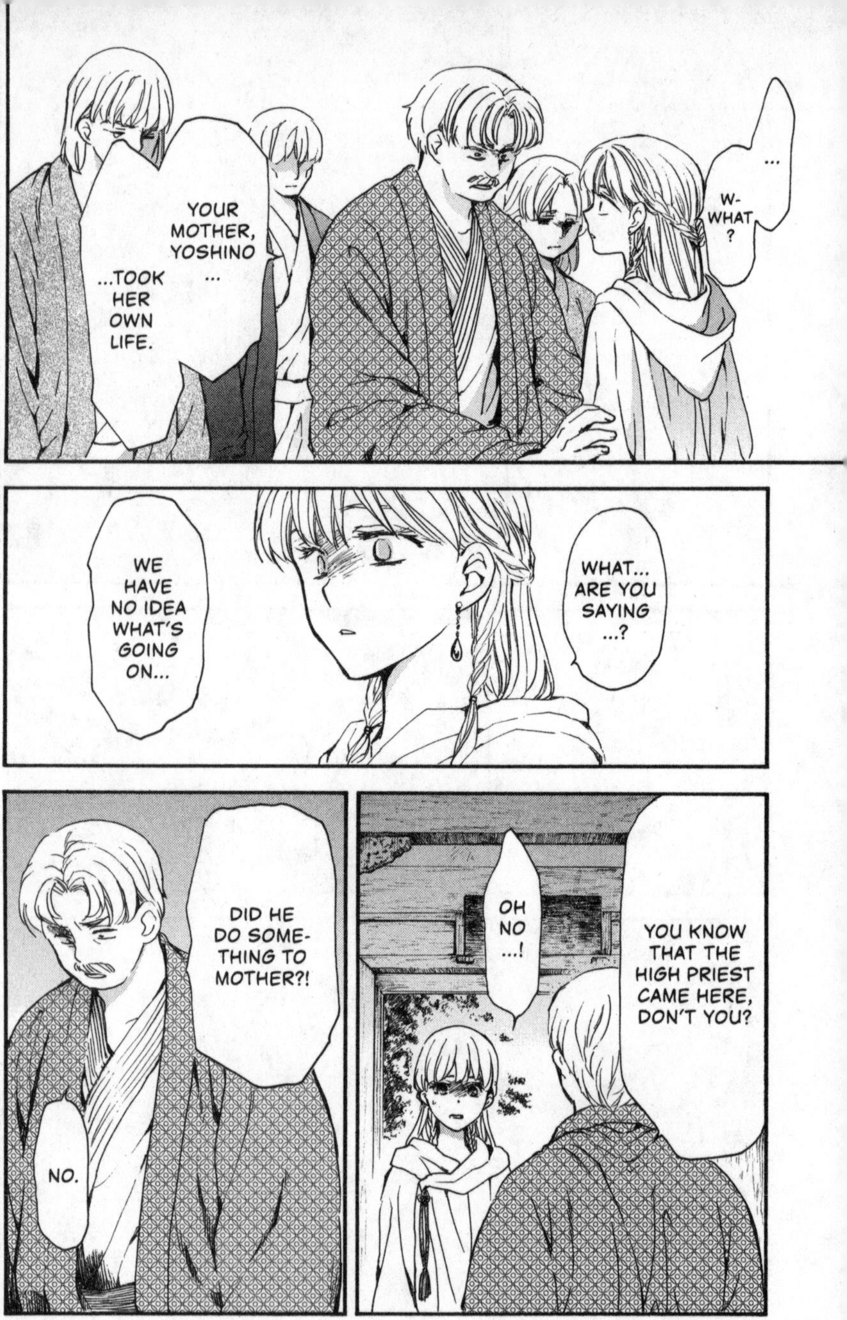
... W-WHAT?
YOUR MOTHER, YOSHINO ...
...TOOK HER OWN LIFE.
WHAT... ARE YOU SAYING ...?
WE HAVE NO IDEA WHAT'S GOING ON...
YOU KNOW THAT THE HIGH PRIEST CAME HERE, DON'T YOU?
OH NO ...!
DID HE DO SOMETHING TO MOTHER?!
NO.

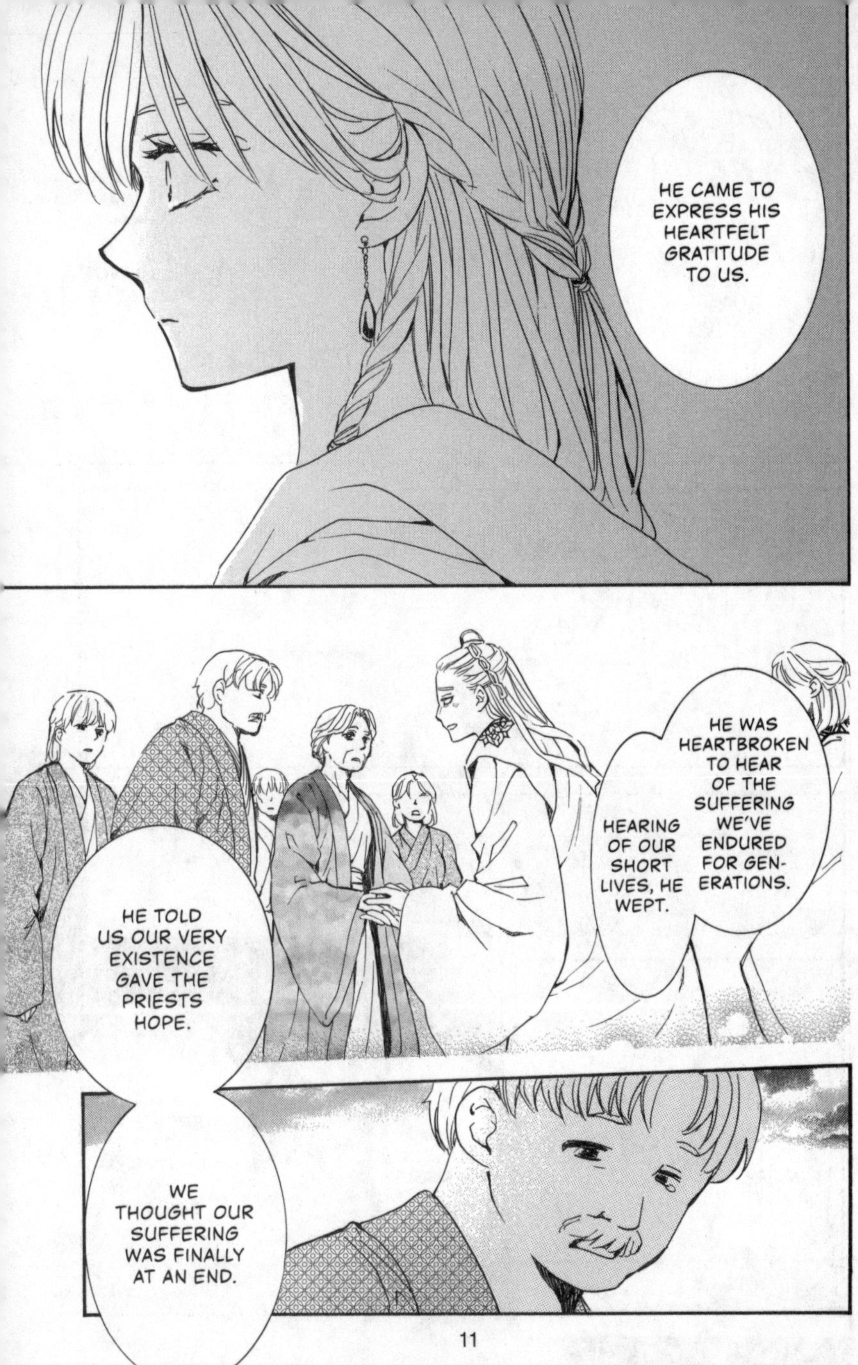
HE CAME TO EXPRESS HIS HEARTFELT GRATITUDE TO US.
HE WAS HEARTBROKEN TO HEAR OF THE SUFFERING WE'VE ENDURED FOR GEN-ERATIONS.
HEARING OF OUR SHORT LIVES, HE WEPT.
HE TOLD US OUR VERY EXISTENCE GAVE THE PRIESTS HOPE.
WE THOUGHT OUR SUFFERING WAS FINALLY AT AN END.

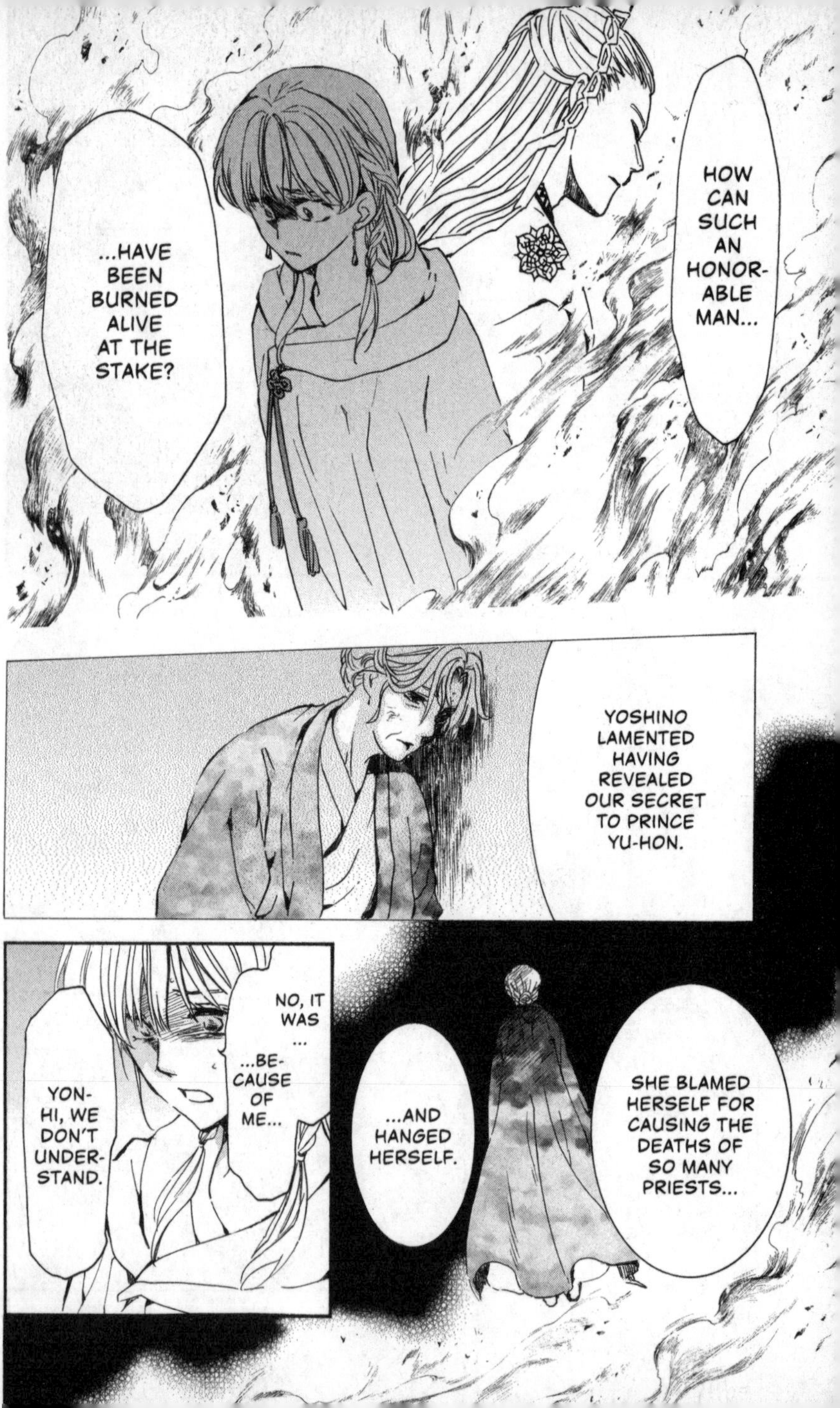
HOW CAN SUCH AN HONOR-ABLE MAN...
...HAVE BEEN BURNED ALIVE AT THE STAKE?
YOSHINO LAMENTED HAVING REVEALED OUR SECRET TO PRINCE YU-HON.
SHE BLAMED HERSELF FOR CAUSING THE DEATHS OF SO MANY PRIESTS...
...AND HANGED HERSELF.
NO, IT WAS ...
...BE-CAUSE OF ME...
YON-HI, WE DON'T UNDER-STAND.

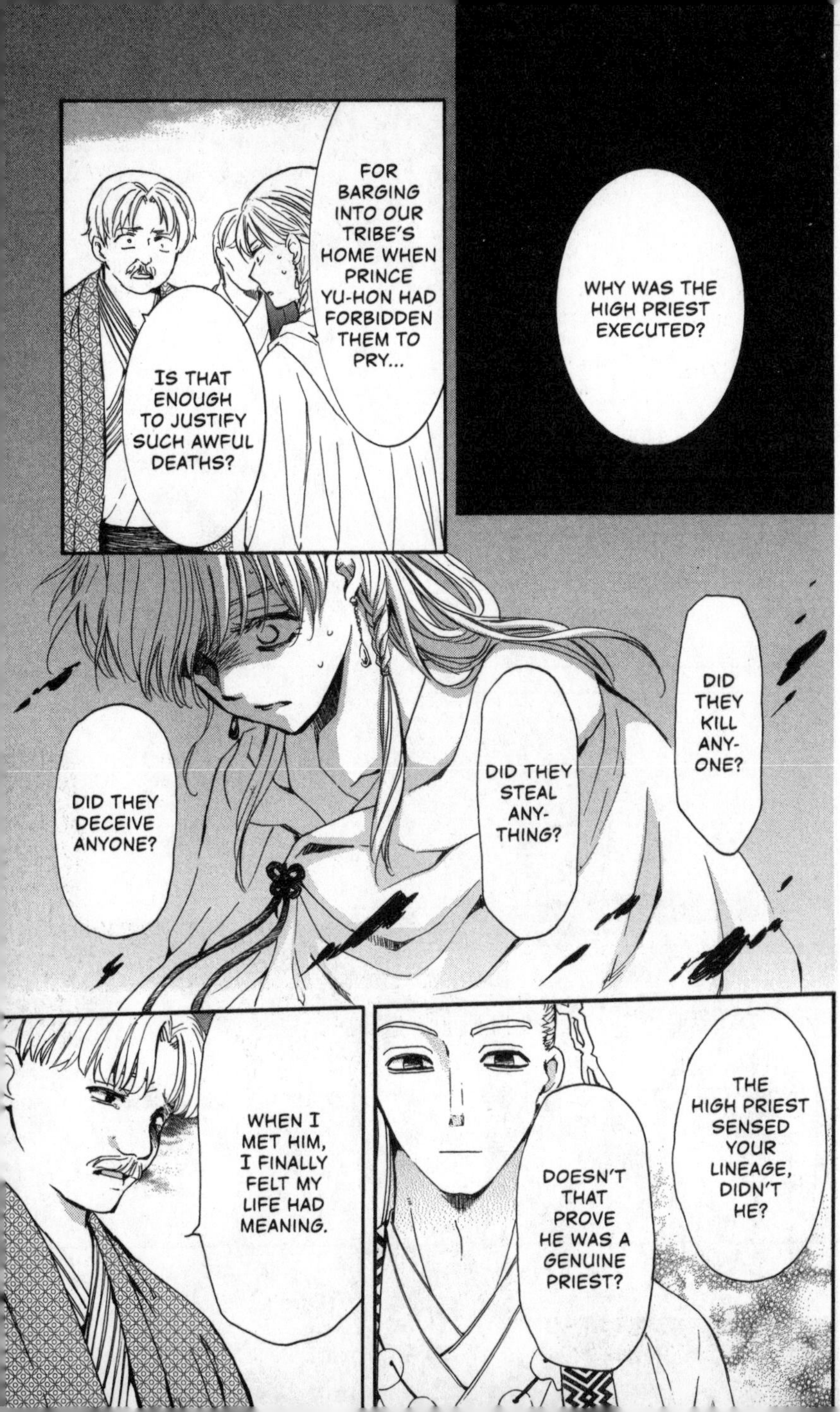
WHY WAS THE HIGH PRIEST EXECUTED?
FOR BARGING INTO OUR TRIBE'S HOME WHEN PRINCE YU-HON HAD FORBIDDEN THEM TO PRY...
IS THAT ENOUGH TO JUSTIFY SUCH AWFUL DEATHS?
DID THEY KILL ANY-ONE?
DID THEY STEAL ANY-THING?
DID THEY DECEIVE ANYONE?
THE HIGH PRIEST SENSED YOUR LINEAGE, DIDN'T HE?
DOESN'T THAT PROVE HE WAS A GENUINE PRIEST?
WHEN I MET HIM, I FINALLY FELT MY LIFE HAD MEANING.

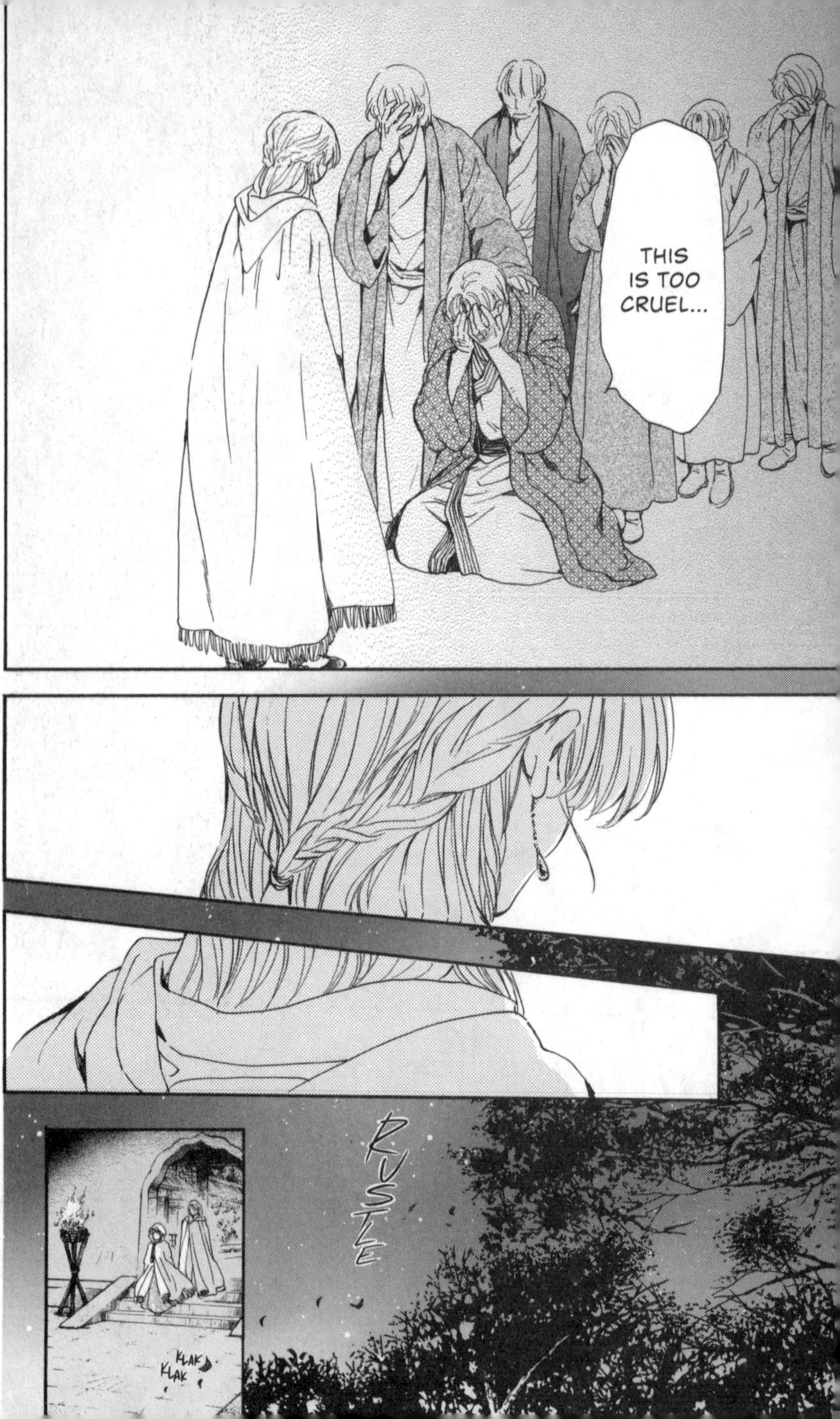
THIS IS TOO CRUEL...
RUSTLE
KLAK KLAK

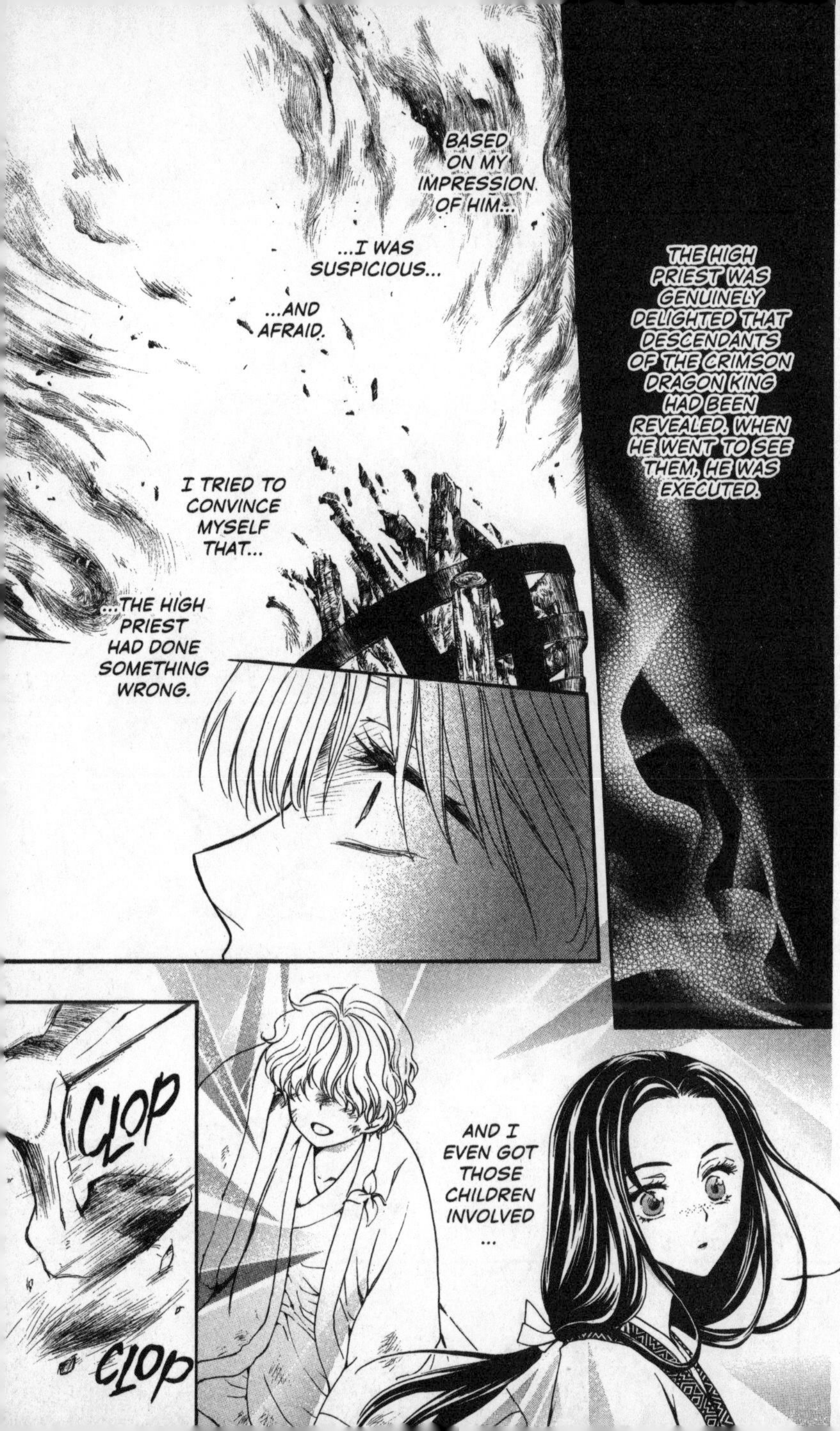
THE HIGH PRIEST WAS GENUINELY DELIGHTED THAT DESCENDANTS OF THE CRIMSON DRAGON KING HAD BEEN REVEALED. WHEN HE WENT TO SEE THEM, HE WAS EXECUTED.
BASED ON MY IMPRESSION OF HIM...
...I WAS SUSPICIOUS...
...AND AFRAID.
I TRIED TO CONVINCE MYSELF THAT...
...THE HIGH PRIEST HAD DONE SOMETHING WRONG.
AND I EVEN GOT THOSE CHILDREN INVOLVED ...
CLOP
CLOP

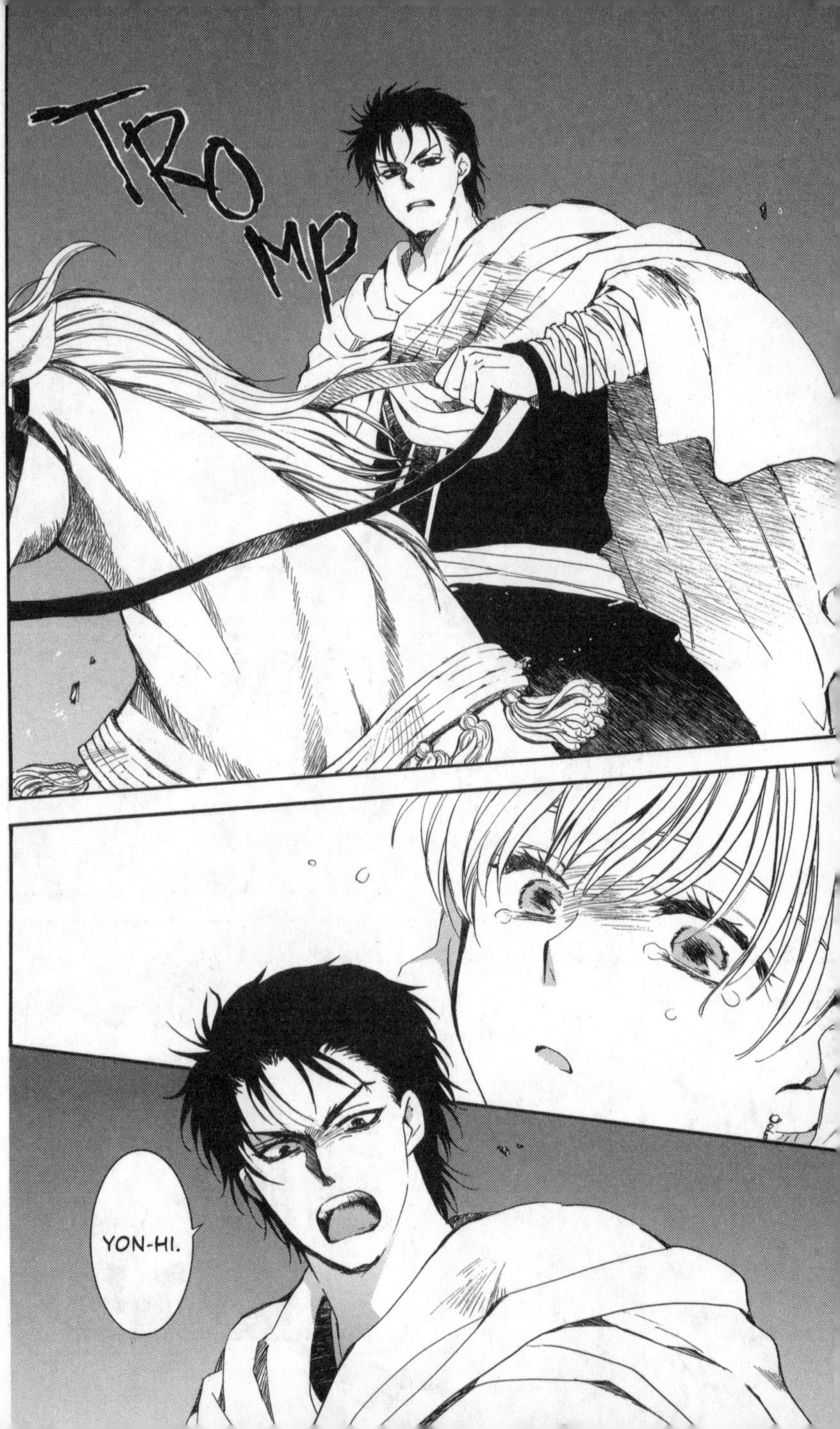
TROMP
YON-HI.

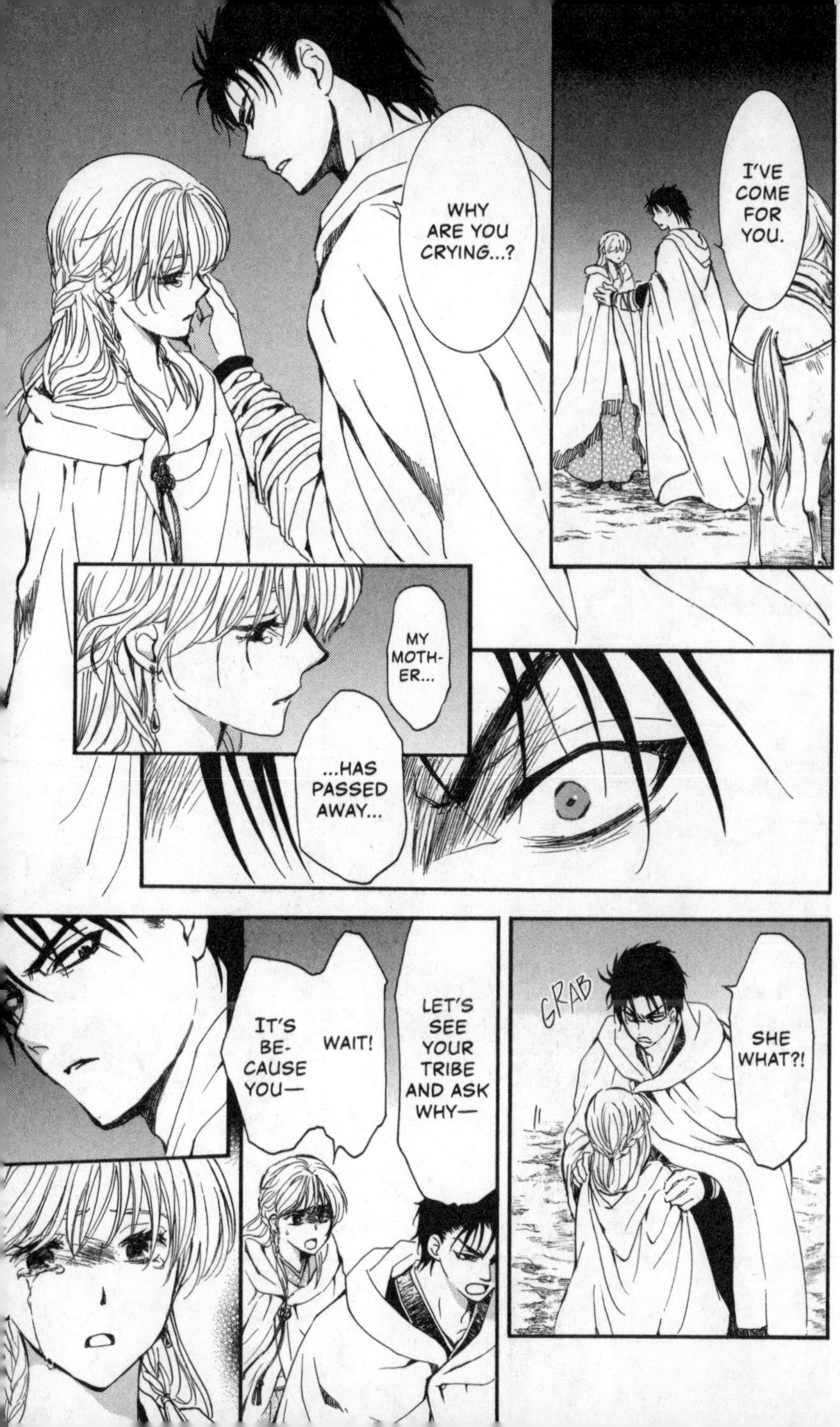
I'VE COME FOR YOU.
WHY ARE YOU CRYING...?
MY MOTHER...
...HAS PASSED AWAY...
GRAB
SHE WHAT?!
LET'S SEE YOUR TRIBE AND ASK WHY—
WAIT!
IT'S BECAUSE YOU—

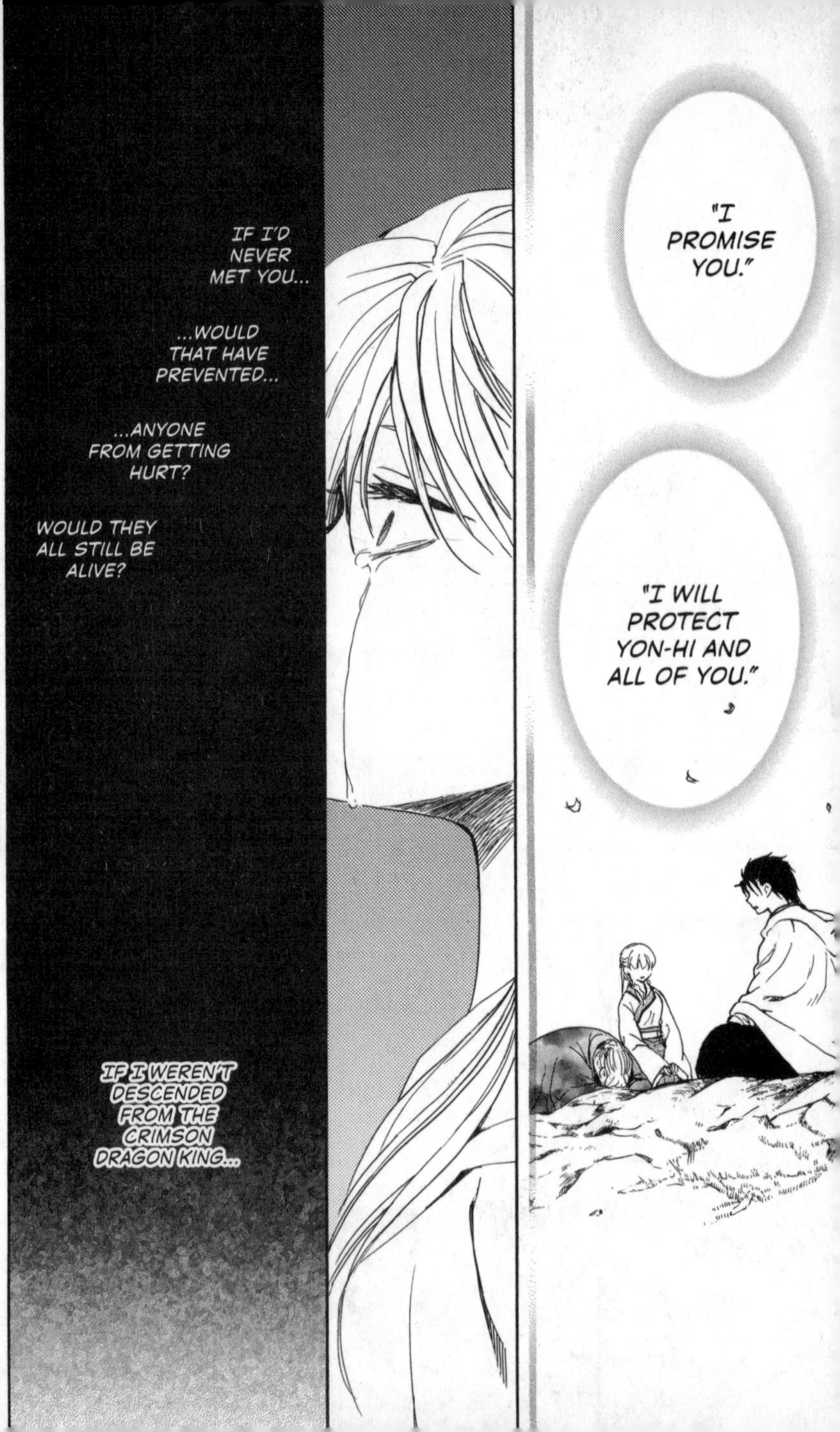
"I PROMISE YOU."
"I WILL PROTECT YON-HI AND ALL OF YOU."
IF I'D NEVER MET YOU...
...WOULD THAT HAVE PREVENTED...
...ANYONE FROM GETTING HURT?
WOULD THEY ALL STILL BE ALIVE?
IF I WEREN'T DESCENDED FROM THE CRIMSON DRAGON KING...

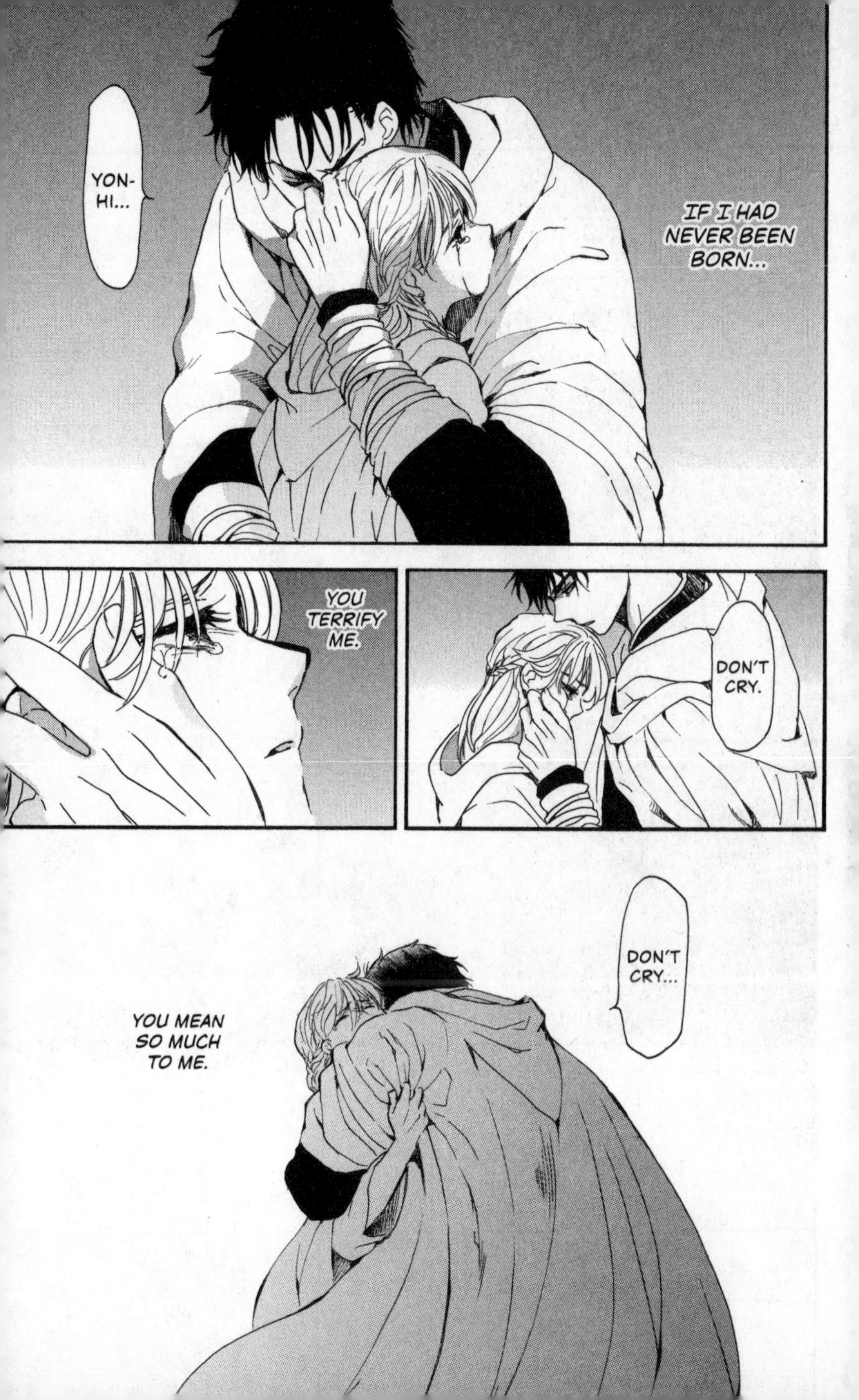
IF I HAD NEVER BEEN BORN...
YON-HI...
DON'T CRY.
YOU TERRIFY ME.
DON'T CRY...
YOU MEAN SO MUCH TO ME.

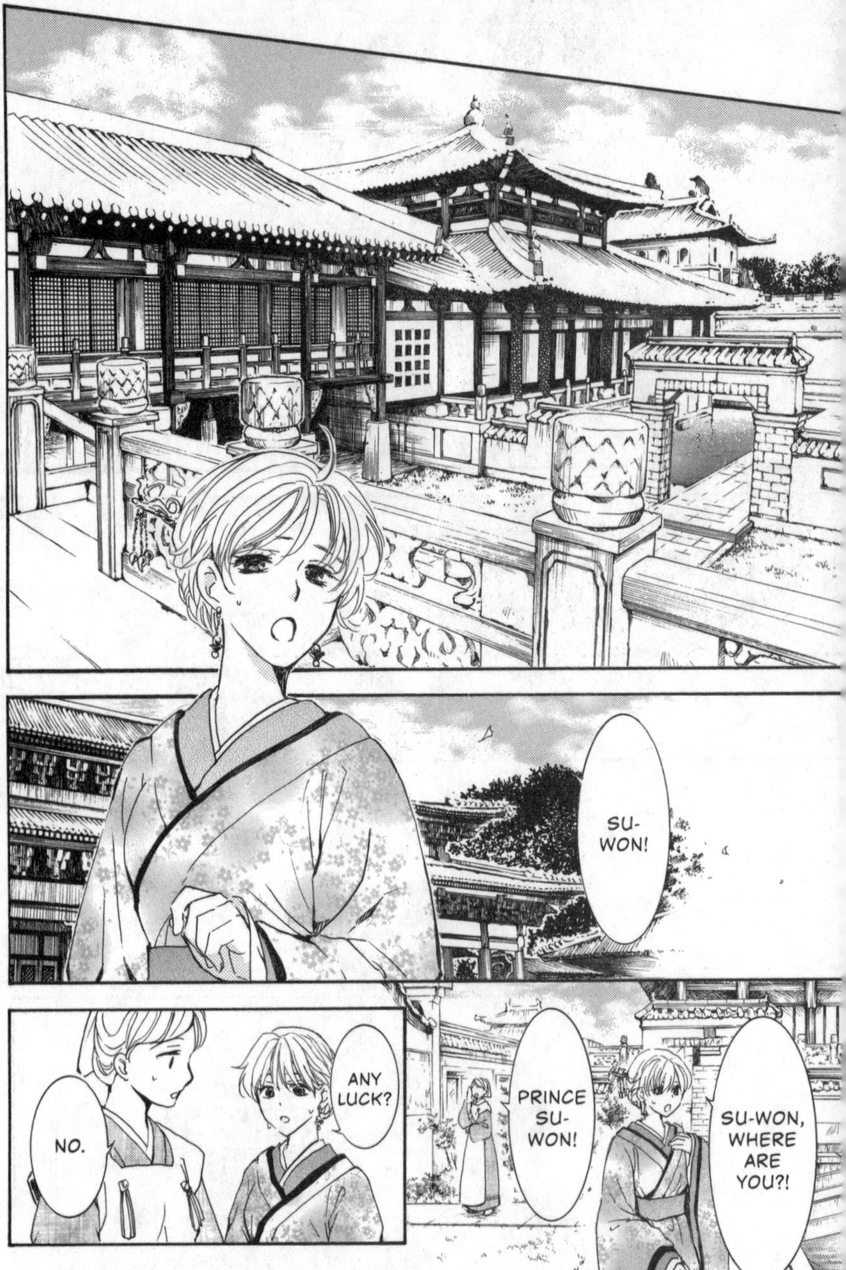
SU-WON!
SU-WON, WHERE ARE YOU?!
PRINCE SU-WON!
ANY LUCK?
NO.

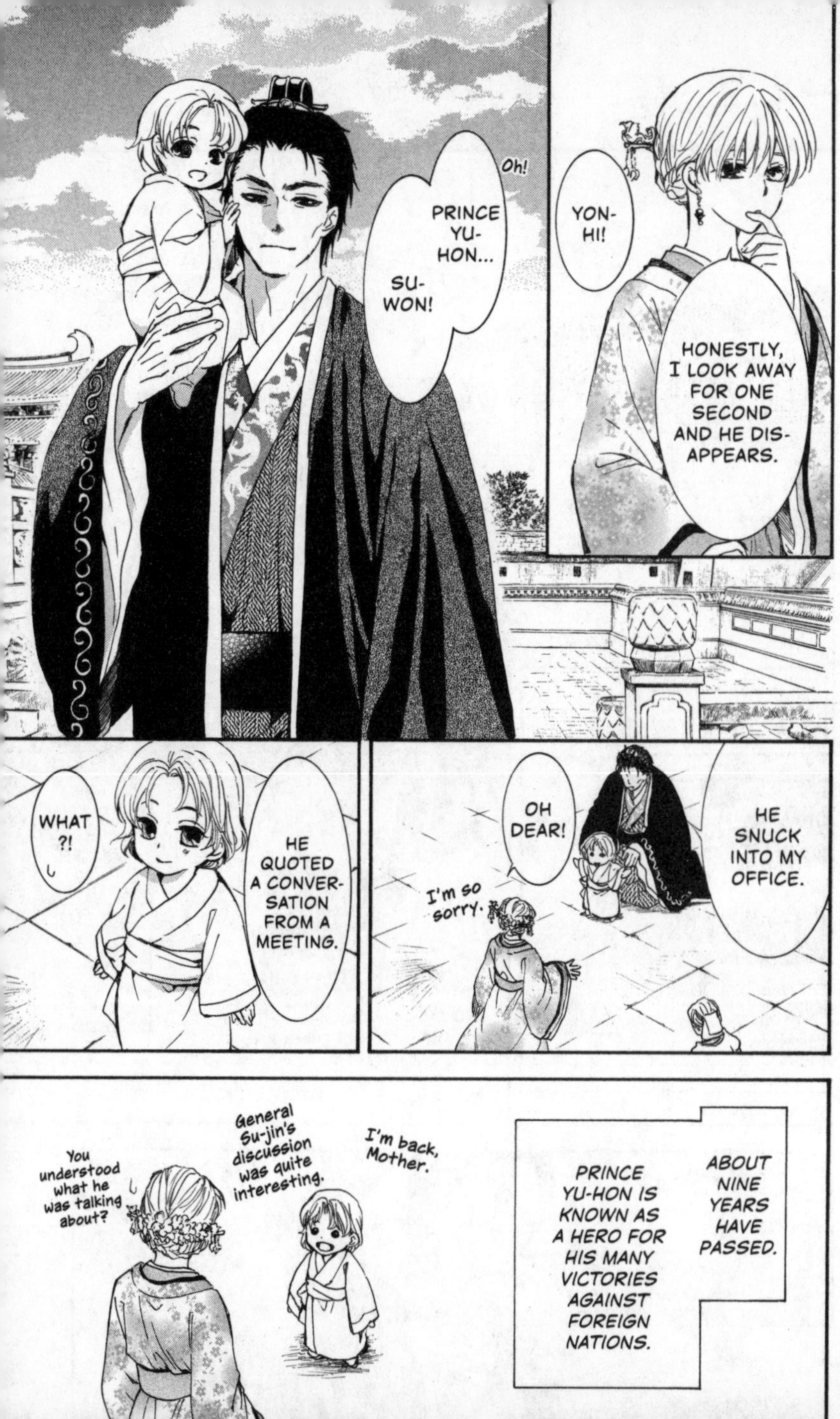
YON-HI!
HONESTLY, I LOOK AWAY FOR ONE SECOND AND HE DIS-APPEARS.
Oh!
PRINCE YU-HON...
SU-WON!
HE SNUCK INTO MY OFFICE.
OH DEAR!
I'm so sorry.
HE QUOTED A CONVERSATION FROM A MEETING.
WHAT?!
ABOUT NINE YEARS HAVE PASSED.
PRINCE YU-HON IS KNOWN AS A HERO FOR HIS MANY VICTORIES AGAINST FOREIGN NATIONS.
I'm back, Mother.
General Su-jin's discussion was quite interesting.
You understood what he was talking about?

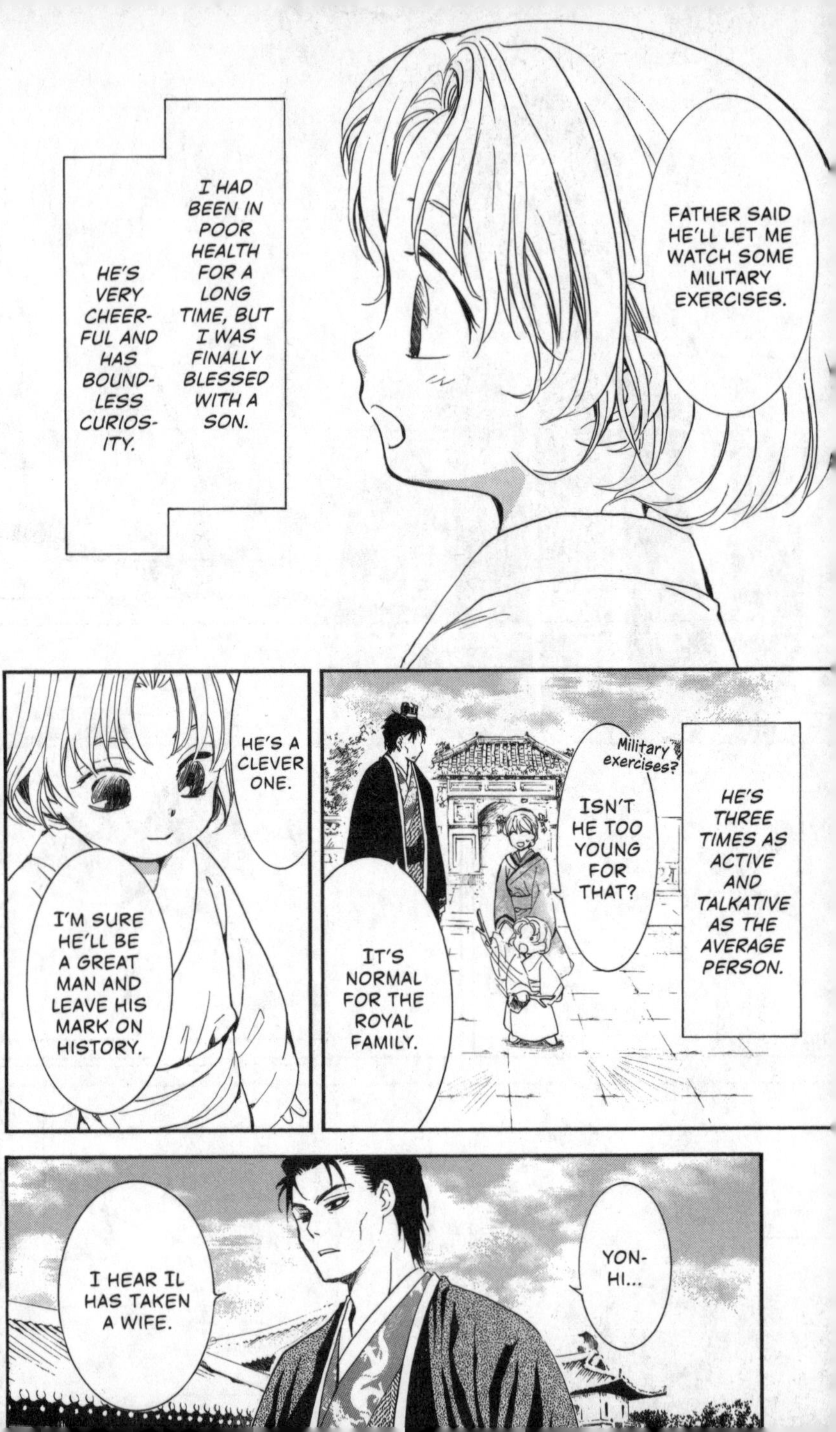
FATHER SAID HE'LL LET ME WATCH SOME MILITARY EXERCISES.
I HAD BEEN IN POOR HEALTH FOR A LONG TIME, BUT I WAS FINALLY BLESSED WITH A SON.
HE'S VERY CHEERFUL AND HAS BOUNDLESS CURIOSITY.
HE'S THREE TIMES AS ACTIVE AND TALKATIVE AS THE AVERAGE PERSON.
Military exercises?
ISN'T HE TOO YOUNG FOR THAT?
IT'S NORMAL FOR THE ROYAL FAMILY.
HE'S A CLEVER ONE.
I'M SURE HE'LL BE A GREAT MAN AND LEAVE HIS MARK ON HISTORY.
YON-HI...
I HEAR IL HAS TAKEN A WIFE.

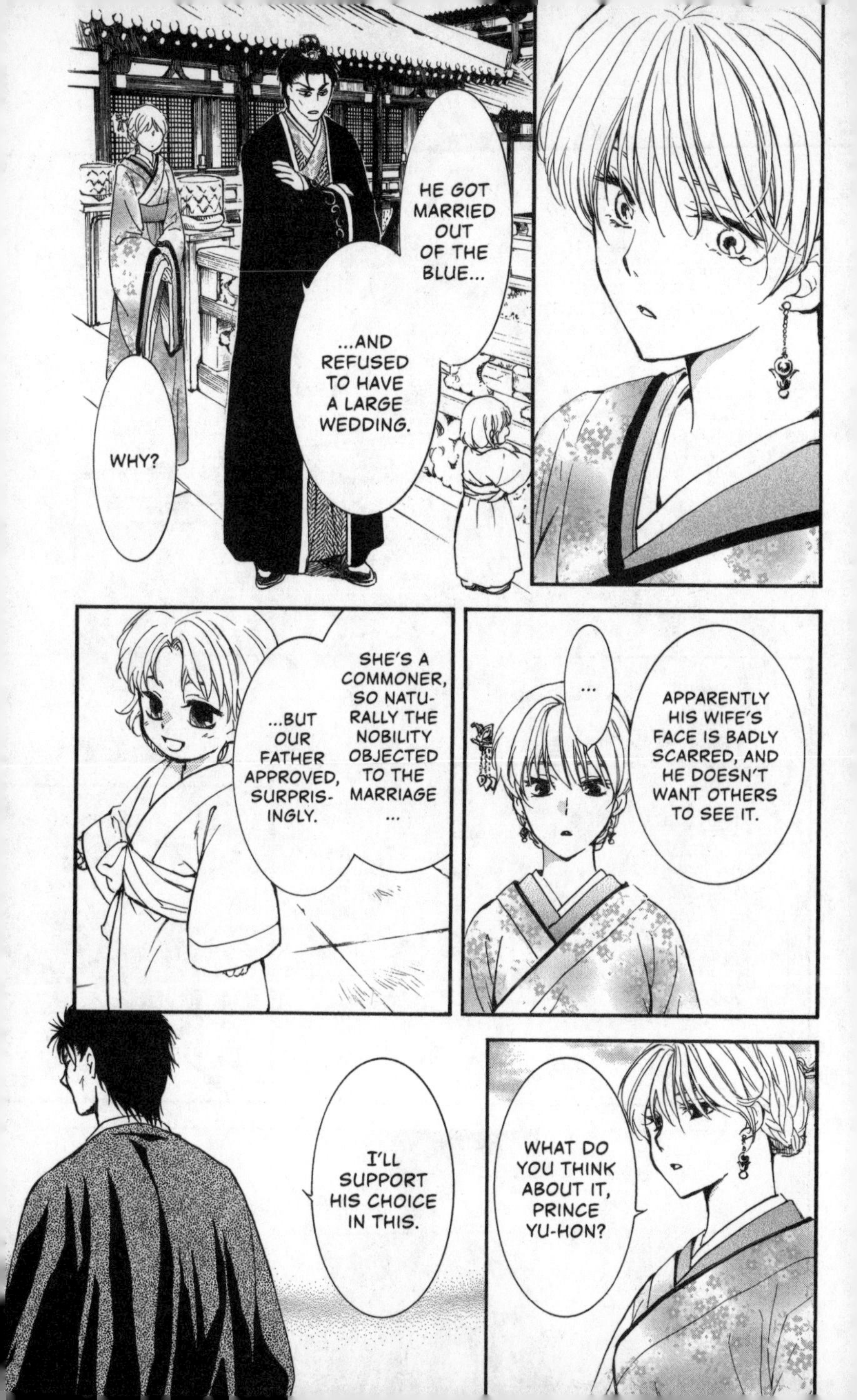
HE GOT MARRIED OUT OF THE BLUE...
...AND REFUSED TO HAVE A LARGE WEDDING.
WHY?
APPARENTLY HIS WIFE'S FACE IS BADLY SCARRED, AND HE DOESN'T WANT OTHERS TO SEE IT.
...
SHE'S A COMMONER, SO NATURALLY THE NOBILITY OBJECTED TO THE MARRIAGE...
...BUT OUR FATHER APPROVED, SURPRISINGLY.
WHAT DO YOU THINK ABOUT IT, PRINCE YU-HON?
I'LL SUPPORT HIS CHOICE IN THIS.

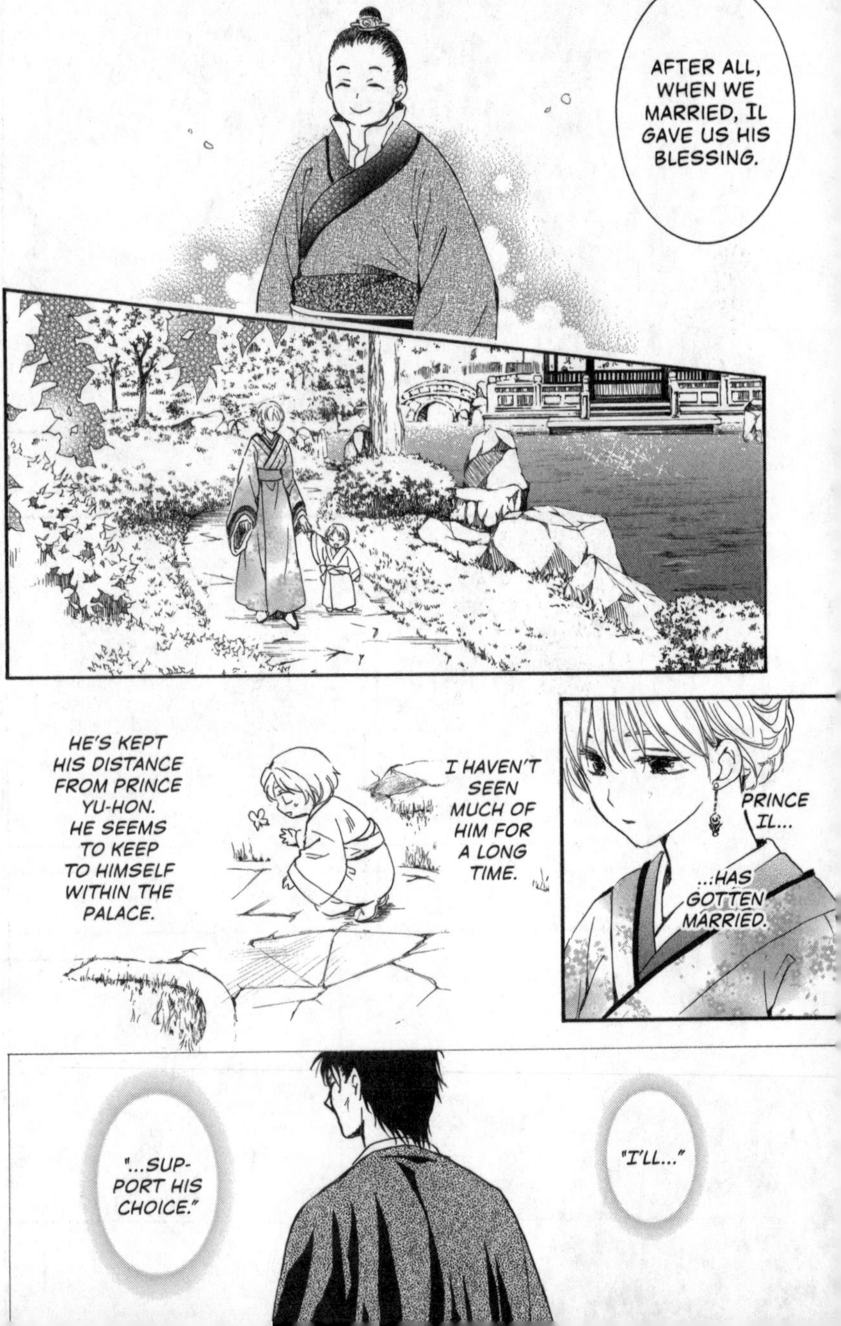
AFTER ALL, WHEN WE MARRIED, IL GAVE US HIS BLESSING.
PRINCE IL...
...HAS GOTTEN MARRIED.
I HAVEN'T SEEN MUCH OF HIM FOR A LONG TIME.
HE'S KEPT HIS DISTANCE FROM PRINCE YU-HON. HE SEEMS TO KEEP TO HIMSELF WITHIN THE PALACE.
"I'LL..."
"...SUP-PORT HIS CHOICE."

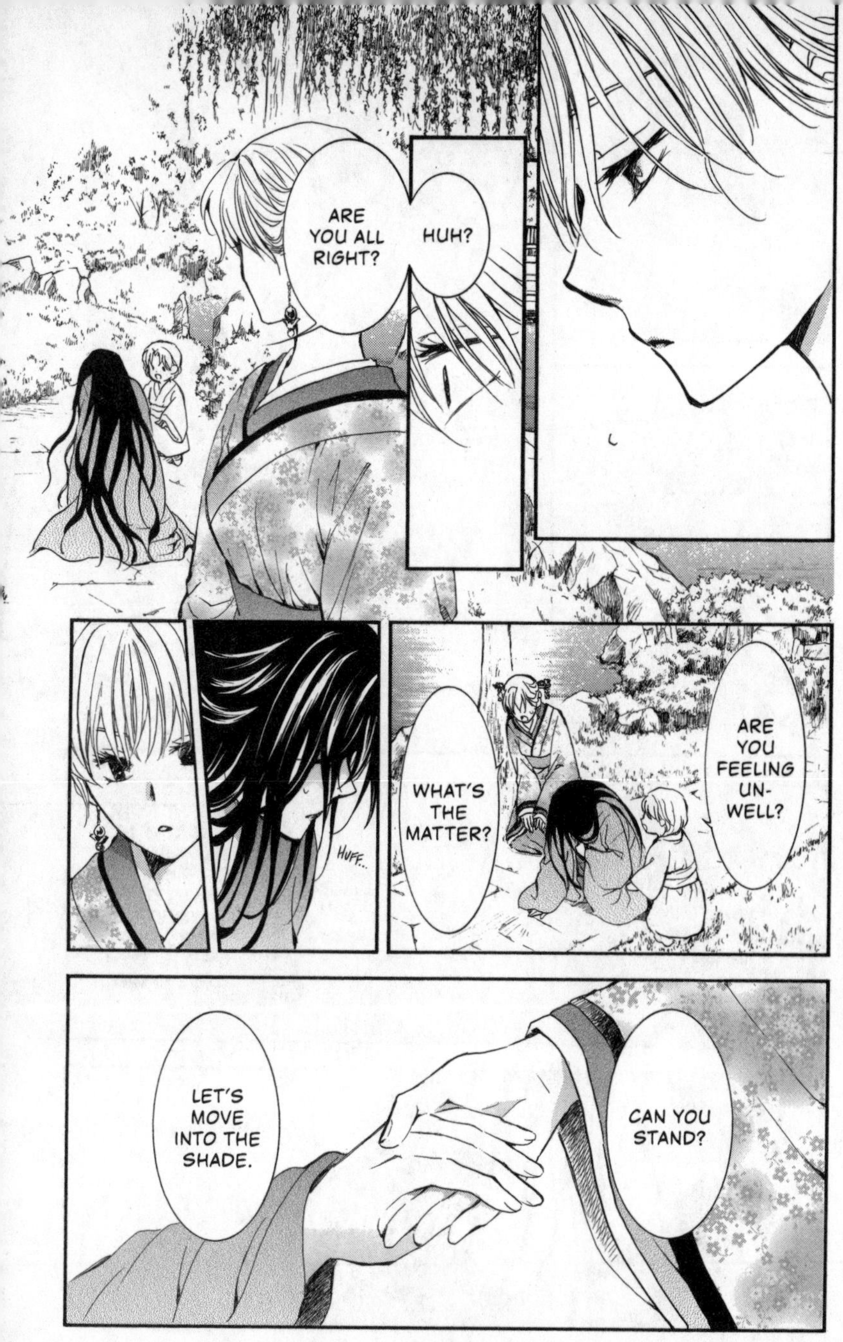
HUH?
ARE YOU ALL RIGHT?
ARE YOU FEELING UN-WELL?
WHAT'S THE MATTER?
HUFF...
CAN YOU STAND?
LET'S MOVE INTO THE SHADE.

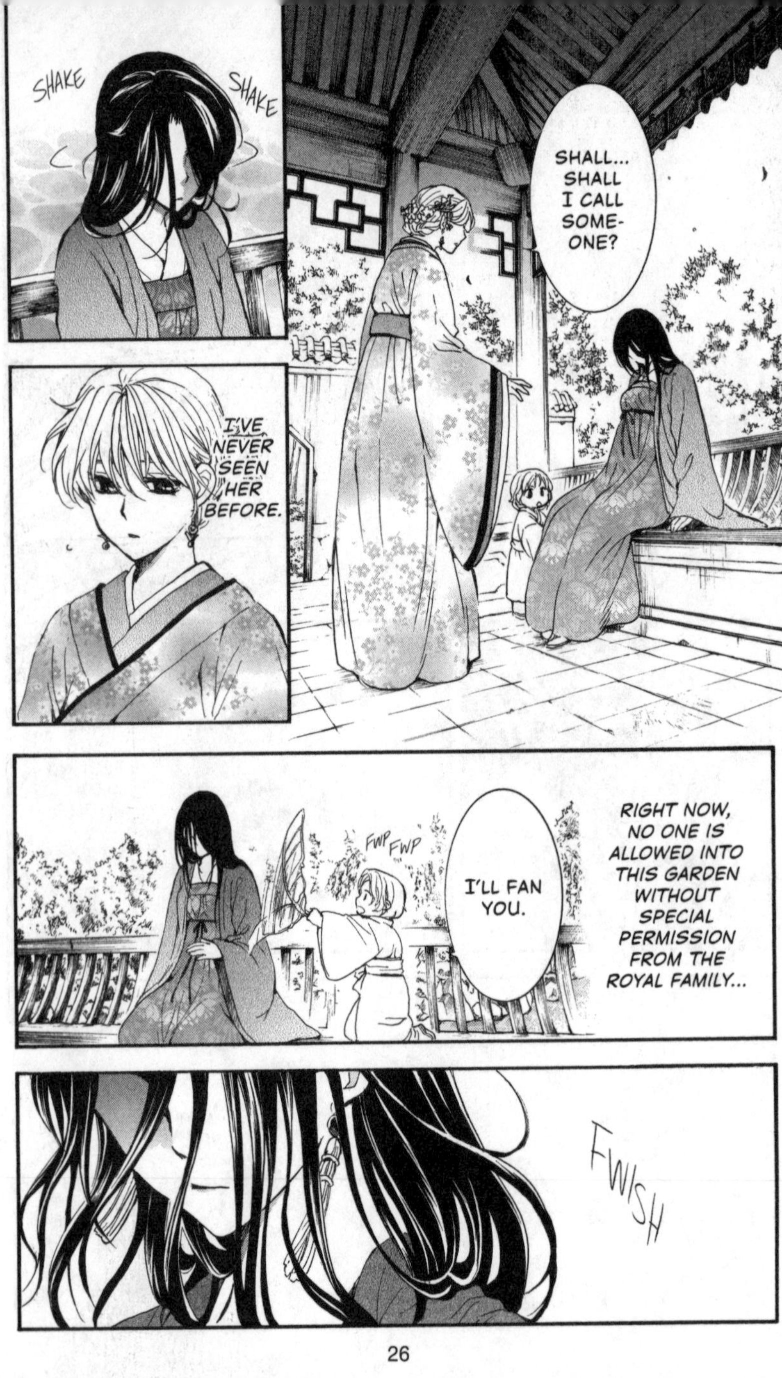
SHALL... SHALL I CALL SOME-ONE?
SHAKE SHAKE
I'VE NEVER SEEN HER BEFORE.
RIGHT NOW, NO ONE IS ALLOWED INTO THIS GARDEN WITHOUT SPECIAL PERMISSION FROM THE ROYAL FAMILY...
I'LL FAN YOU.
FWP FWP
FWISH

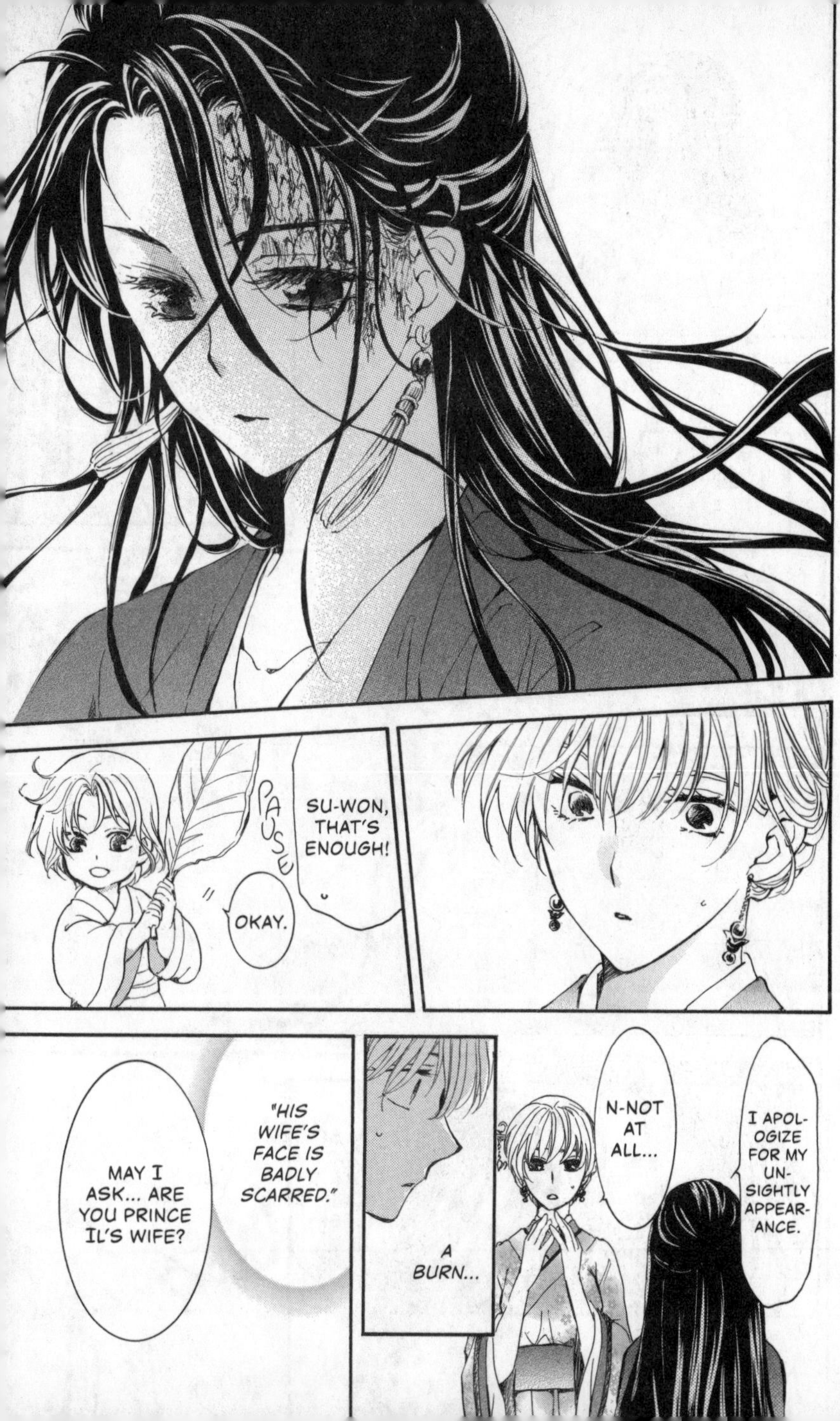
SU-WON, THAT'S ENOUGH!
PAUSE
OKAY.
I APOLOGIZE FOR MY UNSIGHTLY APPEARANCE.
N-NOT AT ALL...
A BURN...
"HIS WIFE'S FACE IS BADLY SCARRED."
MAY I ASK... ARE YOU PRINCE IL'S WIFE?

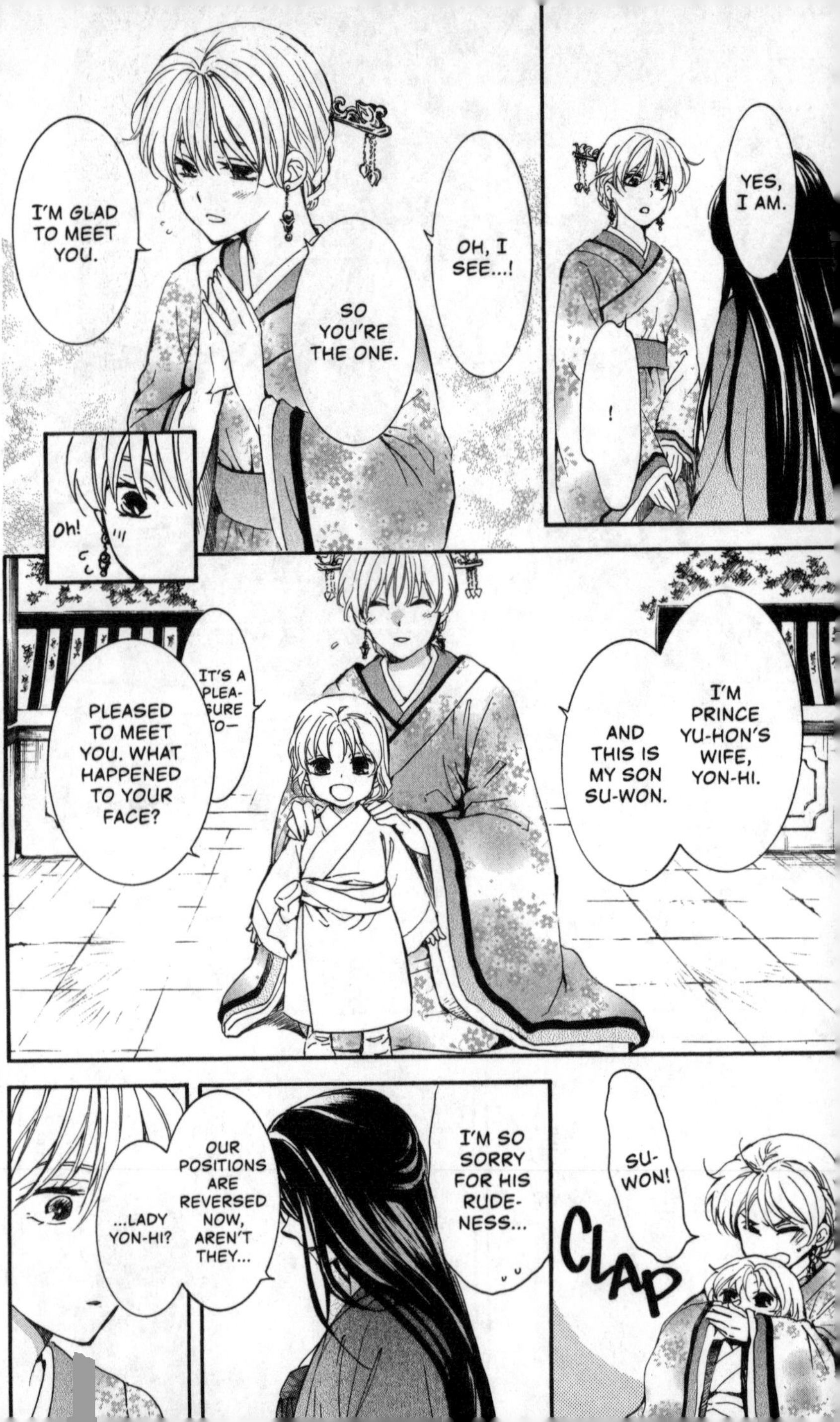
YES, I AM.
!
OH, I SEE...!
SO YOU'RE THE ONE.
I'M GLAD TO MEET YOU.
Oh!
I'M PRINCE YU-HON'S WIFE, YON-HI.
AND THIS IS MY SON SU-WON.
IT'S A PLEA-SURE TO—
PLEASED TO MEET YOU. WHAT HAPPENED TO YOUR FACE?
SU-WON!
CLAP
I'M SO SORRY FOR HIS RUDE-NESS...
OUR POSITIONS ARE REVERSED NOW, AREN'T THEY...
...LADY YON-HI?

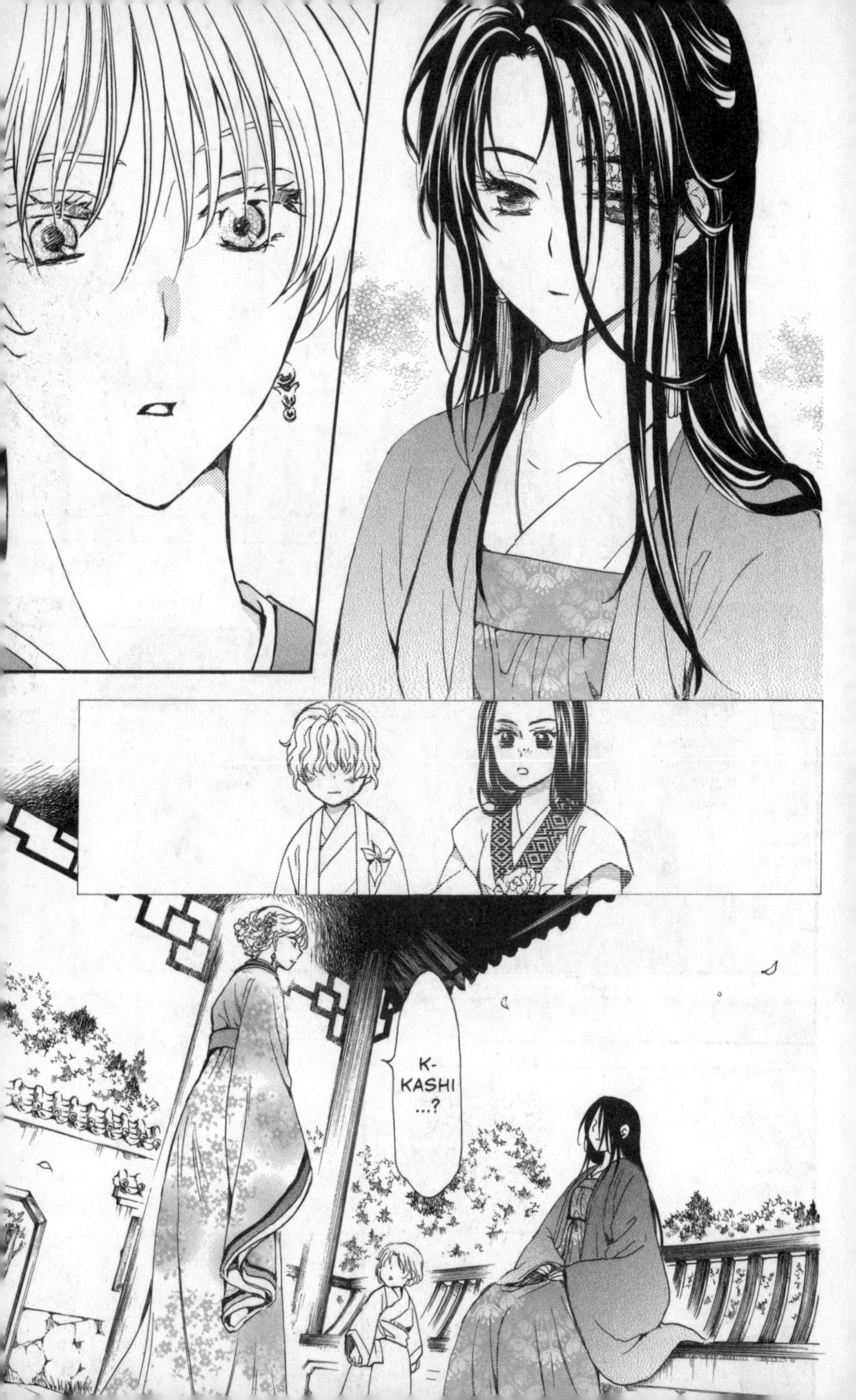
K-KASHI...?

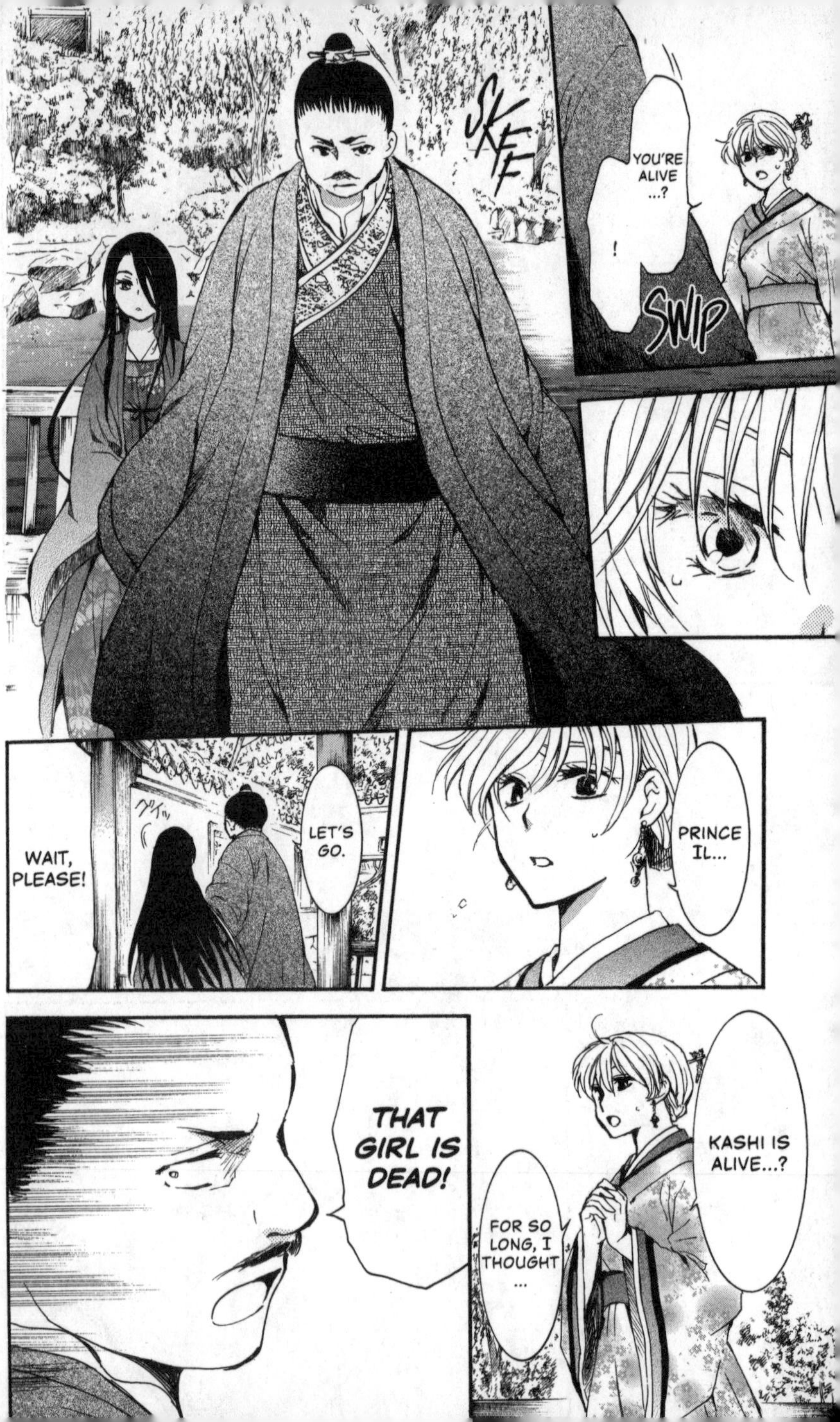
YOU'RE ALIVE ...?
!
SWIP
SKFF
PRINCE IL...
LET'S GO.
WAIT, PLEASE!
KASHI IS ALIVE...?
FOR SO LONG, I THOUGHT ...
THAT GIRL IS DEAD!

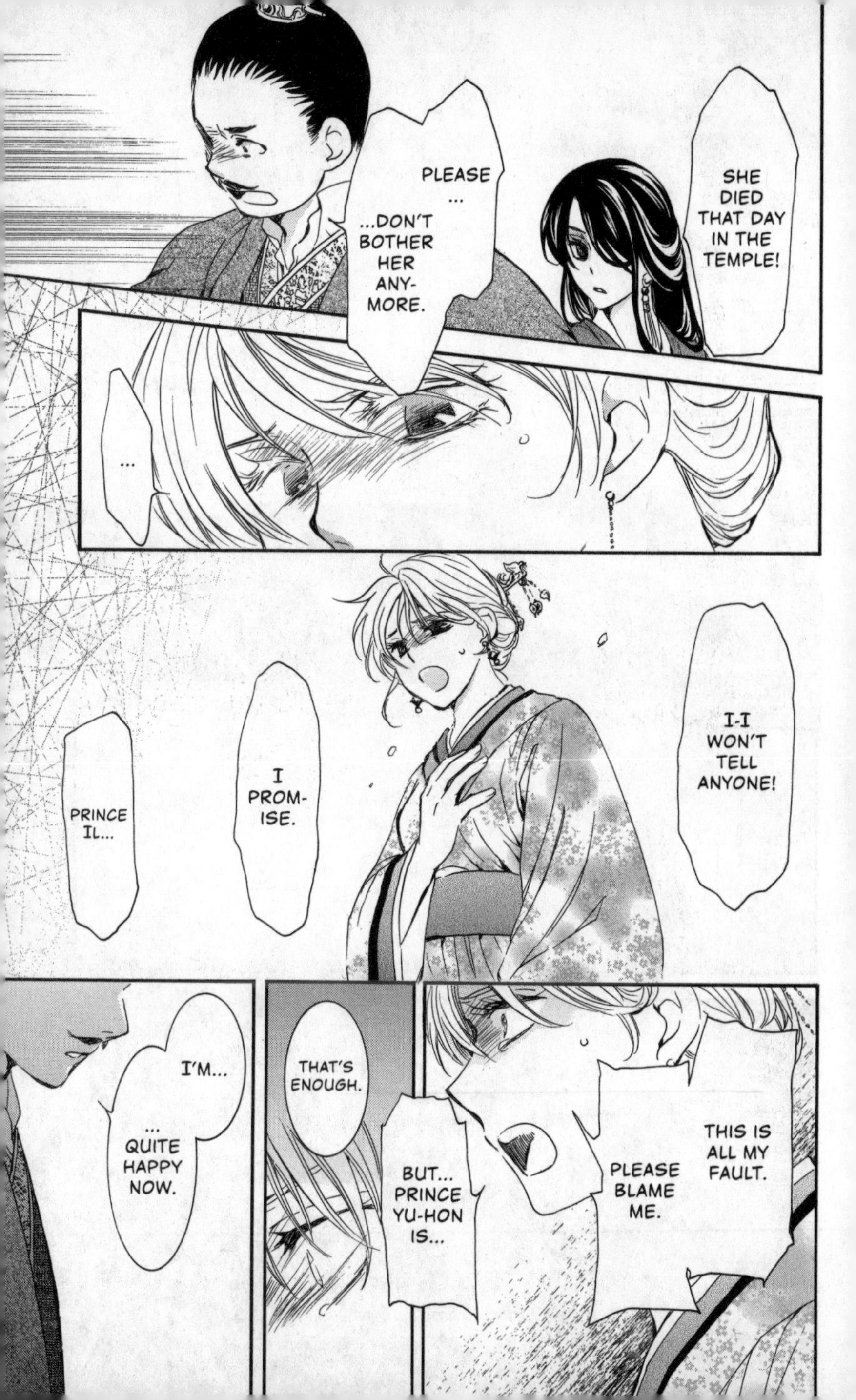

SHE DIED THAT DAY IN THE TEMPLE!
PLEASE ... ...DON'T BOTHER HER ANYMORE.
...
I-I WON'T TELL ANYONE!
I PROMISE.
PRINCE IL...
THIS IS ALL MY FAULT.
PLEASE BLAME ME.
BUT... PRINCE YU-HON IS...
THAT'S ENOUGH.
I'M...
... QUITE HAPPY NOW.

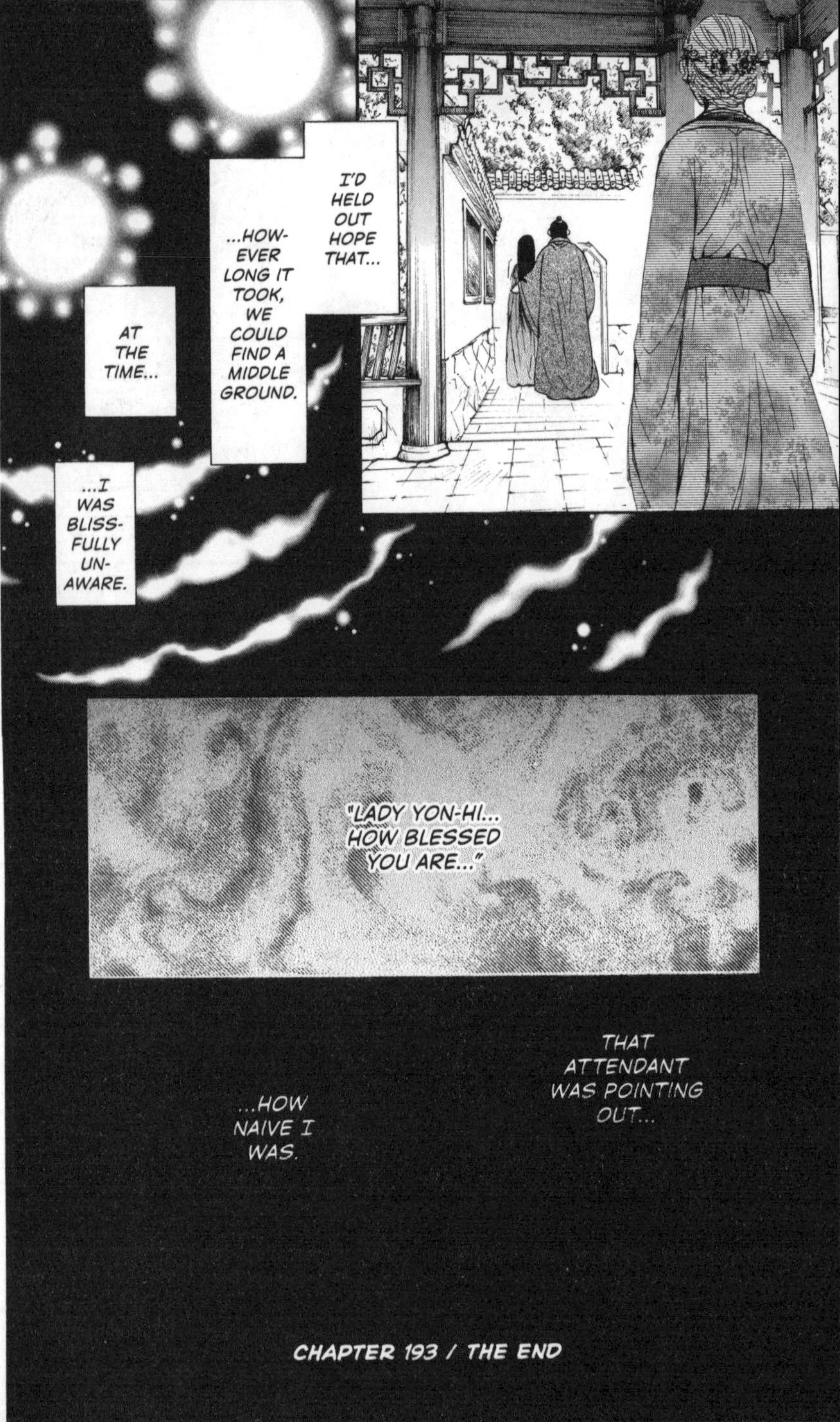
I'D HELD OUT HOPE THAT...
...HOW-EVER LONG IT TOOK, WE COULD FIND A MIDDLE GROUND.
AT THE TIME...
...I WAS BLISS-FULLY UN-AWARE.
"LADY YON-HI... HOW BLESSED YOU ARE..."
THAT ATTENDANT WAS POINTING OUT...
...HOW NAIVE I WAS.
CHAPTER 193 / THE END

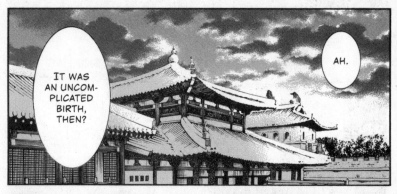

AH.
IT WAS AN UNCOM-PLICATED BIRTH, THEN?
YES. MOTHER AND CHILD ARE BOTH WELL.
PRINCE IL MUST BE DELIGHTED.
THE BABY IS A GIRL NAMED YONA. WE SHOULD SEND THEM A COM-MEMORATIVE GIFT SOON.
YONA ...

Yona of the Dawn

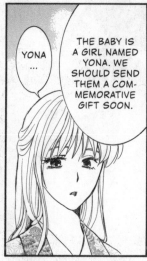

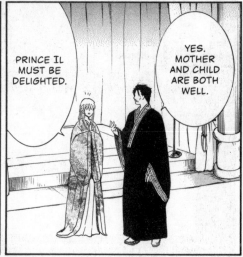

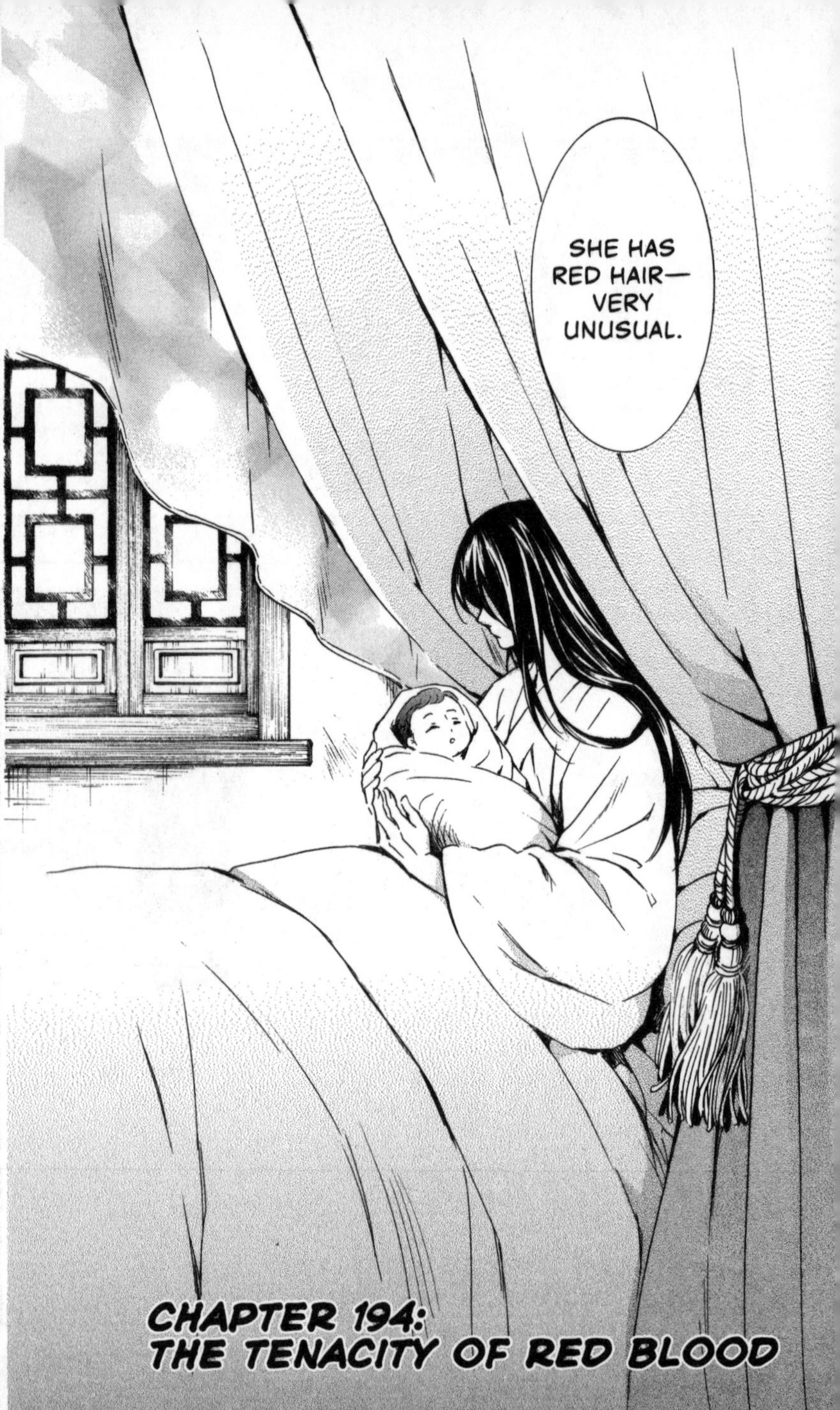
SHE HAS RED HAIR—VERY UNUSUAL.
CHAPTER 194: THE TENACITY OF RED BLOOD

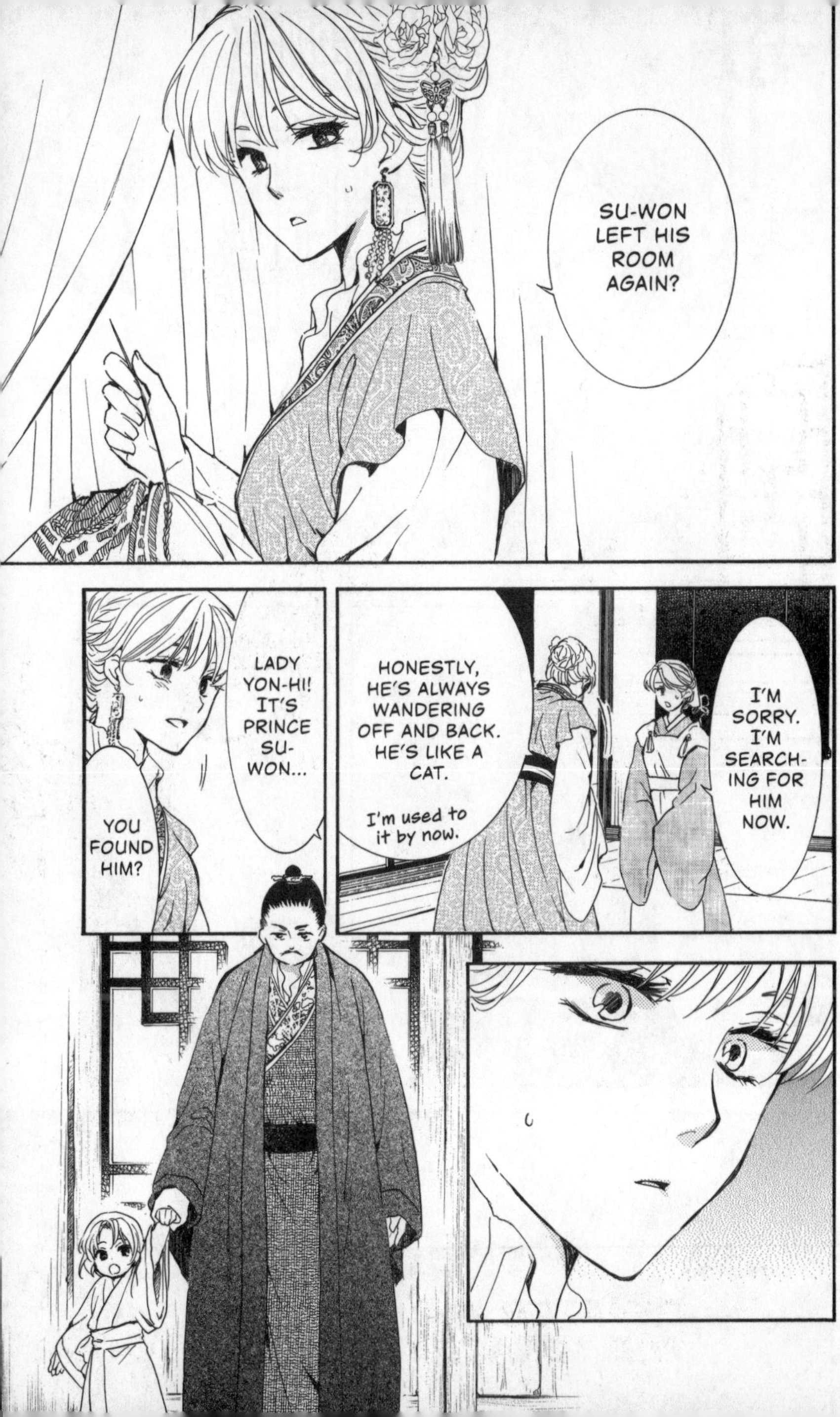
SU-WON LEFT HIS ROOM AGAIN?
I'M SORRY. I'M SEARCHING FOR HIM NOW.
HONESTLY, HE'S ALWAYS WANDERING OFF AND BACK. HE'S LIKE A CAT.
I'm used to it by now.
LADY YON-HI! IT'S PRINCE SU-WON...
YOU FOUND HIM?

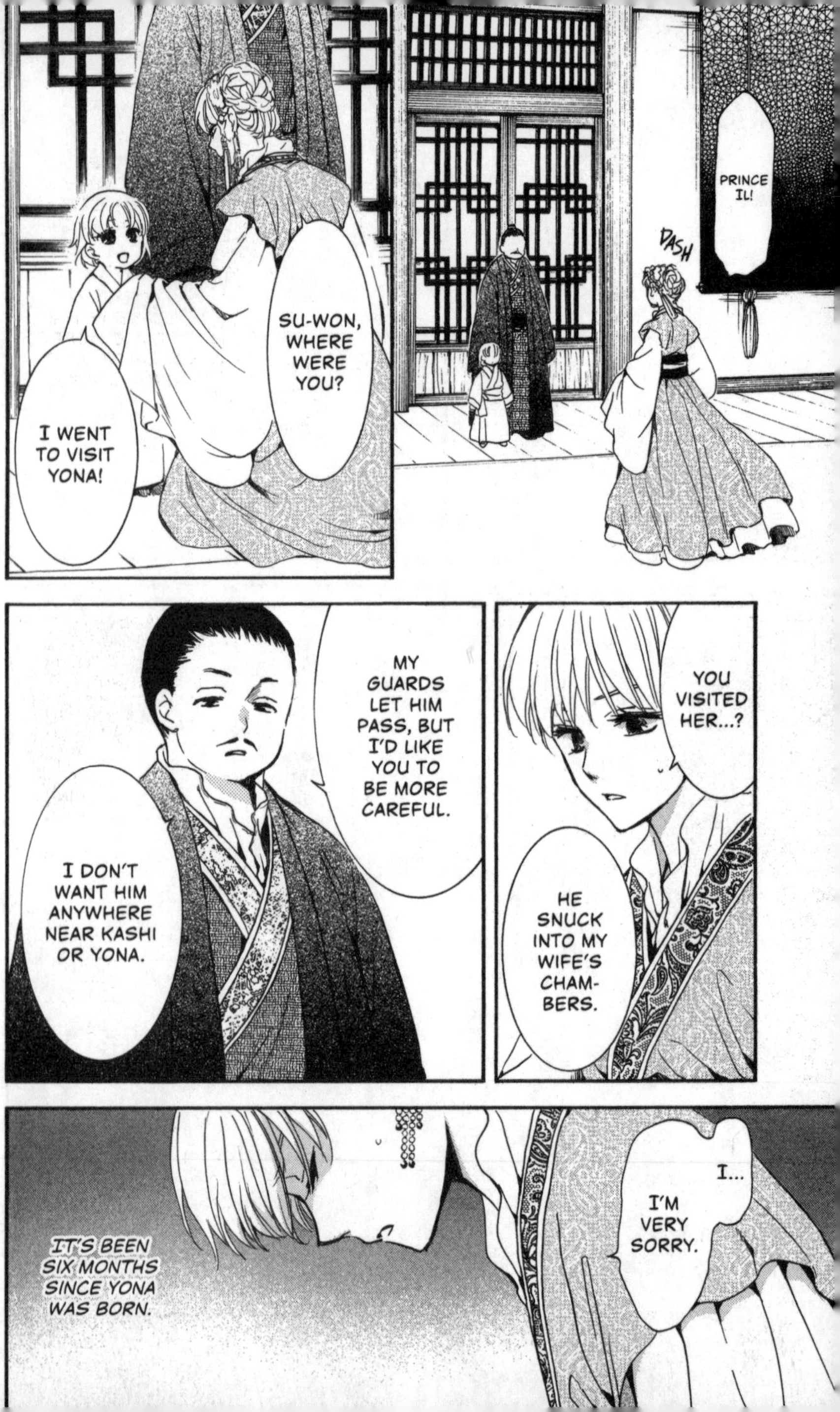
PRINCE IL!
DASH
SU-WON, WHERE WERE YOU?
I WENT TO VISIT YONA!
YOU VISITED HER...?
HE SNUCK INTO MY WIFE'S CHAMBERS.
MY GUARDS LET HIM PASS, BUT I'D LIKE YOU TO BE MORE CAREFUL.
I DON'T WANT HIM ANYWHERE NEAR KASHI OR YONA.
I...
I'M VERY SORRY.
IT'S BEEN SIX MONTHS SINCE YONA WAS BORN.

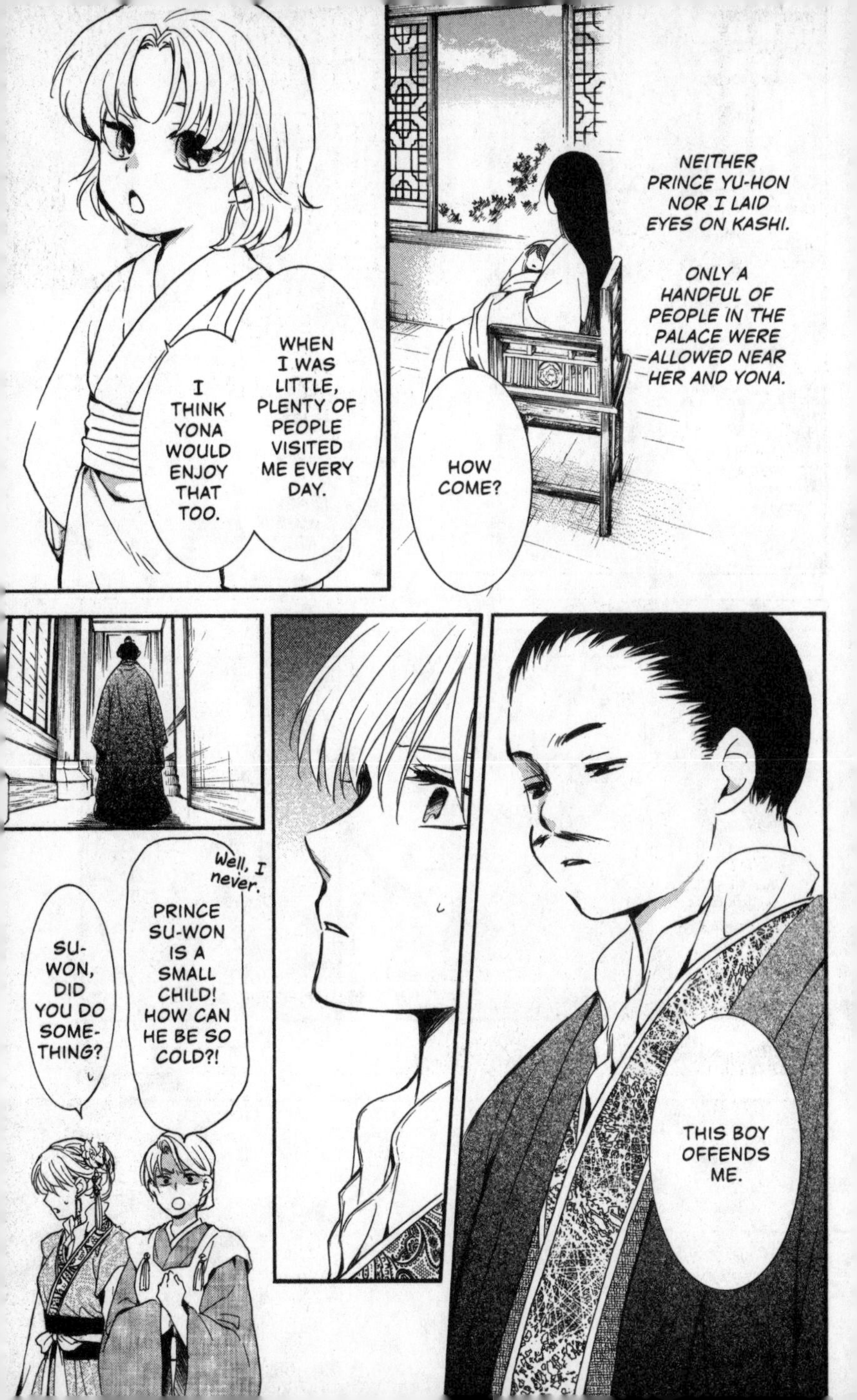
NEITHER PRINCE YU-HON NOR I LAID EYES ON KASHI.
ONLY A HANDFUL OF PEOPLE IN THE PALACE WERE ALLOWED NEAR HER AND YONA.
HOW COME?
WHEN I WAS LITTLE, PLENTY OF PEOPLE VISITED ME EVERY DAY.
I THINK YONA WOULD ENJOY THAT TOO.
THIS BOY OFFENDS ME.
Well, I never.
PRINCE SU-WON IS A SMALL CHILD! HOW CAN HE BE SO COLD?!
SU-WON, DID YOU DO SOME-THING?

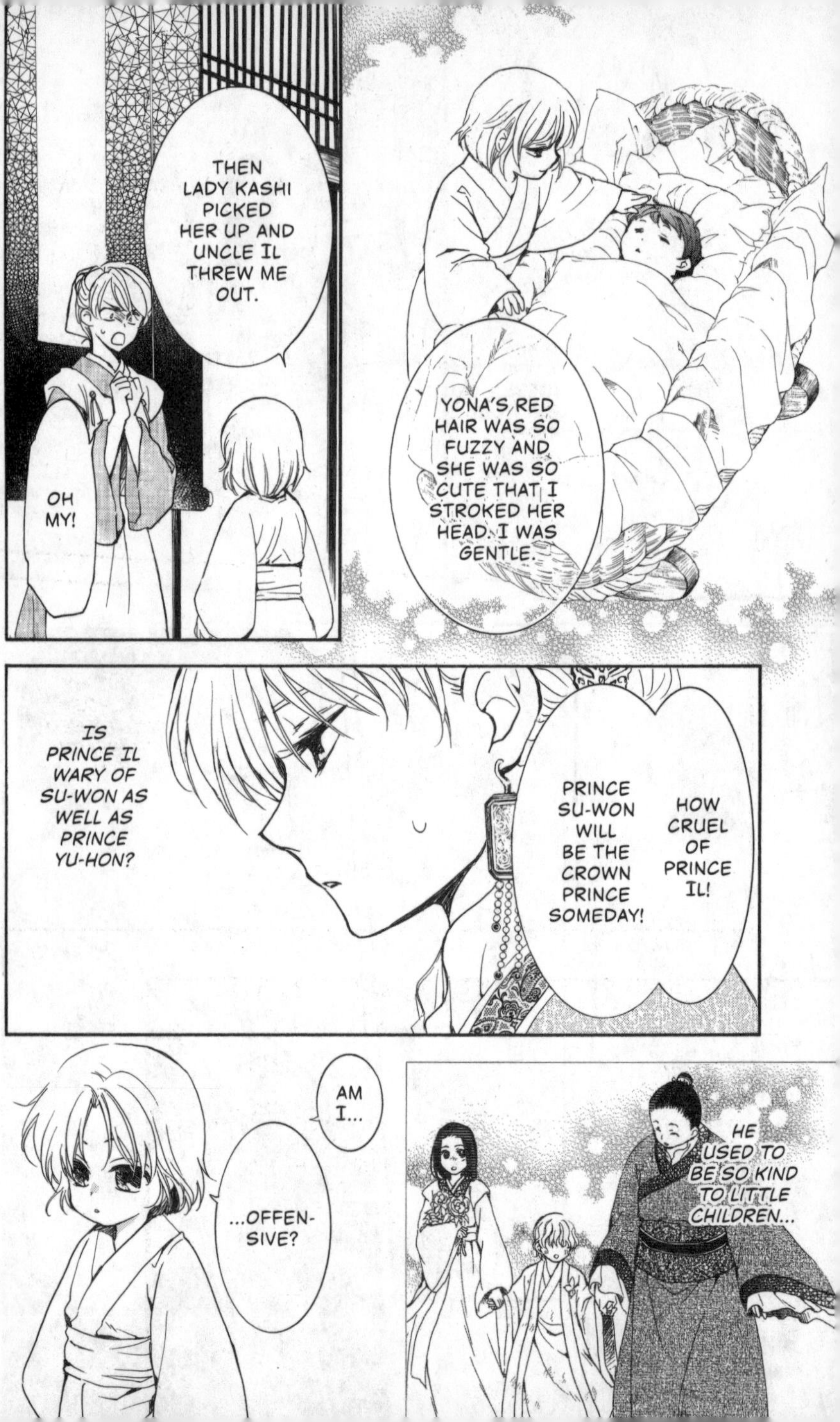
YONA'S RED HAIR WAS SO FUZZY AND SHE WAS SO CUTE THAT I STROKED HER HEAD. I WAS GENTLE.
THEN LADY KASHI PICKED HER UP AND UNCLE IL THREW ME OUT.
OH MY!
HOW CRUEL OF PRINCE IL!
PRINCE SU-WON WILL BE THE CROWN PRINCE SOMEDAY!
IS PRINCE IL WARY OF SU-WON AS WELL AS PRINCE YU-HON?
HE USED TO BE SO KIND TO LITTLE CHILDREN...
AM I...
...OFFEN-SIVE?

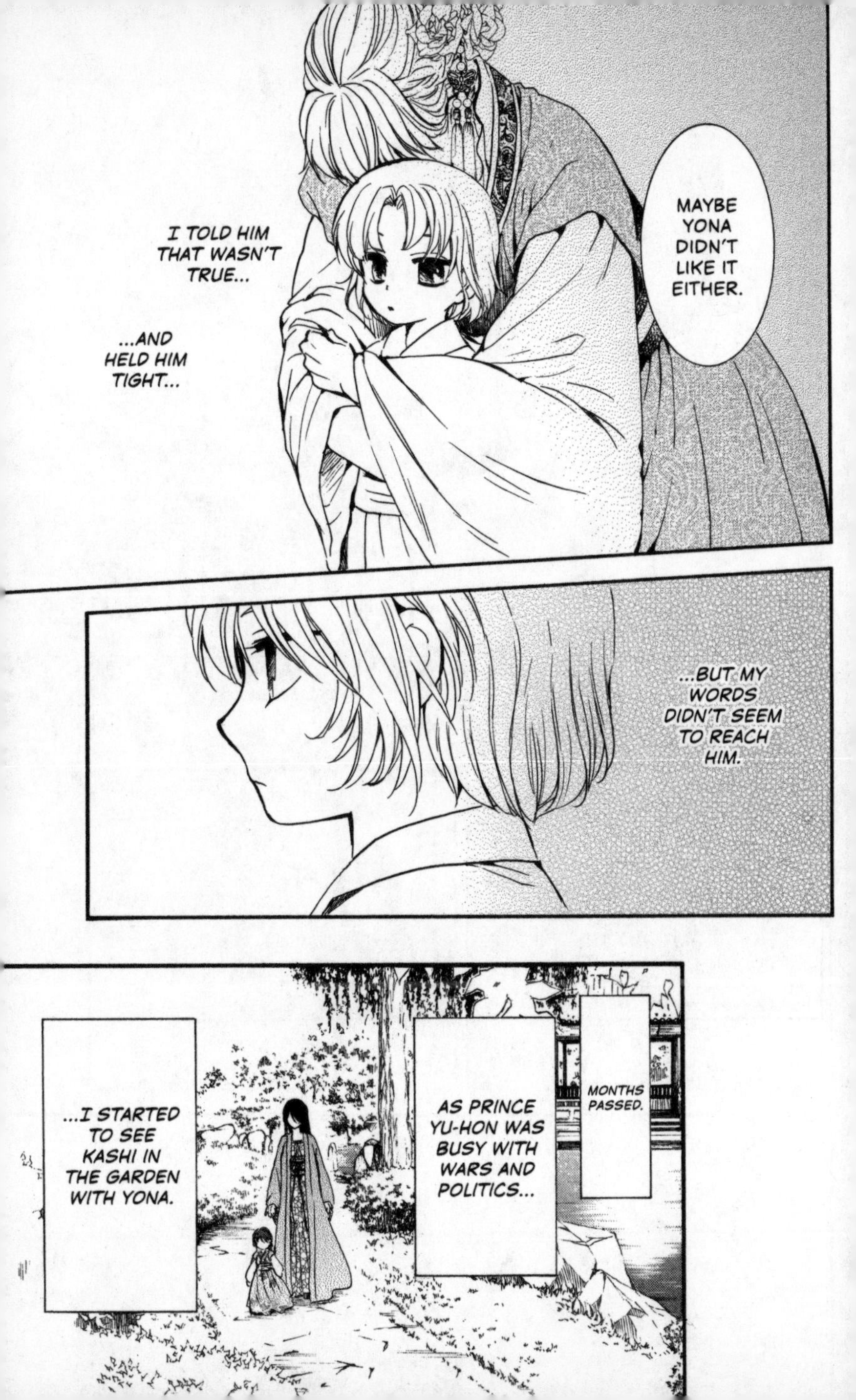
MAYBE YONA DIDN'T LIKE IT EITHER.
I TOLD HIM THAT WASN'T TRUE...
...AND HELD HIM TIGHT...
...BUT MY WORDS DIDN'T SEEM TO REACH HIM.
MONTHS PASSED.
AS PRINCE YU-HON WAS BUSY WITH WARS AND POLITICS...
...I STARTED TO SEE KASHI IN THE GARDEN WITH YONA.

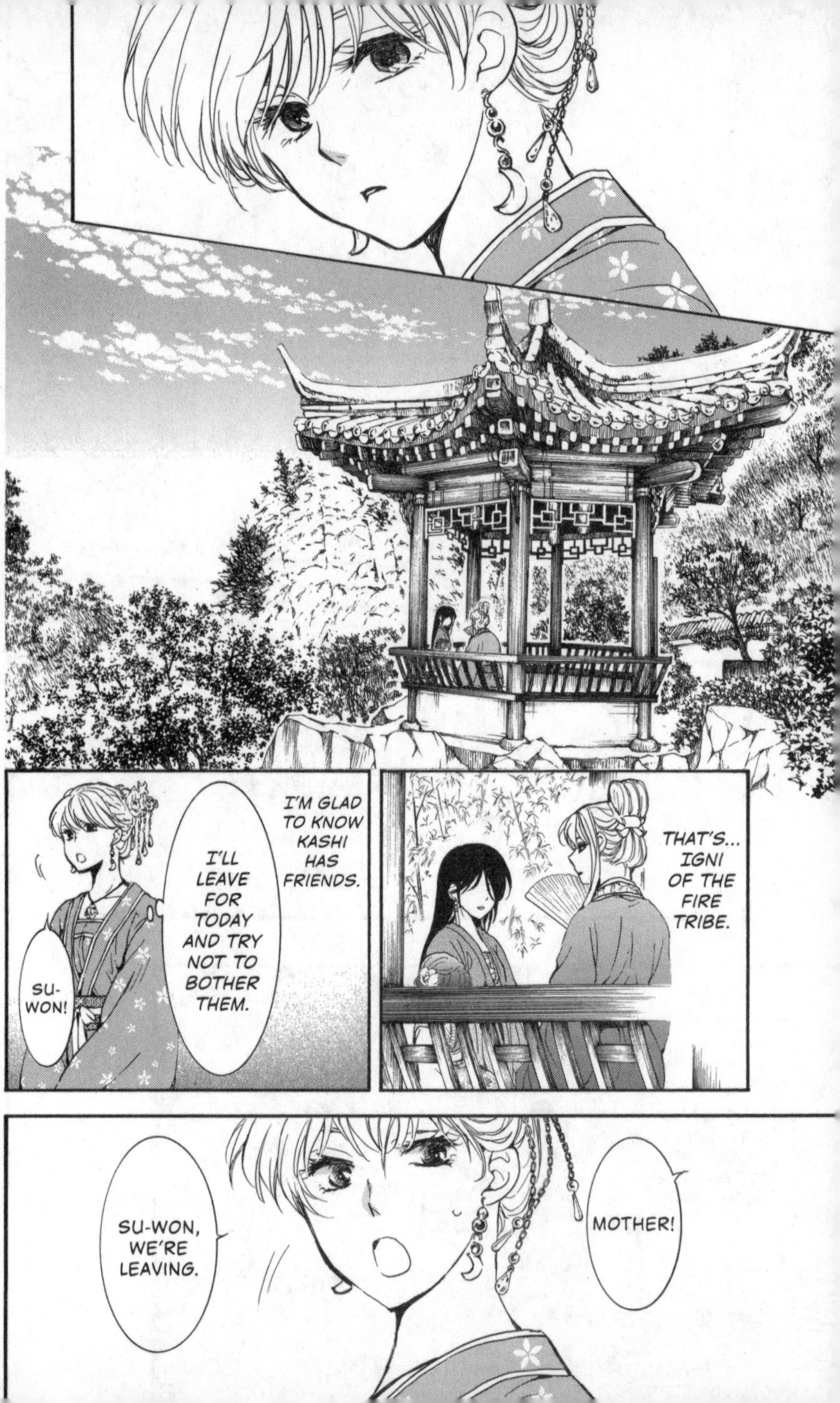
THAT'S... IGNI OF THE FIRE TRIBE.
I'M GLAD TO KNOW KASHI HAS FRIENDS.
I'LL LEAVE FOR TODAY AND TRY NOT TO BOTHER THEM.
SU-WON!
MOTHER!
SU-WON, WE'RE LEAVING.

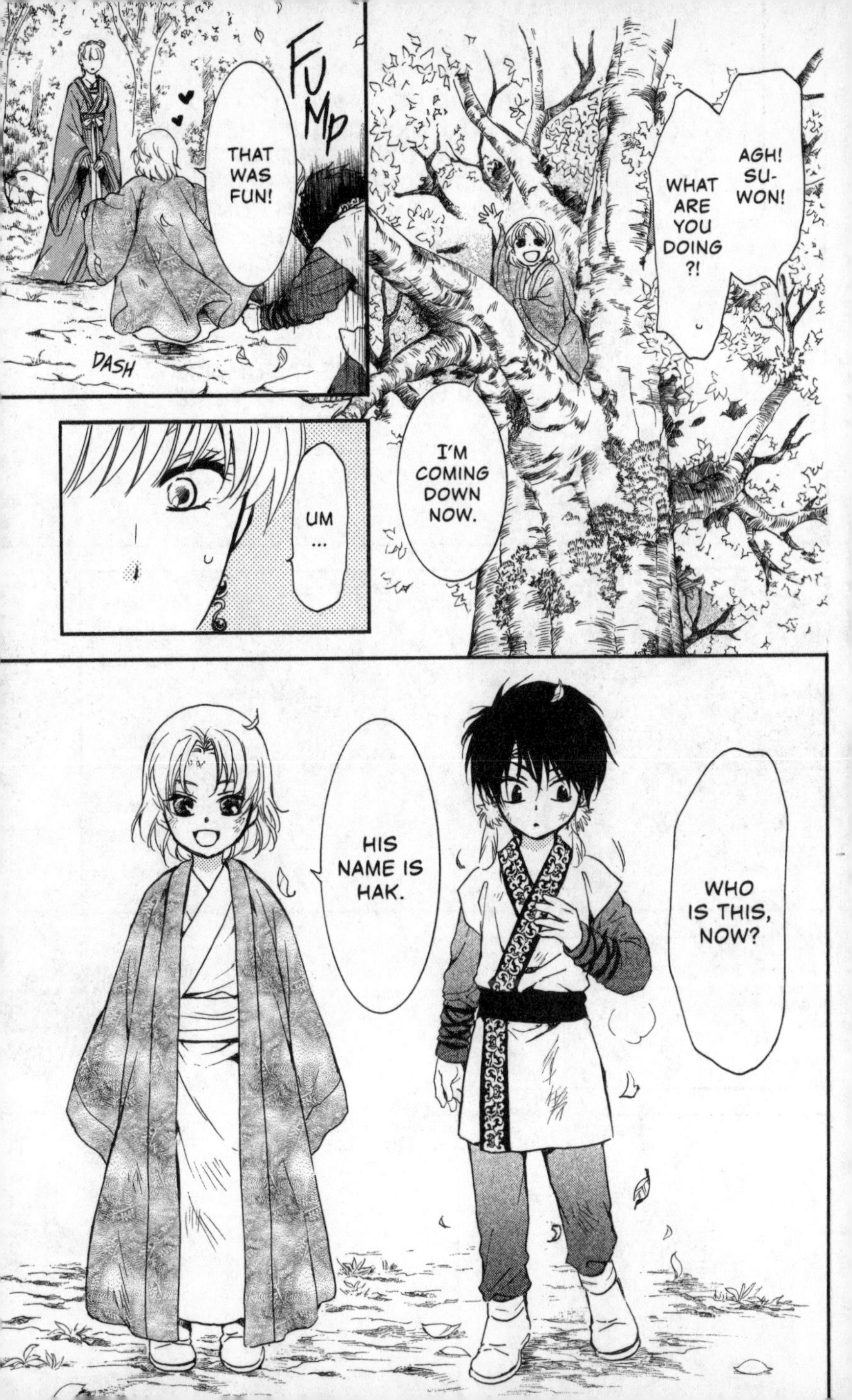

AGH! SU-WON!
WHAT ARE YOU DOING ?!
I'M COMING DOWN NOW.
FUMP
THAT WAS FUN!
DASH
UM ...
WHO IS THIS, NOW?
HIS NAME IS HAK.

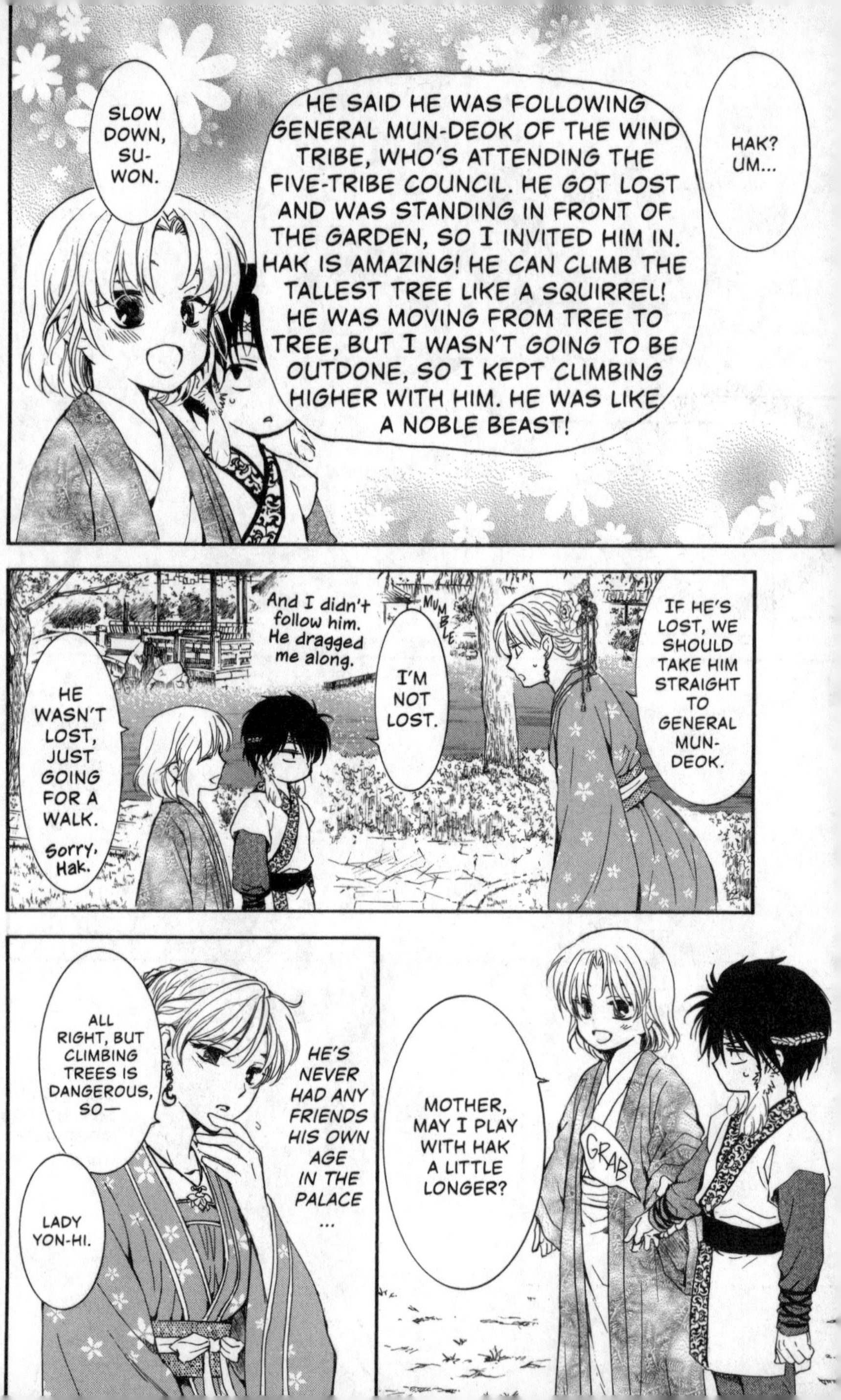
HAK? UM...
HE SAID HE WAS FOLLOWING GENERAL MUN-DEOK OF THE WIND TRIBE, WHO'S ATTENDING THE FIVE-TRIBE COUNCIL. HE GOT LOST AND WAS STANDING IN FRONT OF THE GARDEN, SO I INVITED HIM IN. HAK IS AMAZING! HE CAN CLIMB THE TALLEST TREE LIKE A SQUIRREL! HE WAS MOVING FROM TREE TO TREE, BUT I WASN'T GOING TO BE OUTDONE, SO I KEPT CLIMBING HIGHER WITH HIM. HE WAS LIKE A NOBLE BEAST!
SLOW DOWN, SU-WON.
IF HE'S LOST, WE SHOULD TAKE HIM STRAIGHT TO GENERAL MUN-DEOK.
MUMBLE
I'M NOT LOST.
And I didn't follow him. He dragged me along.
HE WASN'T LOST, JUST GOING FOR A WALK.
Sorry, Hak.
MOTHER, MAY I PLAY WITH HAK A LITTLE LONGER?
GRAB
ALL RIGHT, BUT CLIMBING TREES IS DANGEROUS, SO—
HE'S NEVER HAD ANY FRIENDS HIS OWN AGE IN THE PALACE ...
LADY YON-HI.

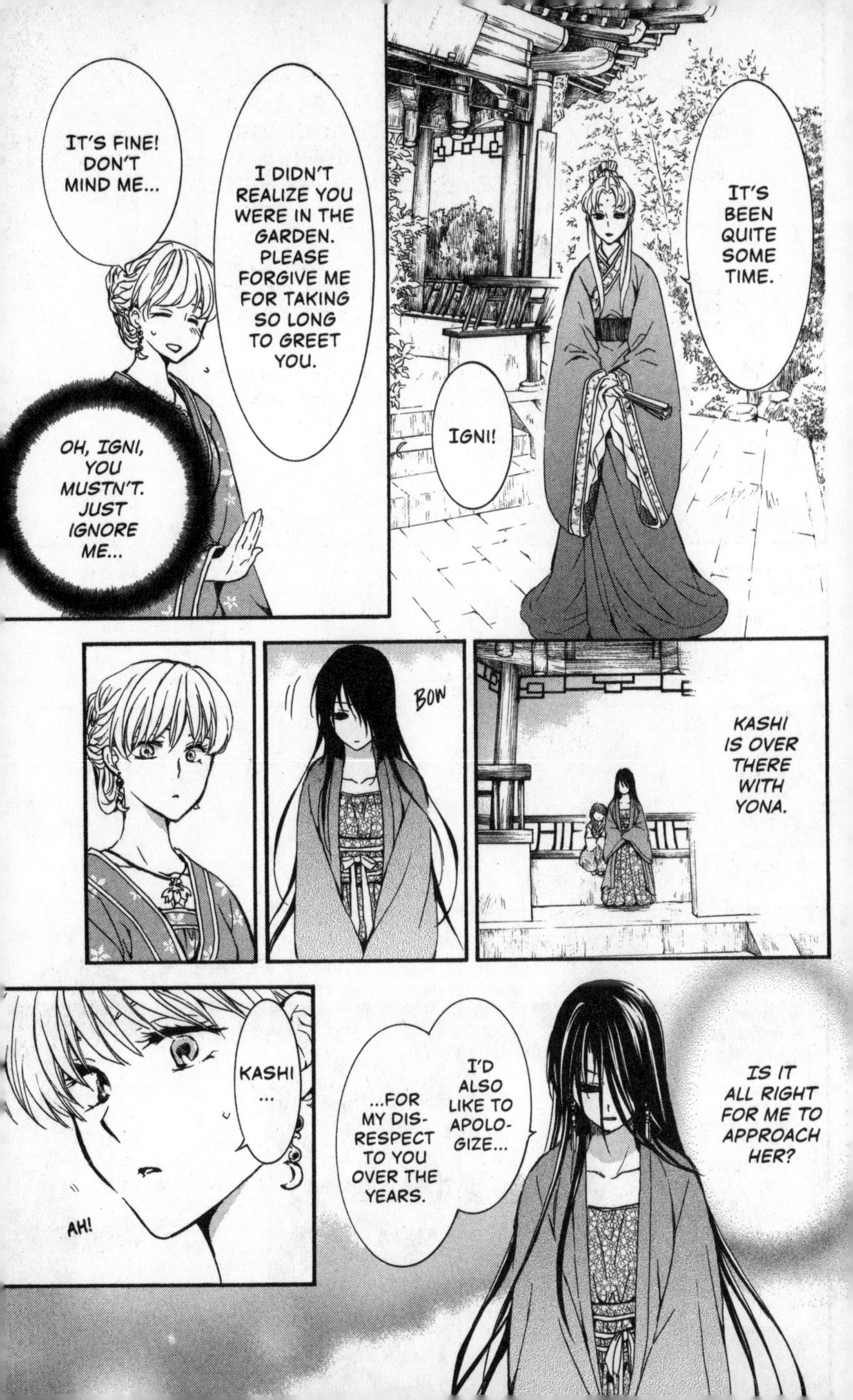
IT'S BEEN QUITE SOME TIME.
IGNI!
I DIDN'T REALIZE YOU WERE IN THE GARDEN. PLEASE FORGIVE ME FOR TAKING SO LONG TO GREET YOU.
IT'S FINE! DON'T MIND ME...
OH, IGNI, YOU MUSTN'T. JUST IGNORE ME...
KASHI IS OVER THERE WITH YONA.
BOW
IS IT ALL RIGHT FOR ME TO APPROACH HER?
I'D ALSO LIKE TO APOLO-GIZE...
...FOR MY DIS-RESPECT TO YOU OVER THE YEARS.
KASHI...
AH!

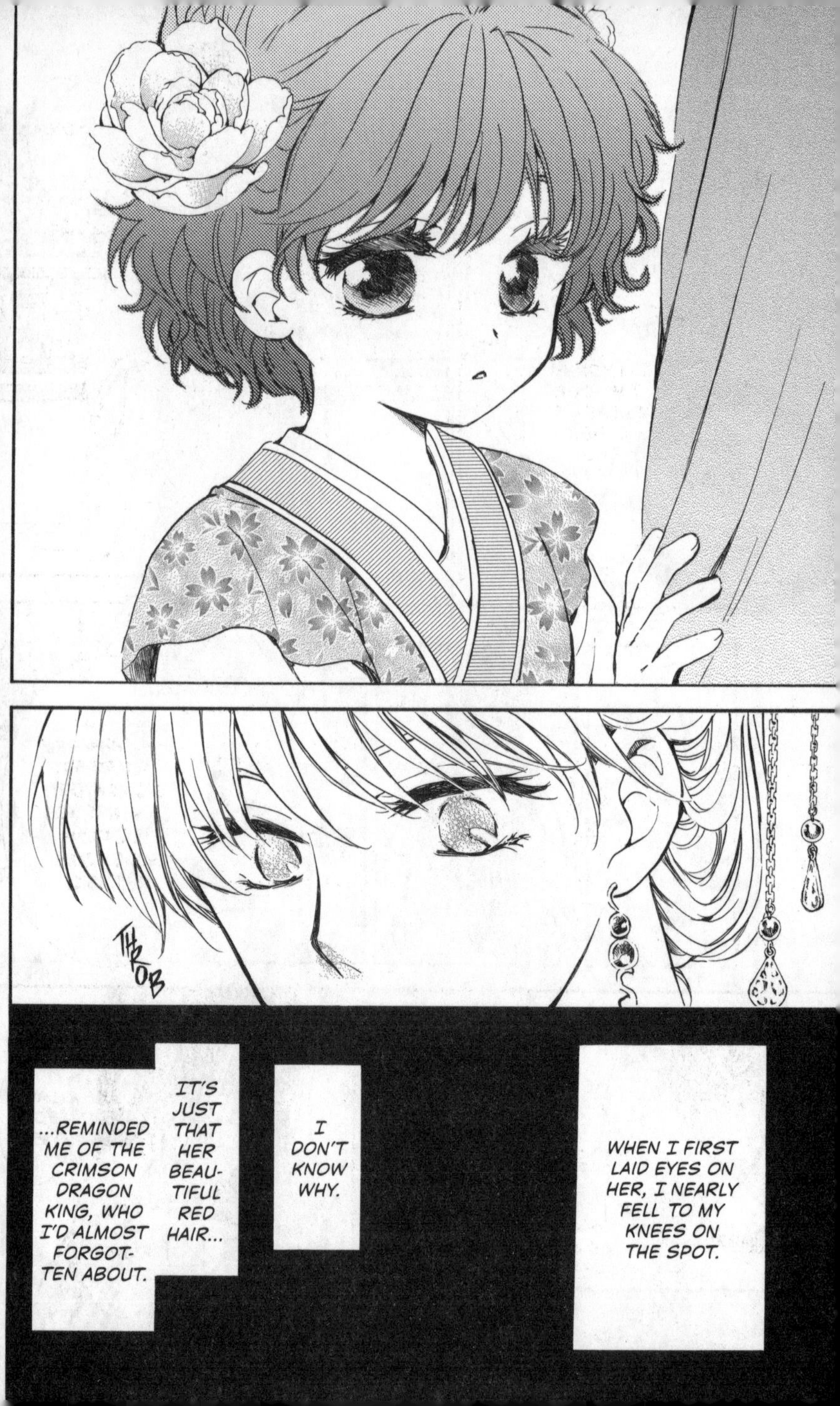
THROB
WHEN I FIRST LAID EYES ON HER, I NEARLY FELL TO MY KNEES ON THE SPOT.
I DON'T KNOW WHY.
IT'S JUST THAT HER BEAU-TIFUL RED HAIR...
...REMINDED ME OF THE CRIMSON DRAGON KING, WHO I'D ALMOST FORGOT-TEN ABOUT.

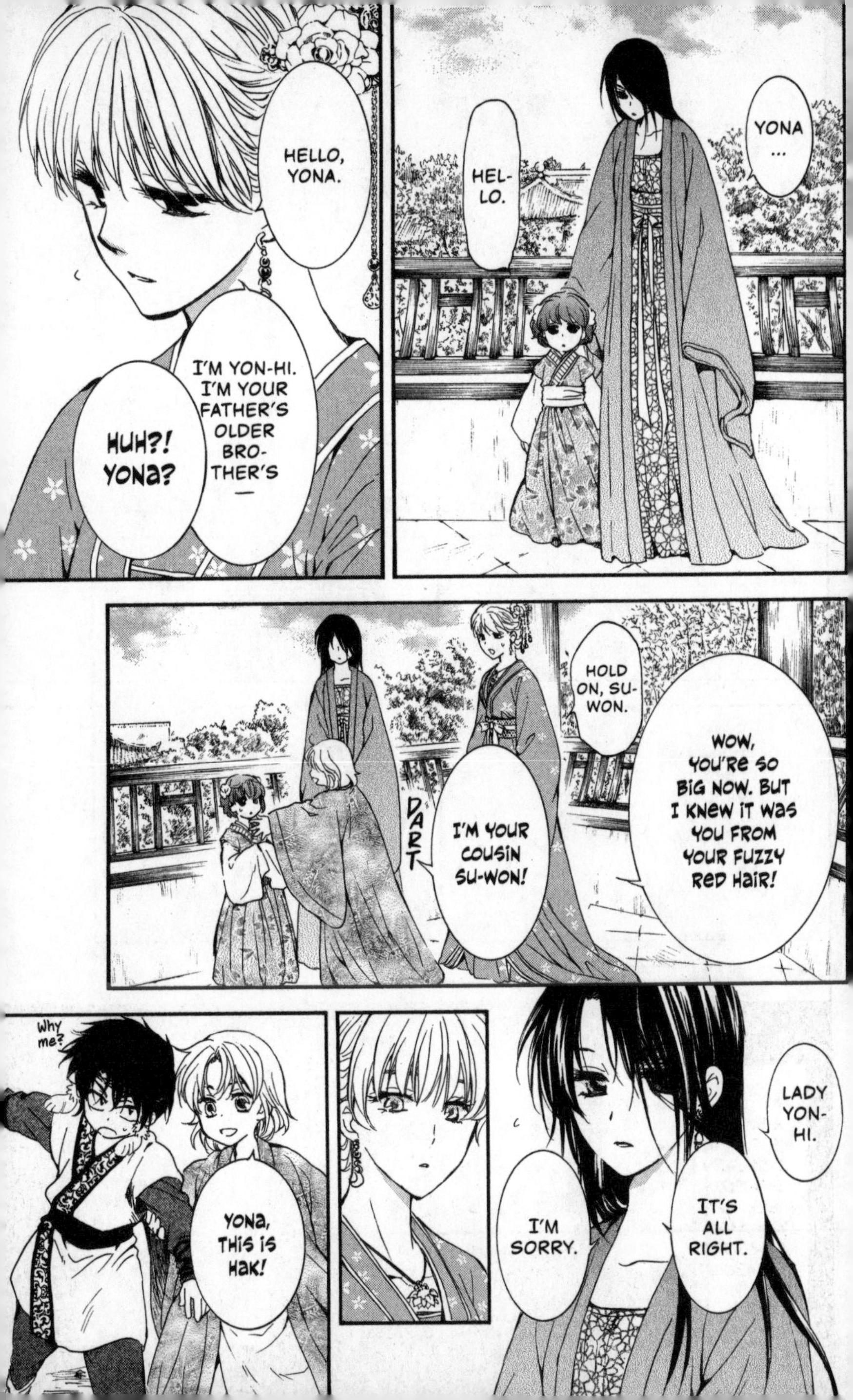
YONA...
HEL-LO.
HELLO, YONA.
I'M YON-HI. I'M YOUR FATHER'S OLDER BRO-THER'S —
HUH?! YONA?
WOW, YOU'RE SO BIG NOW. BUT I KNEW IT WAS YOU FROM YOUR FUZZY RED HAIR!
HOLD ON, SU-WON.
DART
I'M YOUR COUSIN SU-WON!
LADY YON-HI.
IT'S ALL RIGHT.
I'M SORRY.
YONA, THIS IS HAK!
Why me?

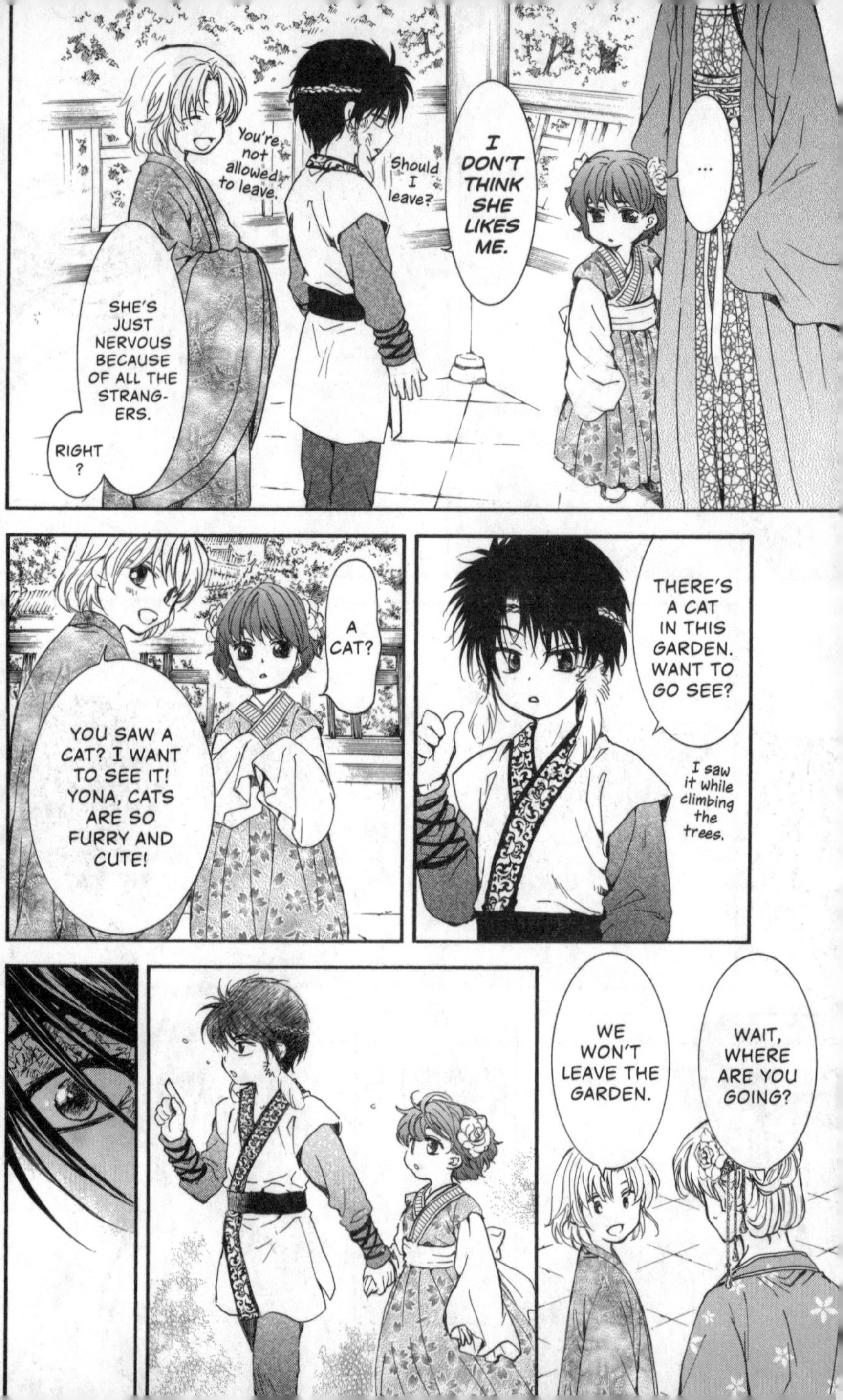
...
I DON'T THINK SHE LIKES ME.
Should I leave?
You're not allowed to leave.
SHE'S JUST NERVOUS BECAUSE OF ALL THE STRANGERS.
RIGHT?
THERE'S A CAT IN THIS GARDEN. WANT TO GO SEE?
I saw it while climbing the trees.
A CAT?
YOU SAW A CAT? I WANT TO SEE IT! YONA, CATS ARE SO FURRY AND CUTE!
WAIT, WHERE ARE YOU GOING?
WE WON'T LEAVE THE GARDEN.

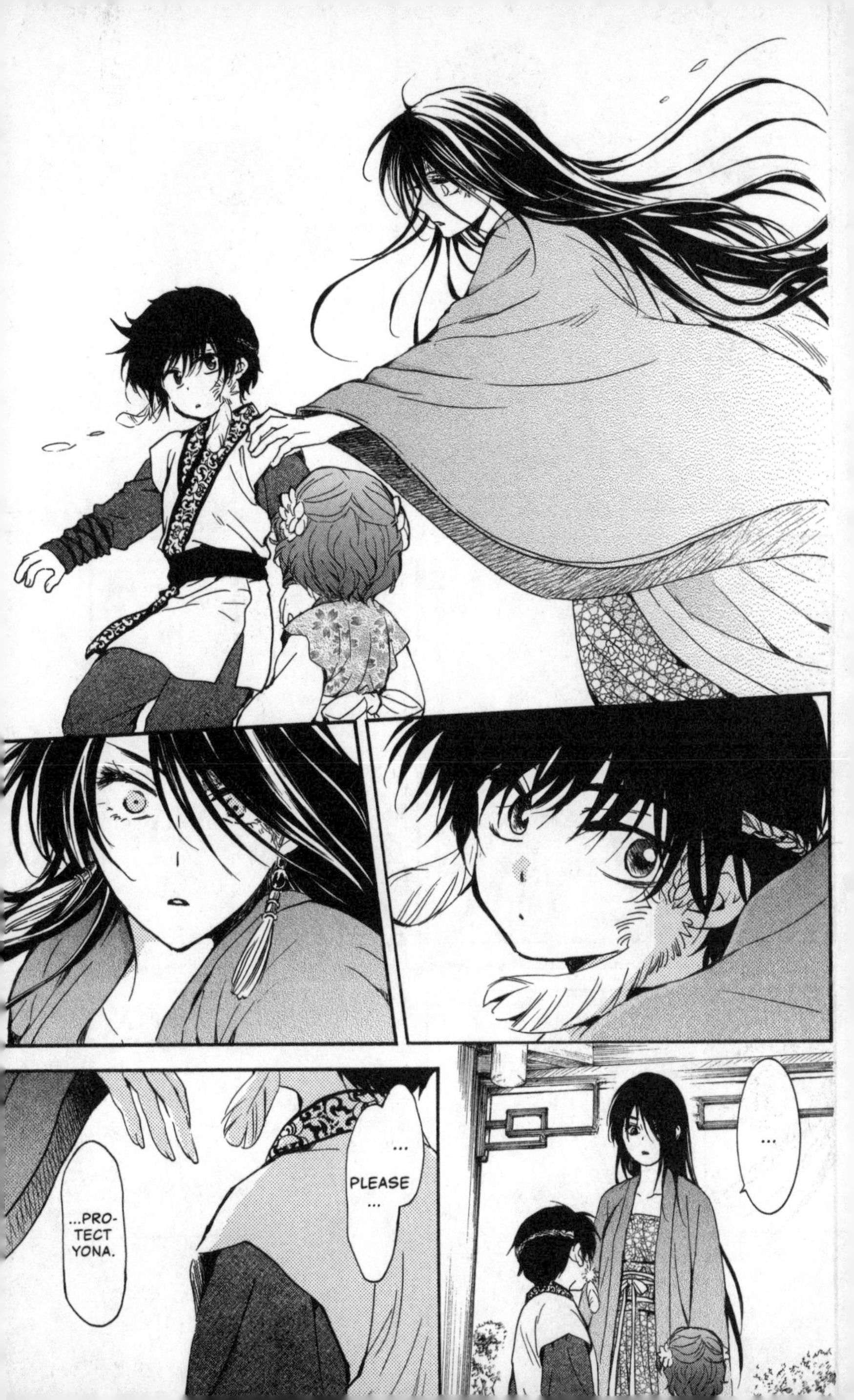
...
... PLEASE ...
...PRO-TECT YONA.

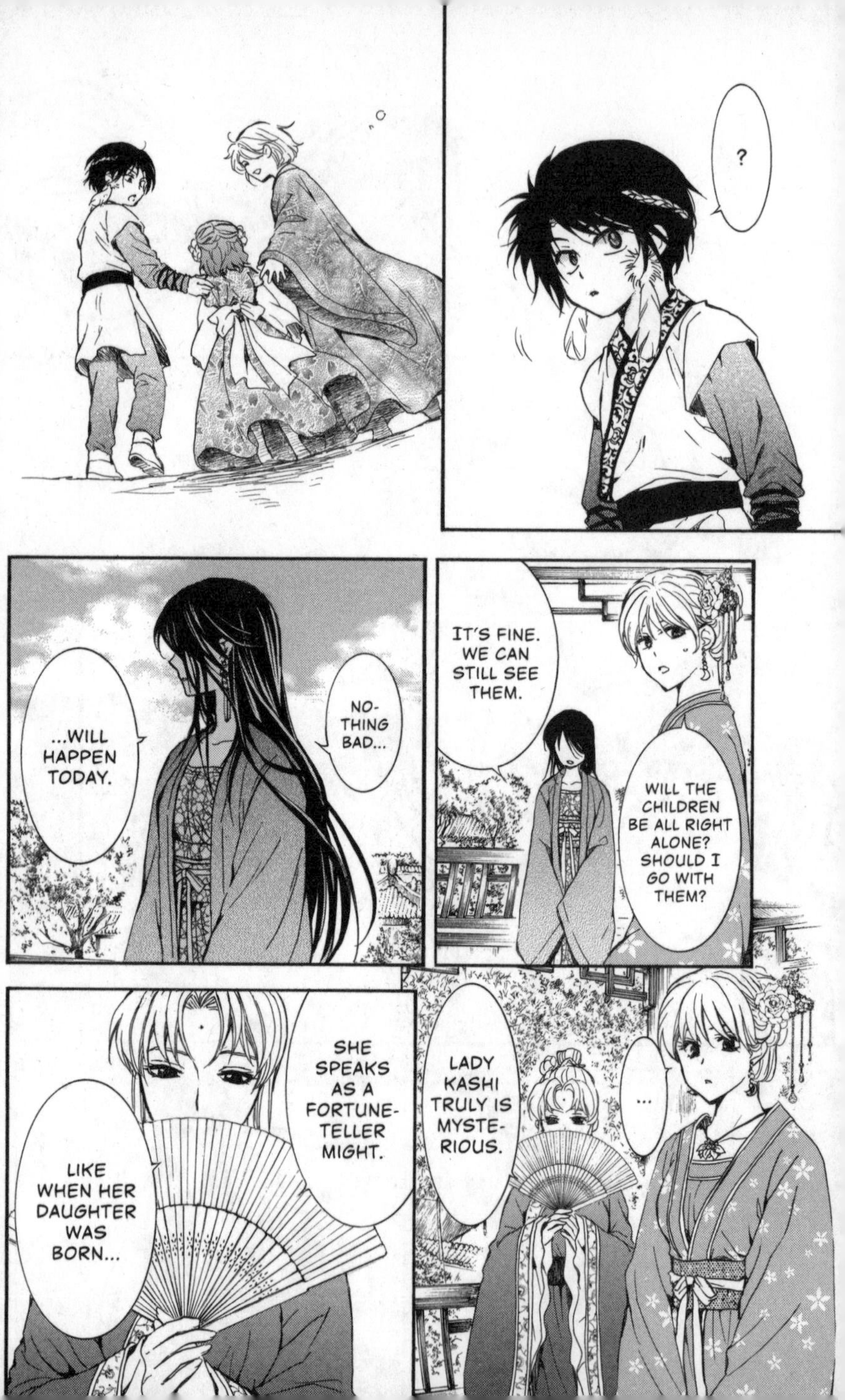
?
WILL THE CHILDREN BE ALL RIGHT ALONE? SHOULD I GO WITH THEM?
IT'S FINE. WE CAN STILL SEE THEM.
NO-THING BAD...
...WILL HAPPEN TODAY.
...
LADY KASHI TRULY IS MYSTE-RIOUS.
SHE SPEAKS AS A FORTUNE-TELLER MIGHT.
LIKE WHEN HER DAUGHTER WAS BORN...

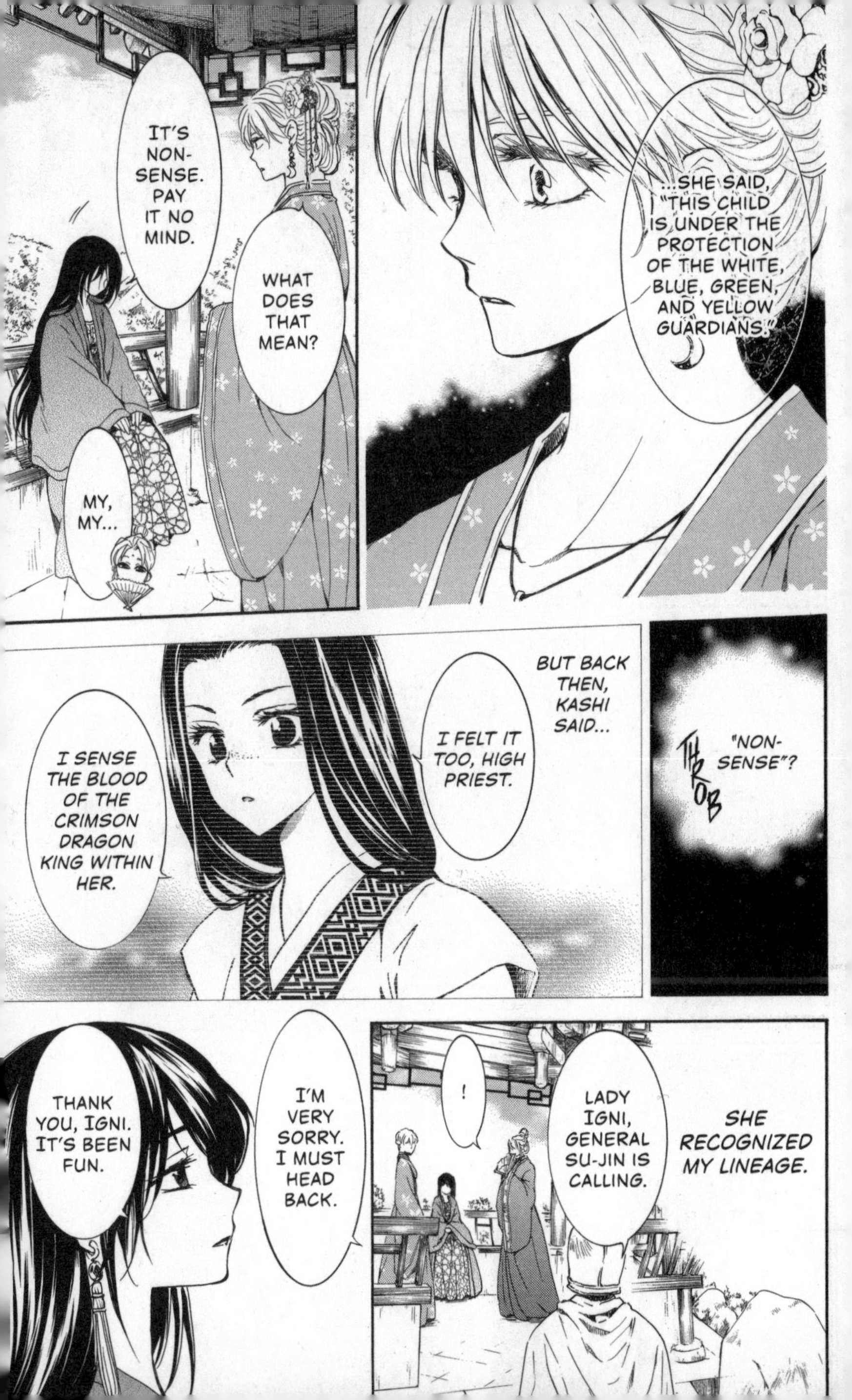
...SHE SAID, "THIS CHILD IS UNDER THE PROTECTION OF THE WHITE, BLUE, GREEN, AND YELLOW GUARDIANS."
WHAT DOES THAT MEAN?
IT'S NON-SENSE. PAY IT NO MIND.
MY, MY...
"NON-SENSE"?
THROB
BUT BACK THEN, KASHI SAID...
I FELT IT TOO, HIGH PRIEST.
I SENSE THE BLOOD OF THE CRIMSON DRAGON KING WITHIN HER.
SHE RECOGNIZED MY LINEAGE.
LADY IGNI, GENERAL SU-JIN IS CALLING.
!
I'M VERY SORRY. I MUST HEAD BACK.
THANK YOU, IGNI. IT'S BEEN FUN.

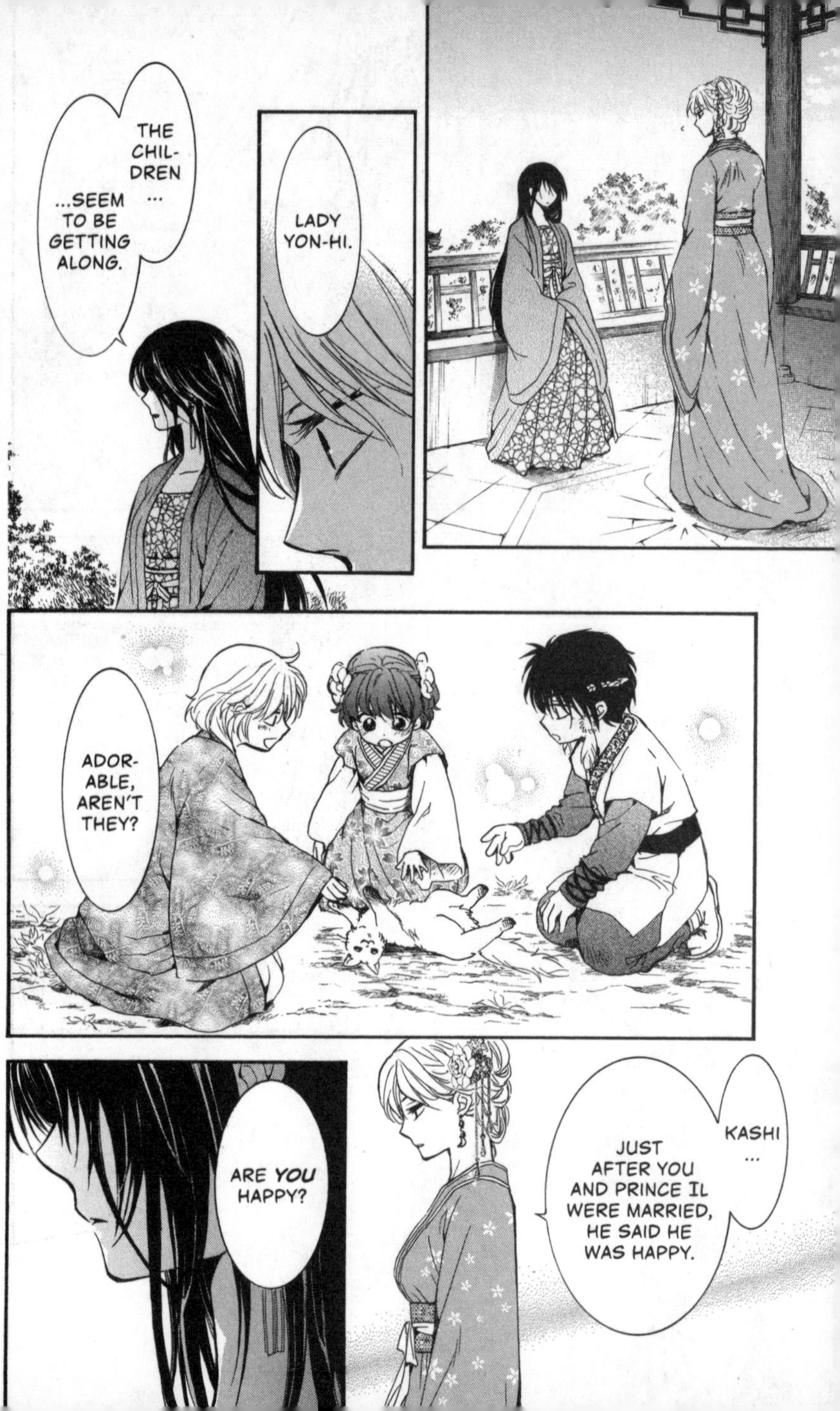
LADY YON-HI.
THE CHILDREN ... ...SEEM TO BE GETTING ALONG.
ADORABLE, AREN'T THEY?
KASHI ...
JUST AFTER YOU AND PRINCE IL WERE MARRIED, HE SAID HE WAS HAPPY.
ARE *YOU* HAPPY?

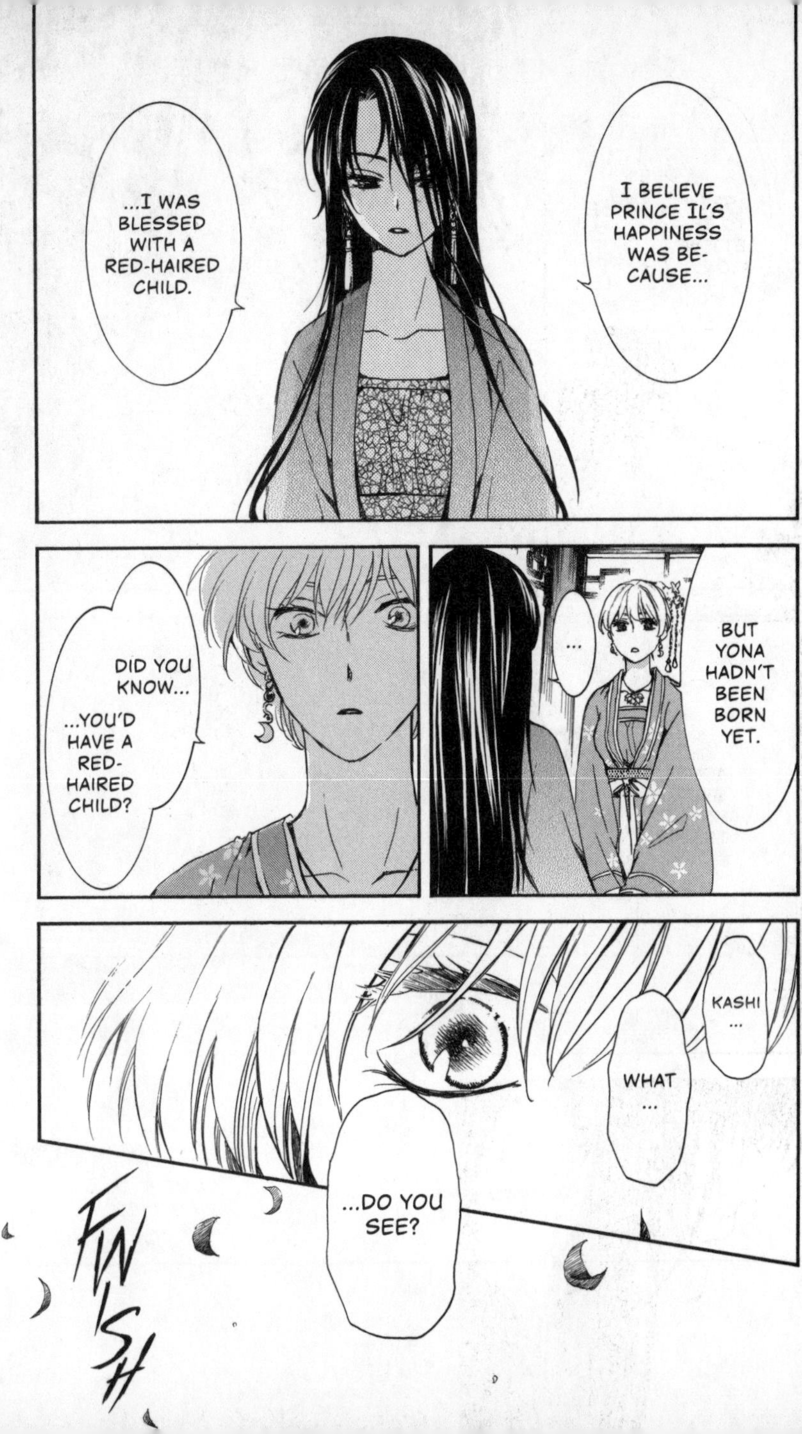
I BELIEVE PRINCE IL'S HAPPINESS WAS BE-CAUSE...
...I WAS BLESSED WITH A RED-HAIRED CHILD.
BUT YONA HADN'T BEEN BORN YET.
...
DID YOU KNOW...
...YOU'D HAVE A RED-HAIRED CHILD?
KASHI...
WHAT...
...DO YOU SEE?
FWISH

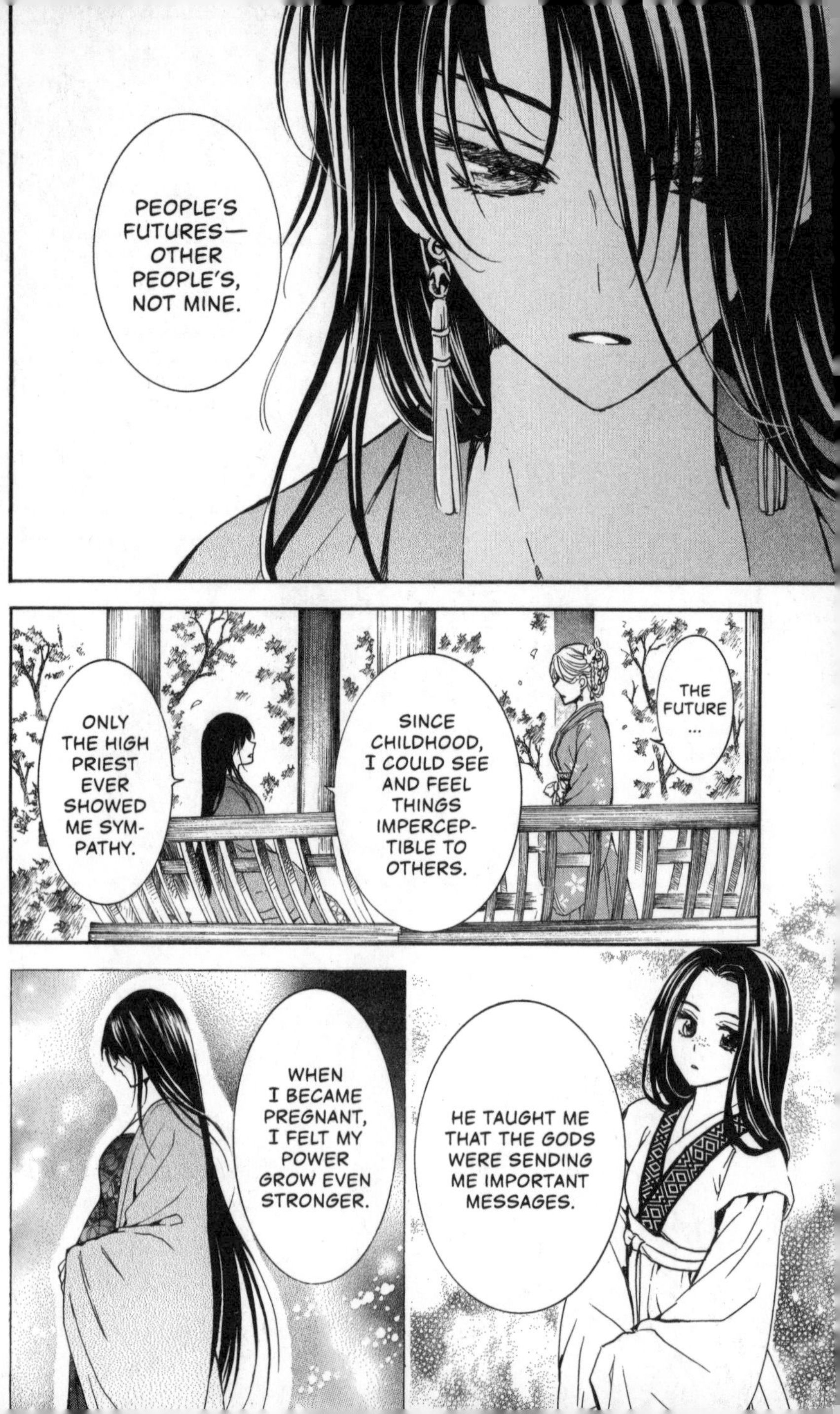
PEOPLE'S FUTURES— OTHER PEOPLE'S, NOT MINE.
THE FUTURE ...
SINCE CHILDHOOD, I COULD SEE AND FEEL THINGS IMPERCEP-TIBLE TO OTHERS.
ONLY THE HIGH PRIEST EVER SHOWED ME SYM-PATHY.
HE TAUGHT ME THAT THE GODS WERE SENDING ME IMPORTANT MESSAGES.
WHEN I BECAME PREGNANT, I FELT MY POWER GROW EVEN STRONGER.

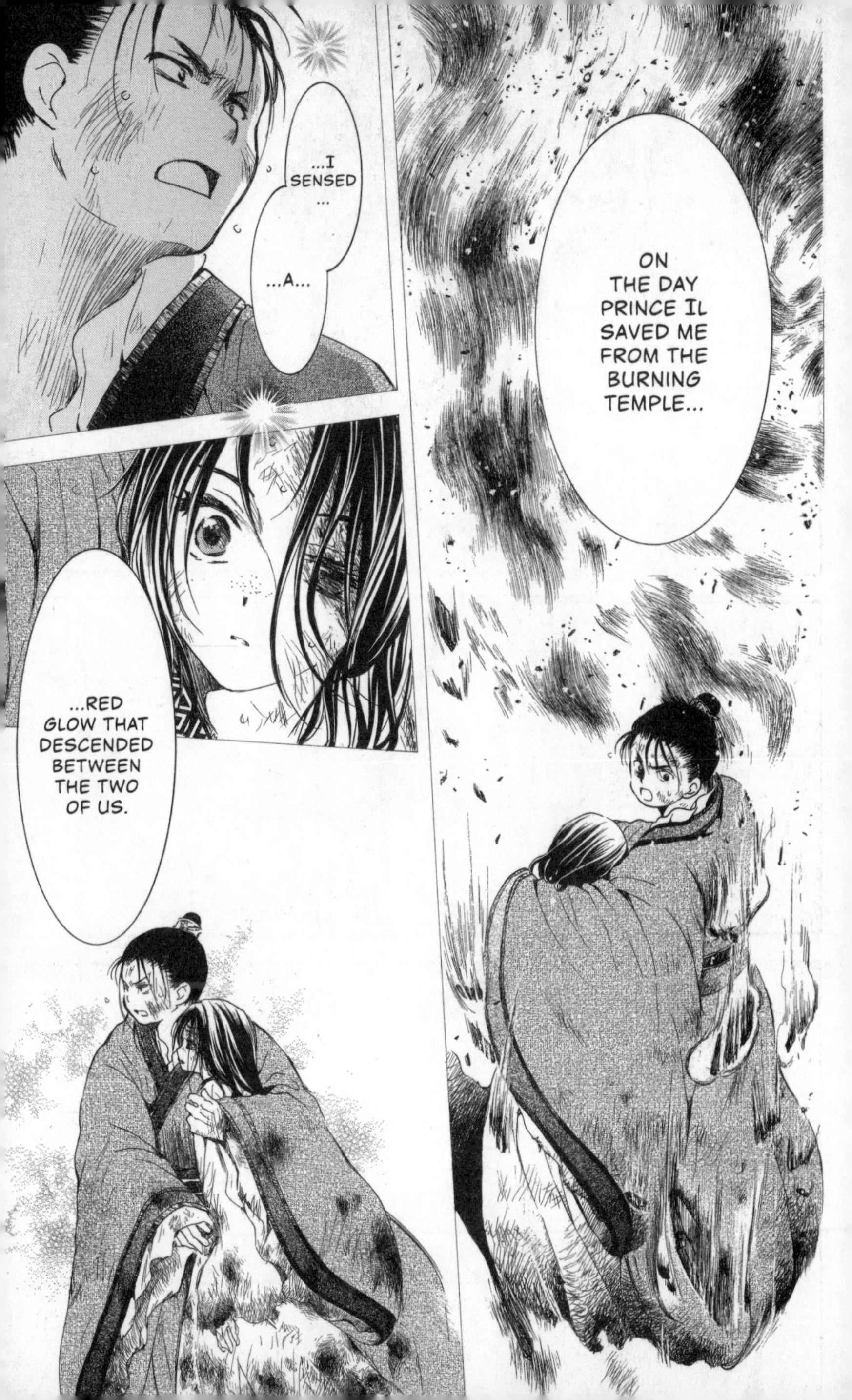
ON THE DAY PRINCE IL SAVED ME FROM THE BURNING TEMPLE...
...I SENSED...
...A...
...RED GLOW THAT DESCENDED BETWEEN THE TWO OF US.

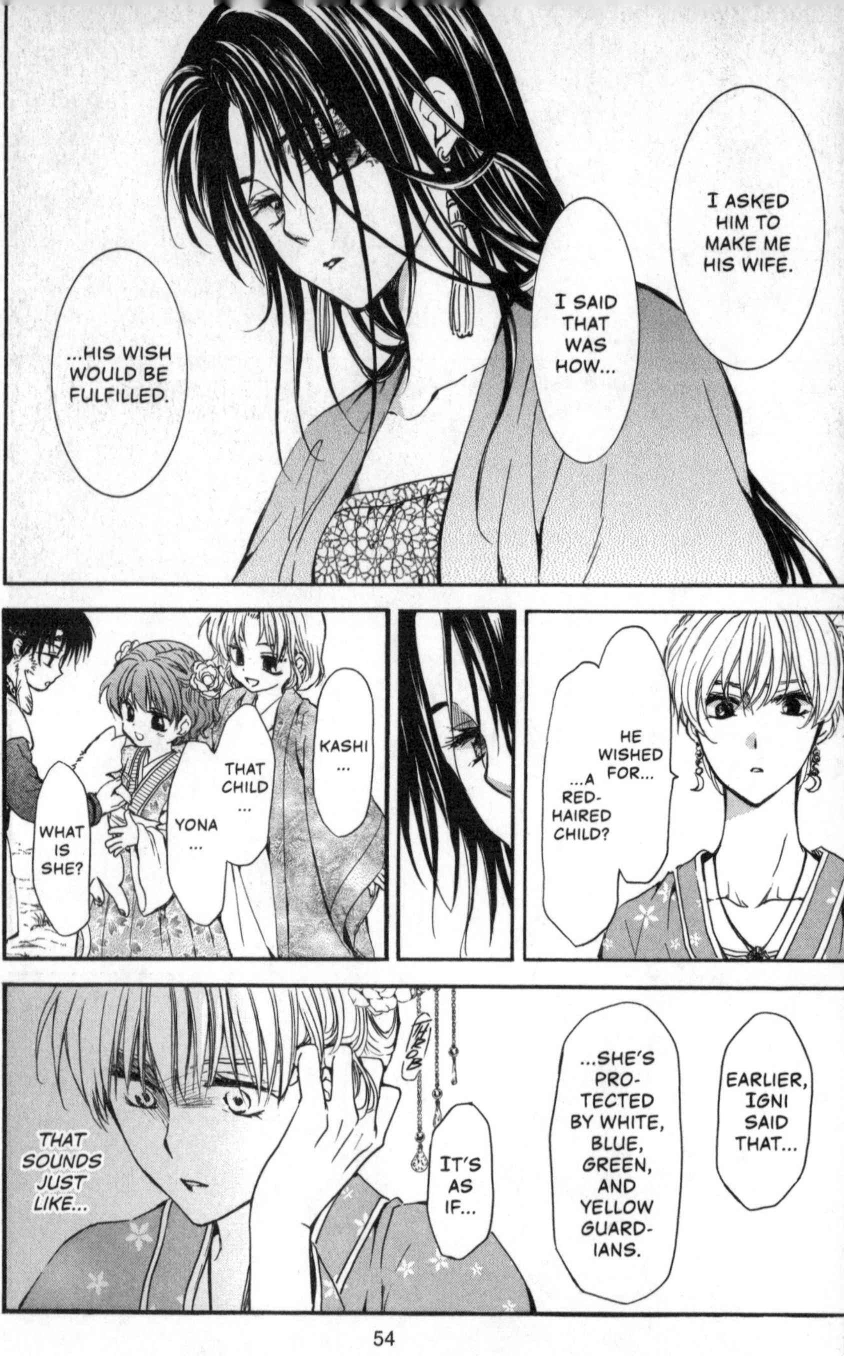
I ASKED HIM TO MAKE ME HIS WIFE.
I SAID THAT WAS HOW...
...HIS WISH WOULD BE FULFILLED.
HE WISHED FOR...
...A RED-HAIRED CHILD?
KASHI ...
THAT CHILD ...
YONA ...
WHAT IS SHE?
EARLIER, IGNI SAID THAT...
...SHE'S PROTECTED BY WHITE, BLUE, GREEN, AND YELLOW GUARDIANS.
THROB
IT'S AS IF...
THAT SOUNDS JUST LIKE...

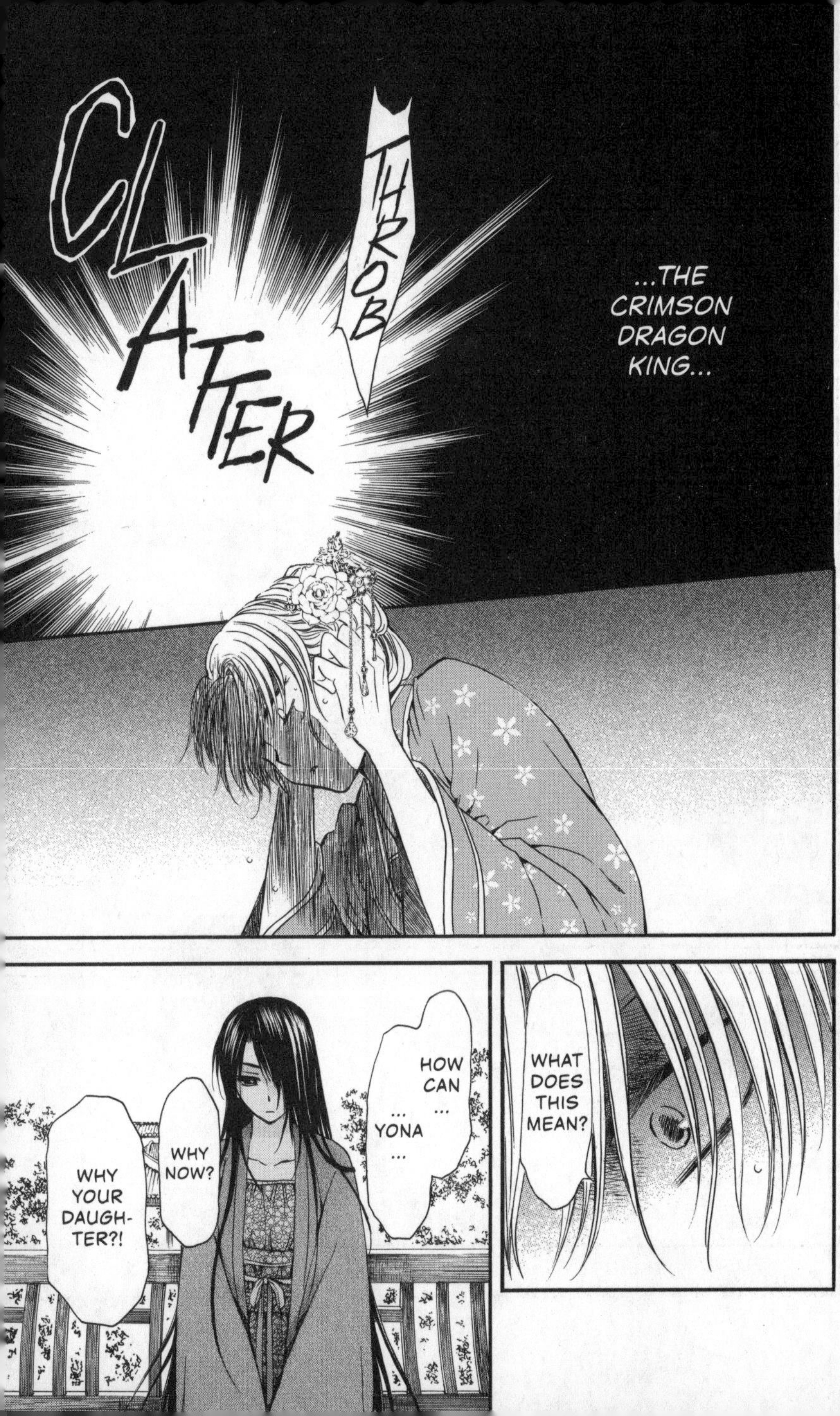
...THE CRIMSON DRAGON KING...
THROB
CLATTER
WHAT DOES THIS MEAN?
HOW CAN ... YONA ...
WHY NOW?
WHY YOUR DAUGHTER?!

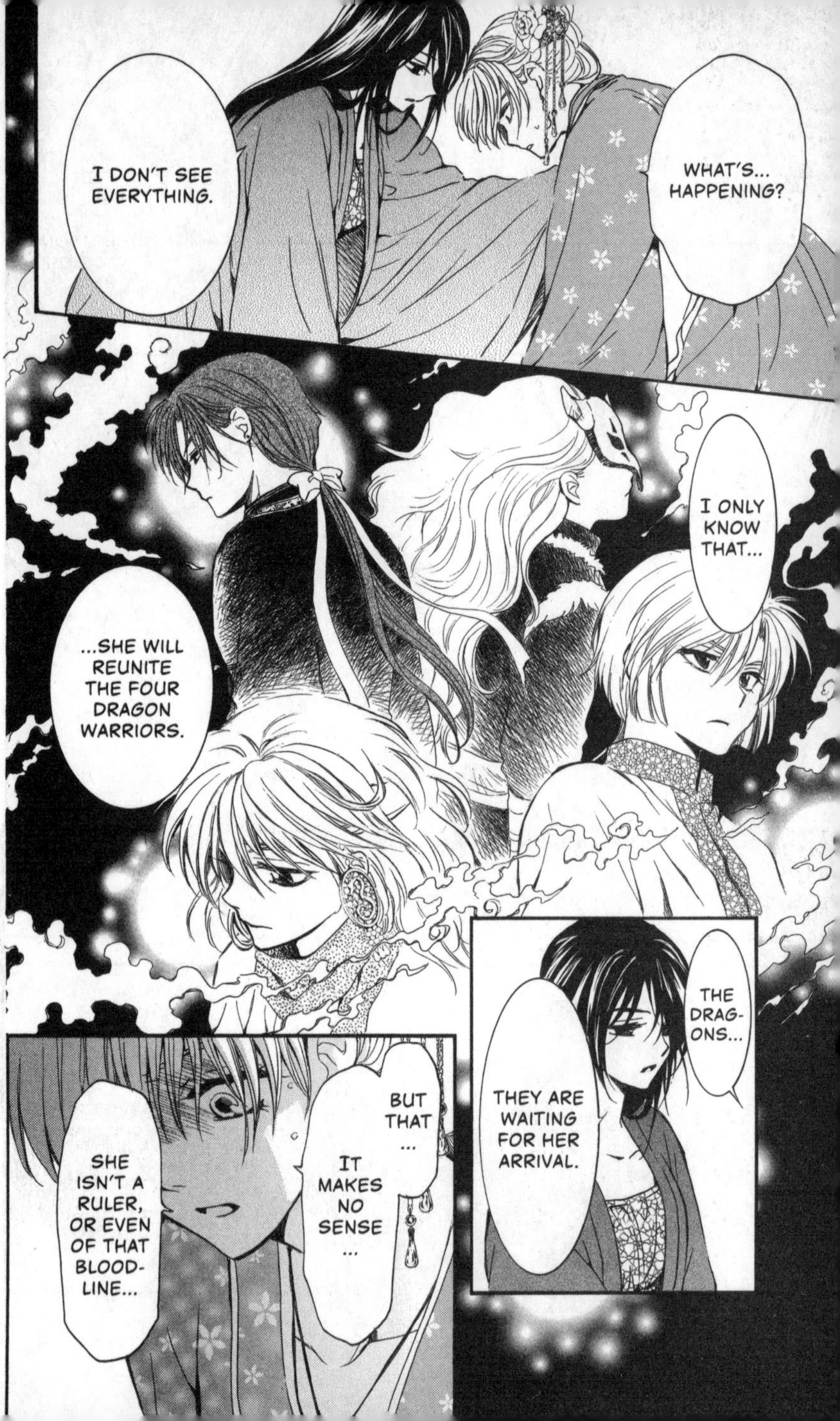
WHAT'S... HAPPENING?
I DON'T SEE EVERYTHING.
I ONLY KNOW THAT...
...SHE WILL REUNITE THE FOUR DRAGON WARRIORS.
THE DRAG-ONS...
THEY ARE WAITING FOR HER ARRIVAL.
BUT THAT ...
IT MAKES NO SENSE ...
SHE ISN'T A RULER, OR EVEN OF THAT BLOOD-LINE...

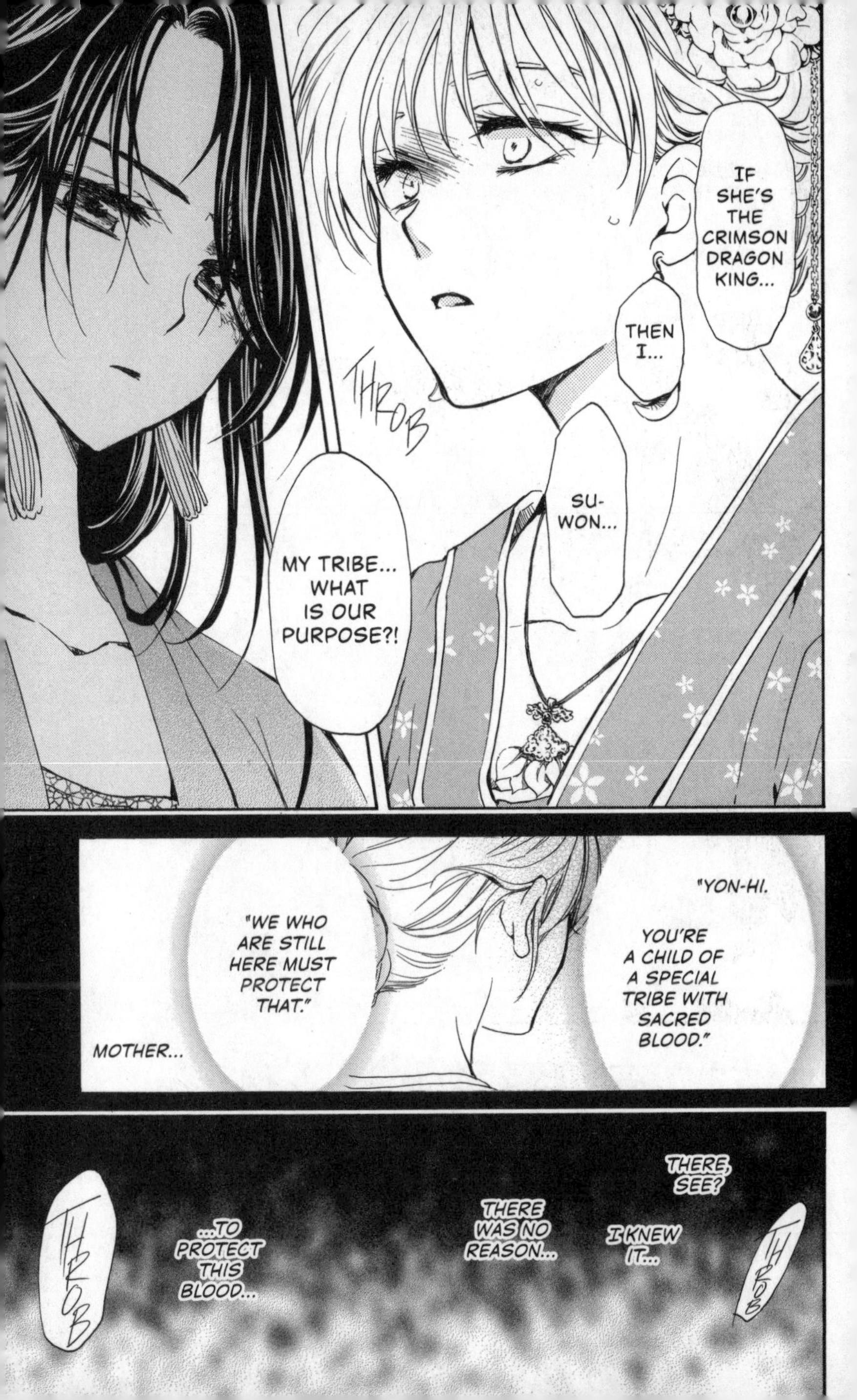
IF SHE'S THE CRIMSON DRAGON KING...
THEN I...
SU-WON...
THROB
MY TRIBE... WHAT IS OUR PURPOSE?!
"YON-HI.
YOU'RE A CHILD OF A SPECIAL TRIBE WITH SACRED BLOOD."
"WE WHO ARE STILL HERE MUST PROTECT THAT."
MOTHER...
THROB
THERE, SEE?
I KNEW IT...
THERE WAS NO REASON...
...TO PROTECT THIS BLOOD...
THROB

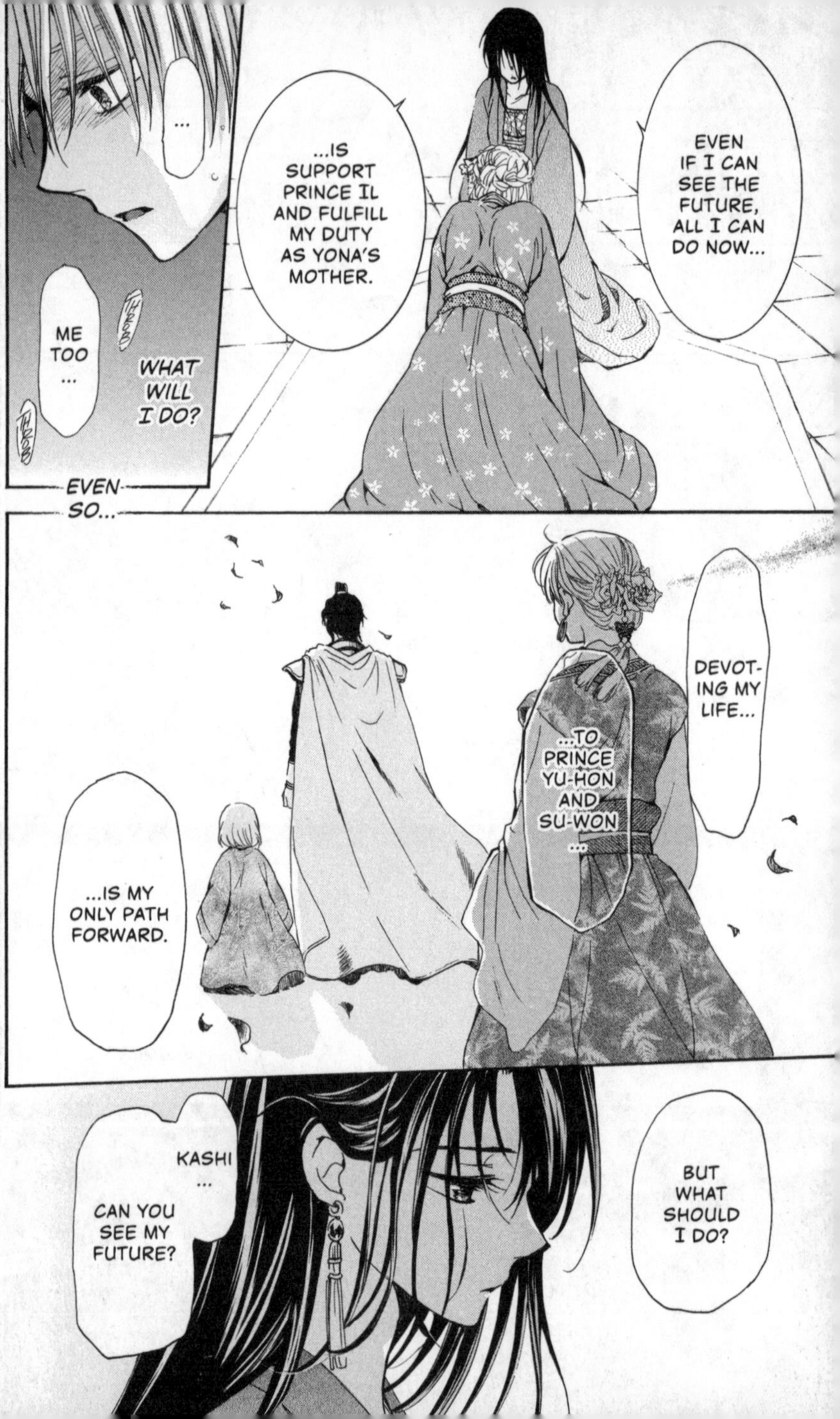
EVEN IF I CAN SEE THE FUTURE, ALL I CAN DO NOW...
...IS SUPPORT PRINCE IL AND FULFILL MY DUTY AS YONA'S MOTHER.
...
THROB
WHAT WILL I DO?
ME TOO ...
THROB
EVEN SO...
DEVOTING MY LIFE...
...TO PRINCE YU-HON AND SU-WON ...
...IS MY ONLY PATH FORWARD.
BUT WHAT SHOULD I DO?
KASHI ...
CAN YOU SEE MY FUTURE?

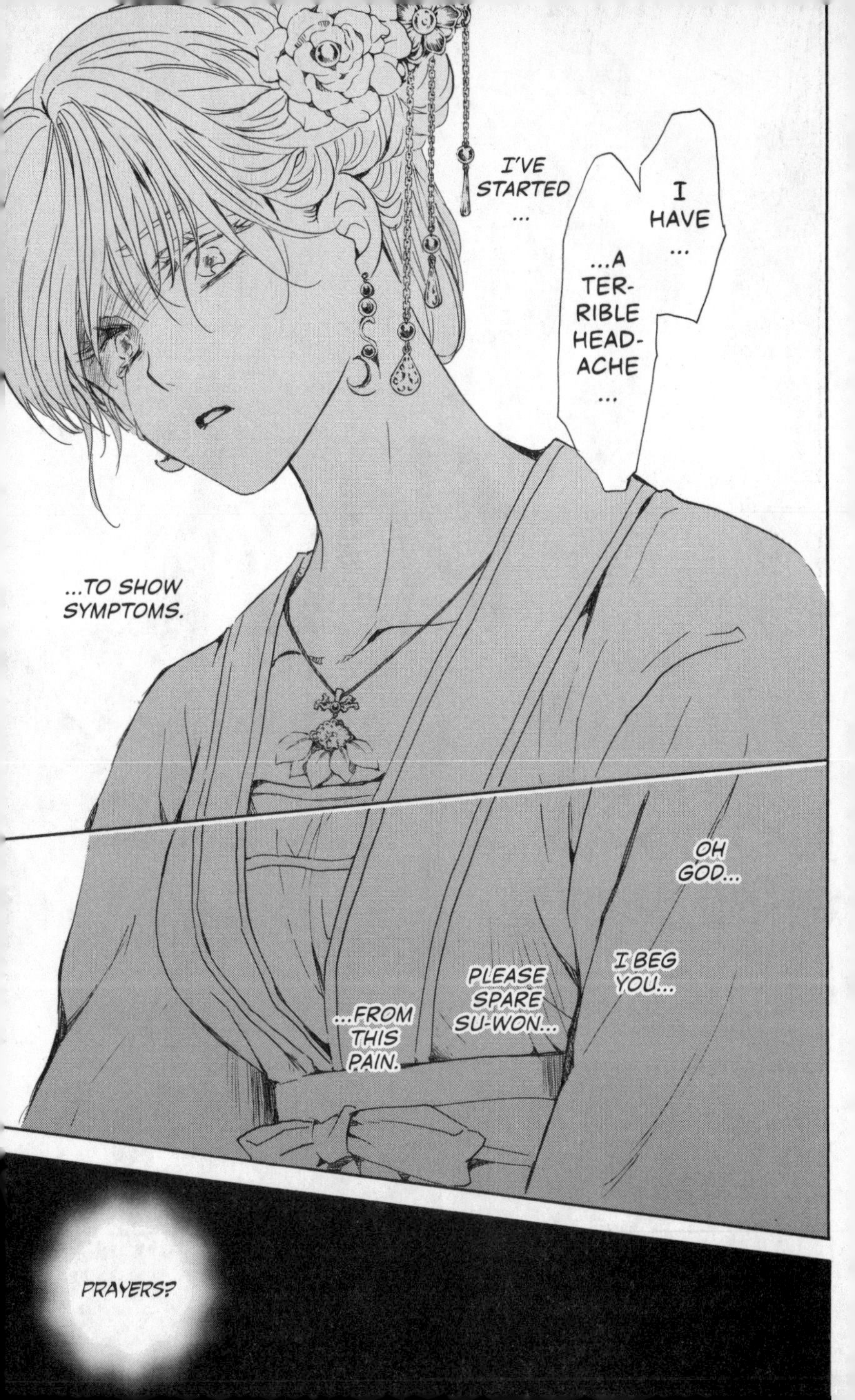
I HAVE ... ...A TERRIBLE HEADACHE ...
I'VE STARTED ...
...TO SHOW SYMPTOMS.
OH GOD...
I BEG YOU...
PLEASE SPARE SU-WON...
...FROM THIS PAIN.
PRAYERS?

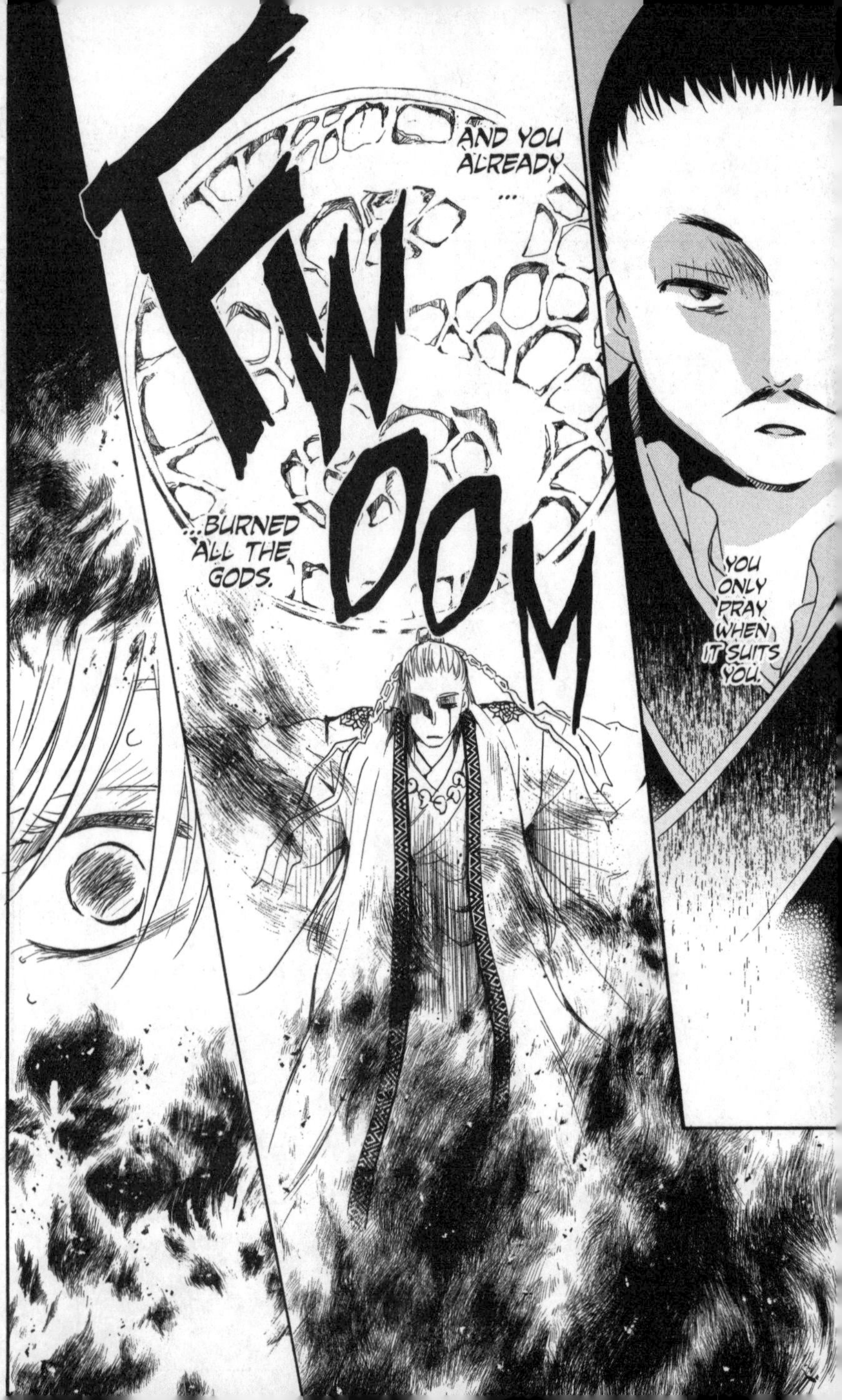
YOU ONLY PRAY WHEN IT SUITS YOU.
AND YOU ALREADY...
FWOOM
...BURNED ALL THE GODS.

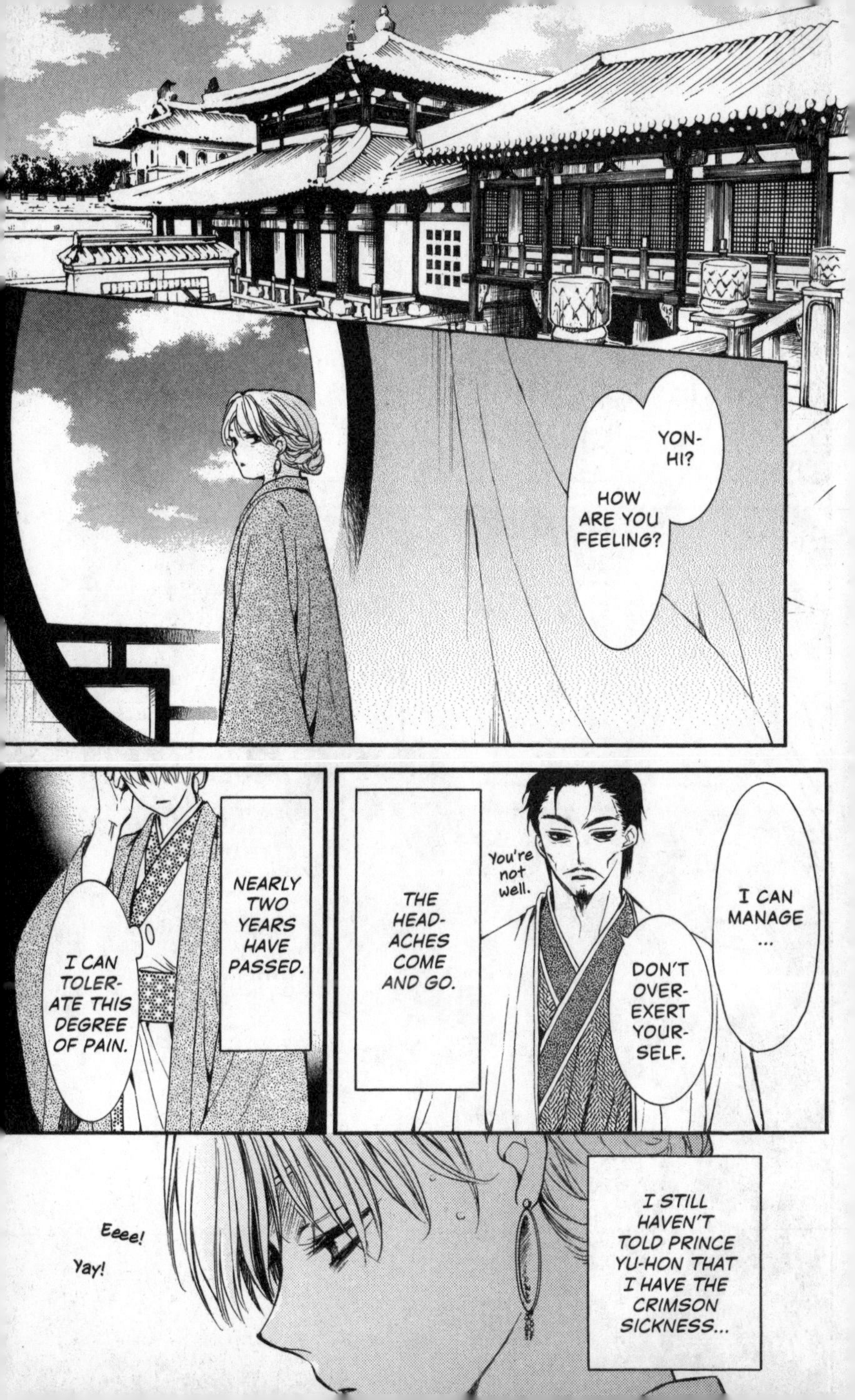
YON-HI?
HOW ARE YOU FEELING?
I CAN MANAGE ...
You're not well.
DON'T OVER-EXERT YOUR-SELF.
THE HEAD-ACHES COME AND GO.
NEARLY TWO YEARS HAVE PASSED.
I CAN TOLER-ATE THIS DEGREE OF PAIN.
I STILL HAVEN'T TOLD PRINCE YU-HON THAT I HAVE THE CRIMSON SICKNESS...
Eeee!
Yay!

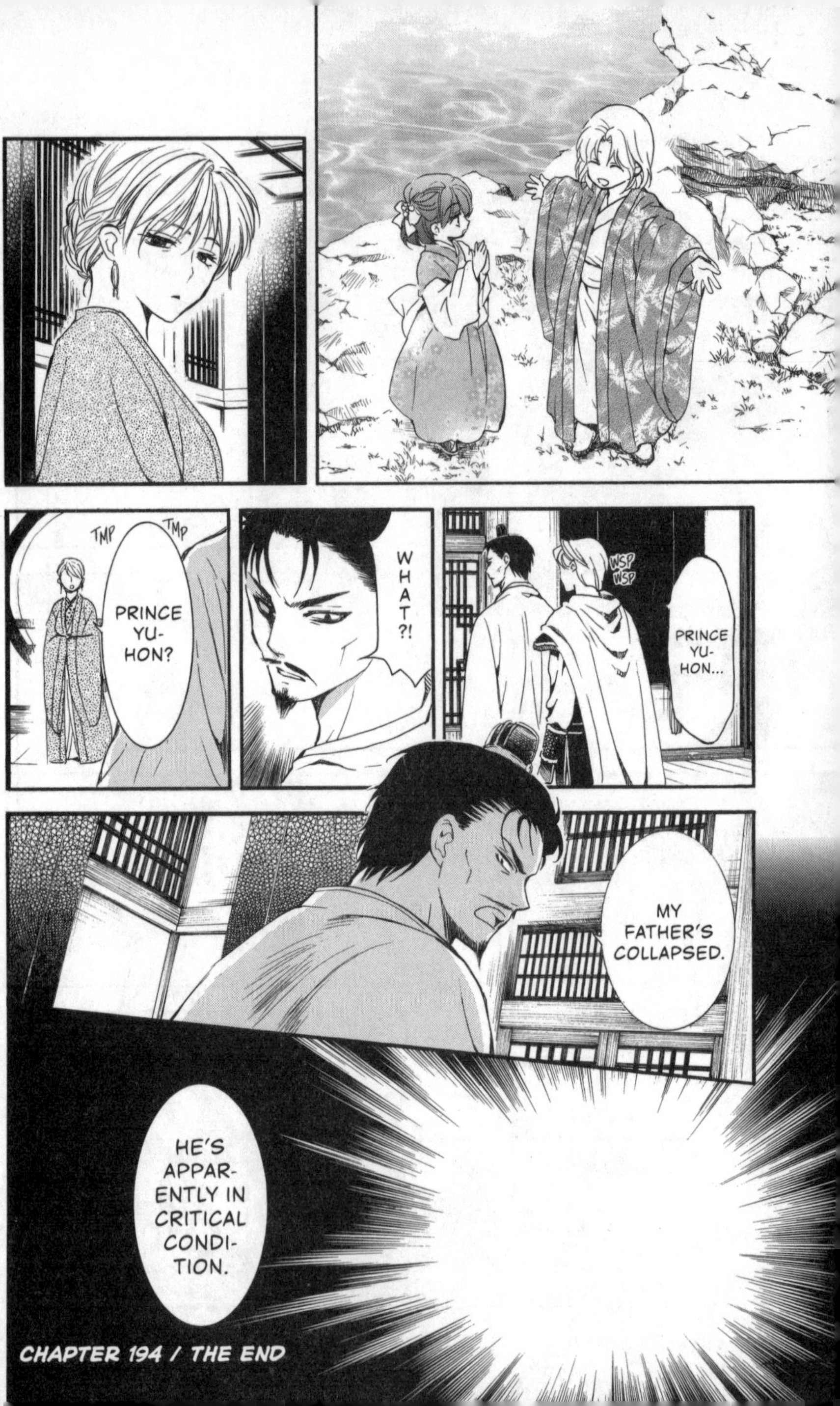
WSP WSP
PRINCE YU-HON...
WHAT?!
TMP TMP
PRINCE YU-HON?
MY FATHER'S COLLAPSED.
HE'S APPARENTLY IN CRITICAL CONDITION.
CHAPTER 194 / THE END

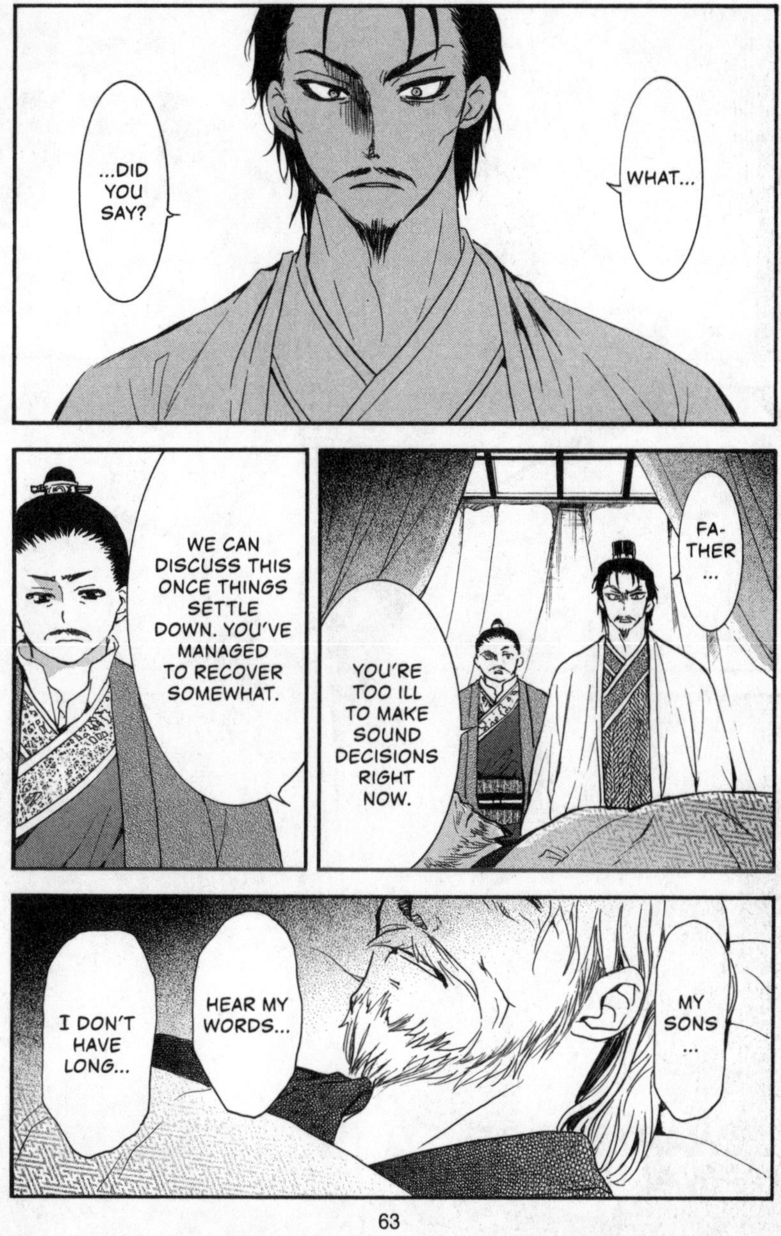
WHAT...
...DID YOU SAY?
FA-THER...
YOU'RE TOO ILL TO MAKE SOUND DECISIONS RIGHT NOW.
WE CAN DISCUSS THIS ONCE THINGS SETTLE DOWN. YOU'VE MANAGED TO RECOVER SOMEWHAT.
MY SONS...
HEAR MY WORDS...
I DON'T HAVE LONG...

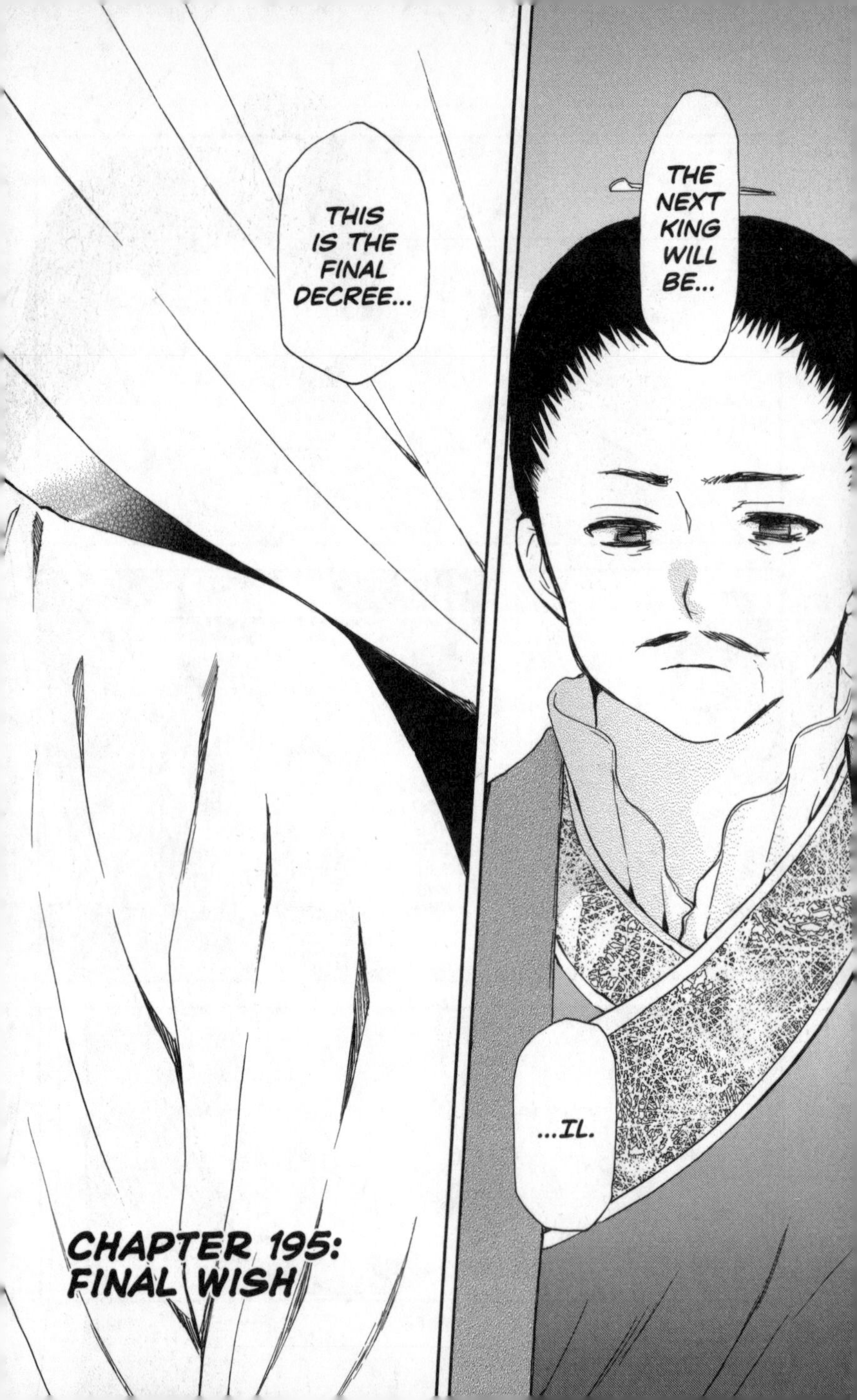
THE NEXT KING WILL BE...
...IL.
THIS IS THE FINAL DECREE...
CHAPTER 195: FINAL WISH

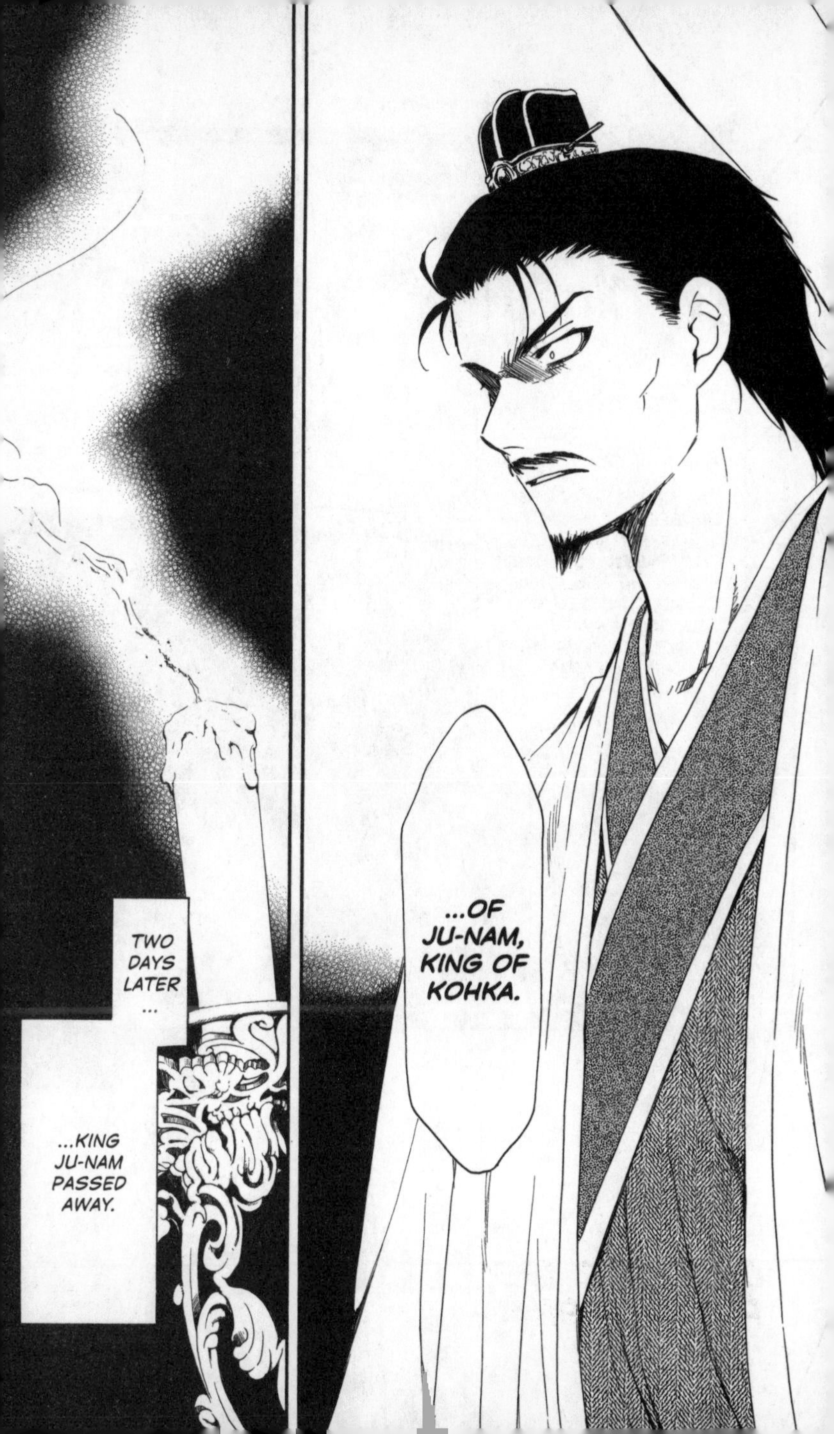
...OF JU-NAM, KING OF KOHKA.
TWO DAYS LATER ...
...KING JU-NAM PASSED AWAY.

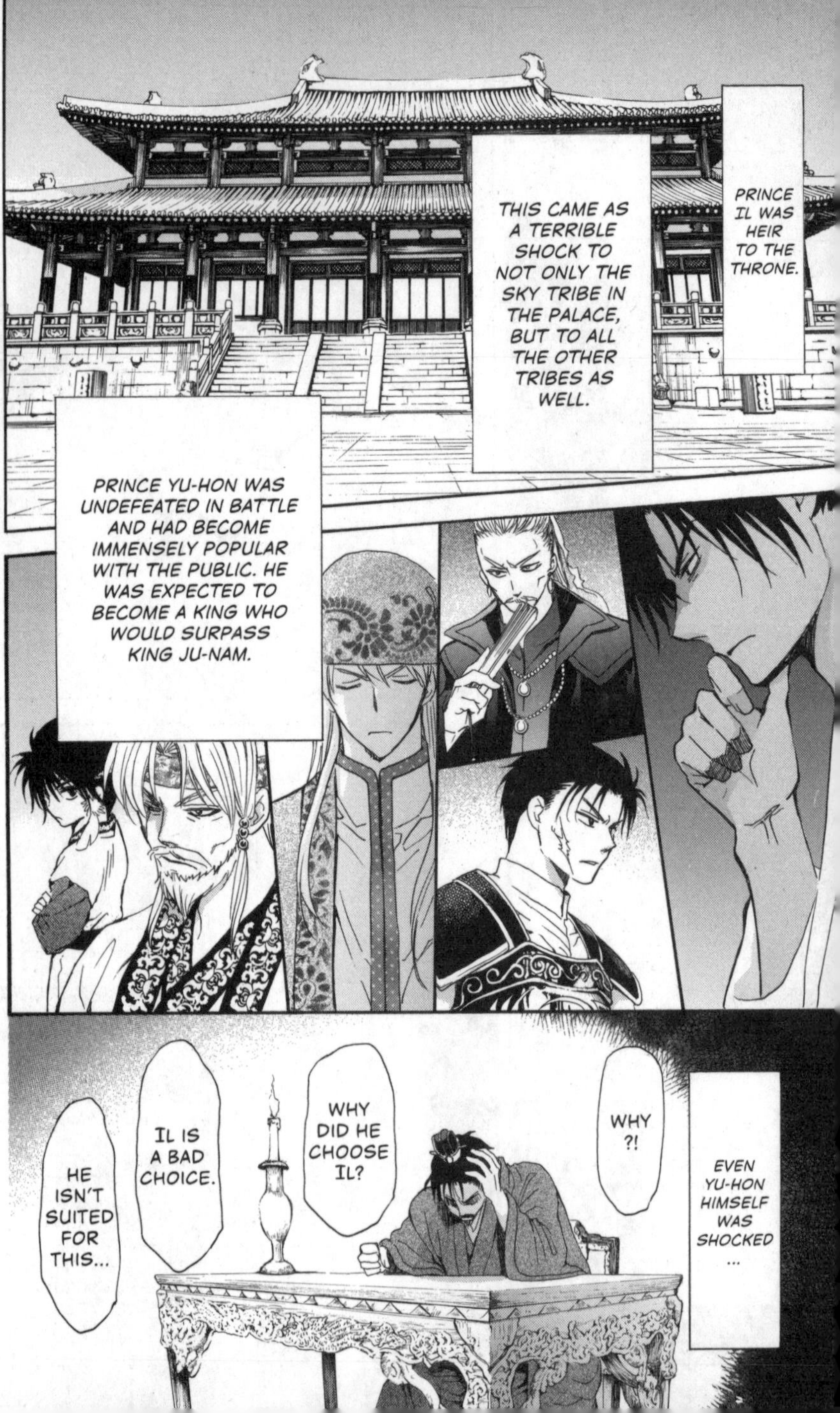
PRINCE IL WAS HEIR TO THE THRONE.
THIS CAME AS A TERRIBLE SHOCK TO NOT ONLY THE SKY TRIBE IN THE PALACE, BUT TO ALL THE OTHER TRIBES AS WELL.
PRINCE YU-HON WAS UNDEFEATED IN BATTLE AND HAD BECOME IMMENSELY POPULAR WITH THE PUBLIC. HE WAS EXPECTED TO BECOME A KING WHO WOULD SURPASS KING JU-NAM.
EVEN YU-HON HIMSELF WAS SHOCKED ...
WHY?!
WHY DID HE CHOOSE IL?
IL IS A BAD CHOICE.
HE ISN'T SUITED FOR THIS...

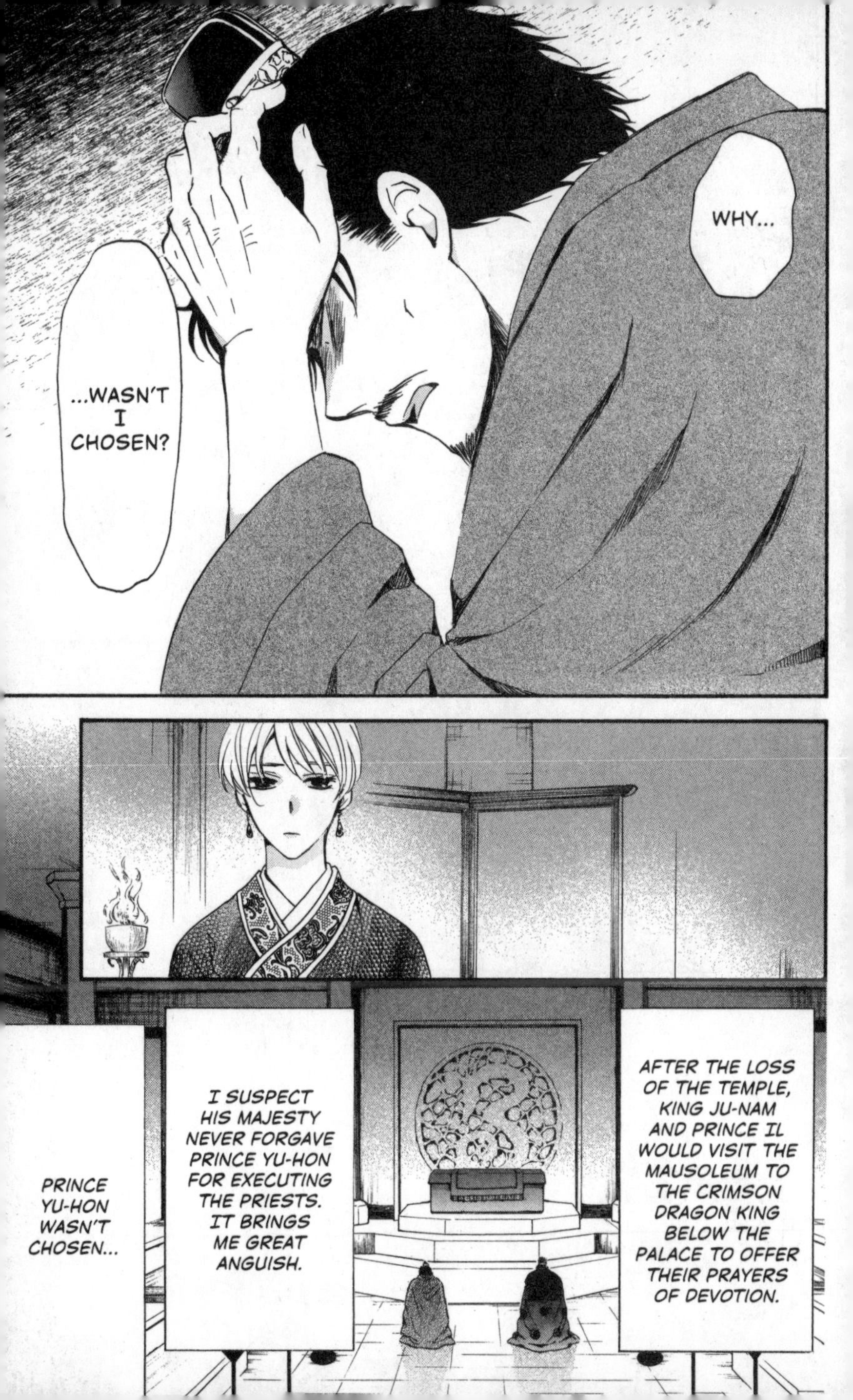
WHY...
...WASN'T I CHOSEN?
AFTER THE LOSS OF THE TEMPLE, KING JU-NAM AND PRINCE IL WOULD VISIT THE MAUSOLEUM TO THE CRIMSON DRAGON KING BELOW THE PALACE TO OFFER THEIR PRAYERS OF DEVOTION.
I SUSPECT HIS MAJESTY NEVER FORGAVE PRINCE YU-HON FOR EXECUTING THE PRIESTS. IT BRINGS ME GREAT ANGUISH.
PRINCE YU-HON WASN'T CHOSEN...

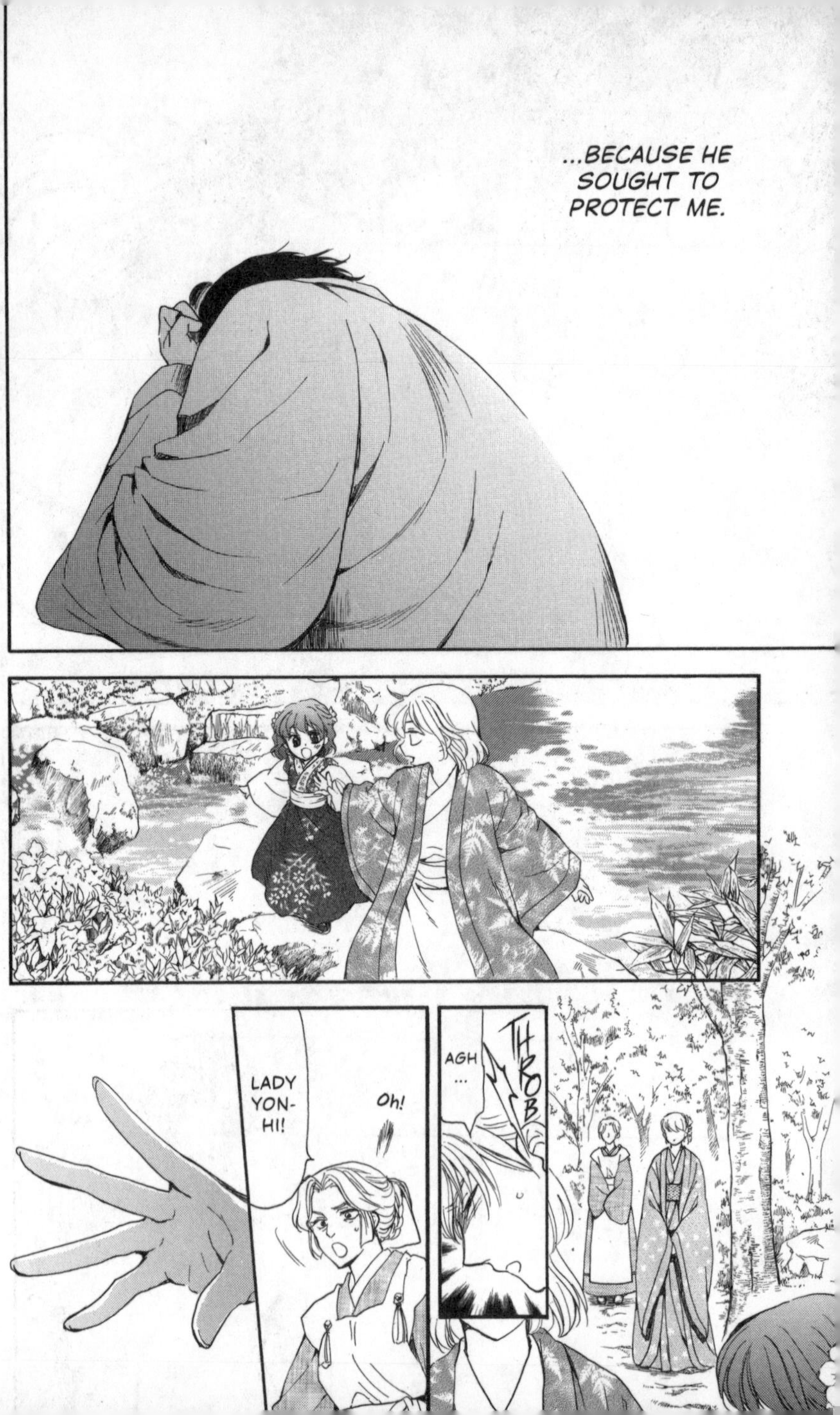
...BECAUSE HE SOUGHT TO PROTECT ME.
AGH ...
THROB
Oh!
LADY YON-HI!

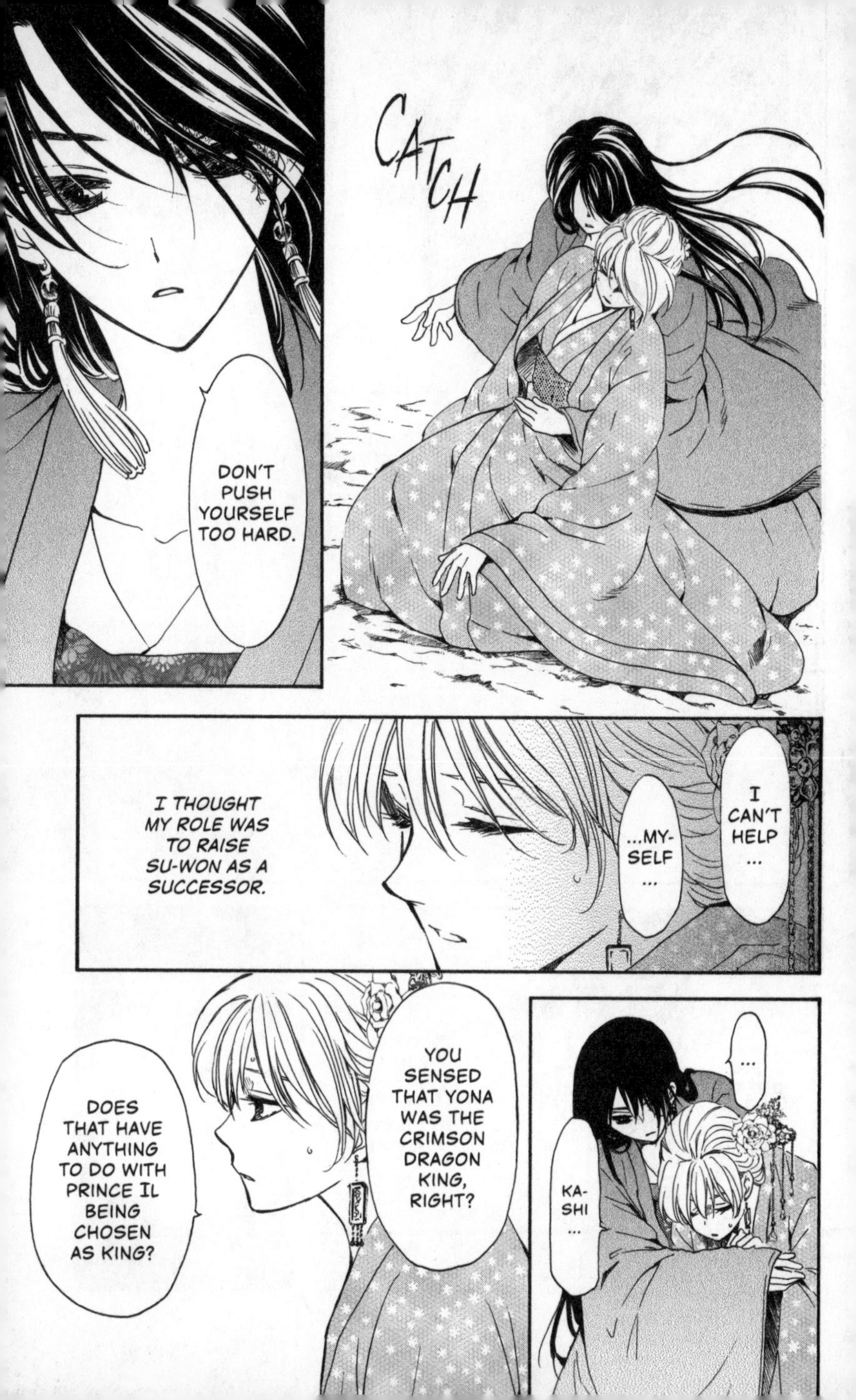
CATCH
DON'T PUSH YOURSELF TOO HARD.
I CAN'T HELP ...
...MYSELF ...
I THOUGHT MY ROLE WAS TO RAISE SU-WON AS A SUCCESSOR.
...
KA-SHI ...
YOU SENSED THAT YONA WAS THE CRIMSON DRAGON KING, RIGHT?
DOES THAT HAVE ANYTHING TO DO WITH PRINCE IL BEING CHOSEN AS KING?

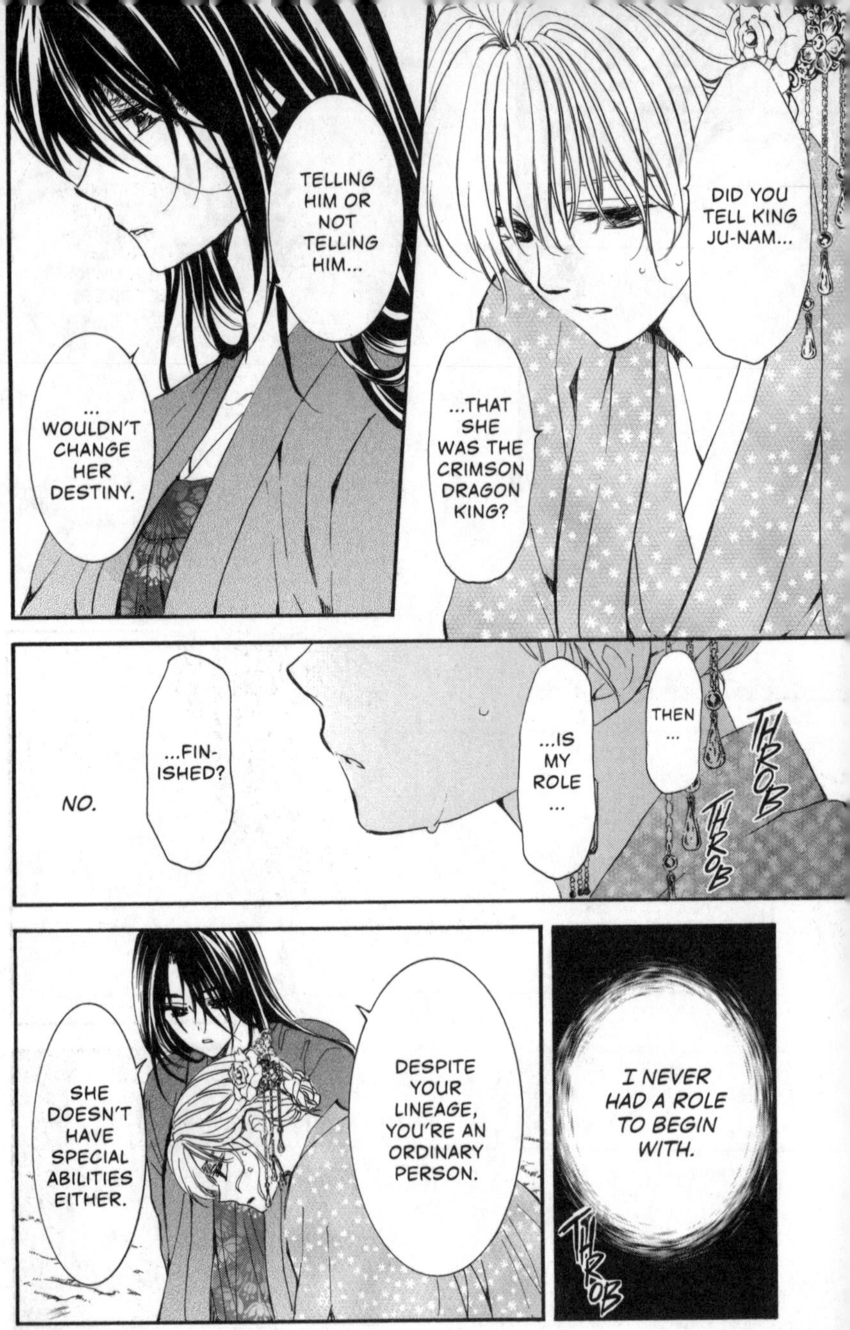
DID YOU TELL KING JU-NAM...
...THAT SHE WAS THE CRIMSON DRAGON KING?
TELLING HIM OR NOT TELLING HIM...
...WOULDN'T CHANGE HER DESTINY.
THROB
THROB
THEN...
...IS MY ROLE...
...FIN-ISHED?
NO.
I NEVER HAD A ROLE TO BEGIN WITH.
THROB
DESPITE YOUR LINEAGE, YOU'RE AN ORDINARY PERSON.
SHE DOESN'T HAVE SPECIAL ABILITIES EITHER.

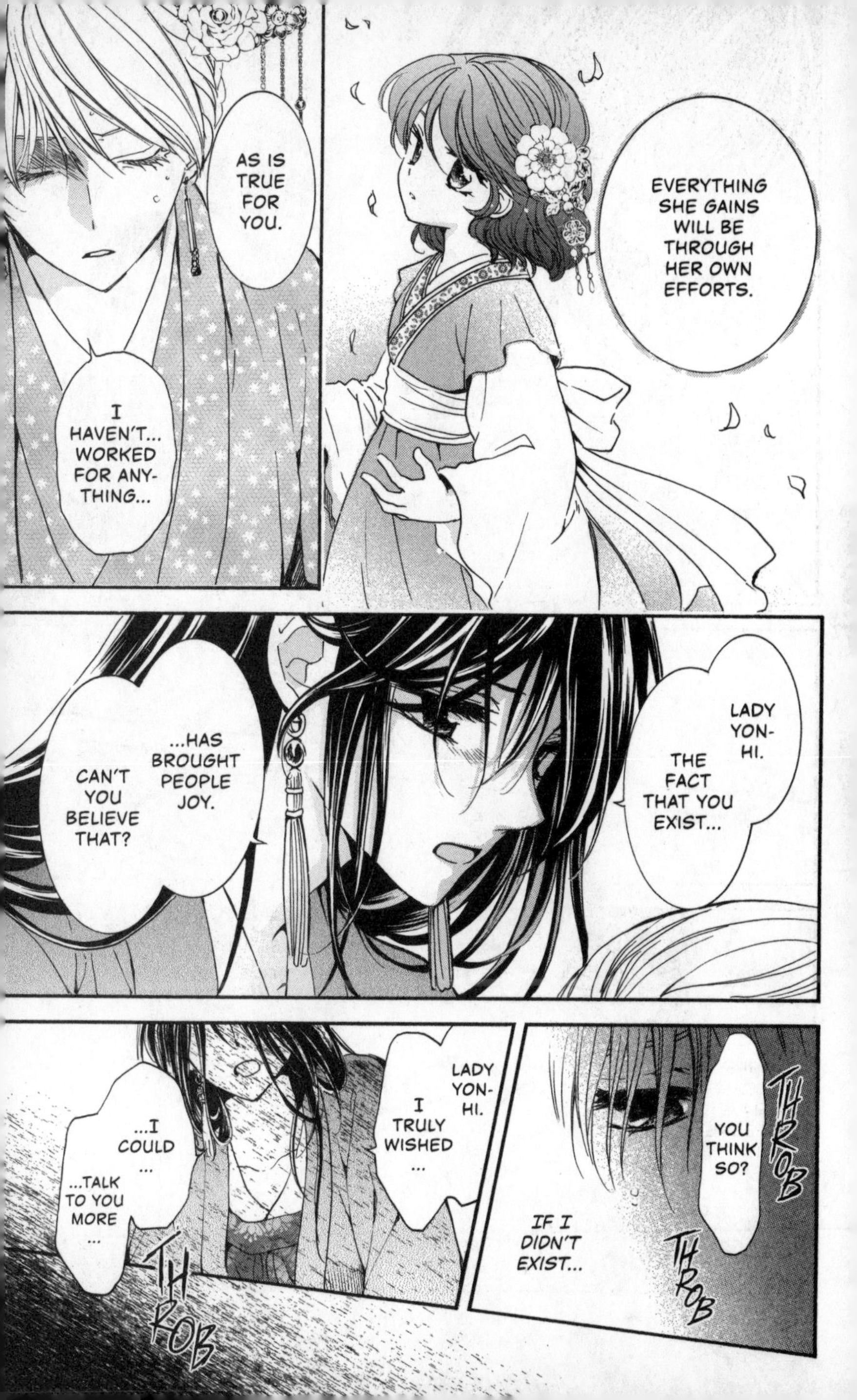
EVERYTHING SHE GAINS WILL BE THROUGH HER OWN EFFORTS.
AS IS TRUE FOR YOU.
I HAVEN'T... WORKED FOR ANY-THING...
LADY YON-HI.
THE FACT THAT YOU EXIST...
...HAS BROUGHT PEOPLE JOY.
CAN'T YOU BELIEVE THAT?
THROB
YOU THINK SO?
THROB
IF I DIDN'T EXIST...
LADY YON-HI.
I TRULY WISHED ...
...I COULD ...
...TALK TO YOU MORE ...
THROB

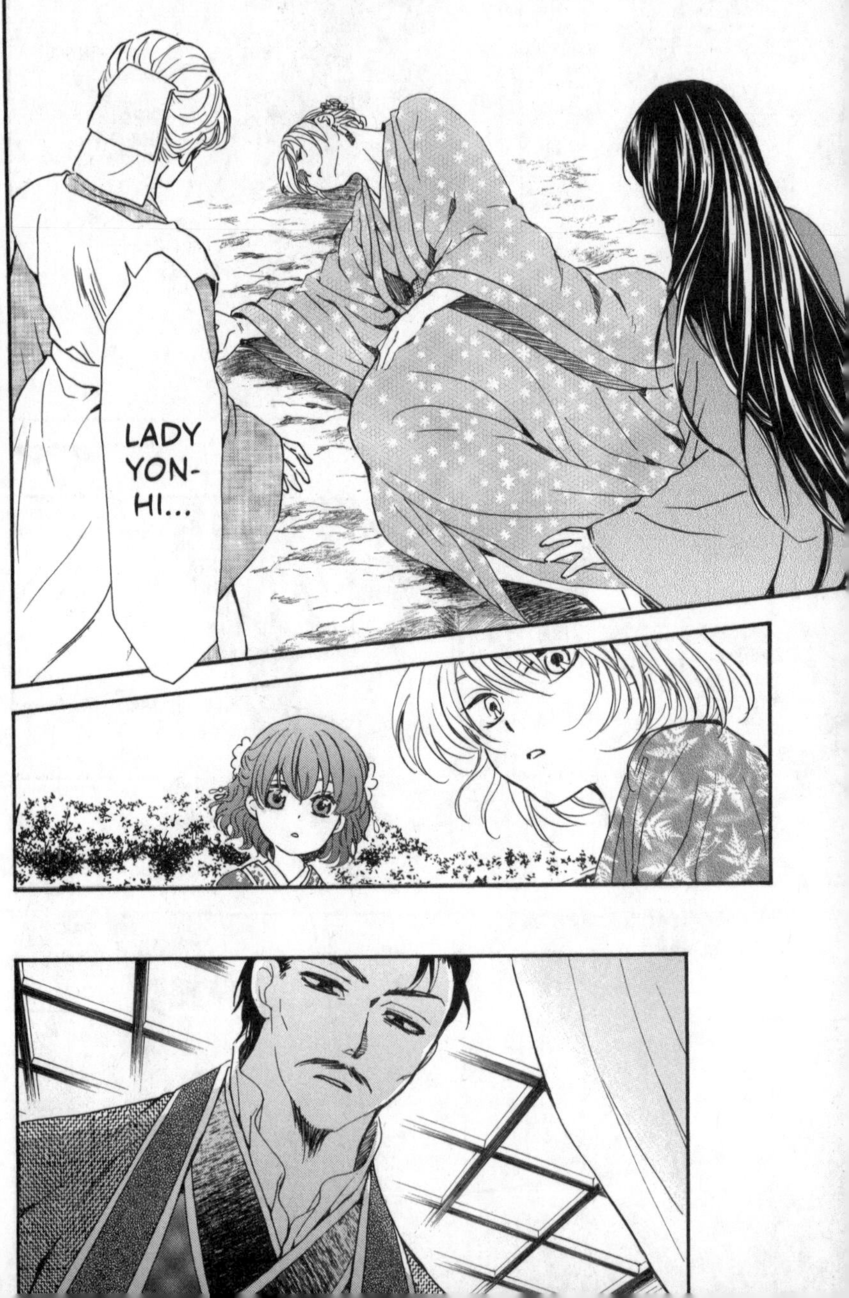
LADY YON-HI...

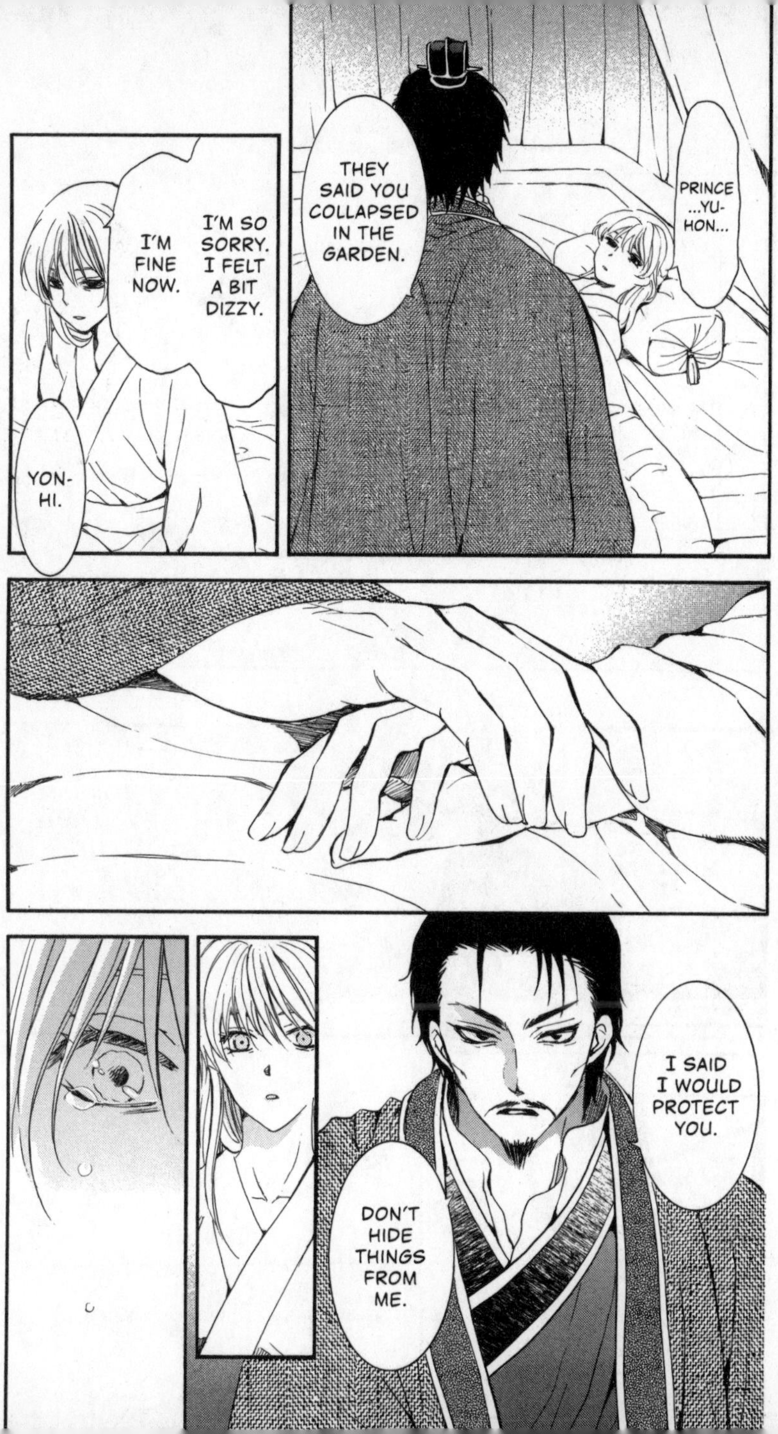
PRINCE ...YU-HON...
THEY SAID YOU COLLAPSED IN THE GARDEN.
I'M SO SORRY. I FELT A BIT DIZZY.
I'M FINE NOW.
YON-HI.
I SAID I WOULD PROTECT YOU.
DON'T HIDE THINGS FROM ME.

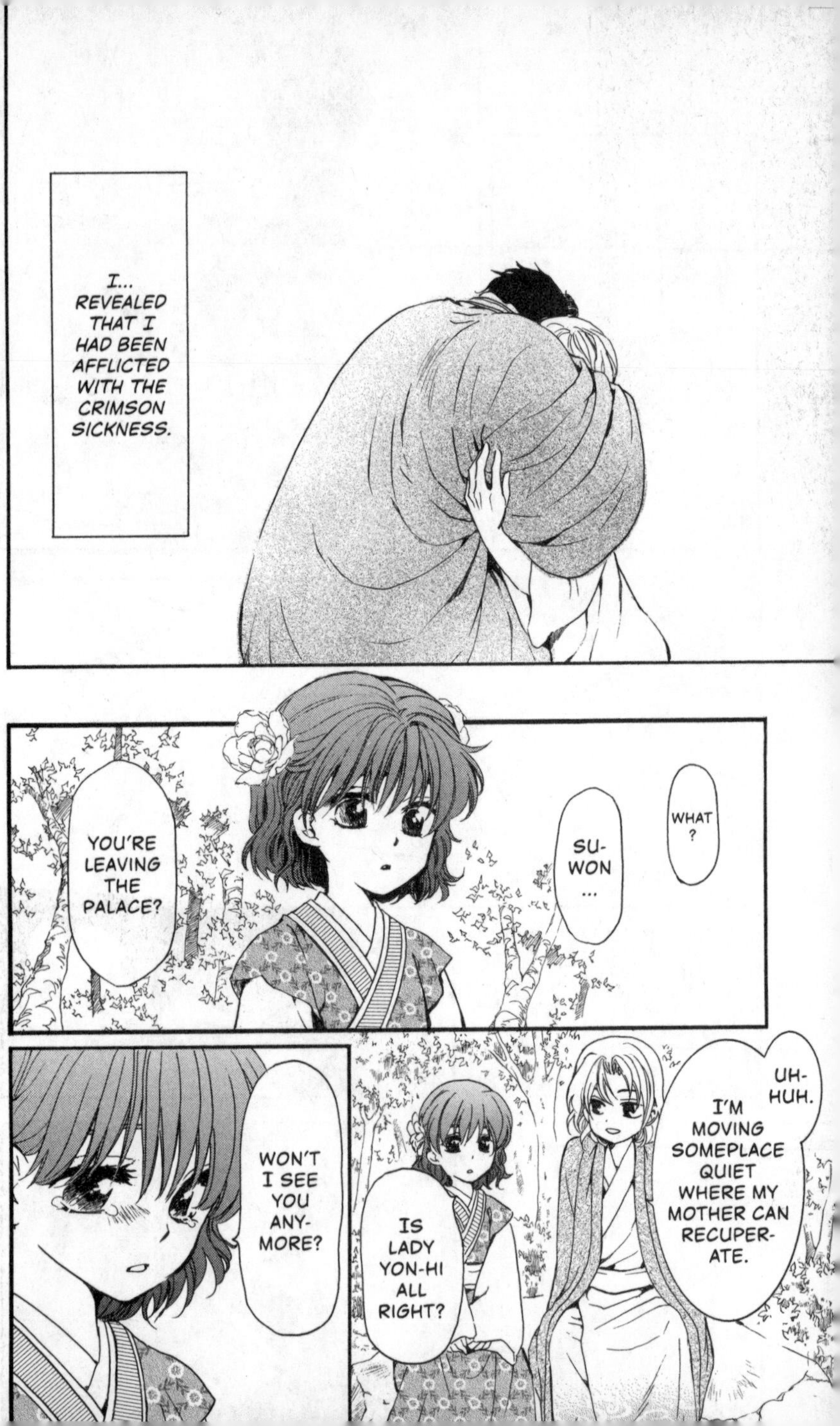
I... REVEALED THAT I HAD BEEN AFFLICTED WITH THE CRIMSON SICKNESS.
WHAT?
SU-WON...
YOU'RE LEAVING THE PALACE?
UH-HUH. I'M MOVING SOMEPLACE QUIET WHERE MY MOTHER CAN RECUPERATE.
IS LADY YON-HI ALL RIGHT?
WON'T I SEE YOU ANYMORE?

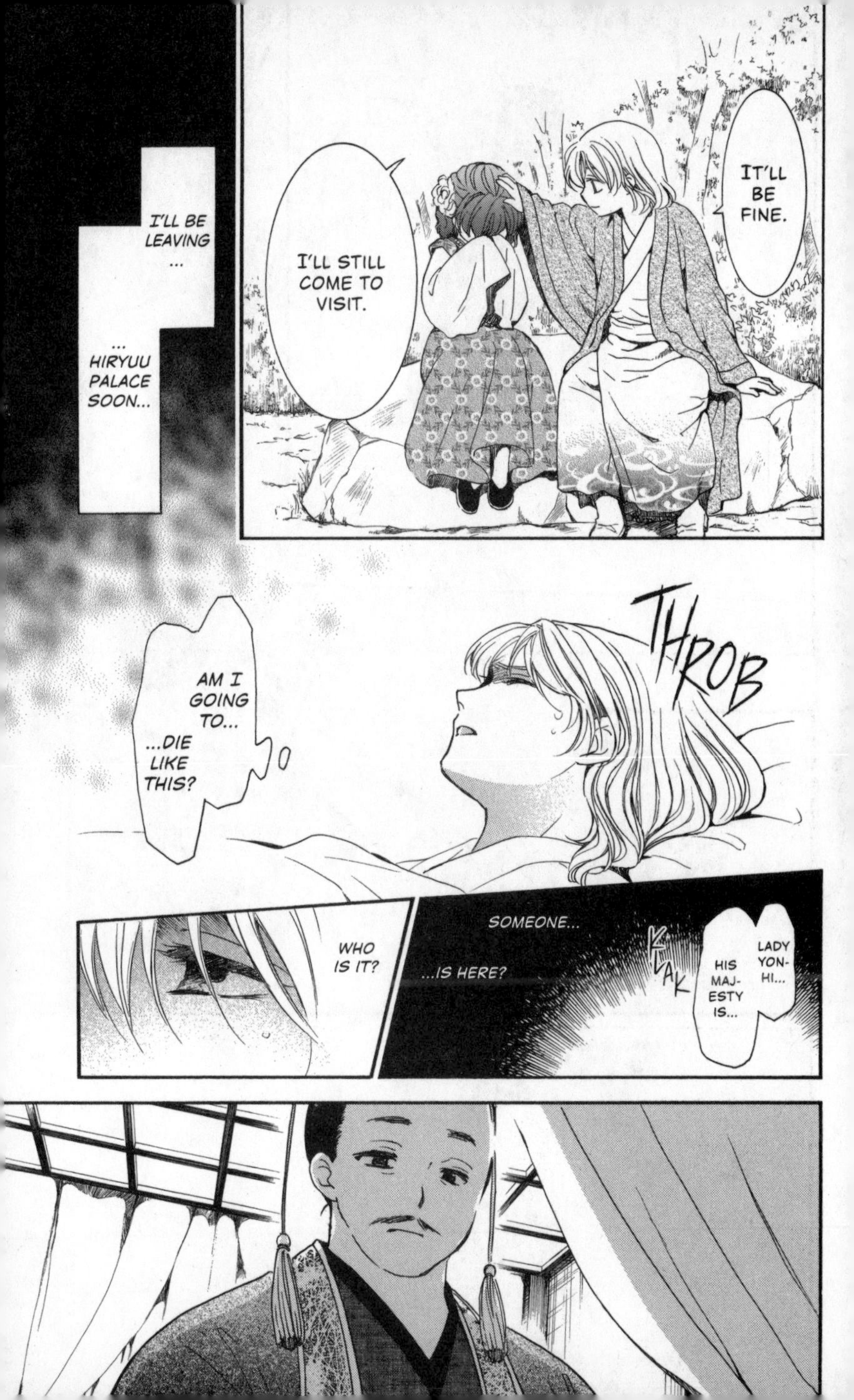
IT'LL BE FINE.
I'LL STILL COME TO VISIT.
I'LL BE LEAVING ...
... HIRYUU PALACE SOON...
THROB
AM I GOING TO... ...DIE LIKE THIS?
LADY YON-HI...
HIS MAJ-ESTY IS...
KLAK
SOMEONE...
...IS HERE?
WHO IS IT?

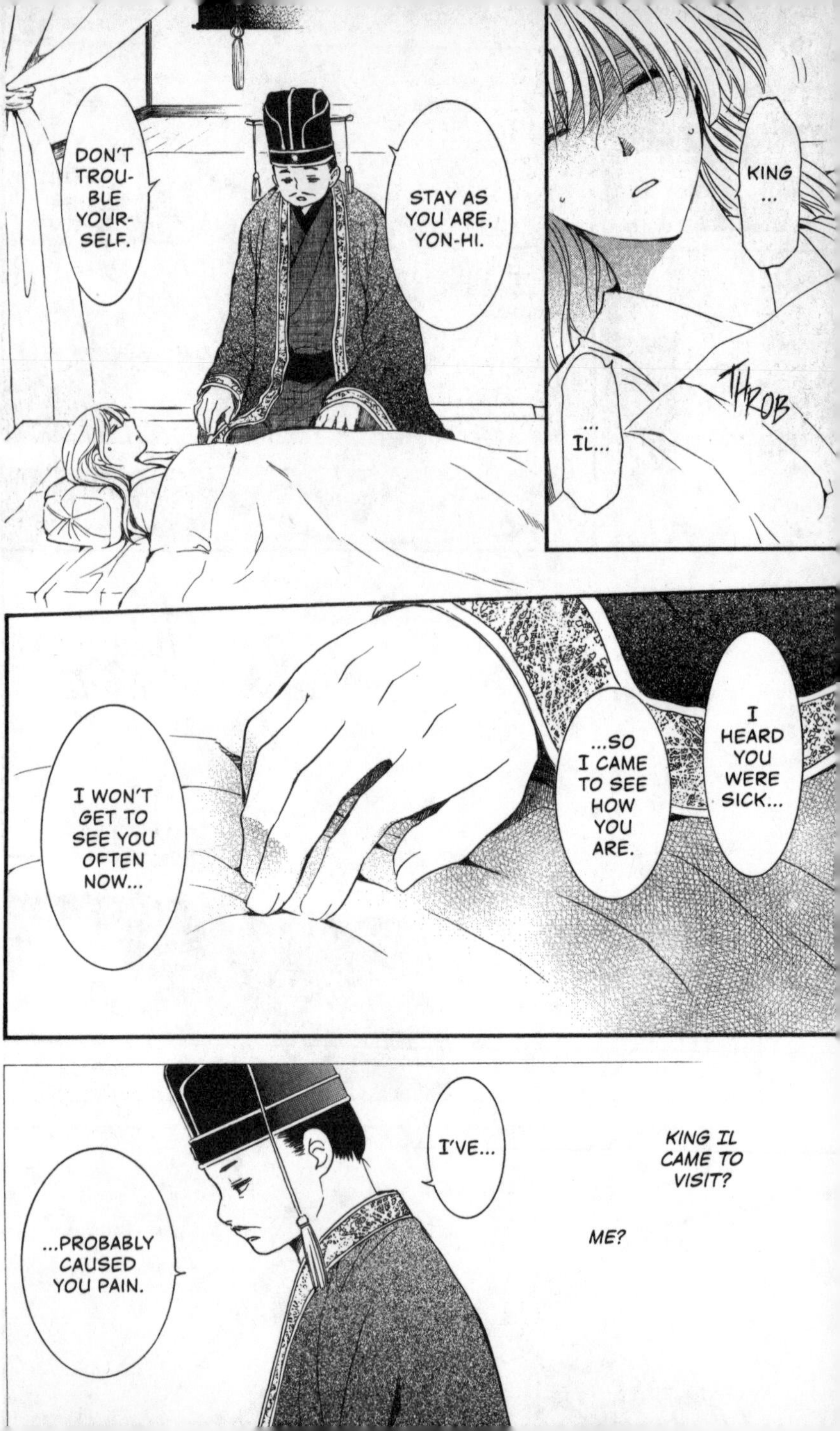
KING ...
... IL...
THROB
STAY AS YOU ARE, YON-HI.
DON'T TROUBLE YOURSELF.
I HEARD YOU WERE SICK...
...SO I CAME TO SEE HOW YOU ARE.
I WON'T GET TO SEE YOU OFTEN NOW...
KING IL CAME TO VISIT?
ME?
I'VE...
...PROBABLY CAUSED YOU PAIN.

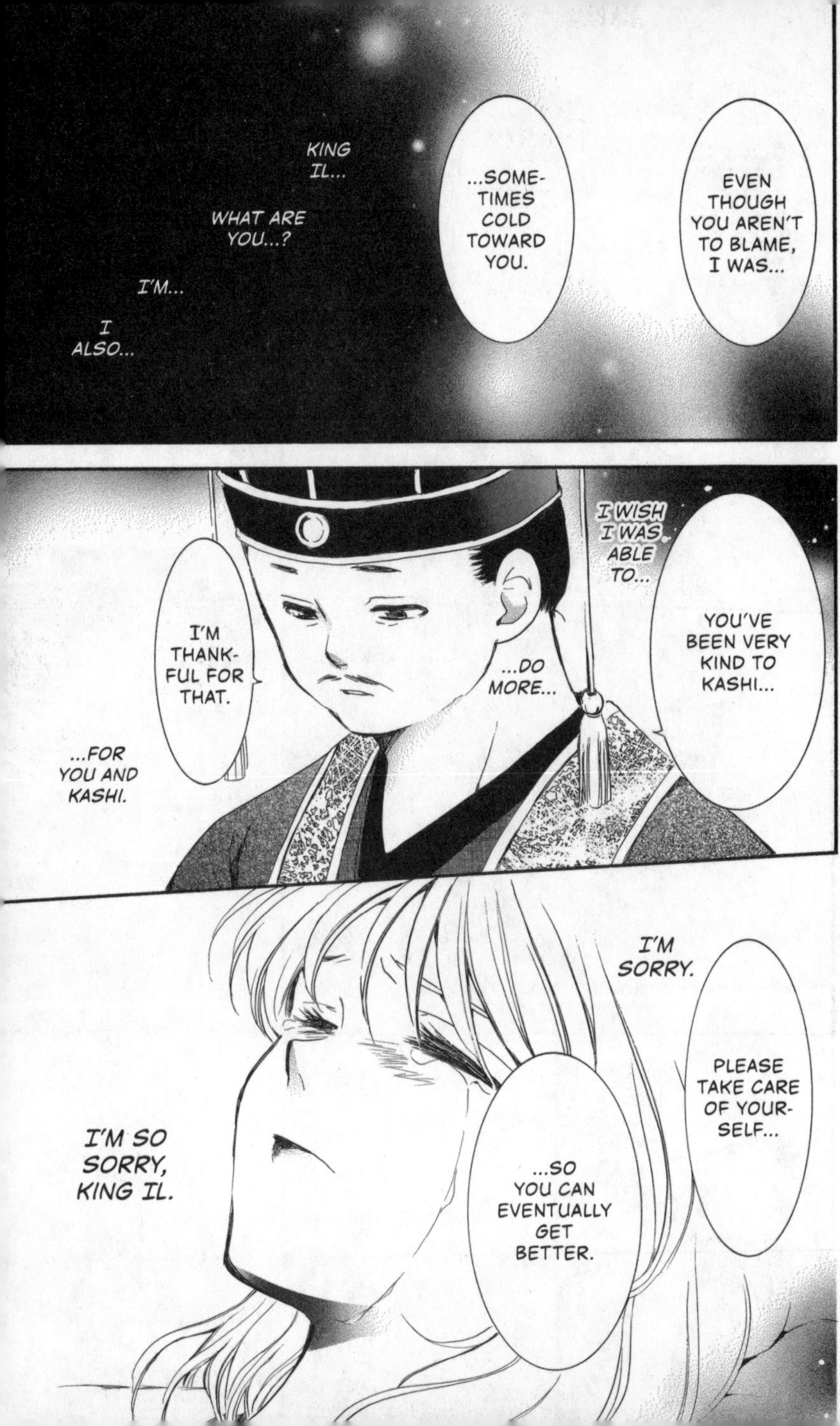
EVEN THOUGH YOU AREN'T TO BLAME, I WAS...
...SOME-TIMES COLD TOWARD YOU.
KING IL...
WHAT ARE YOU...?
I'M...
I ALSO...
I WISH I WAS ABLE TO...
YOU'VE BEEN VERY KIND TO KASHI...
...DO MORE...
I'M THANKFUL FOR THAT.
...FOR YOU AND KASHI.
I'M SORRY.
PLEASE TAKE CARE OF YOUR-SELF...
...SO YOU CAN EVENTUALLY GET BETTER.
I'M SO SORRY, KING IL.

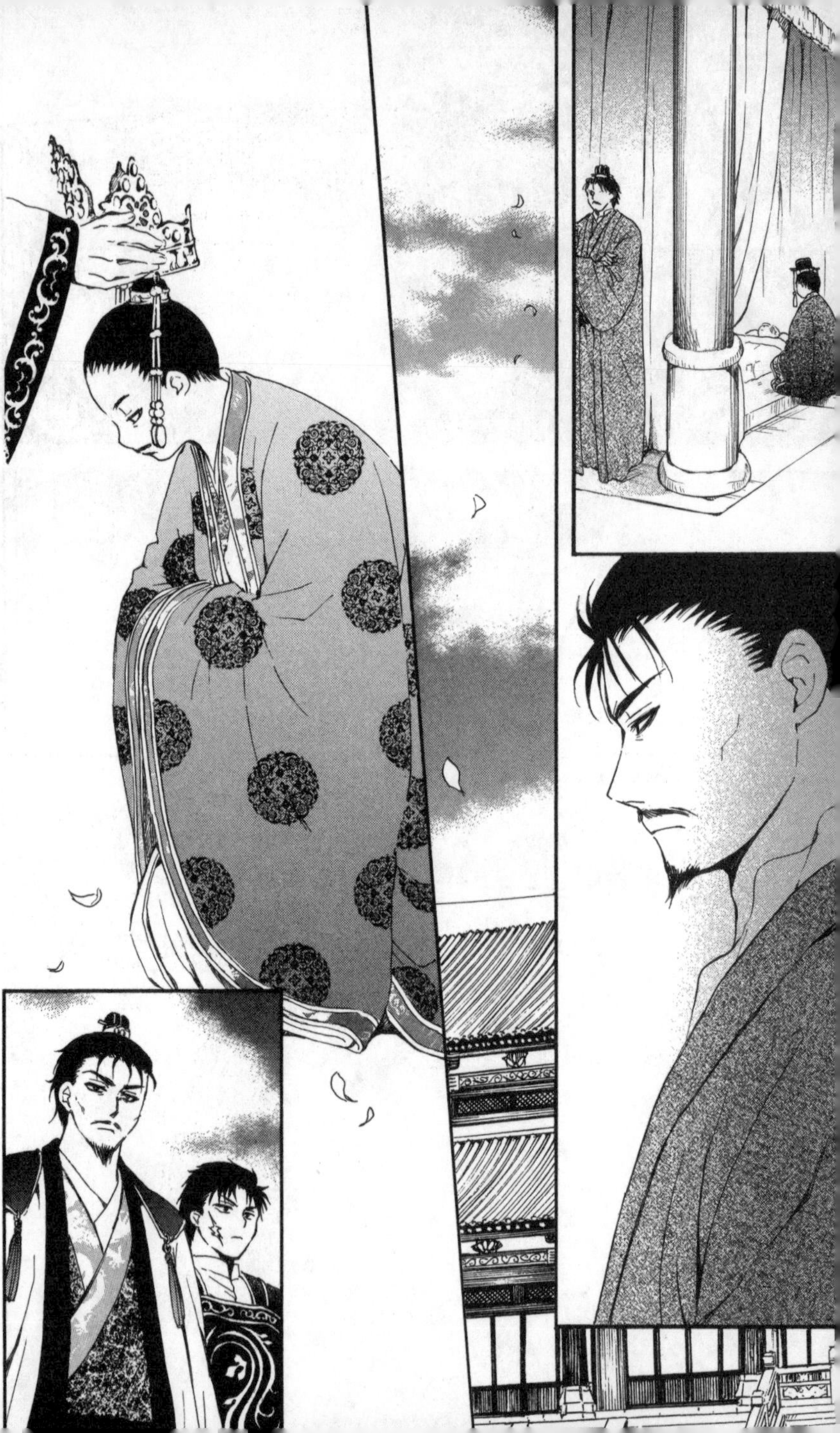

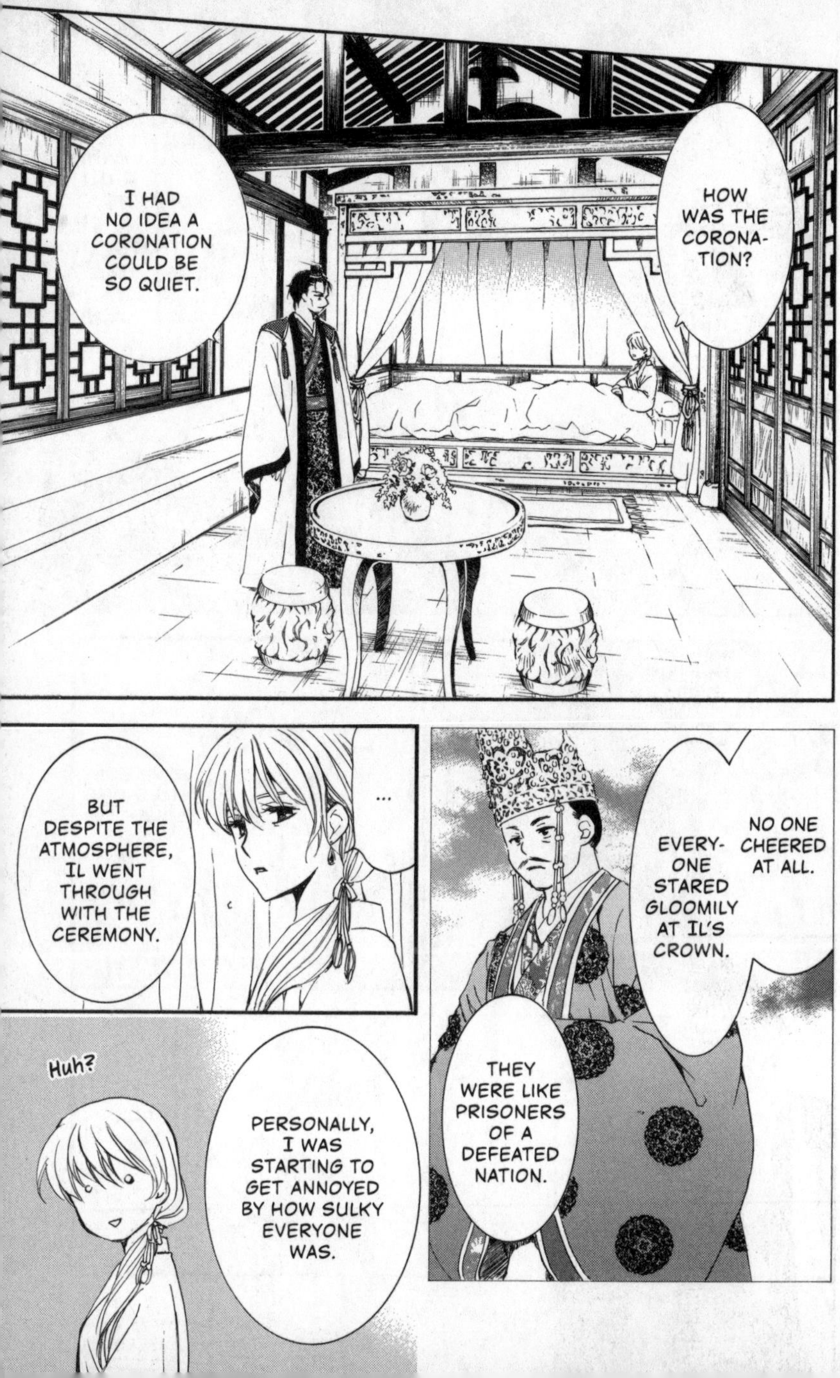
HOW WAS THE CORONATION?
I HAD NO IDEA A CORONATION COULD BE SO QUIET.
NO ONE CHEERED AT ALL.
EVERYONE STARED GLOOMILY AT IL'S CROWN.
THEY WERE LIKE PRISONERS OF A DEFEATED NATION.
...
BUT DESPITE THE ATMOSPHERE, IL WENT THROUGH WITH THE CEREMONY.
PERSONALLY, I WAS STARTING TO GET ANNOYED BY HOW SULKY EVERYONE WAS.
Huh?

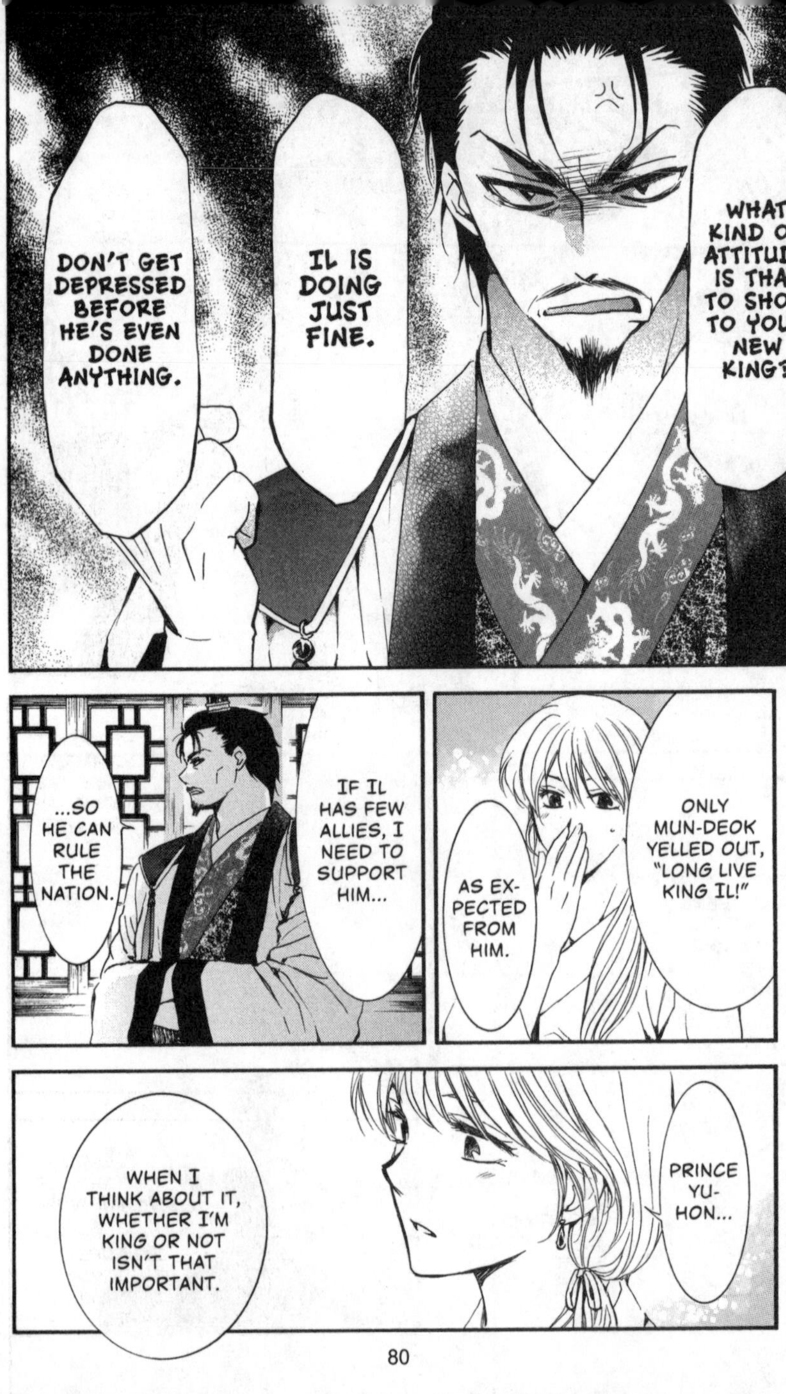
WHAT KIND OF ATTITUDE IS THAT TO SHOW TO YOUR NEW KING?
IL IS DOING JUST FINE.
DON'T GET DEPRESSED BEFORE HE'S EVEN DONE ANYTHING.
ONLY MUN-DEOK YELLED OUT, "LONG LIVE KING IL!"
AS EX-PECTED FROM HIM.
IF IL HAS FEW ALLIES, I NEED TO SUPPORT HIM...
...SO HE CAN RULE THE NATION.
PRINCE YU-HON...
WHEN I THINK ABOUT IT, WHETHER I'M KING OR NOT ISN'T THAT IMPORTANT.

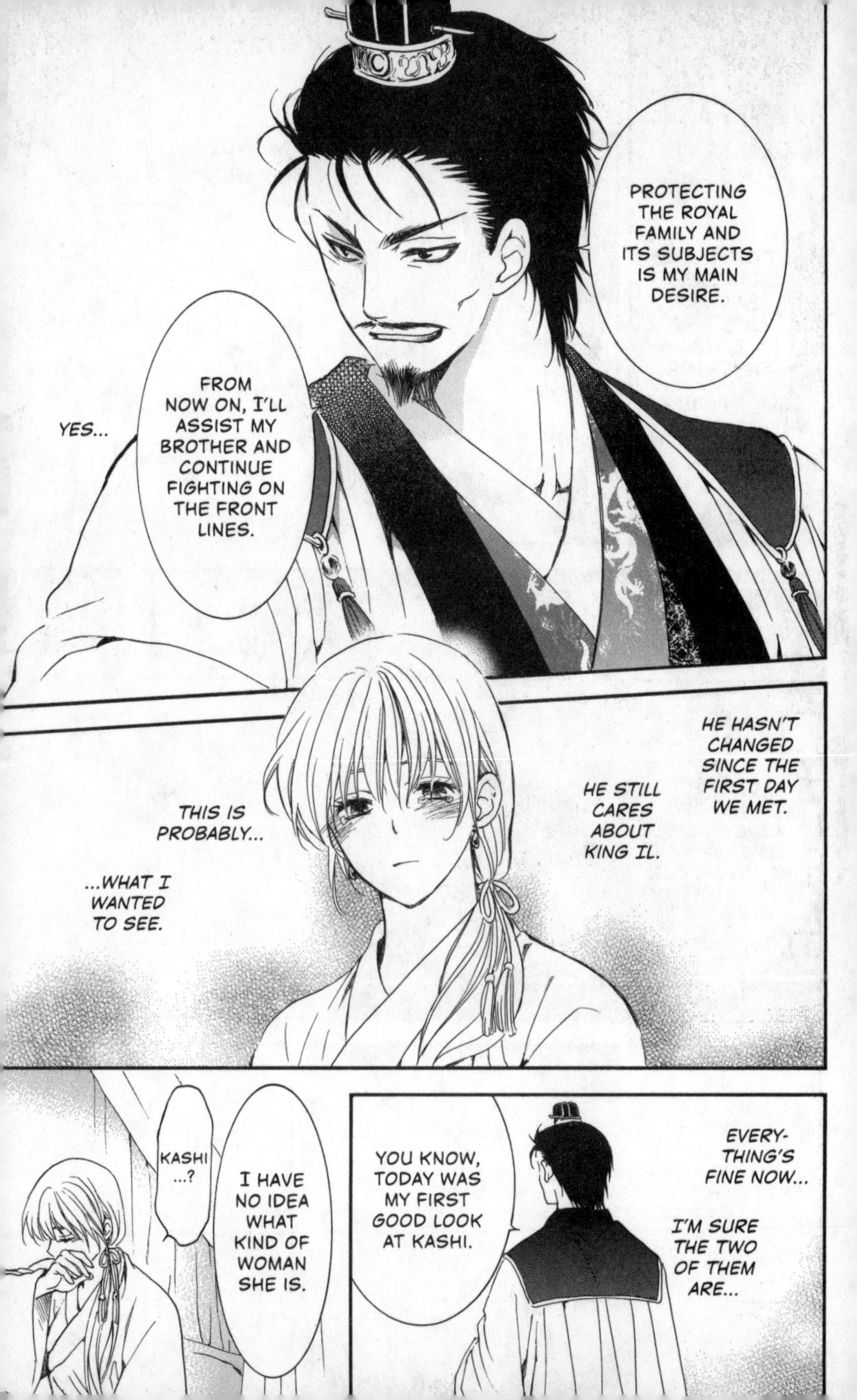
PROTECTING THE ROYAL FAMILY AND ITS SUBJECTS IS MY MAIN DESIRE.
FROM NOW ON, I'LL ASSIST MY BROTHER AND CONTINUE FIGHTING ON THE FRONT LINES.
YES...
HE HASN'T CHANGED SINCE THE FIRST DAY WE MET.
HE STILL CARES ABOUT KING IL.
THIS IS PROBABLY...
...WHAT I WANTED TO SEE.
EVERY-THING'S FINE NOW...
I'M SURE THE TWO OF THEM ARE...
YOU KNOW, TODAY WAS MY FIRST GOOD LOOK AT KASHI.
I HAVE NO IDEA WHAT KIND OF WOMAN SHE IS.
KASHI ...?

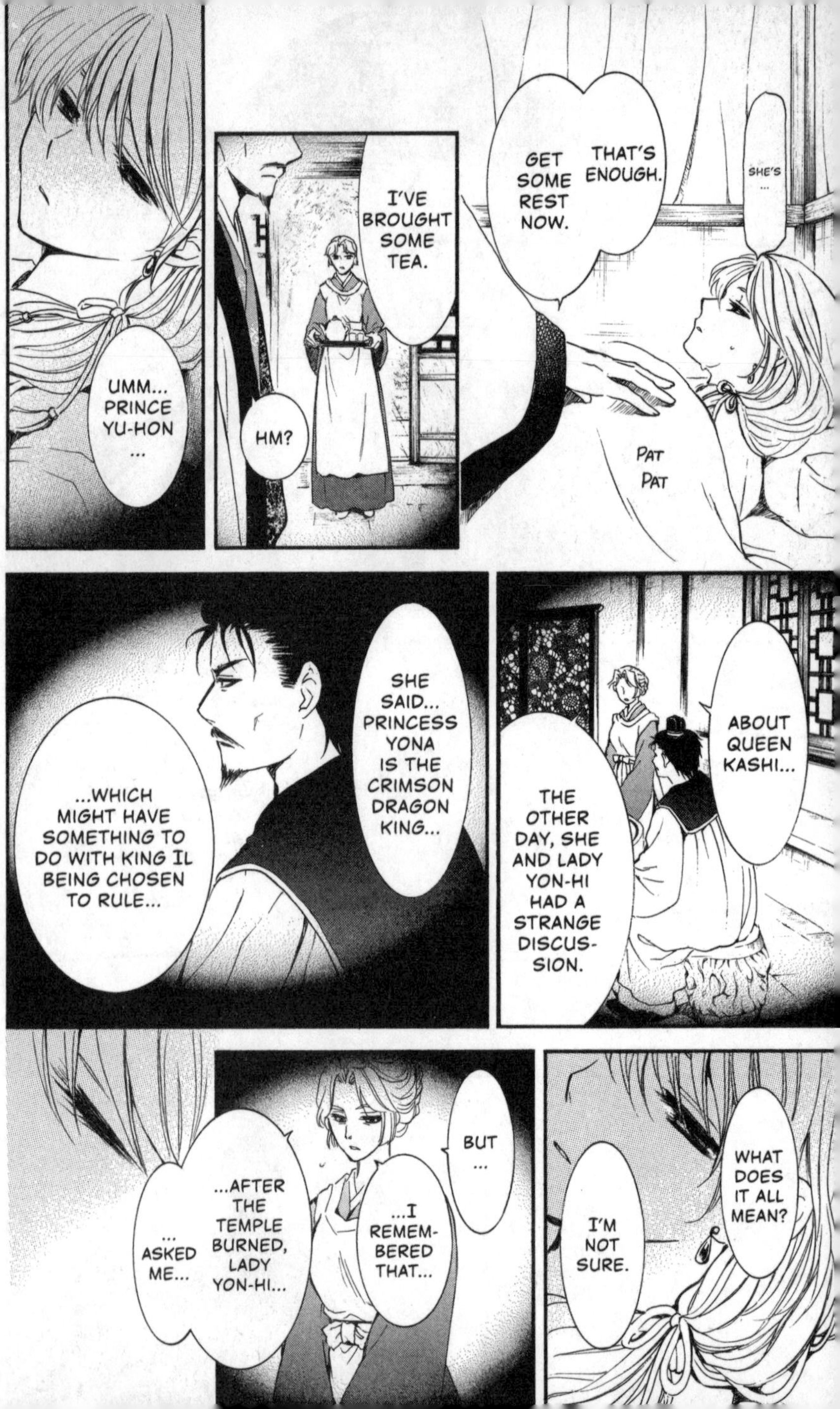
SHE'S ...
THAT'S ENOUGH.
GET SOME REST NOW.
PAT PAT
I'VE BROUGHT SOME TEA.
HM?
UMM... PRINCE YU-HON ...
ABOUT QUEEN KASHI...
THE OTHER DAY, SHE AND LADY YON-HI HAD A STRANGE DISCUSSION.
SHE SAID... PRINCESS YONA IS THE CRIMSON DRAGON KING...
...WHICH MIGHT HAVE SOMETHING TO DO WITH KING IL BEING CHOSEN TO RULE...
WHAT DOES IT ALL MEAN?
I'M NOT SURE.
BUT ...
...I REMEMBERED THAT...
...AFTER THE TEMPLE BURNED, LADY YON-HI...
... ASKED ME...

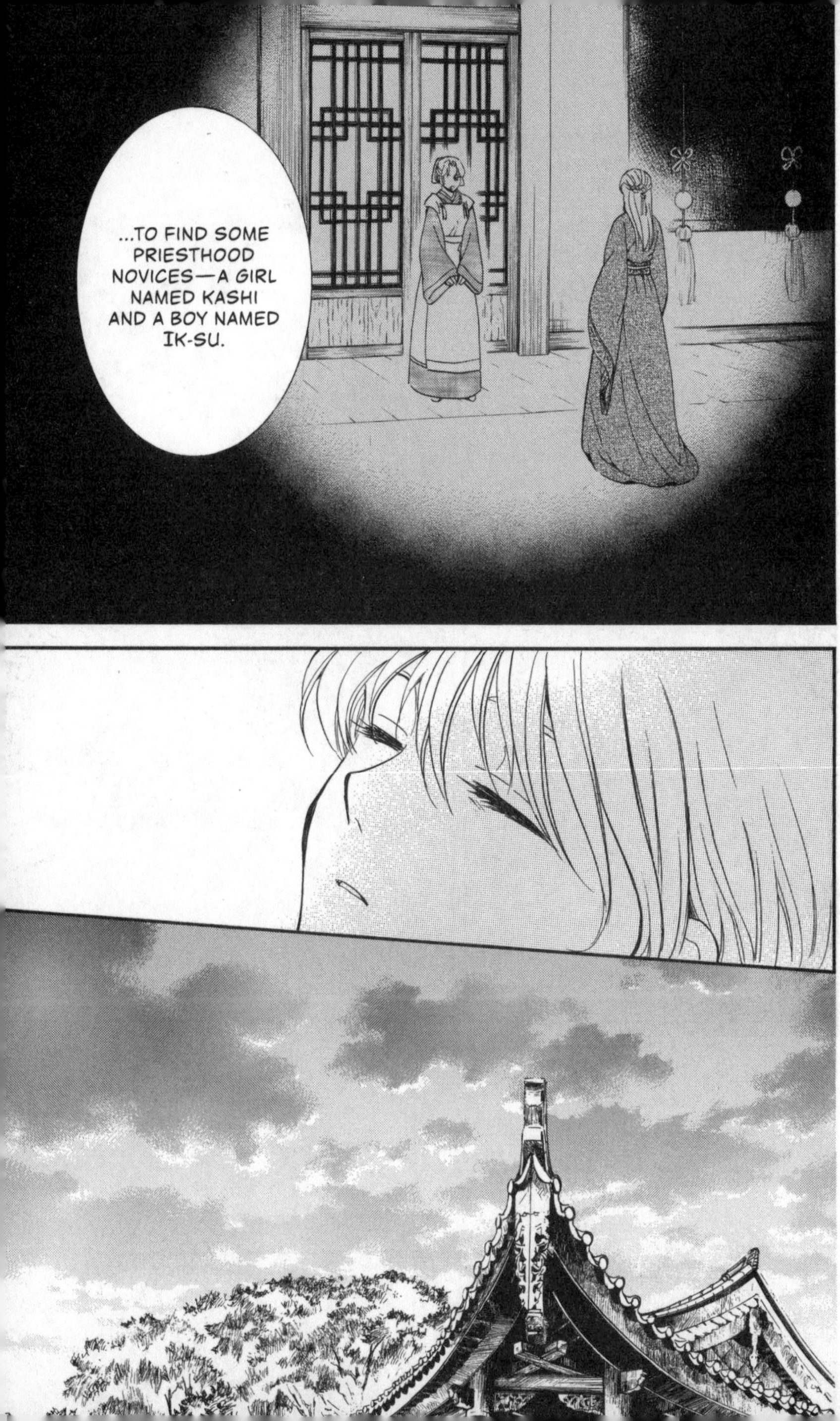
...TO FIND SOME PRIESTHOOD NOVICES—A GIRL NAMED KASHI AND A BOY NAMED IK-SU.

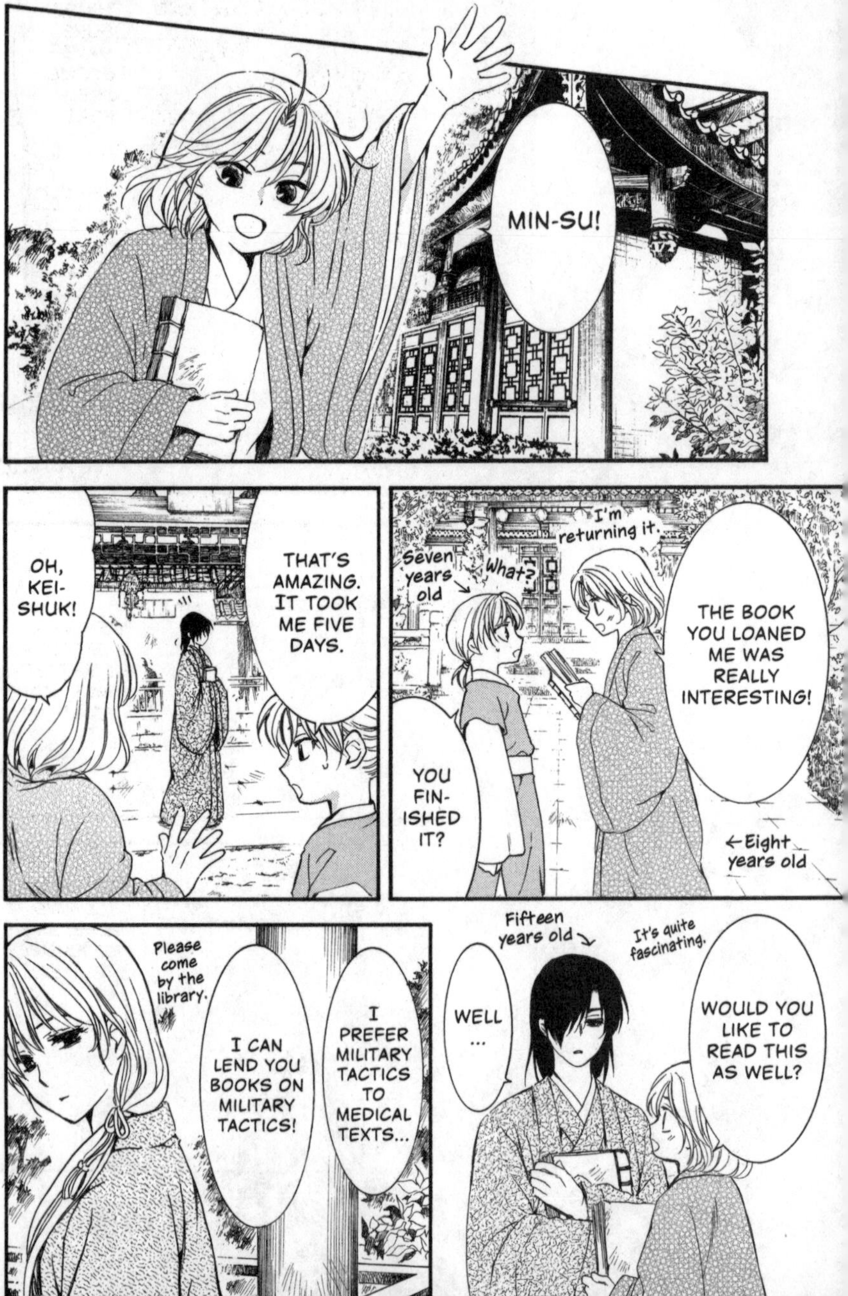
MIN-SU!
I'm returning it.
THE BOOK YOU LOANED ME WAS REALLY INTERESTING!
What?
Seven years old
YOU FIN-ISHED IT?
←Eight years old
THAT'S AMAZING. IT TOOK ME FIVE DAYS.
OH, KEI-SHUK!
WOULD YOU LIKE TO READ THIS AS WELL?
It's quite fascinating.
Fifteen years old
WELL...
I PREFER MILITARY TACTICS TO MEDICAL TEXTS...
I CAN LEND YOU BOOKS ON MILITARY TACTICS!
Please come by the library.

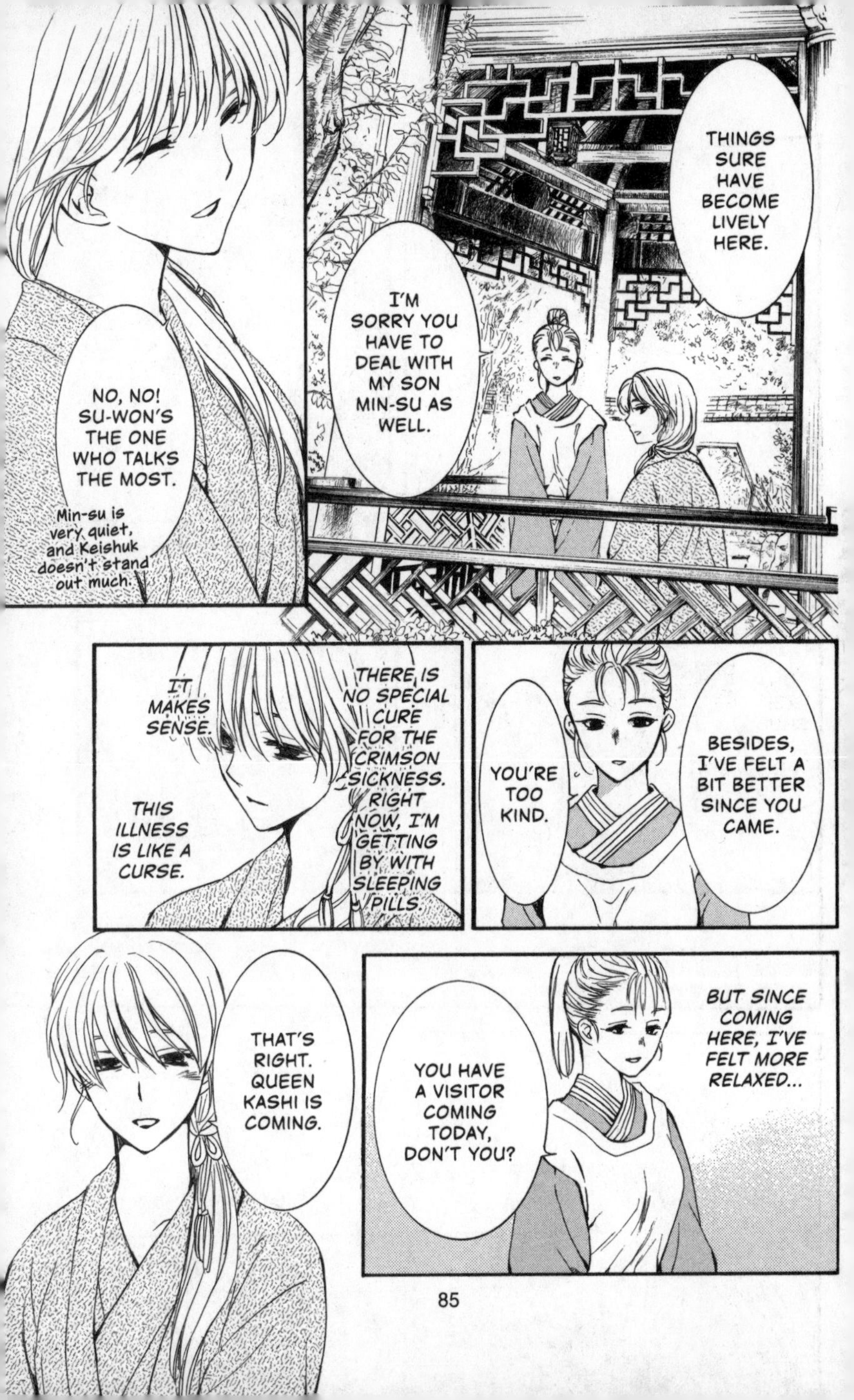
THINGS SURE HAVE BECOME LIVELY HERE.
I'M SORRY YOU HAVE TO DEAL WITH MY SON MIN-SU AS WELL.
NO, NO! SU-WON'S THE ONE WHO TALKS THE MOST.
Min-su is very quiet, and Keishuk doesn't stand out much.
BESIDES, I'VE FELT A BIT BETTER SINCE YOU CAME.
YOU'RE TOO KIND.
THERE IS NO SPECIAL CURE FOR THE CRIMSON SICKNESS. RIGHT NOW, I'M GETTING BY WITH SLEEPING PILLS.
IT MAKES SENSE.
THIS ILLNESS IS LIKE A CURSE.
BUT SINCE COMING HERE, I'VE FELT MORE RELAXED...
YOU HAVE A VISITOR COMING TODAY, DON'T YOU?
THAT'S RIGHT. QUEEN KASHI IS COMING.

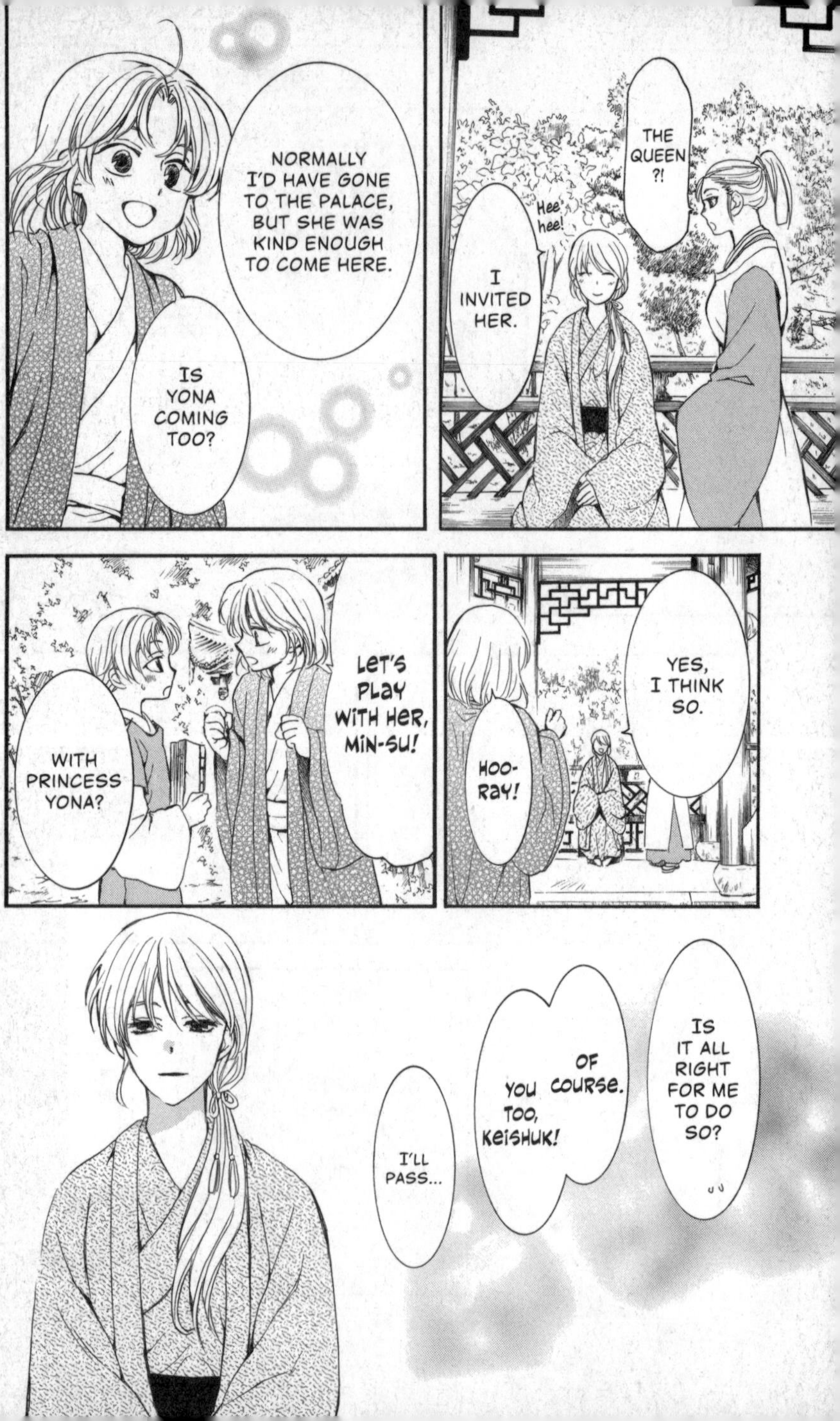
THE QUEEN?!
Hee hee!
I INVITED HER.
NORMALLY I'D HAVE GONE TO THE PALACE, BUT SHE WAS KIND ENOUGH TO COME HERE.
IS YONA COMING TOO?
YES, I THINK SO.
HOO-RAY!
LET'S PLAY WITH HER, MIN-SU!
WITH PRINCESS YONA?
IS IT ALL RIGHT FOR ME TO DO SO?
OF COURSE.
YOU TOO, KEISHUK!
I'LL PASS...

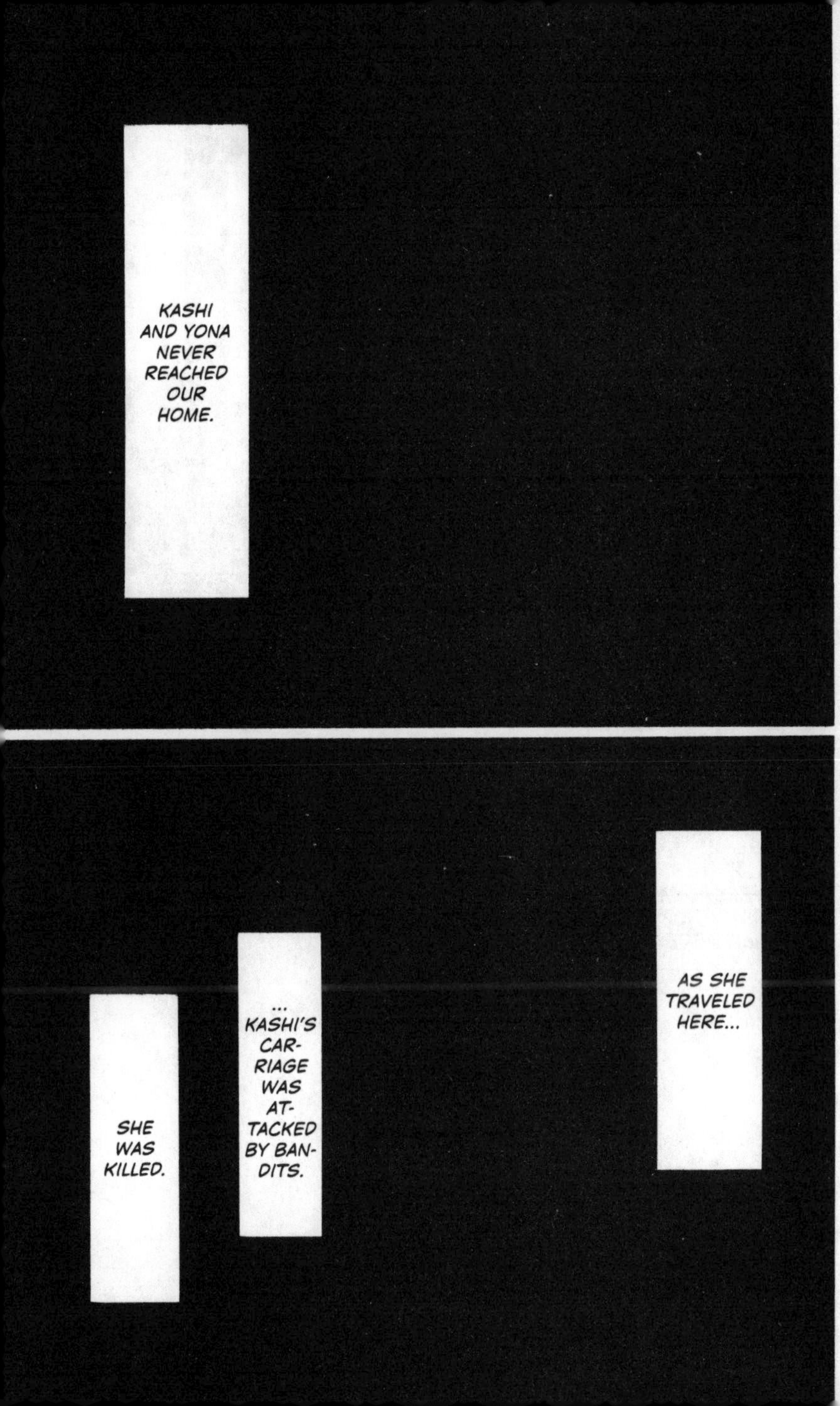
KASHI AND YONA NEVER REACHED OUR HOME.
AS SHE TRAVELED HERE...
...KASHI'S CARRIAGE WAS ATTACKED BY BANDITS.
SHE WAS KILLED.

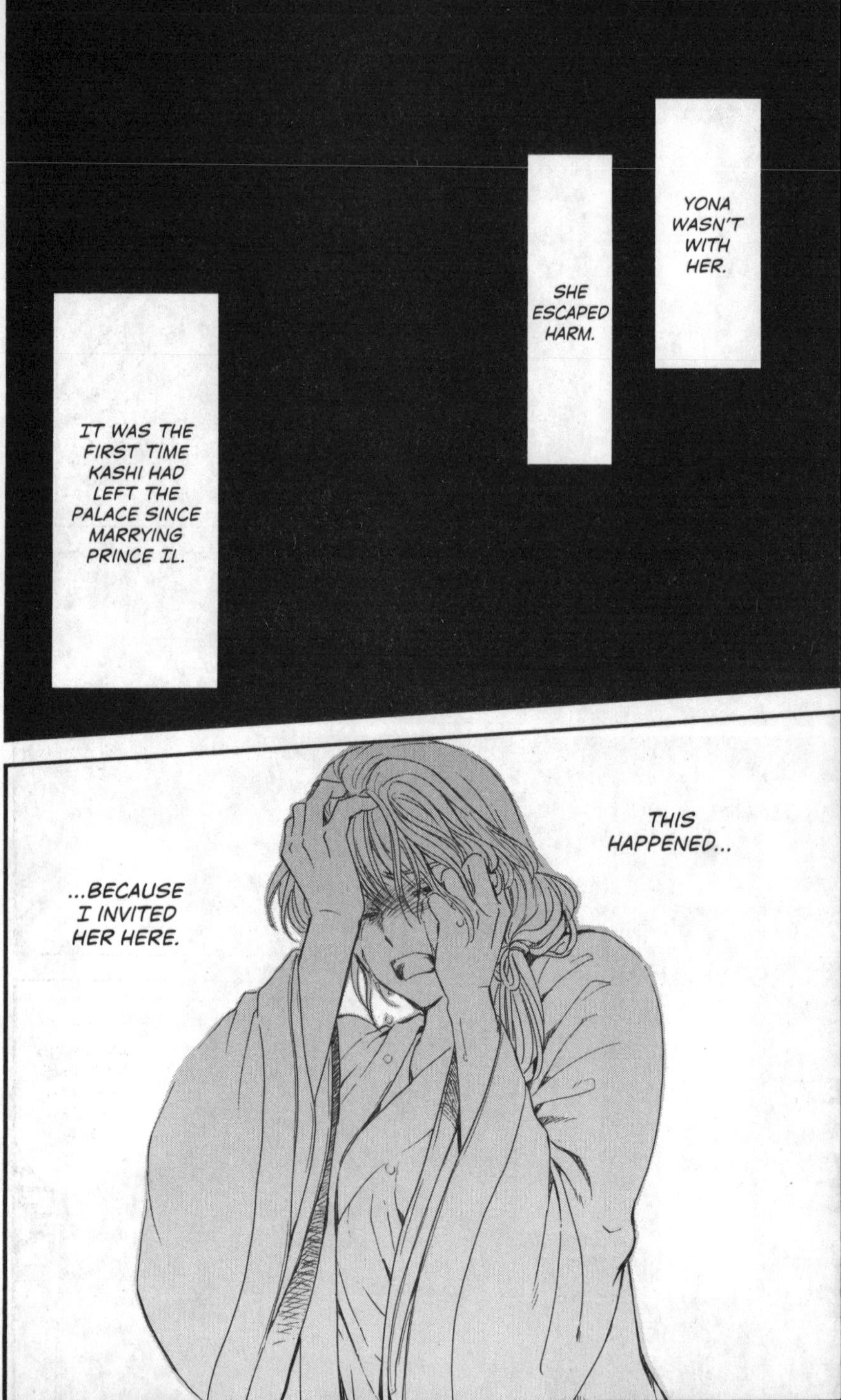
YONA WASN'T WITH HER.
SHE ESCAPED HARM.
IT WAS THE FIRST TIME KASHI HAD LEFT THE PALACE SINCE MARRYING PRINCE IL.
THIS HAPPENED...
...BECAUSE I INVITED HER HERE.

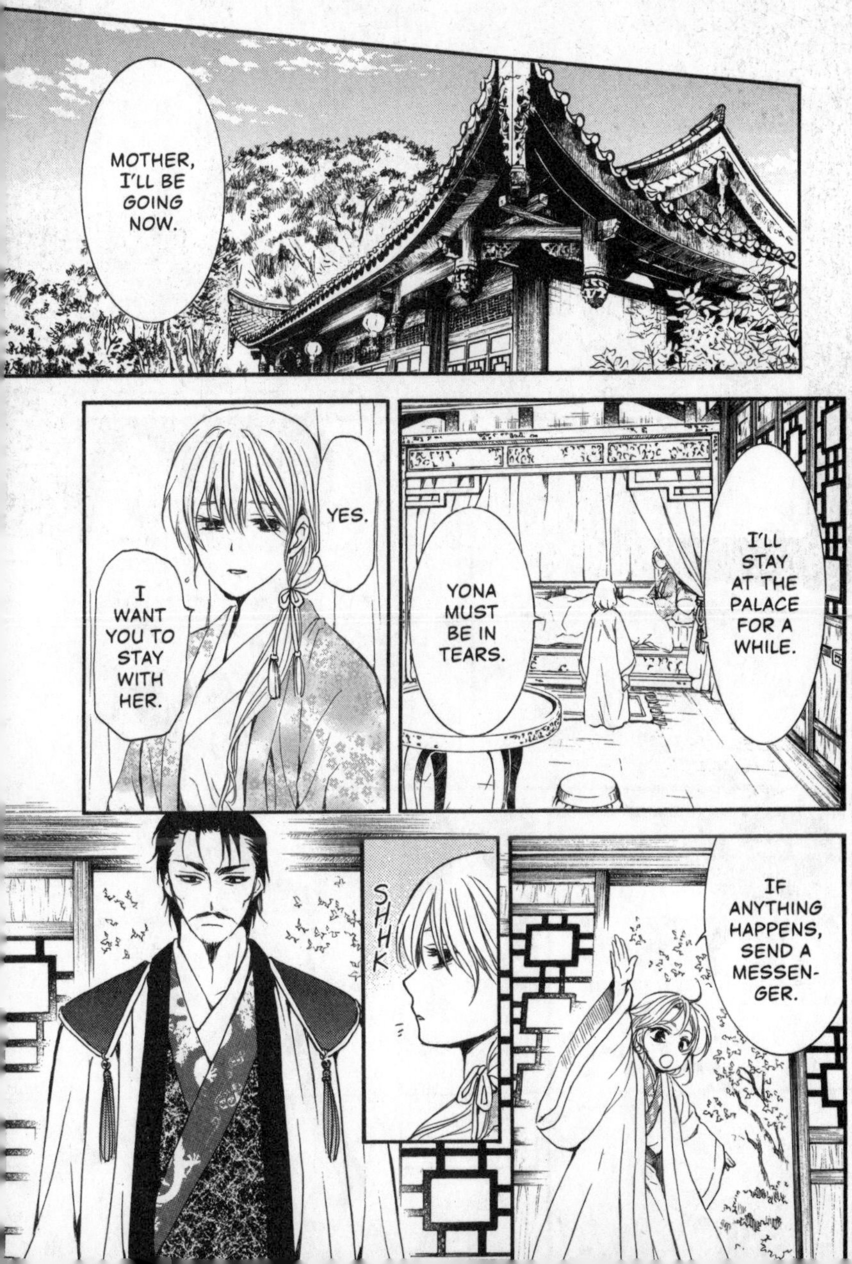
MOTHER, I'LL BE GOING NOW.
I'LL STAY AT THE PALACE FOR A WHILE.
YONA MUST BE IN TEARS.
YES.
I WANT YOU TO STAY WITH HER.
IF ANYTHING HAPPENS, SEND A MESSENGER.
SHHK

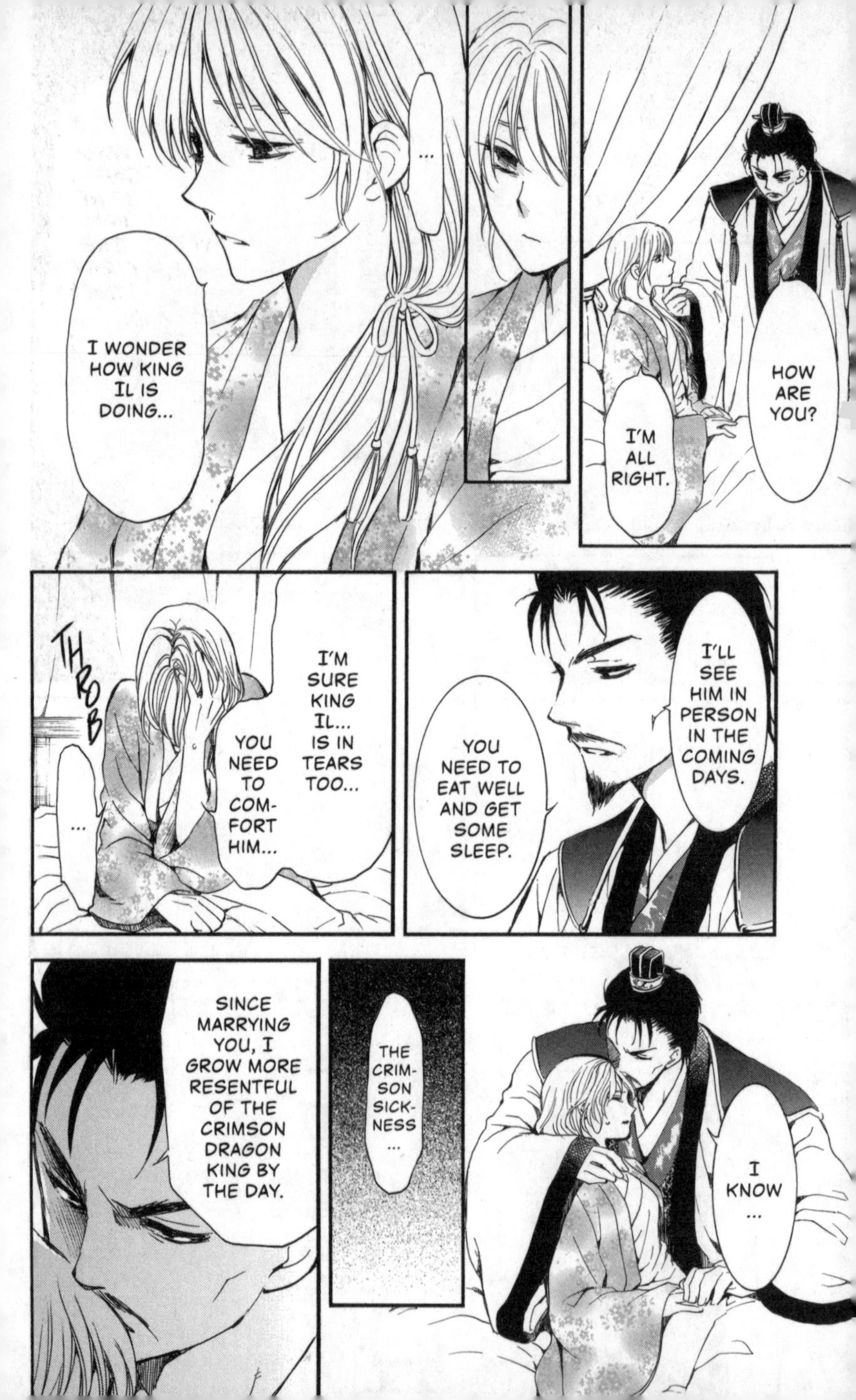
HOW ARE YOU?
I'M ALL RIGHT.
...
I WONDER HOW KING IL IS DOING...
I'LL SEE HIM IN PERSON IN THE COMING DAYS.
YOU NEED TO EAT WELL AND GET SOME SLEEP.
I'M SURE KING IL... IS IN TEARS TOO...
YOU NEED TO COM-FORT HIM...
THROB
...
I KNOW...
THE CRIM-SON SICK-NESS...
SINCE MARRYING YOU, I GROW MORE RESENTFUL OF THE CRIMSON DRAGON KING BY THE DAY.

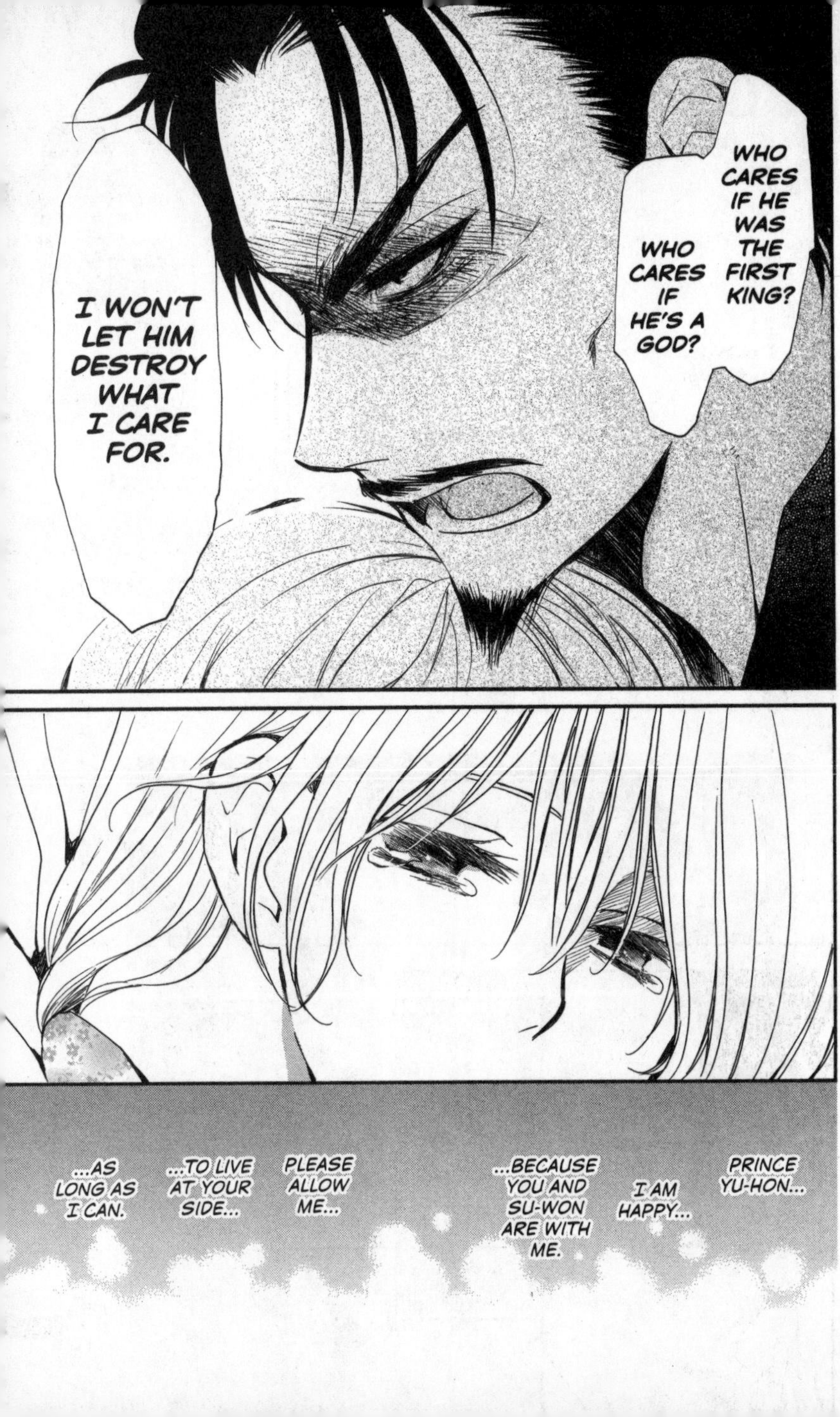
WHO CARES IF HE WAS THE FIRST KING?
WHO CARES IF HE'S A GOD?
I WON'T LET HIM DESTROY WHAT I CARE FOR.
PRINCE YU-HON...
I AM HAPPY...
...BECAUSE YOU AND SU-WON ARE WITH ME.
PLEASE ALLOW ME...
...TO LIVE AT YOUR SIDE...
...AS LONG AS I CAN.

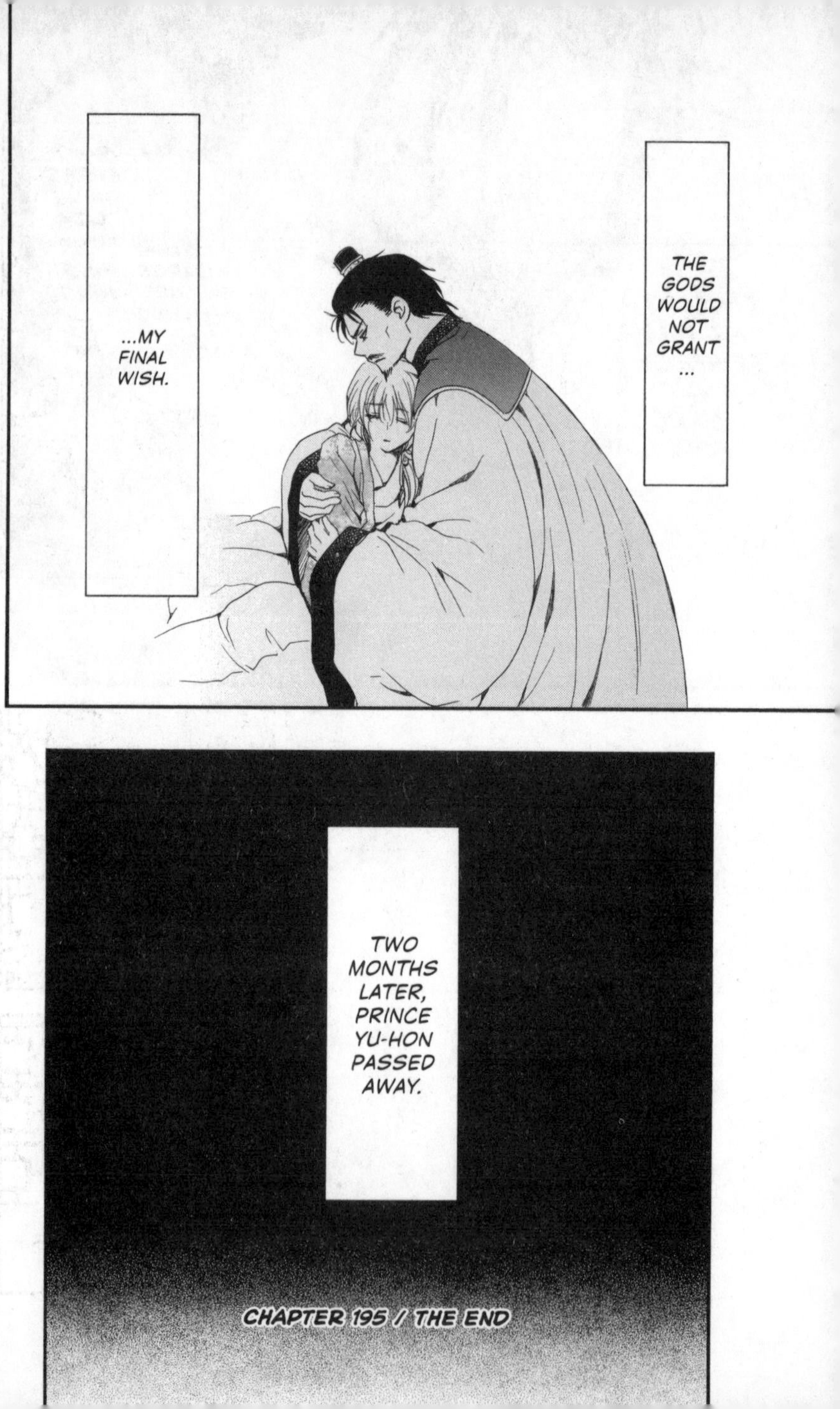
THE GODS WOULD NOT GRANT...
...MY FINAL WISH.
TWO MONTHS LATER, PRINCE YU-HON PASSED AWAY.
CHAPTER 195 / THE END

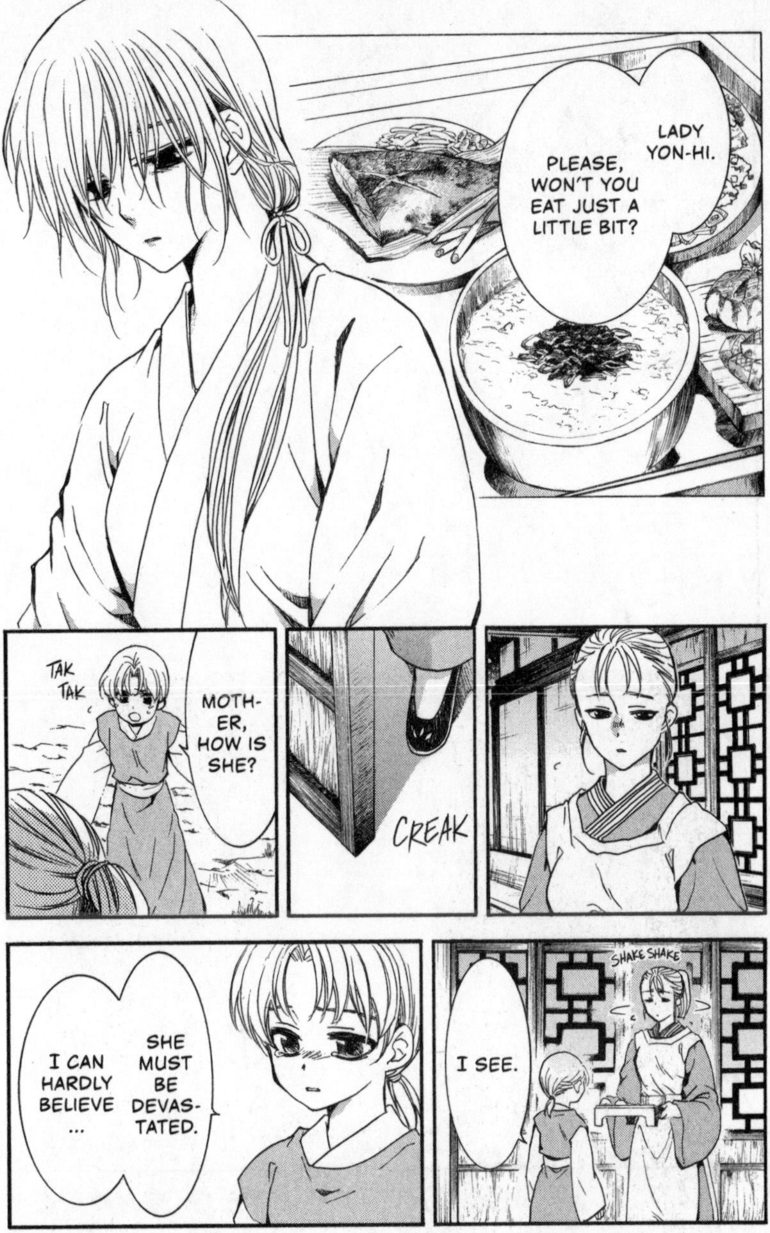
LADY YON-HI.
PLEASE, WON'T YOU EAT JUST A LITTLE BIT?
CREAK
TAK TAK
MOTHER, HOW IS SHE?
SHAKE SHAKE
I SEE.
SHE MUST BE DEVASTATED.
I CAN HARDLY BELIEVE ...

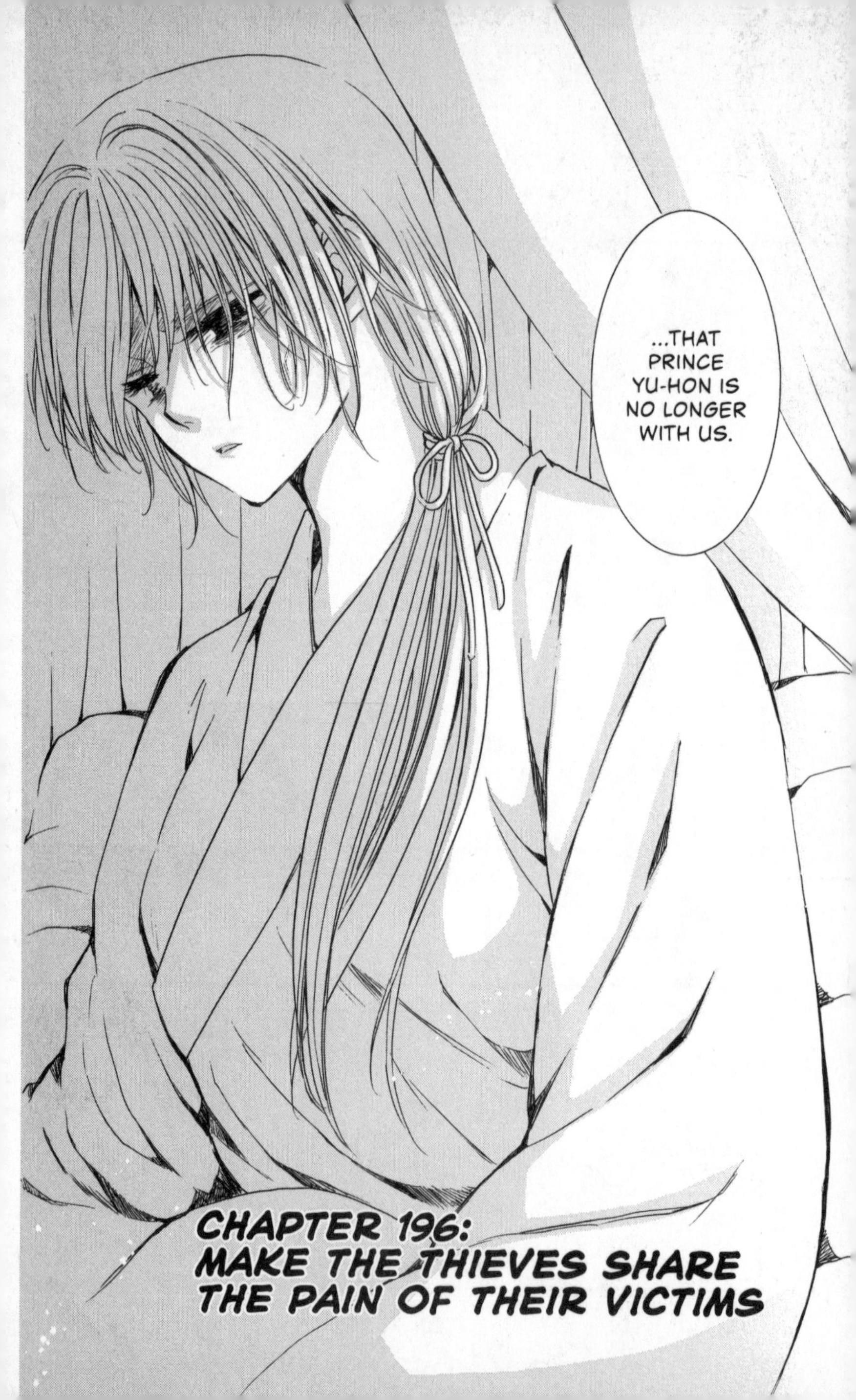
...THAT PRINCE YU-HON IS NO LONGER WITH US.
CHAPTER 196: MAKE THE THIEVES SHARE THE PAIN OF THEIR VICTIMS

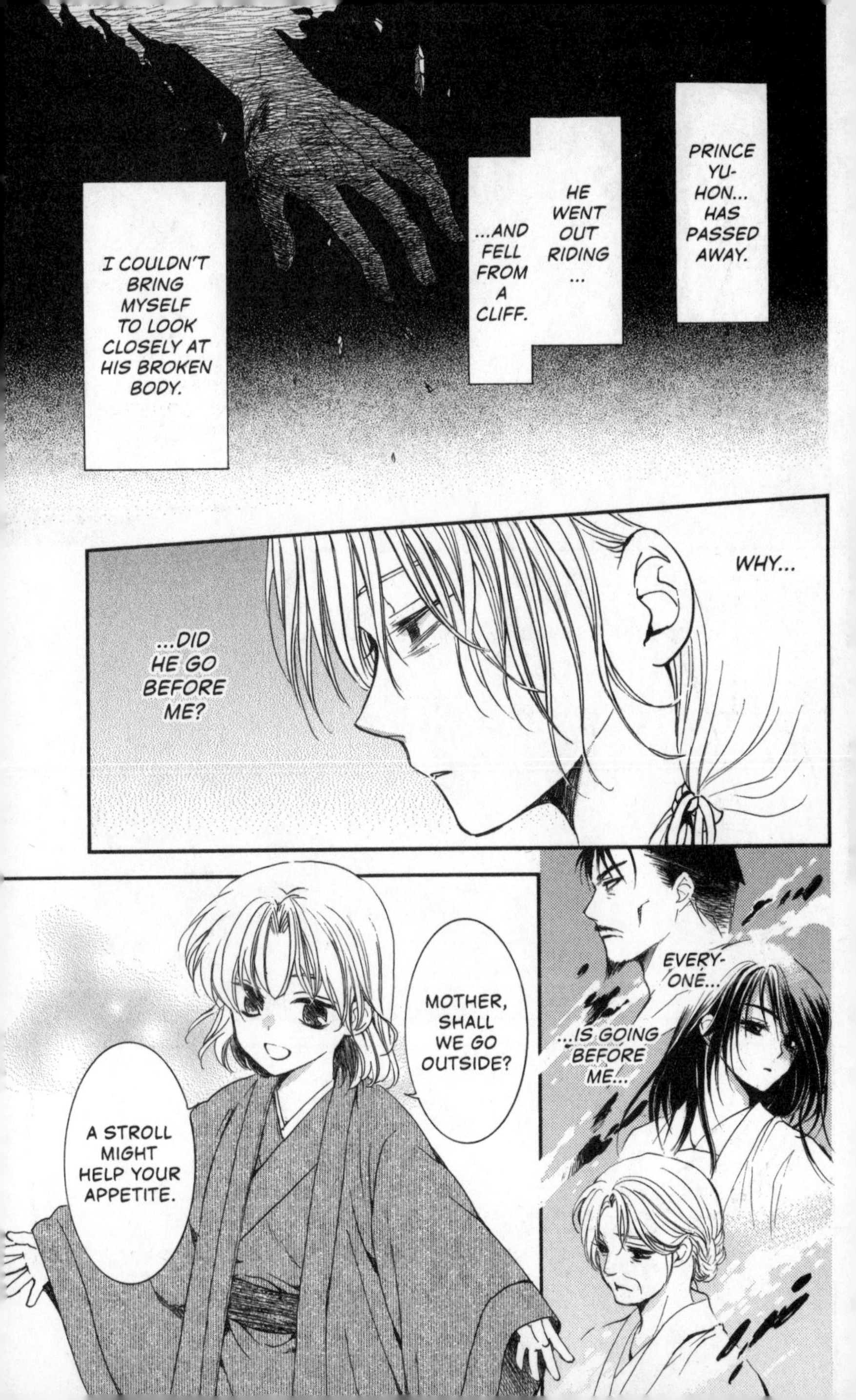
PRINCE YU-HON... HAS PASSED AWAY.
HE WENT OUT RIDING...
...AND FELL FROM A CLIFF.
I COULDN'T BRING MYSELF TO LOOK CLOSELY AT HIS BROKEN BODY.
WHY...
...DID HE GO BEFORE ME?
EVERY-ONE...
...IS GOING BEFORE ME...
MOTHER, SHALL WE GO OUTSIDE?
A STROLL MIGHT HELP YOUR APPETITE.

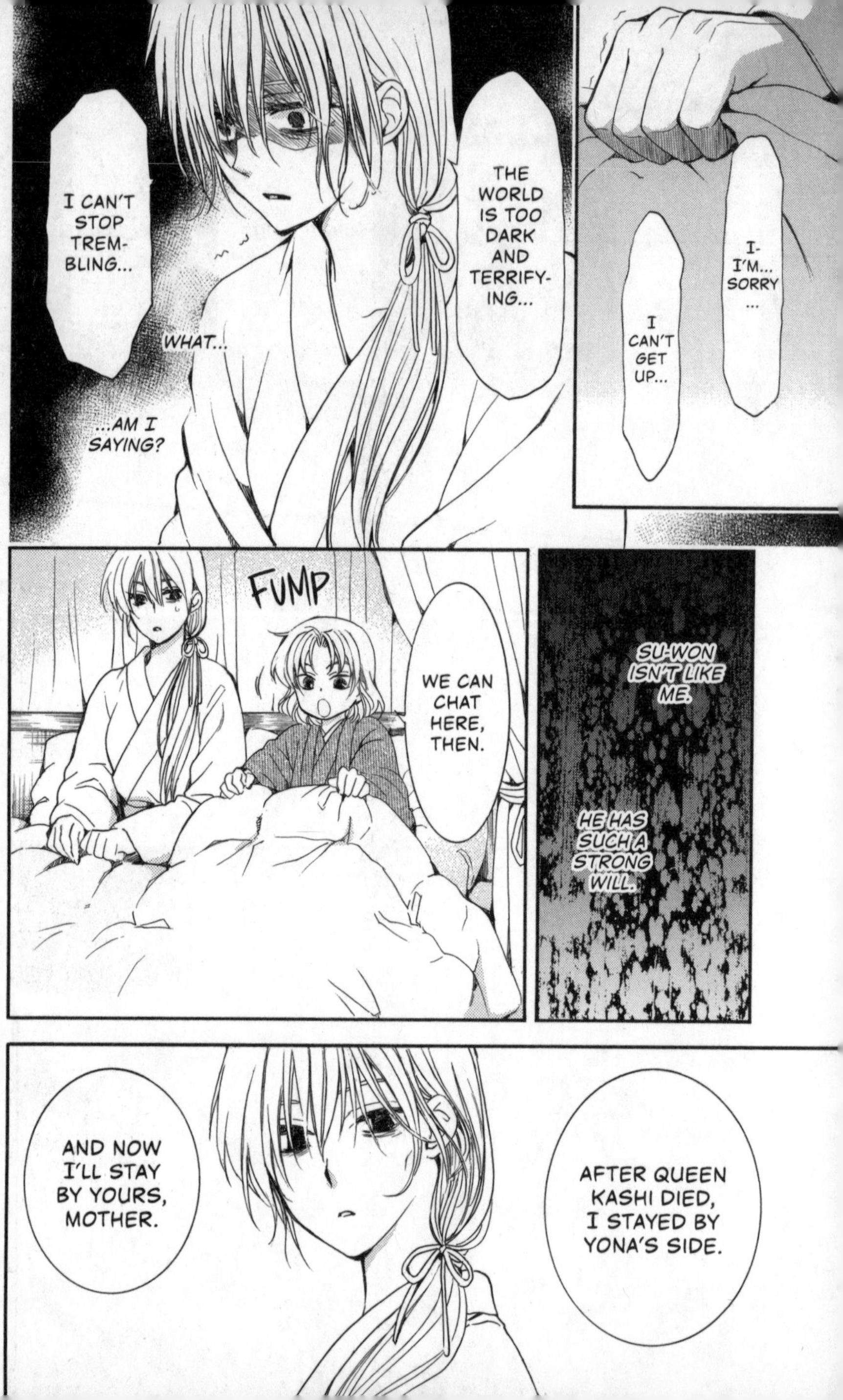
I- I'M... SORRY ...
I CAN'T GET UP...
THE WORLD IS TOO DARK AND TERRIFYING...
I CAN'T STOP TREMBLING...
WHAT...
...AM I SAYING?
SU-WON ISN'T LIKE ME.
HE HAS SUCH A STRONG WILL.
FUMP
WE CAN CHAT HERE, THEN.
AFTER QUEEN KASHI DIED, I STAYED BY YONA'S SIDE.
AND NOW I'LL STAY BY YOURS, MOTHER.

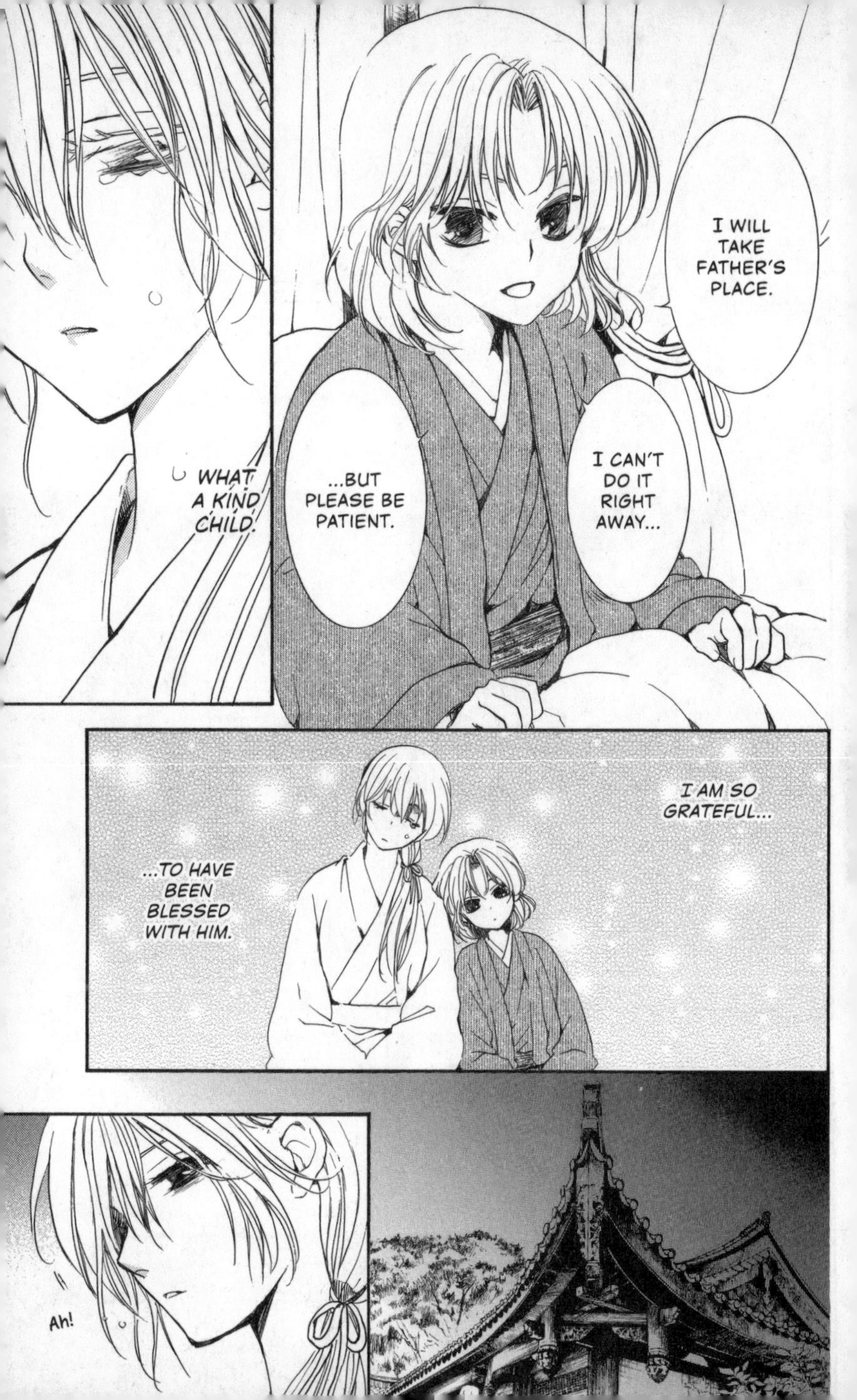
I WILL TAKE FATHER'S PLACE.
I CAN'T DO IT RIGHT AWAY...
...BUT PLEASE BE PATIENT.
WHAT A KIND CHILD.
I AM SO GRATEFUL...
...TO HAVE BEEN BLESSED WITH HIM.
Ah!

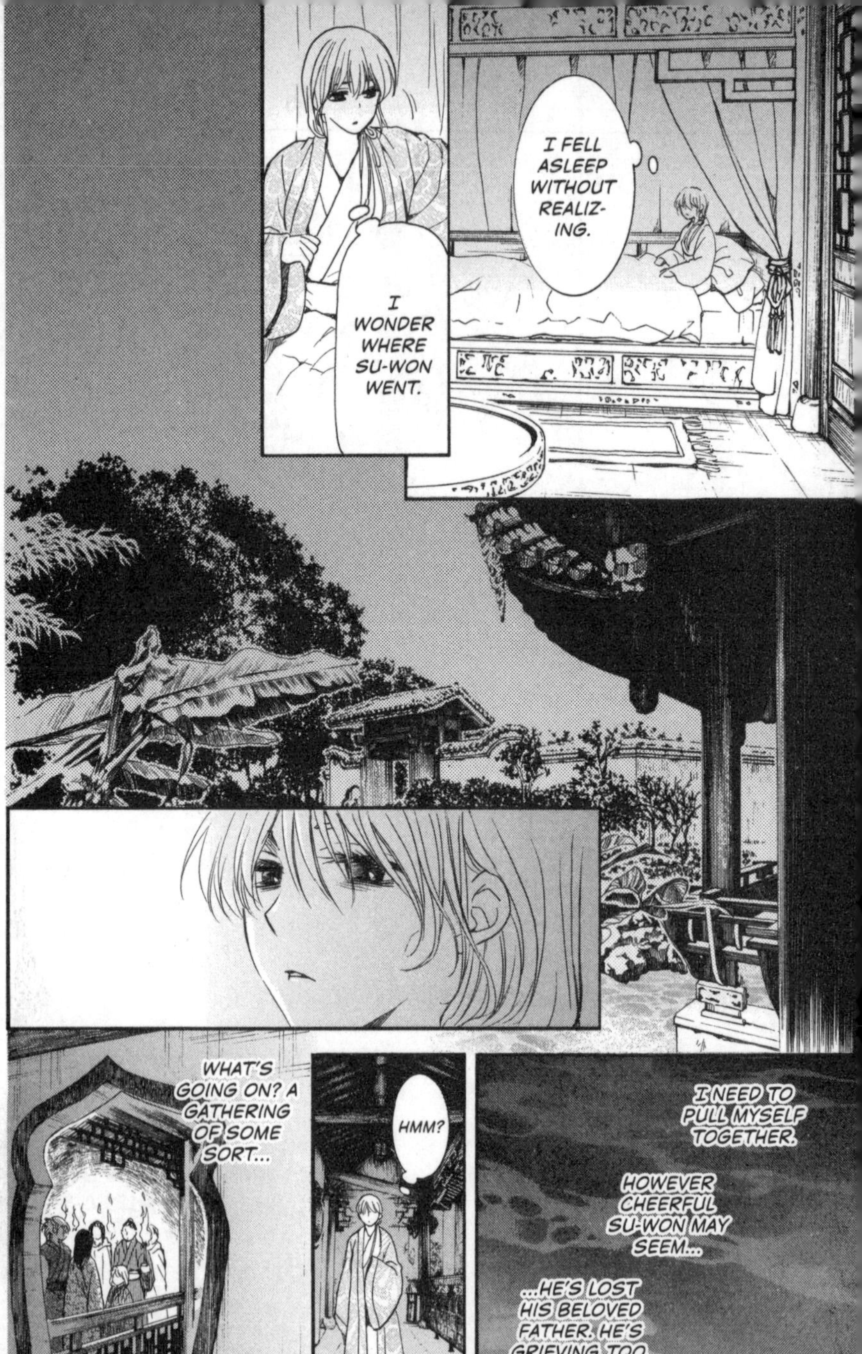
I FELL ASLEEP WITHOUT REALIZ-ING.
I WONDER WHERE SU-WON WENT.
I NEED TO PULL MYSELF TOGETHER.
HOWEVER CHEERFUL SU-WON MAY SEEM...
...HE'S LOST HIS BELOVED FATHER. HE'S GRIEVING TOO.
HMM?
WHAT'S GOING ON? A GATHERING OF SOME SORT...

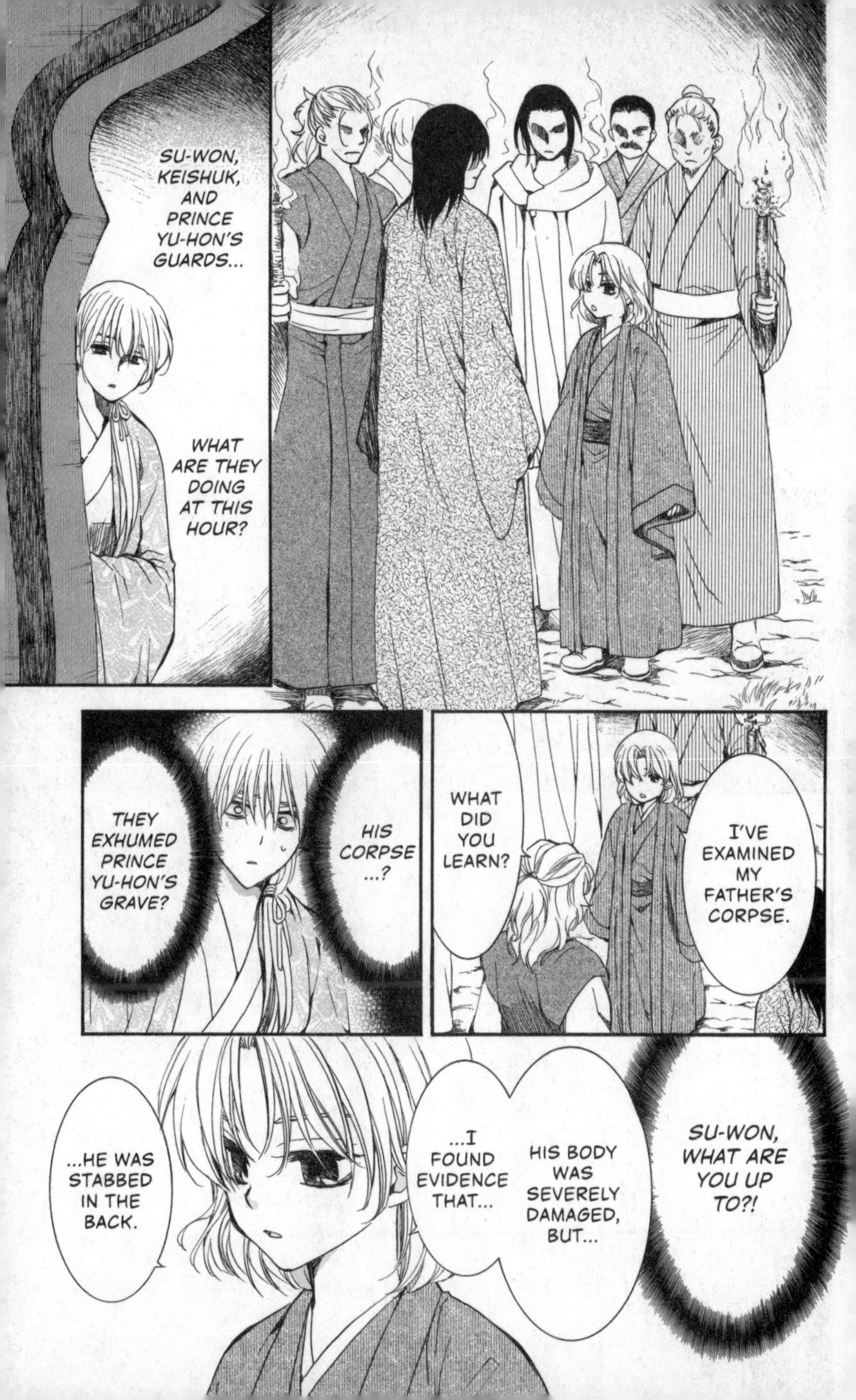
SU-WON, KEISHUK, AND PRINCE YU-HON'S GUARDS...
WHAT ARE THEY DOING AT THIS HOUR?
I'VE EXAMINED MY FATHER'S CORPSE.
WHAT DID YOU LEARN?
HIS CORPSE ...?
THEY EXHUMED PRINCE YU-HON'S GRAVE?
SU-WON, WHAT ARE YOU UP TO?!
HIS BODY WAS SEVERELY DAMAGED, BUT...
...I FOUND EVIDENCE THAT...
...HE WAS STABBED IN THE BACK.

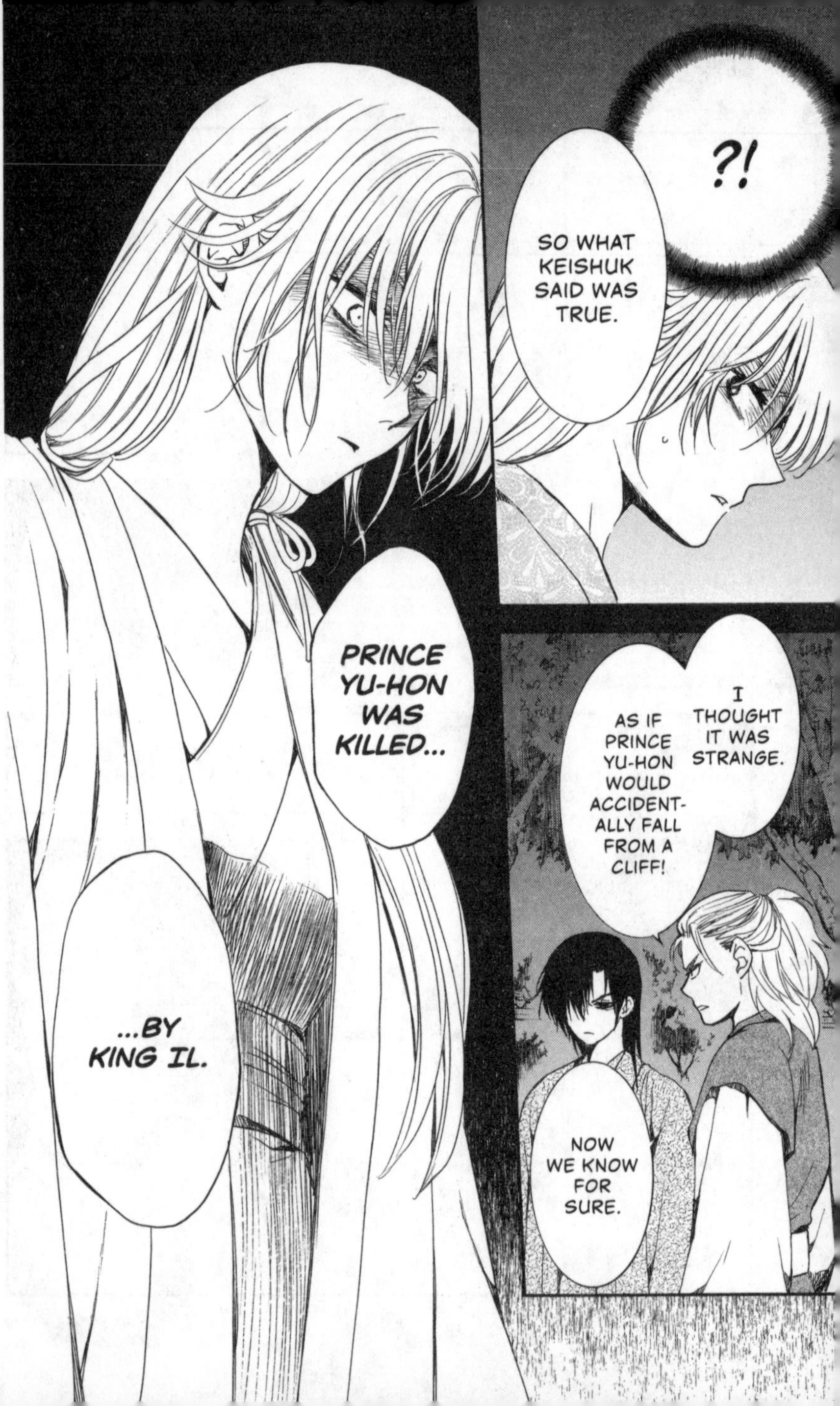
?!
SO WHAT KEISHUK SAID WAS TRUE.
I THOUGHT IT WAS STRANGE.
AS IF PRINCE YU-HON WOULD ACCIDENTALLY FALL FROM A CLIFF!
NOW WE KNOW FOR SURE.
PRINCE YU-HON WAS KILLED...
...BY KING IL.

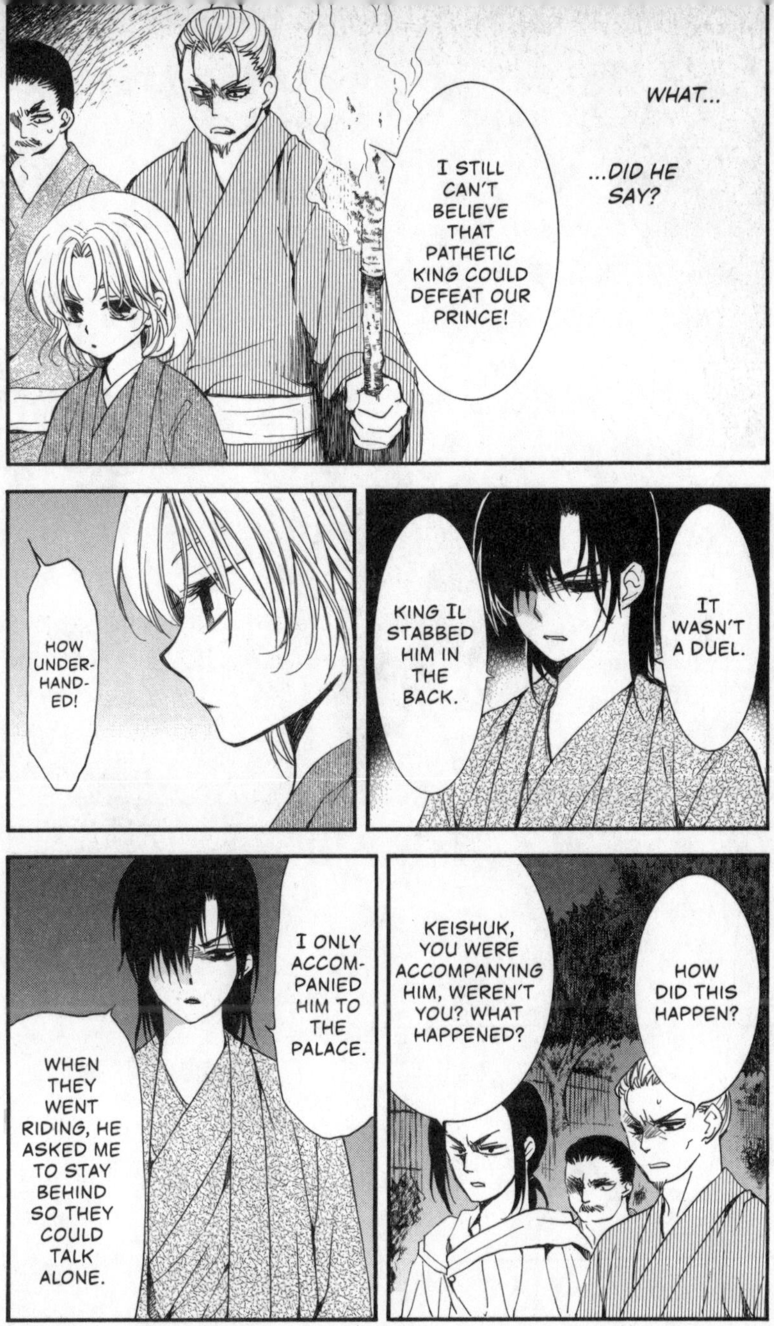
WHAT...
...DID HE SAY?
I STILL CAN'T BELIEVE THAT PATHETIC KING COULD DEFEAT OUR PRINCE!
IT WASN'T A DUEL.
KING IL STABBED HIM IN THE BACK.
HOW UNDER-HAND-ED!
HOW DID THIS HAPPEN?
KEISHUK, YOU WERE ACCOMPANYING HIM, WEREN'T YOU? WHAT HAPPENED?
I ONLY ACCOM-PANIED HIM TO THE PALACE.
WHEN THEY WENT RIDING, HE ASKED ME TO STAY BEHIND SO THEY COULD TALK ALONE.

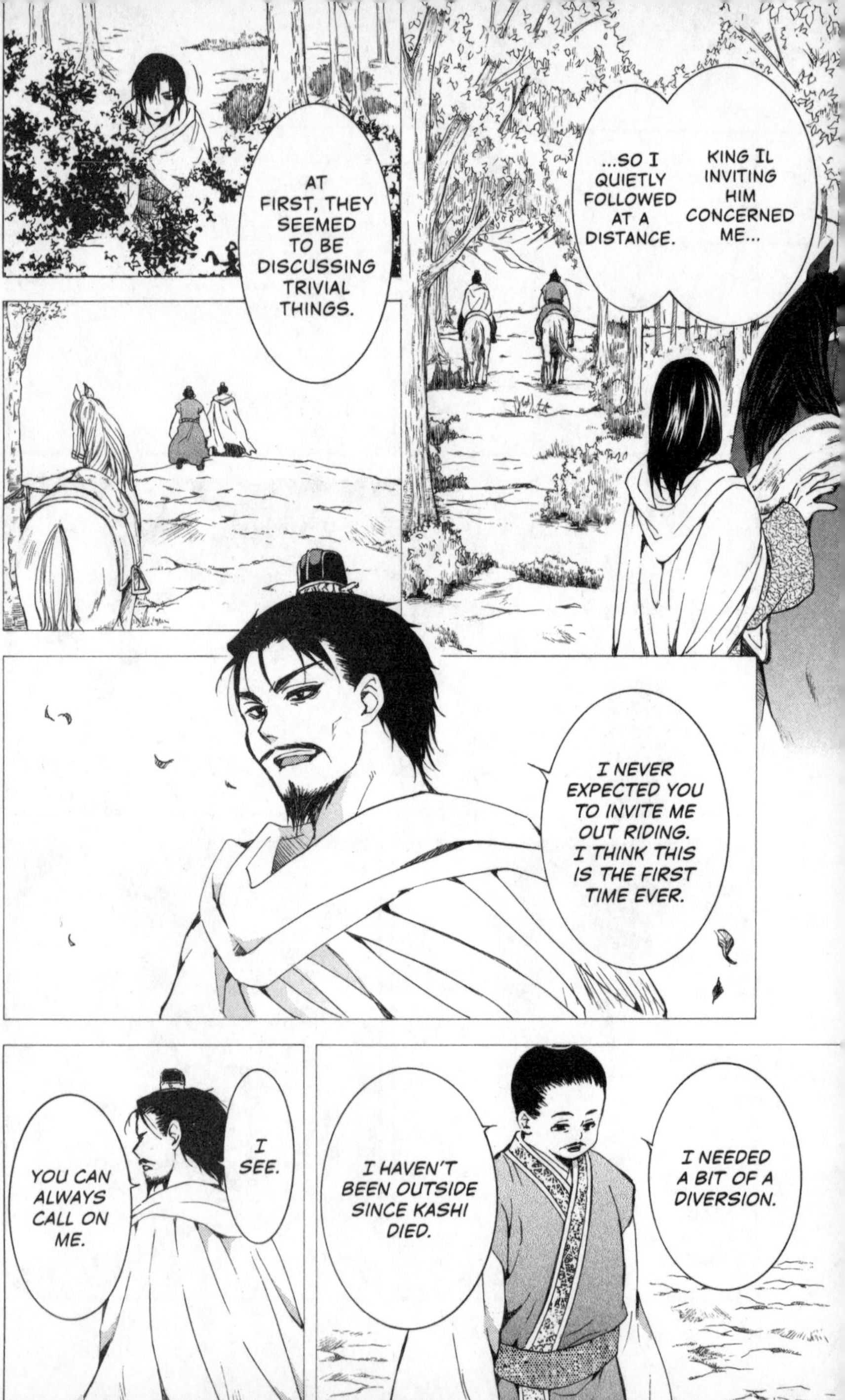
KING IL INVITING HIM CONCERNED ME...
...SO I QUIETLY FOLLOWED AT A DISTANCE.
AT FIRST, THEY SEEMED TO BE DISCUSSING TRIVIAL THINGS.
I NEVER EXPECTED YOU TO INVITE ME OUT RIDING. I THINK THIS IS THE FIRST TIME EVER.
I NEEDED A BIT OF A DIVERSION.
I HAVEN'T BEEN OUTSIDE SINCE KASHI DIED.
I SEE.
YOU CAN ALWAYS CALL ON ME.

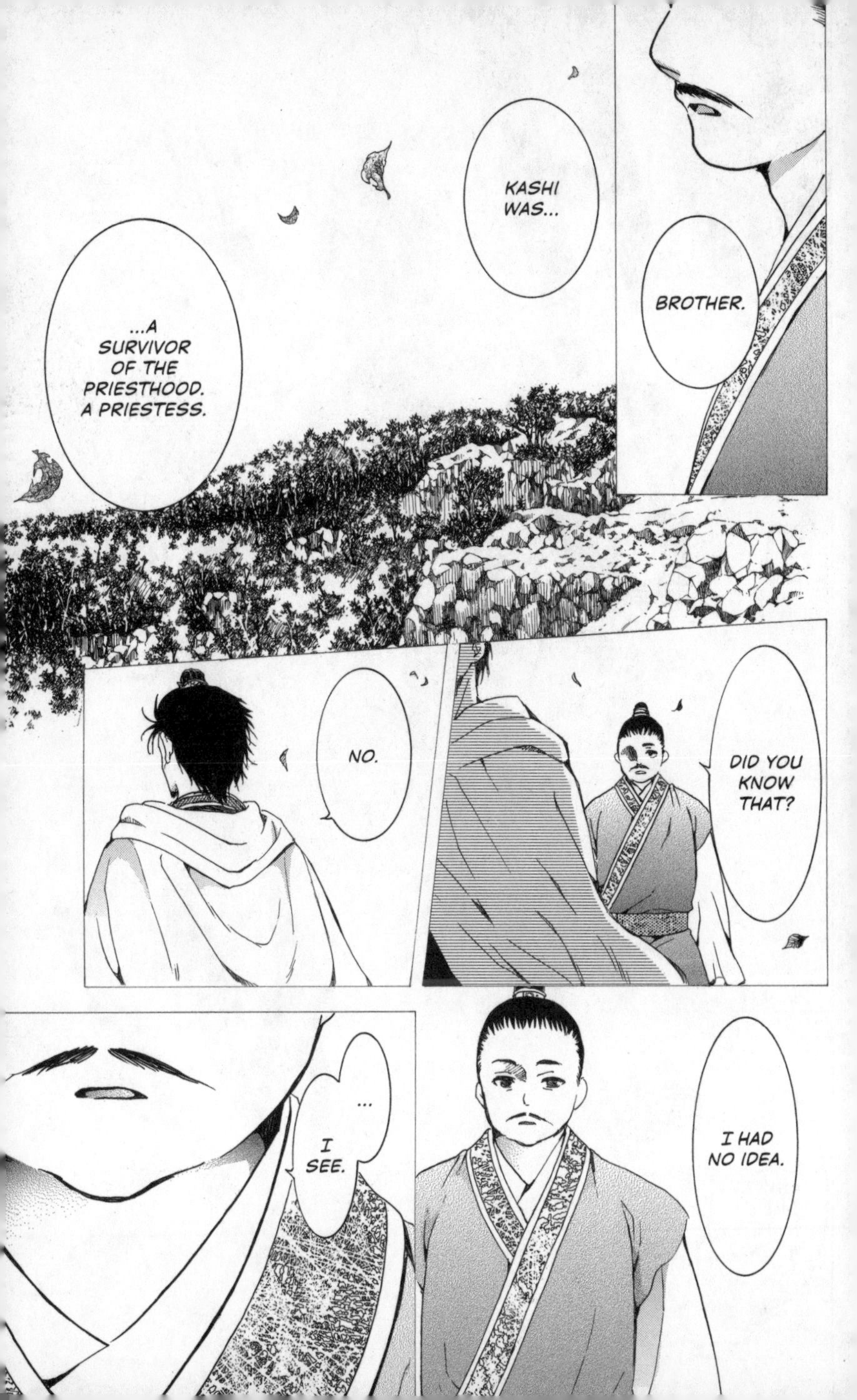
BROTHER.
KASHI WAS...
...A SURVIVOR OF THE PRIESTHOOD. A PRIESTESS.
DID YOU KNOW THAT?
NO.
I HAD NO IDEA.
... I SEE.

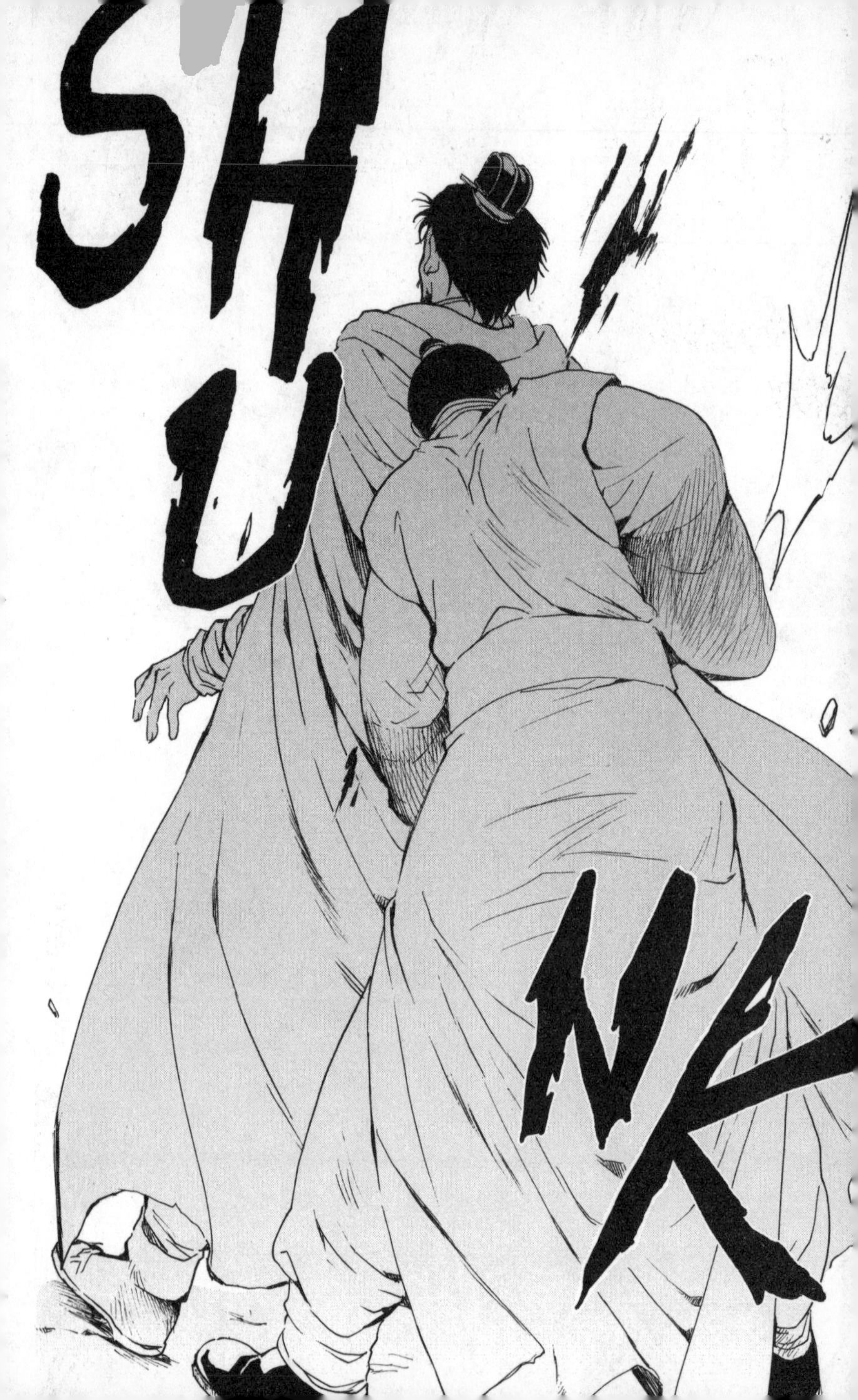
SHUNK

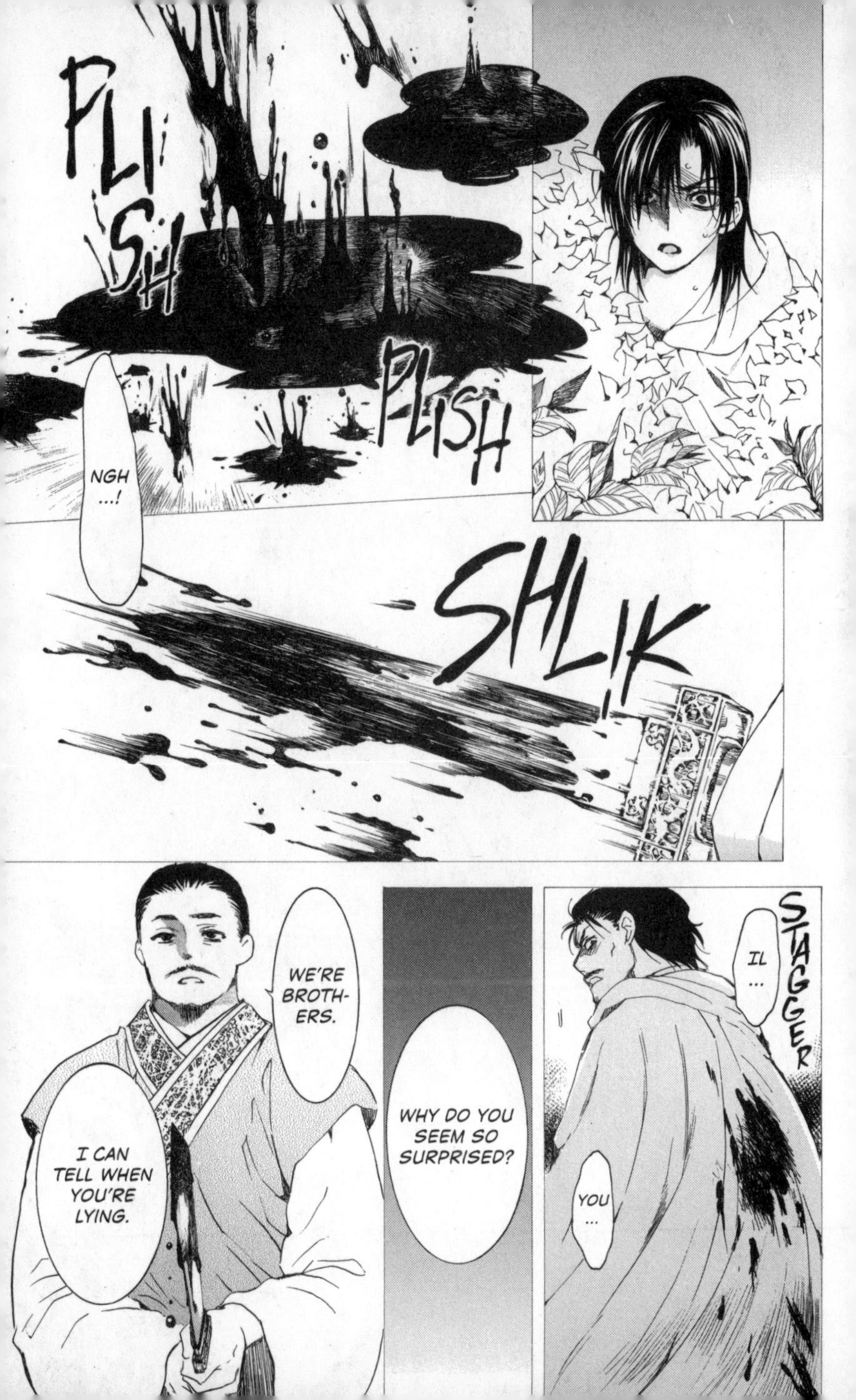
PLISH
PLISH
NGH ...!
SHLIK
STAGGER
IL ...
YOU ...
WHY DO YOU SEEM SO SURPRISED?
WE'RE BROTH-ERS.
I CAN TELL WHEN YOU'RE LYING.

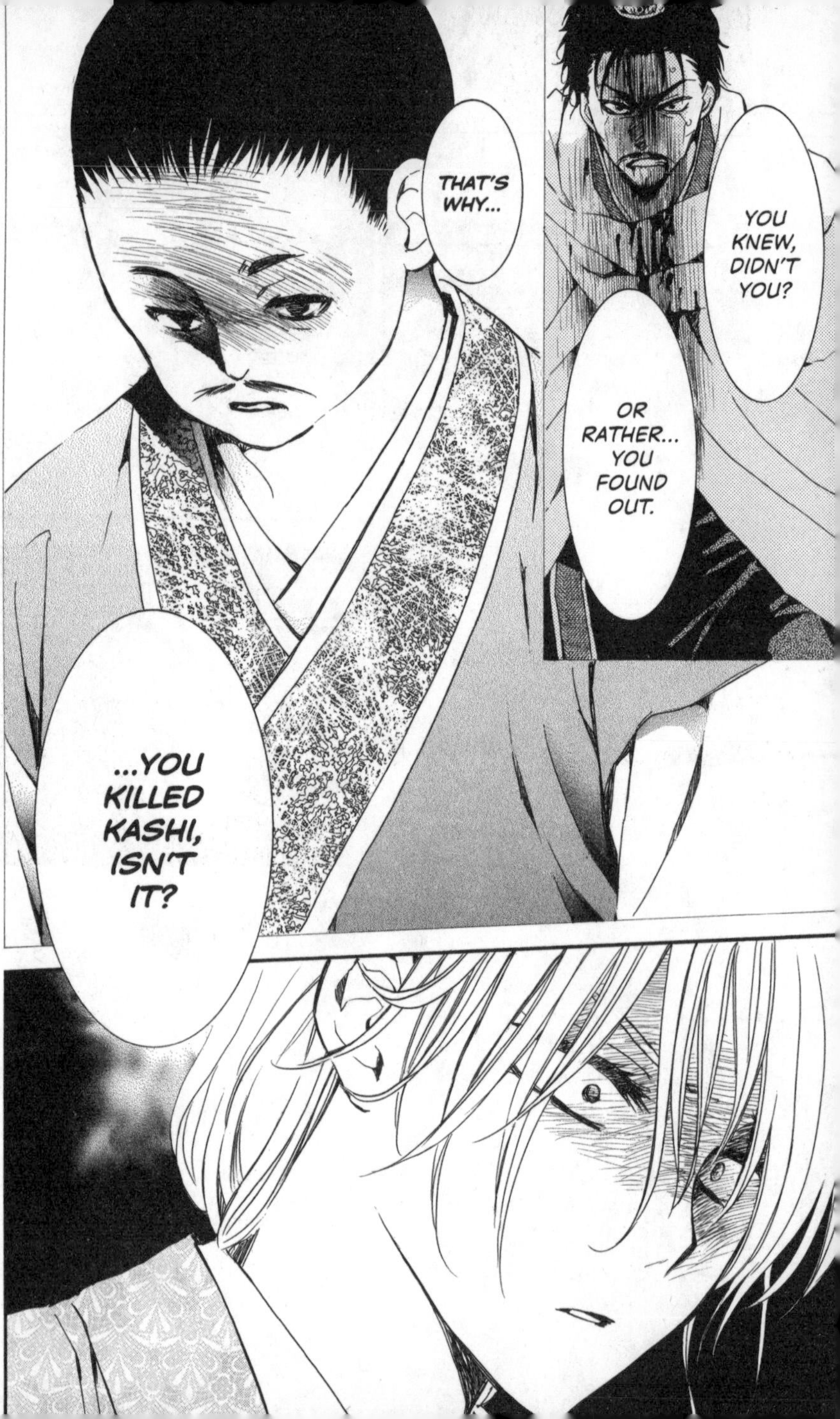
YOU KNEW, DIDN'T YOU?
OR RATHER... YOU FOUND OUT.
THAT'S WHY...
...YOU KILLED KASHI, ISN'T IT?

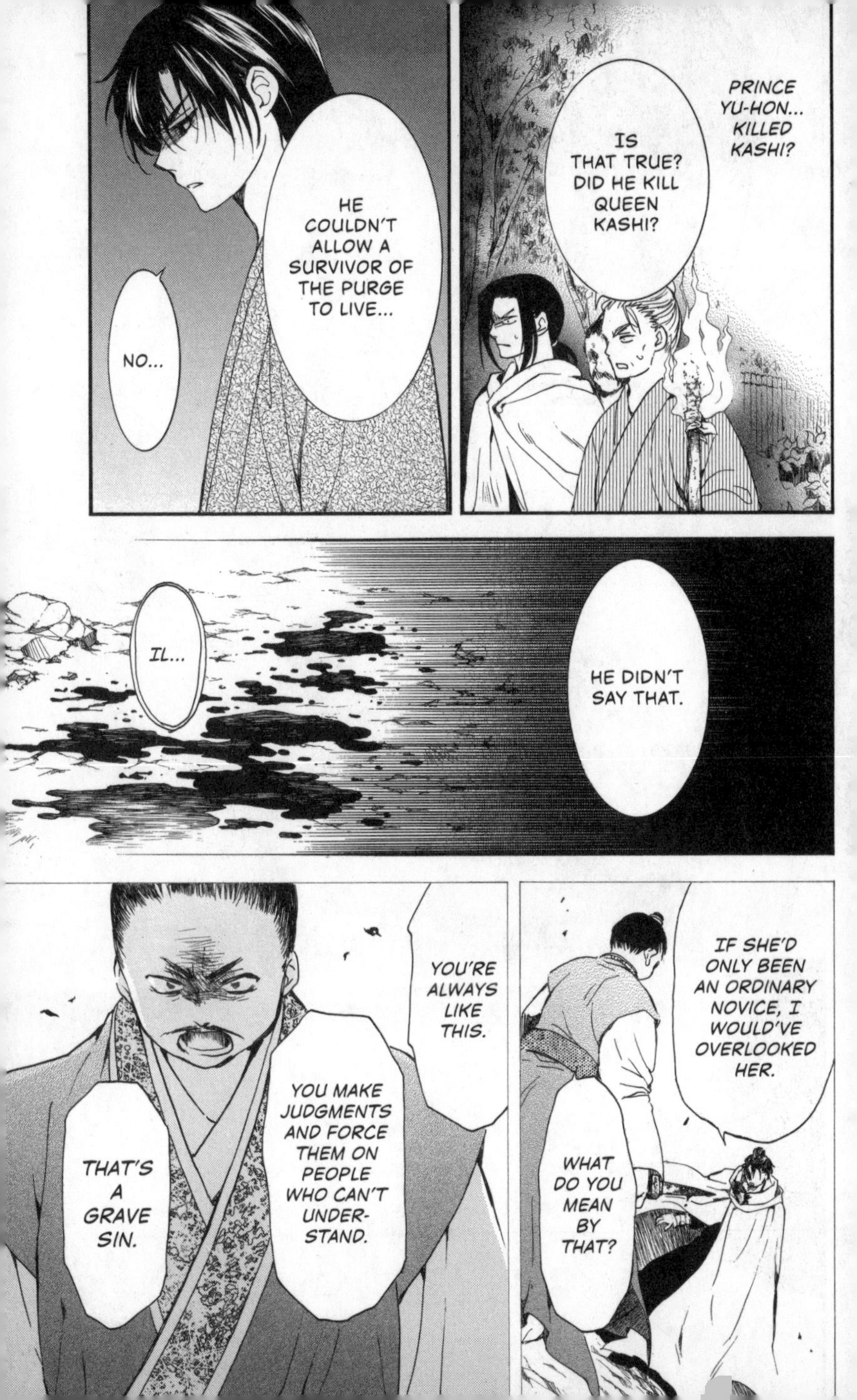
PRINCE YU-HON... KILLED KASHI?
IS THAT TRUE? DID HE KILL QUEEN KASHI?
HE COULDN'T ALLOW A SURVIVOR OF THE PURGE TO LIVE...
NO...
HE DIDN'T SAY THAT.
IL...
IF SHE'D ONLY BEEN AN ORDINARY NOVICE, I WOULD'VE OVERLOOKED HER.
WHAT DO YOU MEAN BY THAT?
YOU'RE ALWAYS LIKE THIS.
YOU MAKE JUDGMENTS AND FORCE THEM ON PEOPLE WHO CAN'T UNDER-STAND.
THAT'S A GRAVE SIN.

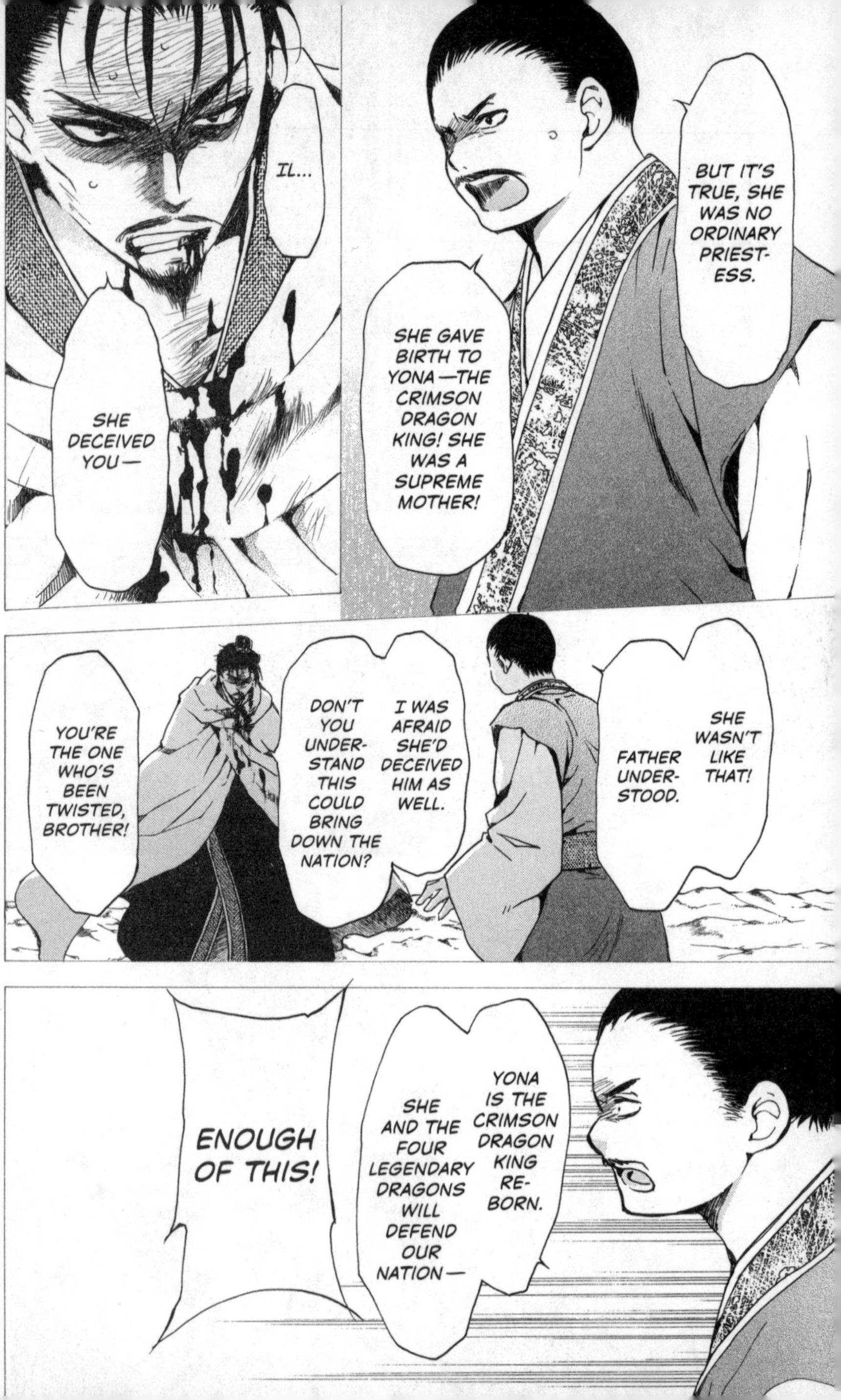
BUT IT'S TRUE, SHE WAS NO ORDINARY PRIEST-ESS.
SHE GAVE BIRTH TO YONA—THE CRIMSON DRAGON KING! SHE WAS A SUPREME MOTHER!
IL...
SHE DECEIVED YOU—
SHE WASN'T LIKE THAT!
FATHER UNDER-STOOD.
I WAS AFRAID SHE'D DECEIVED HIM AS WELL.
DON'T YOU UNDER-STAND THIS COULD BRING DOWN THE NATION?
YOU'RE THE ONE WHO'S BEEN TWISTED, BROTHER!
YONA IS THE CRIMSON DRAGON KING RE-BORN.
SHE AND THE FOUR LEGENDARY DRAGONS WILL DEFEND OUR NATION—
ENOUGH OF THIS!

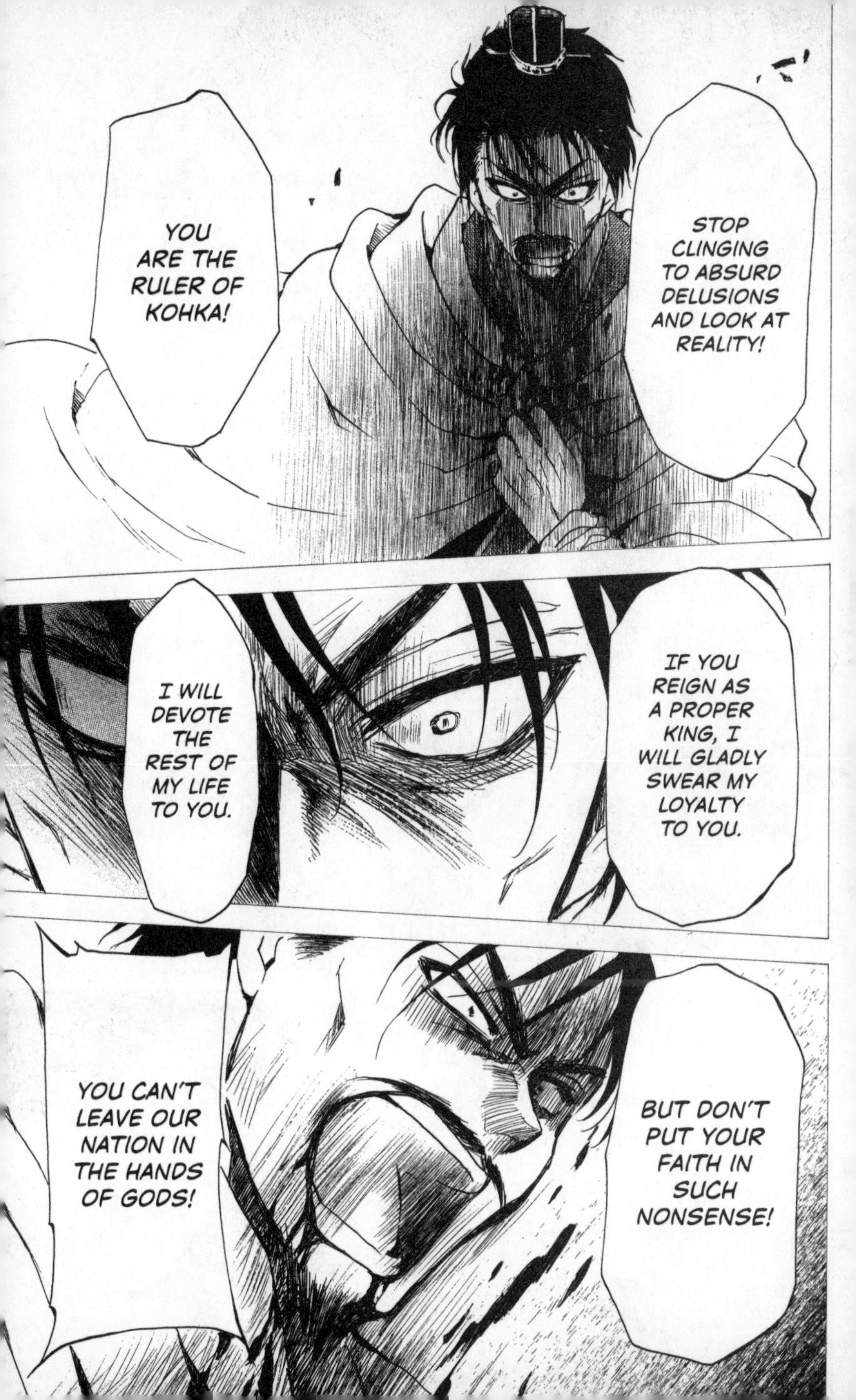
STOP CLINGING TO ABSURD DELUSIONS AND LOOK AT REALITY!
YOU ARE THE RULER OF KOHKA!
IF YOU REIGN AS A PROPER KING, I WILL GLADLY SWEAR MY LOYALTY TO YOU.
I WILL DEVOTE THE REST OF MY LIFE TO YOU.
BUT DON'T PUT YOUR FAITH IN SUCH NONSENSE!
YOU CAN'T LEAVE OUR NATION IN THE HANDS OF GODS!

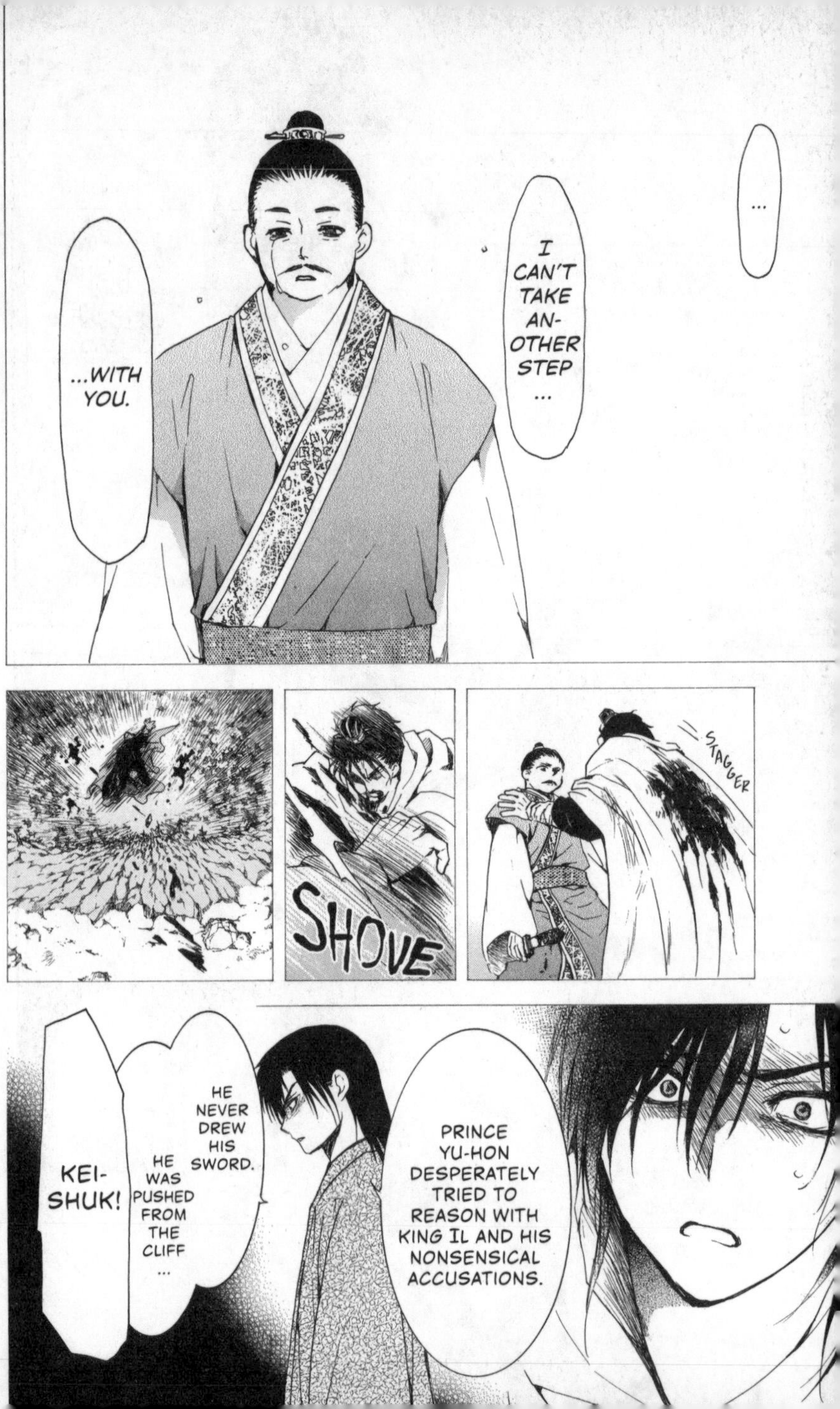
...
I CAN'T TAKE AN-OTHER STEP ...
...WITH YOU.
STAGGER
SHOVE
PRINCE YU-HON DESPERATELY TRIED TO REASON WITH KING IL AND HIS NONSENSICAL ACCUSATIONS.
HE NEVER DREW HIS SWORD.
HE WAS PUSHED FROM THE CLIFF ...
KEI-SHUK!

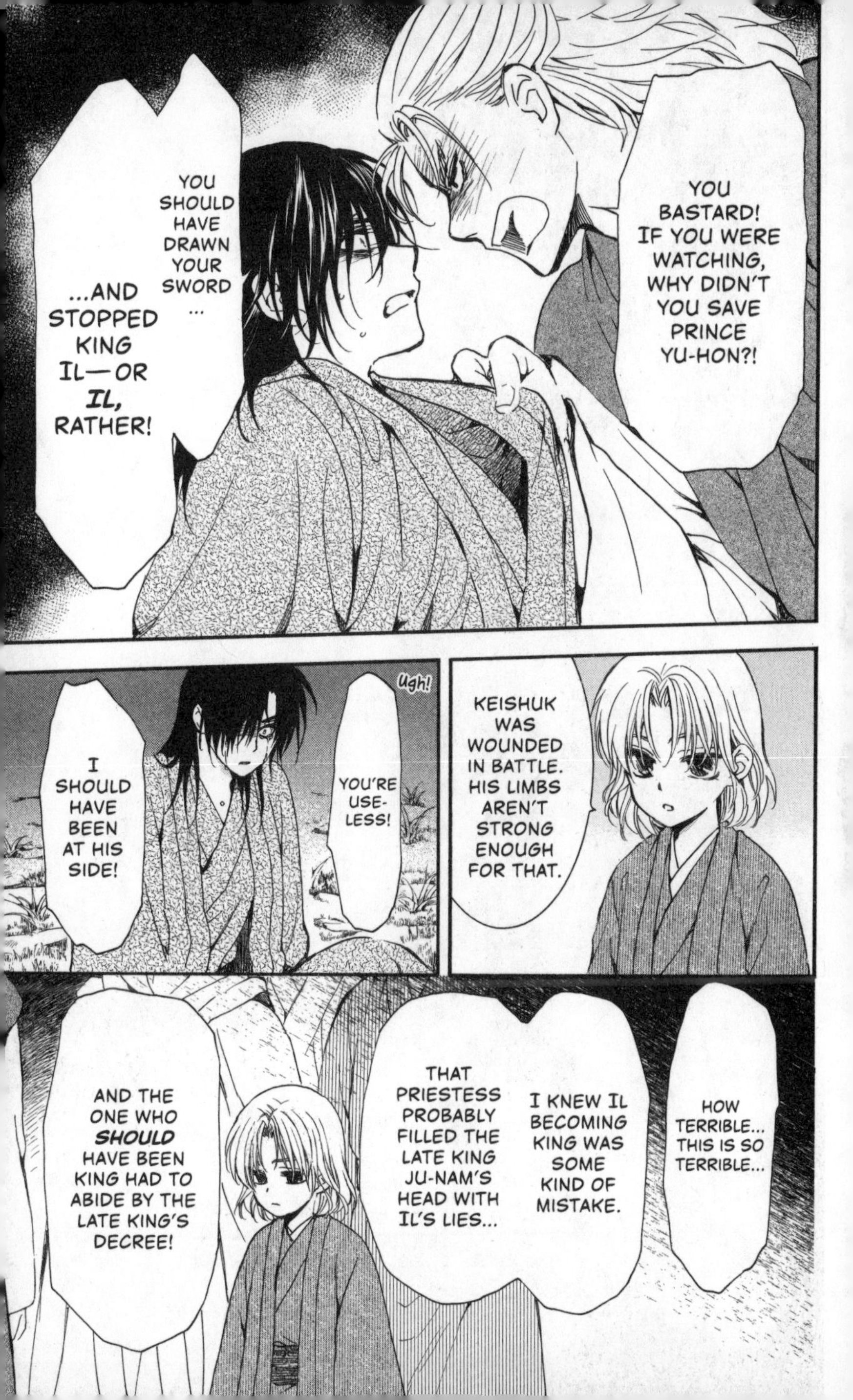
YOU BASTARD! IF YOU WERE WATCHING, WHY DIDN'T YOU SAVE PRINCE YU-HON?!
YOU SHOULD HAVE DRAWN YOUR SWORD ...
...AND STOPPED KING IL—OR *IL,* RATHER!
KEISHUK WAS WOUNDED IN BATTLE. HIS LIMBS AREN'T STRONG ENOUGH FOR THAT.
Ugh!
YOU'RE USE-LESS!
I SHOULD HAVE BEEN AT HIS SIDE!
HOW TERRIBLE... THIS IS SO TERRIBLE...
I KNEW IL BECOMING KING WAS SOME KIND OF MISTAKE.
THAT PRIESTESS PROBABLY FILLED THE LATE KING JU-NAM'S HEAD WITH IL'S LIES...
AND THE ONE WHO ***SHOULD*** HAVE BEEN KING HAD TO ABIDE BY THE LATE KING'S DECREE!

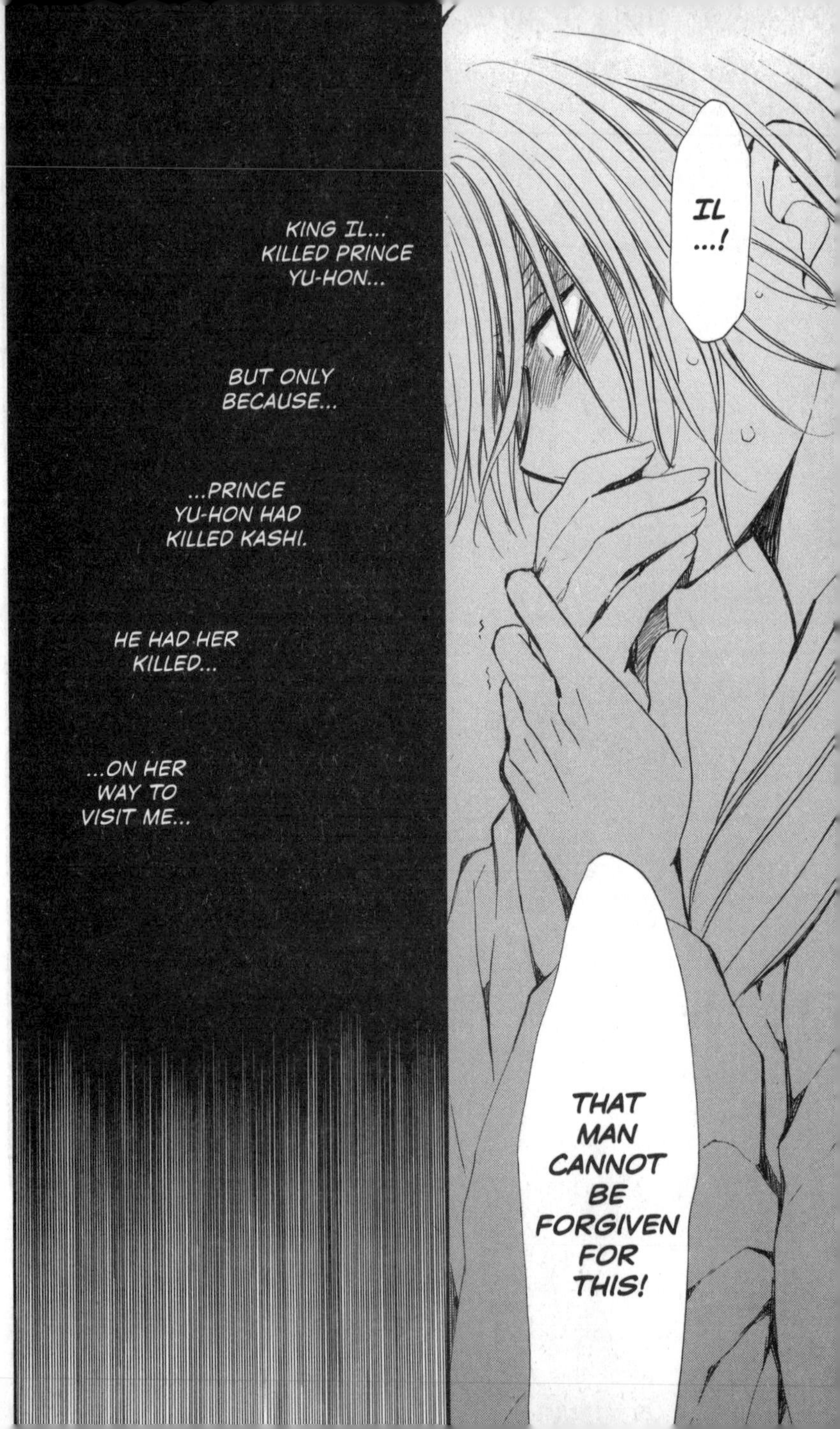
IL ...!
THAT MAN CANNOT BE FORGIVEN FOR THIS!
KING IL... KILLED PRINCE YU-HON...
BUT ONLY BECAUSE...
...PRINCE YU-HON HAD KILLED KASHI.
HE HAD HER KILLED...
...ON HER WAY TO VISIT ME...

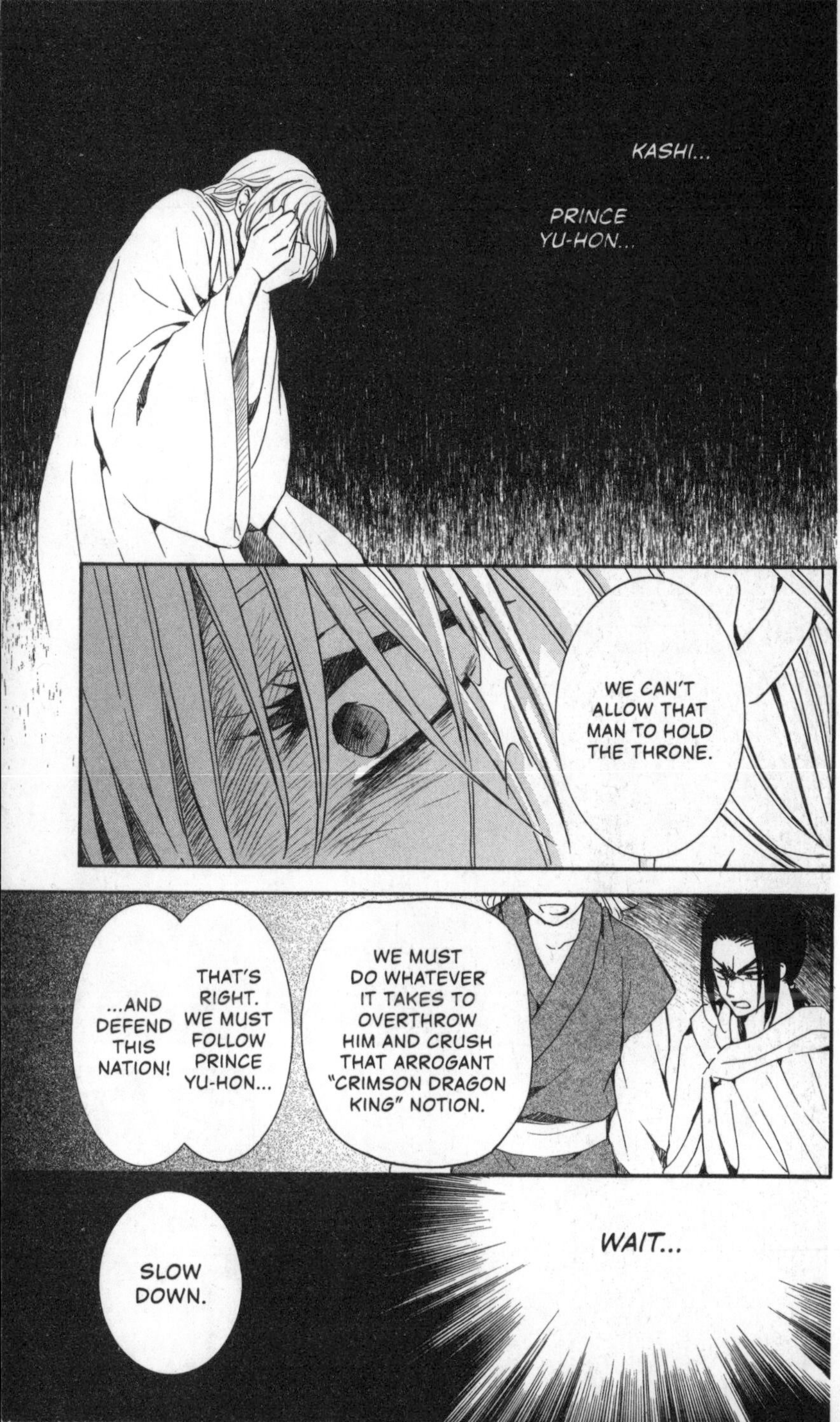
KASHI...
PRINCE YU-HON...
WE CAN'T ALLOW THAT MAN TO HOLD THE THRONE.
WE MUST DO WHATEVER IT TAKES TO OVERTHROW HIM AND CRUSH THAT ARROGANT "CRIMSON DRAGON KING" NOTION.
THAT'S RIGHT. WE MUST FOLLOW PRINCE YU-HON...
...AND DEFEND THIS NATION!
WAIT...
SLOW DOWN.

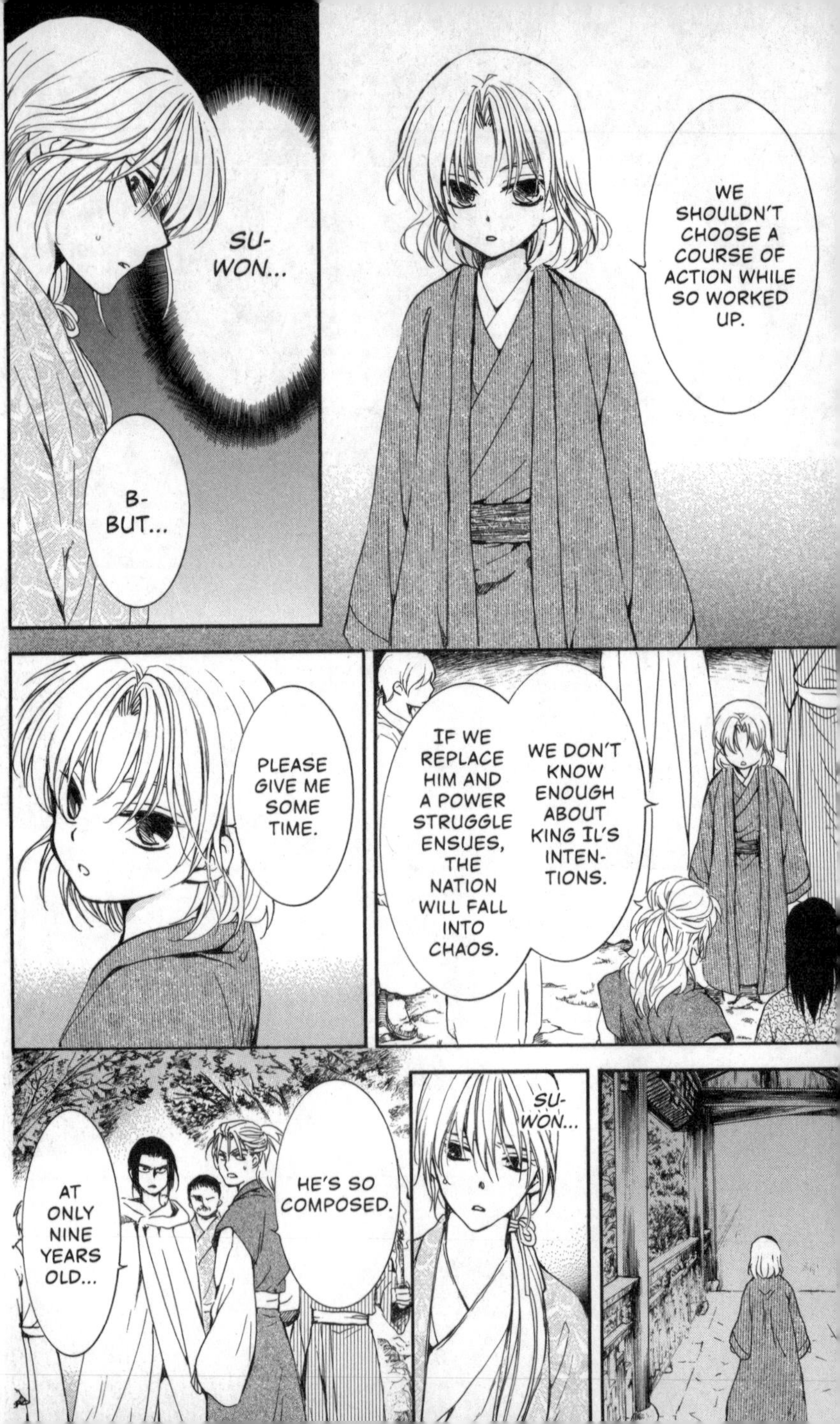
WE SHOULDN'T CHOOSE A COURSE OF ACTION WHILE SO WORKED UP.
SU-WON...
B-BUT...
WE DON'T KNOW ENOUGH ABOUT KING IL'S INTENTIONS.
IF WE REPLACE HIM AND A POWER STRUGGLE ENSUES, THE NATION WILL FALL INTO CHAOS.
PLEASE GIVE ME SOME TIME.
SU-WON...
HE'S SO COMPOSED.
AT ONLY NINE YEARS OLD...

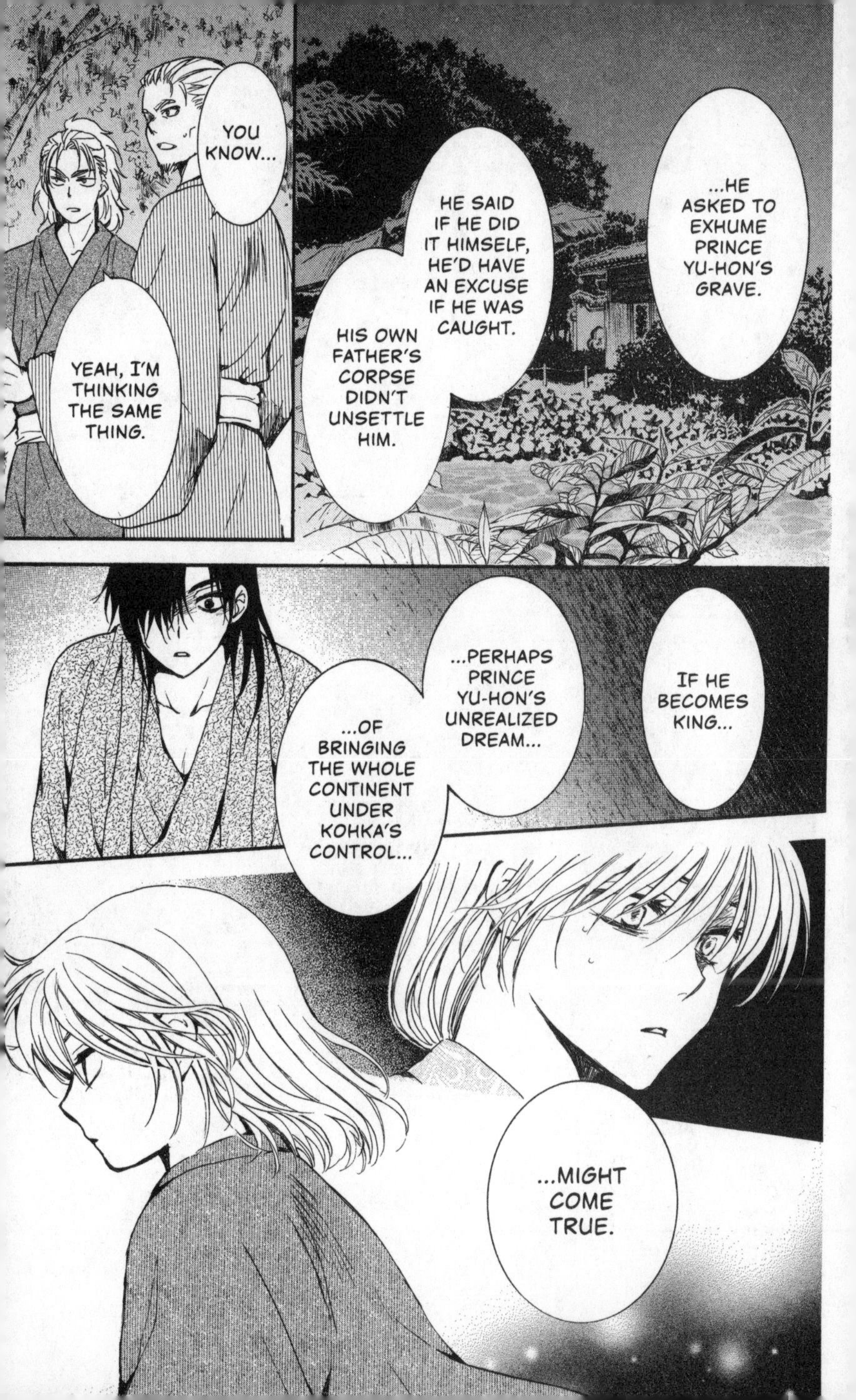
...HE ASKED TO EXHUME PRINCE YU-HON'S GRAVE.
HE SAID IF HE DID IT HIMSELF, HE'D HAVE AN EXCUSE IF HE WAS CAUGHT.
HIS OWN FATHER'S CORPSE DIDN'T UNSETTLE HIM.
YOU KNOW...
YEAH, I'M THINKING THE SAME THING.
IF HE BECOMES KING...
...PERHAPS PRINCE YU-HON'S UNREALIZED DREAM...
...OF BRINGING THE WHOLE CONTINENT UNDER KOHKA'S CONTROL...
...MIGHT COME TRUE.

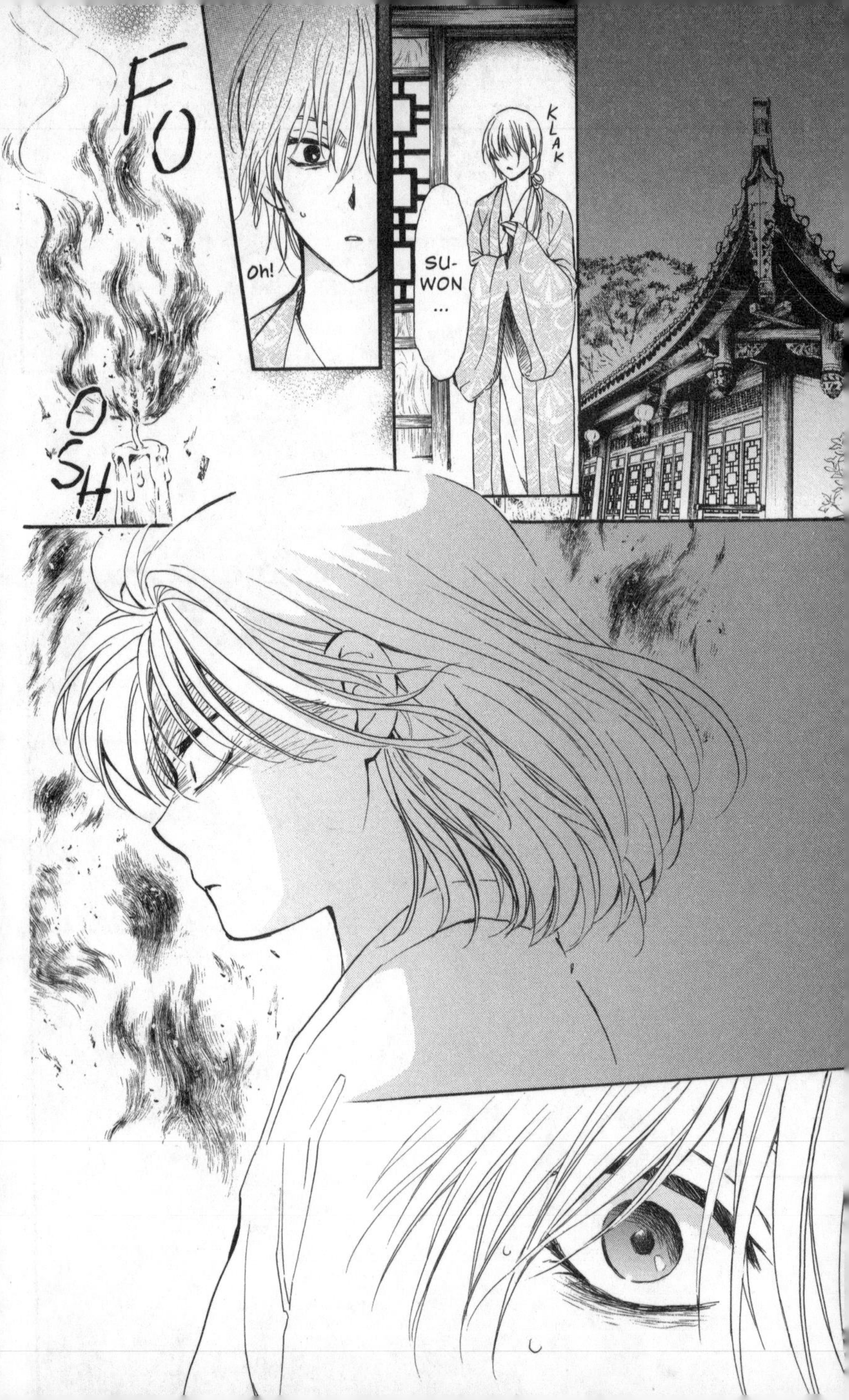
KLAK
SU-WON ...
Oh!
FOOSH

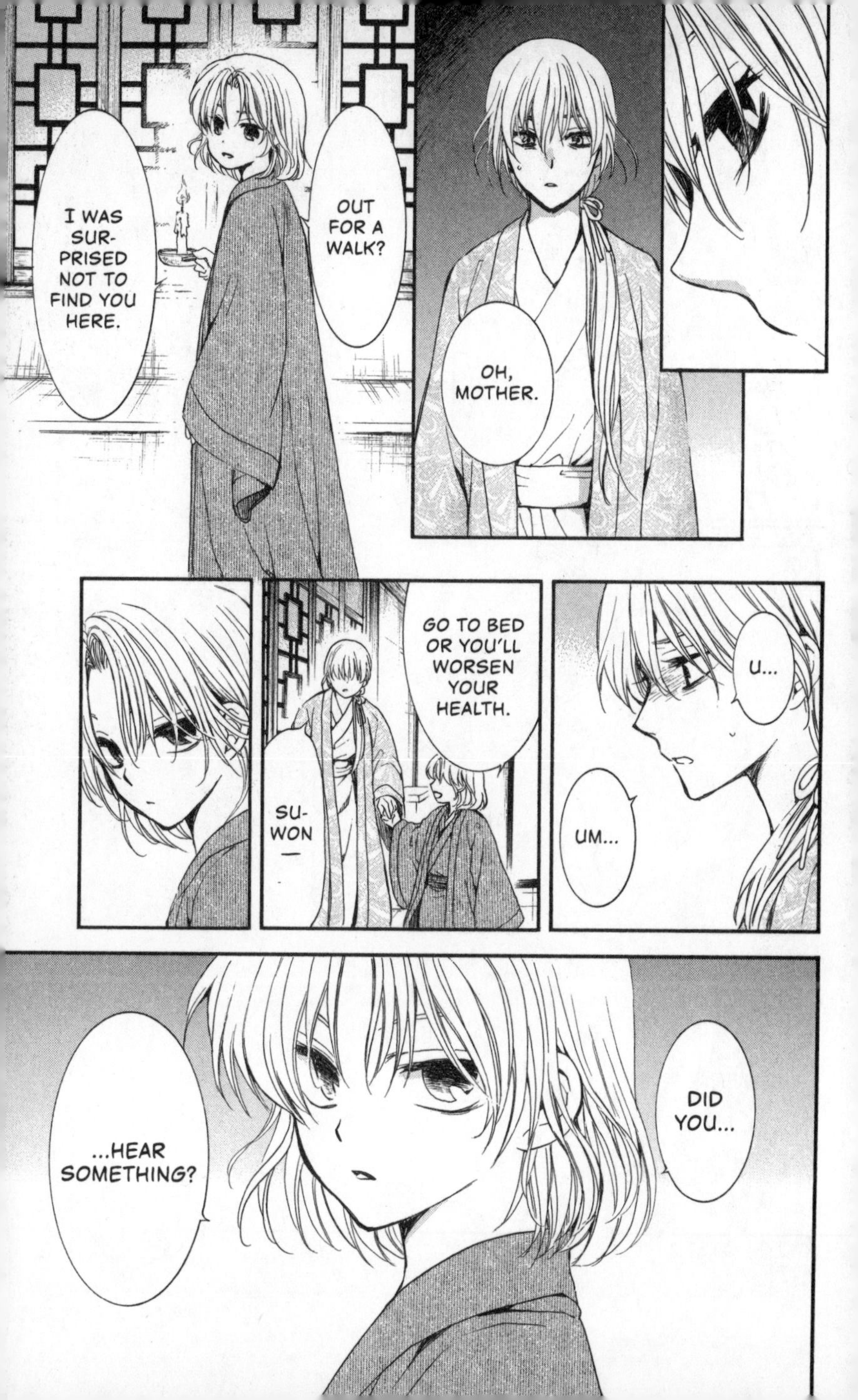
OH, MOTHER.
OUT FOR A WALK?
I WAS SUR-PRISED NOT TO FIND YOU HERE.
U...
UM...
GO TO BED OR YOU'LL WORSEN YOUR HEALTH.
SU-WON—
DID YOU...
...HEAR SOMETHING?

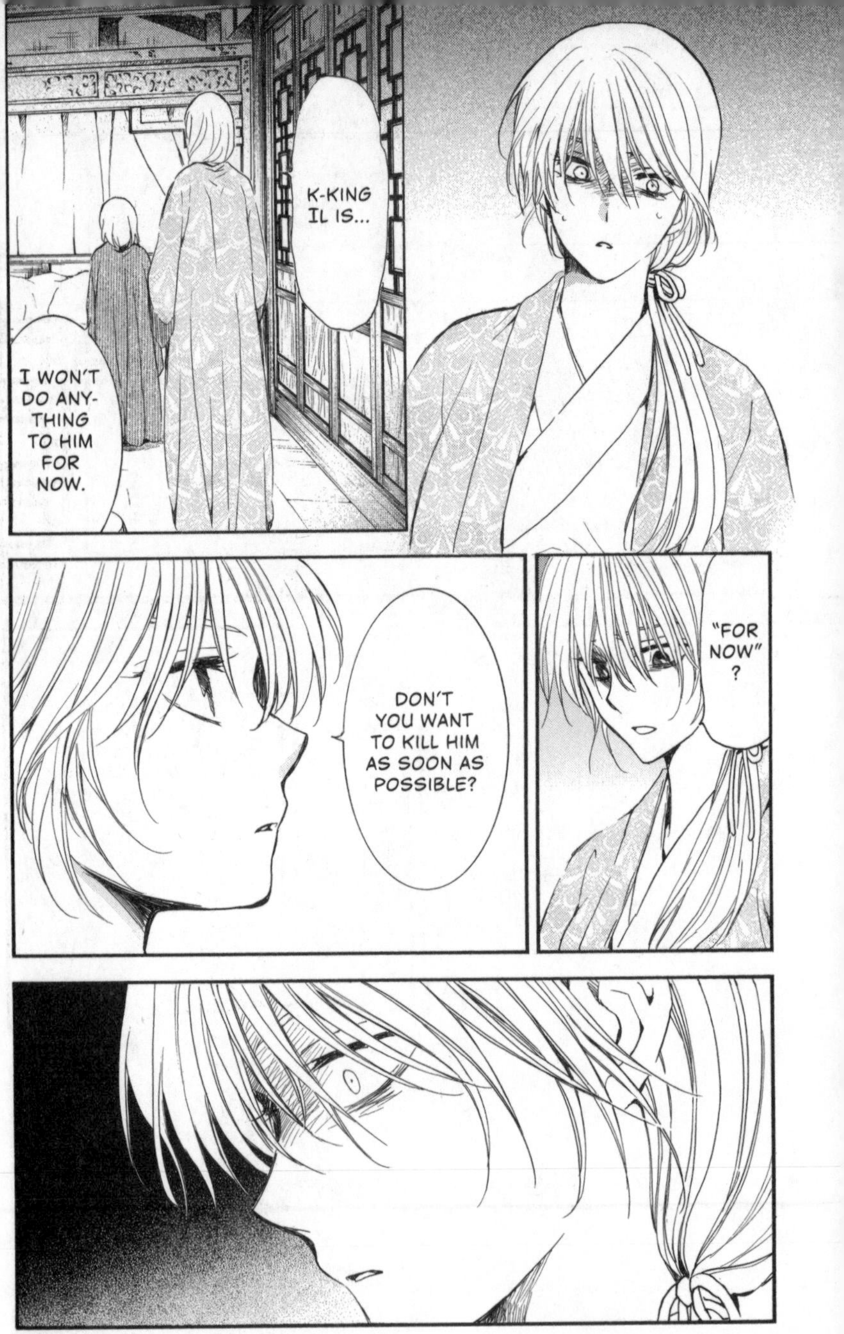
K-KING IL IS...
I WON'T DO ANYTHING TO HIM FOR NOW.
"FOR NOW"?
DON'T YOU WANT TO KILL HIM AS SOON AS POSSIBLE?

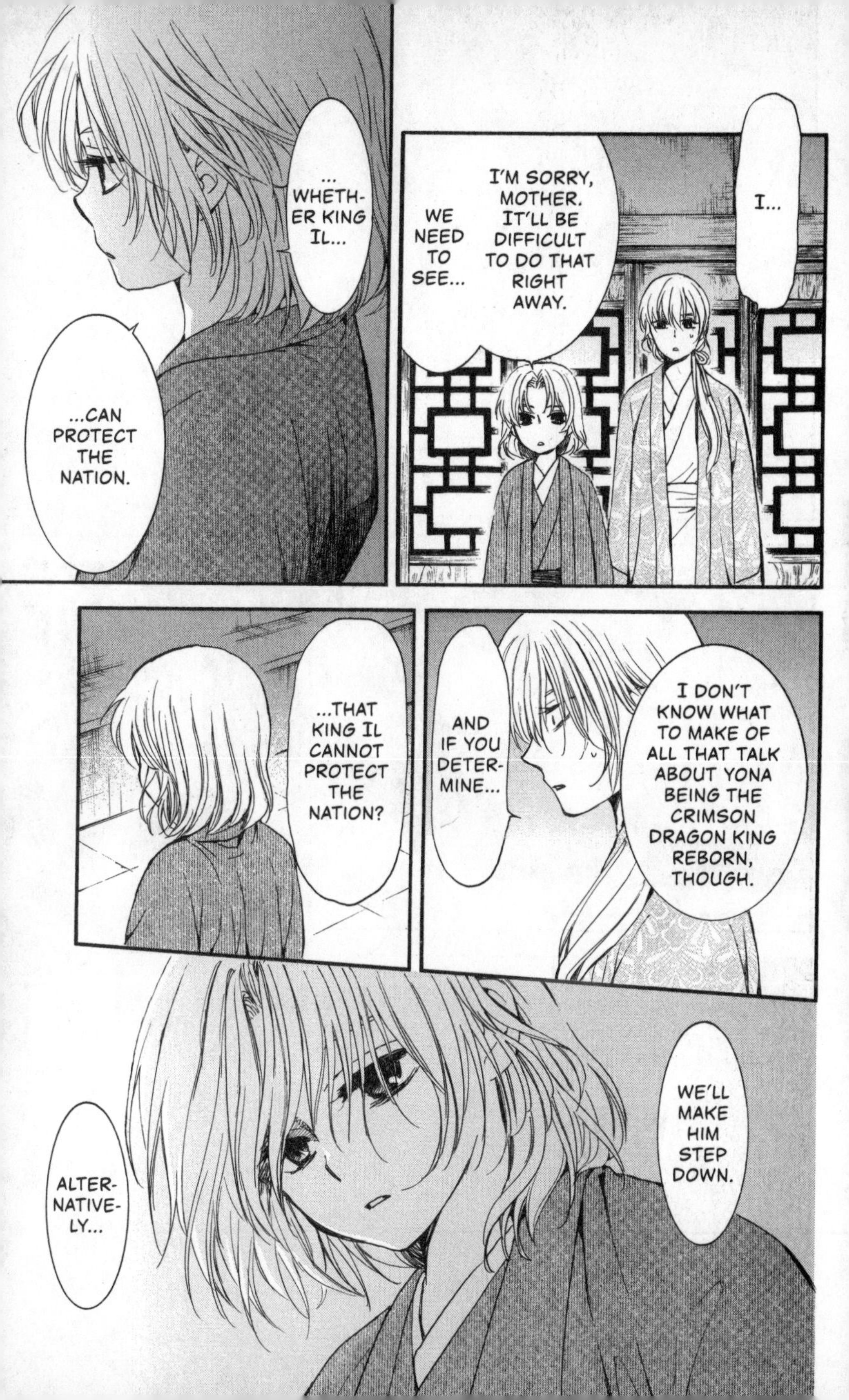
I...
I'M SORRY, MOTHER. IT'LL BE DIFFICULT TO DO THAT RIGHT AWAY.
WE NEED TO SEE...
...WHETHER KING IL...
...CAN PROTECT THE NATION.
I DON'T KNOW WHAT TO MAKE OF ALL THAT TALK ABOUT YONA BEING THE CRIMSON DRAGON KING REBORN, THOUGH.
AND IF YOU DETERMINE...
...THAT KING IL CANNOT PROTECT THE NATION?
WE'LL MAKE HIM STEP DOWN.
ALTERNATIVELY...

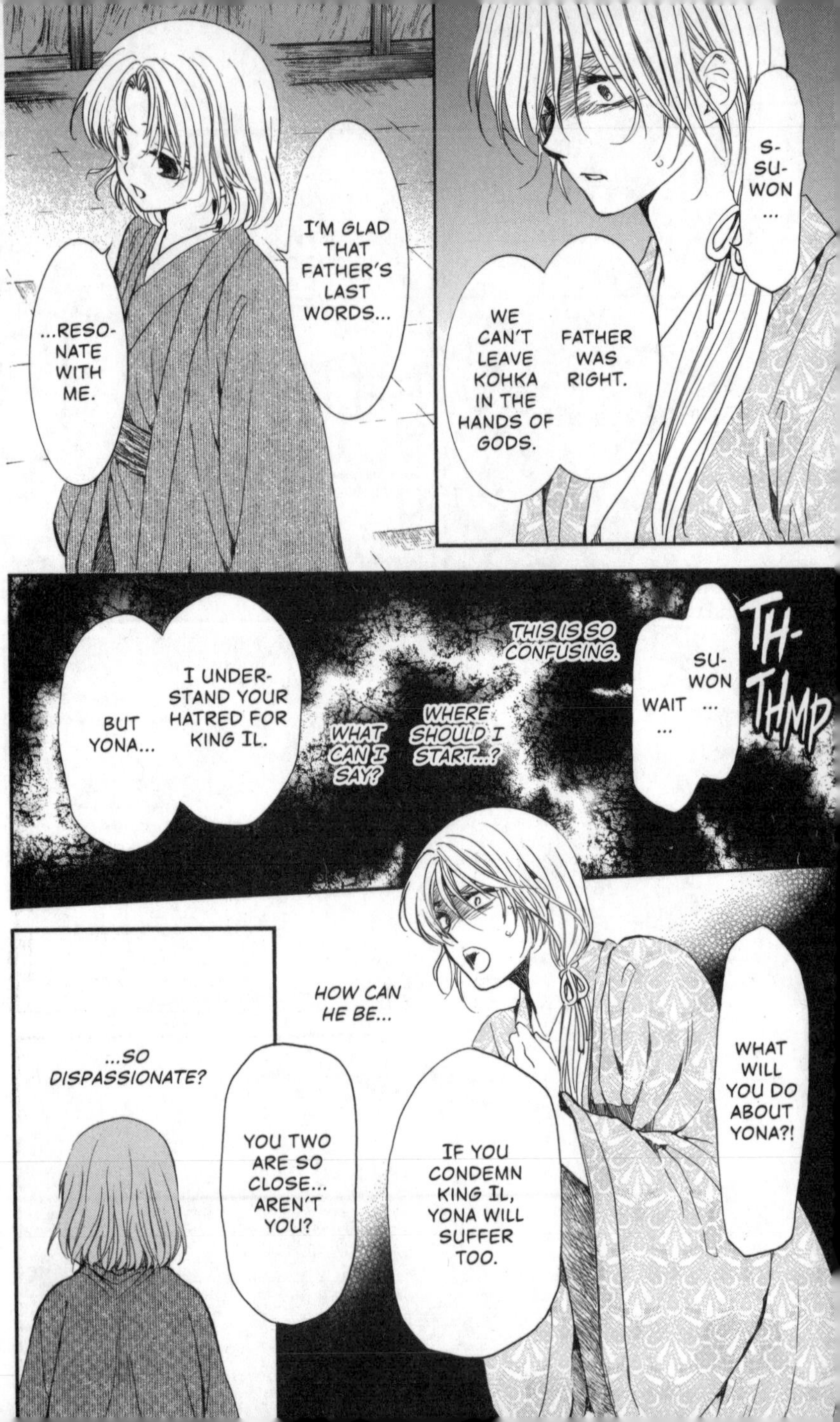
S-SU-WON...
FATHER WAS RIGHT.
WE CAN'T LEAVE KOHKA IN THE HANDS OF GODS.
I'M GLAD THAT FATHER'S LAST WORDS...
...RESONATE WITH ME.
TH-THMP
SU-WON ...
WAIT ...
THIS IS SO CONFUSING.
WHERE SHOULD I START...?
WHAT CAN I SAY?
I UNDERSTAND YOUR HATRED FOR KING IL.
BUT YONA...
WHAT WILL YOU DO ABOUT YONA?!
IF YOU CONDEMN KING IL, YONA WILL SUFFER TOO.
YOU TWO ARE SO CLOSE... AREN'T YOU?
HOW CAN HE BE...
...SO DISPASSIONATE?

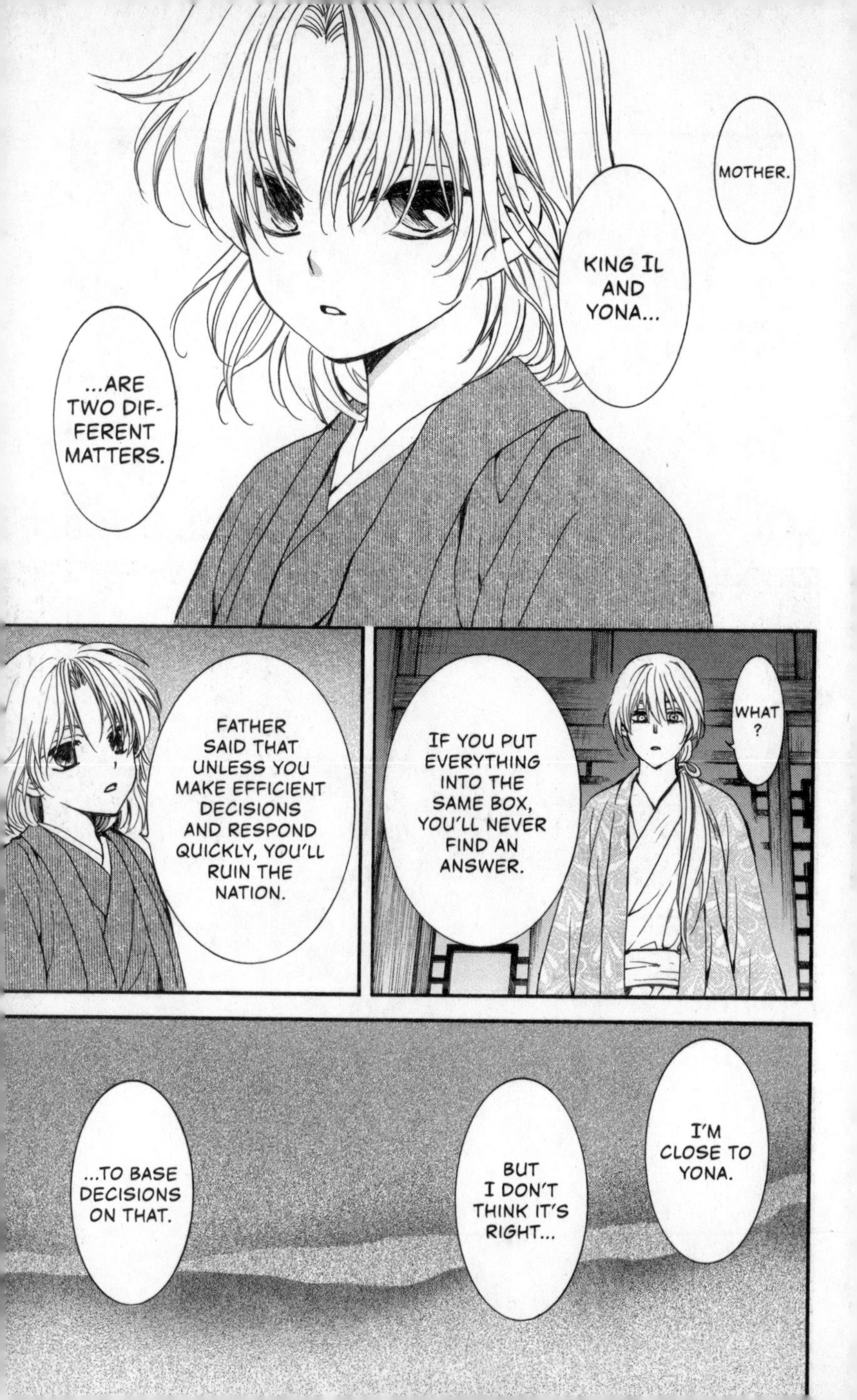
MOTHER.
KING IL AND YONA...
...ARE TWO DIF-FERENT MATTERS.
WHAT?
IF YOU PUT EVERYTHING INTO THE SAME BOX, YOU'LL NEVER FIND AN ANSWER.
FATHER SAID THAT UNLESS YOU MAKE EFFICIENT DECISIONS AND RESPOND QUICKLY, YOU'LL RUIN THE NATION.
I'M CLOSE TO YONA.
BUT I DON'T THINK IT'S RIGHT...
...TO BASE DECISIONS ON THAT.

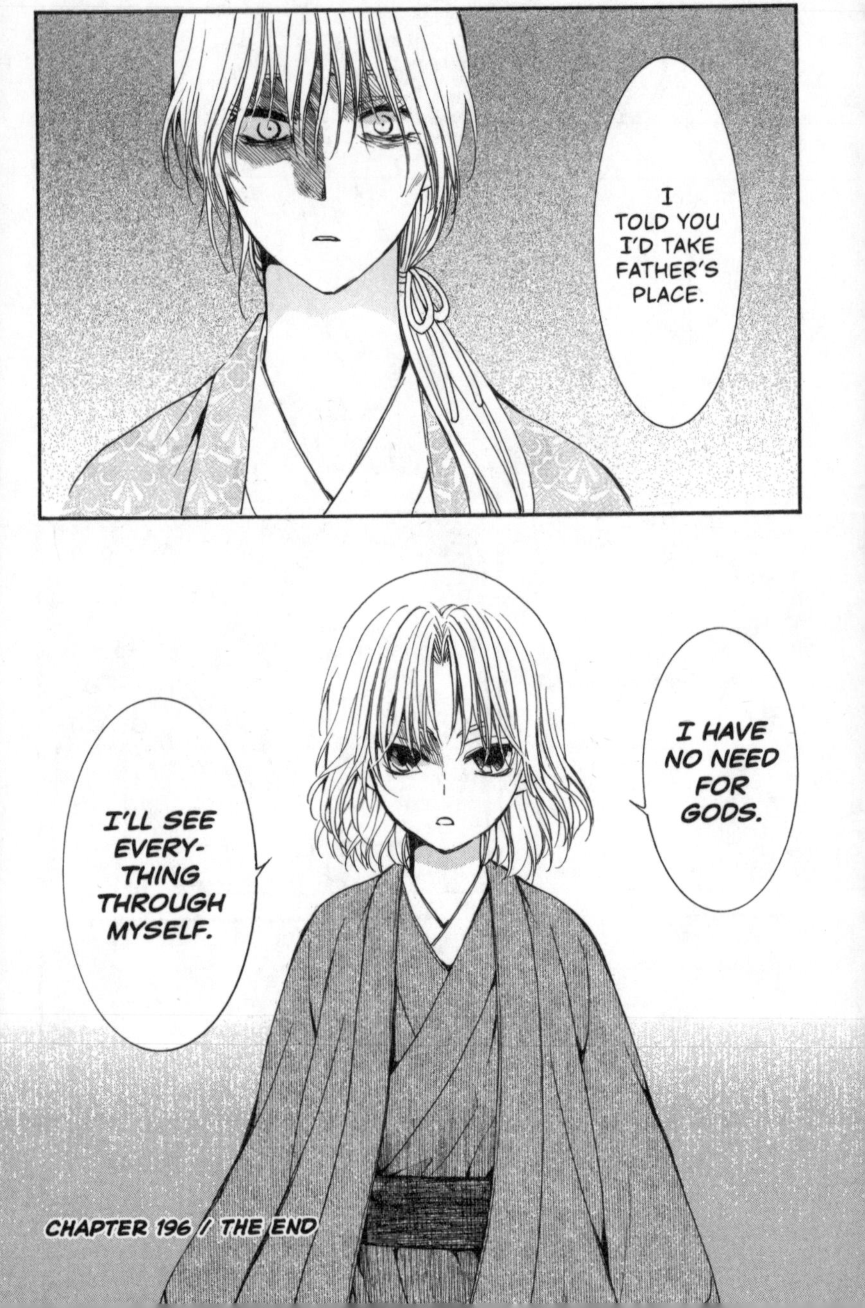
I TOLD YOU I'D TAKE FATHER'S PLACE.
I HAVE NO NEED FOR GODS.
I'LL SEE EVERY-THING THROUGH MYSELF.
CHAPTER 196 / THE END

A special thanks to the people who help me!

My assistants who have worked with me → Mikorun, C.F., Ryo Sakura, Ryo,
                                                                                          and my little sister...
My editors → Hasegawa, my previous editors, and the *Hana to Yume* editorial
office...
Everyone who is involved with selling *Yona*...
My family and friends who always encourage and support me...
My cats for soothing me...
My longtime readers and those who have only recently started reading...
Everyone who has sent me letters and art or messaged me over social media...

Thank you so much for helping me focus on my manga! I'll try my best not to
overwork myself. I hope that all of you enjoy my choices.

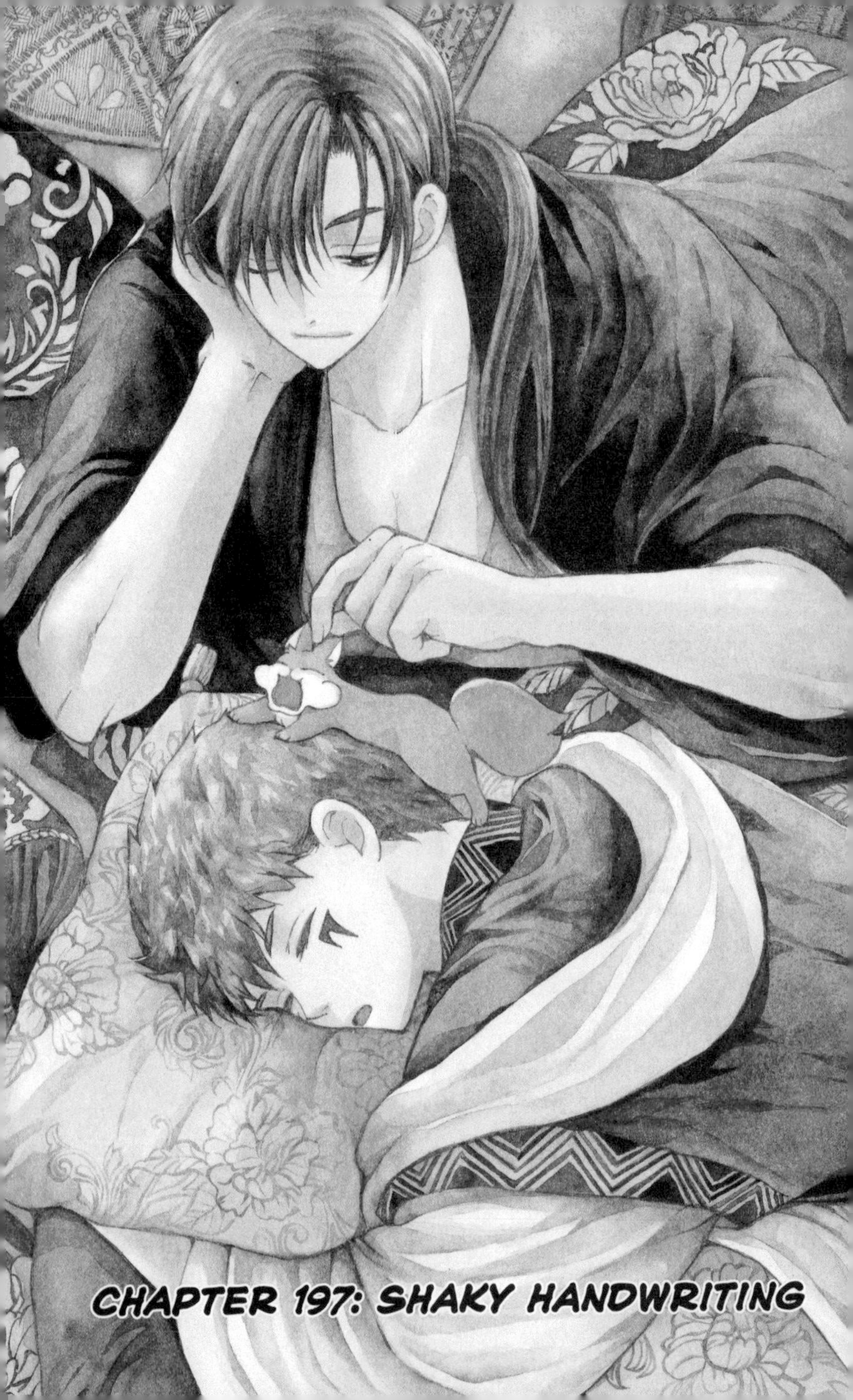

CHAPTER 197: SHAKY HANDWRITING

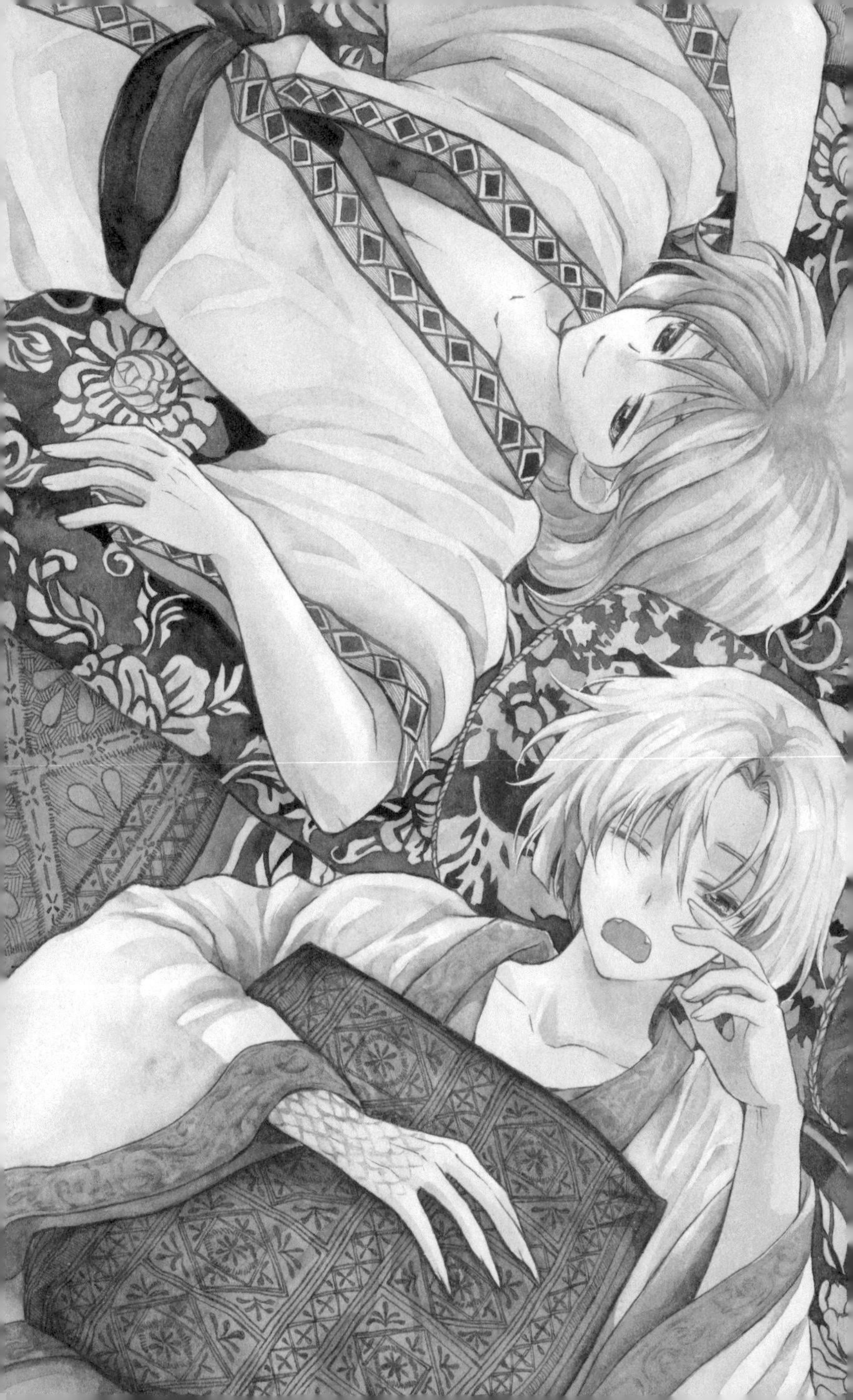

Desk calendar art from the special edition of volume 34. The September illustration had an Arabian theme, and I wasn't sure whether to go with Jaeha or Gija. I ended up going with Jaeha. I figured I'd take this chance to show the Gija version.

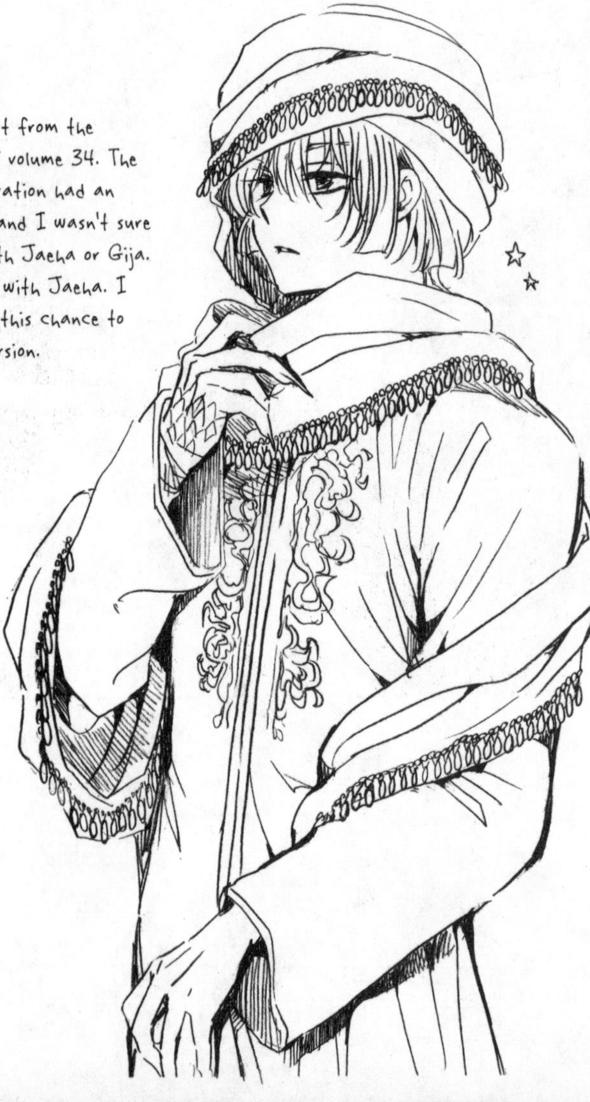

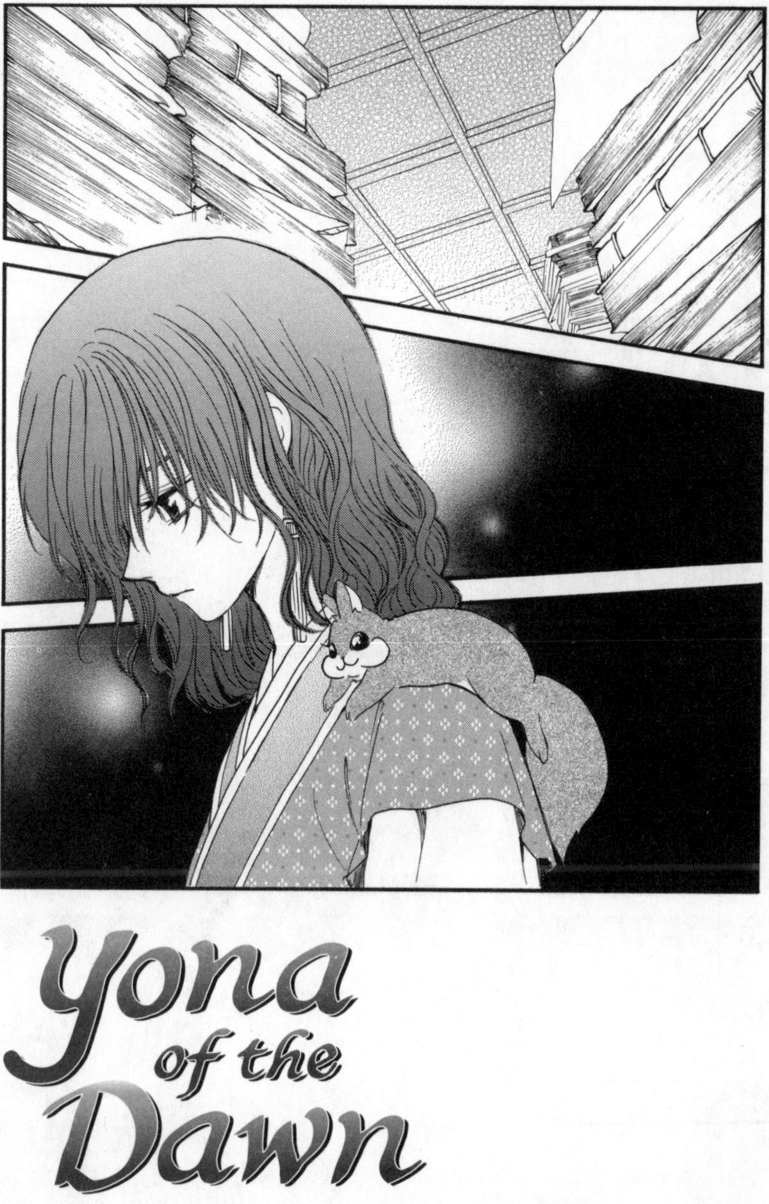

Yona of the Dawn

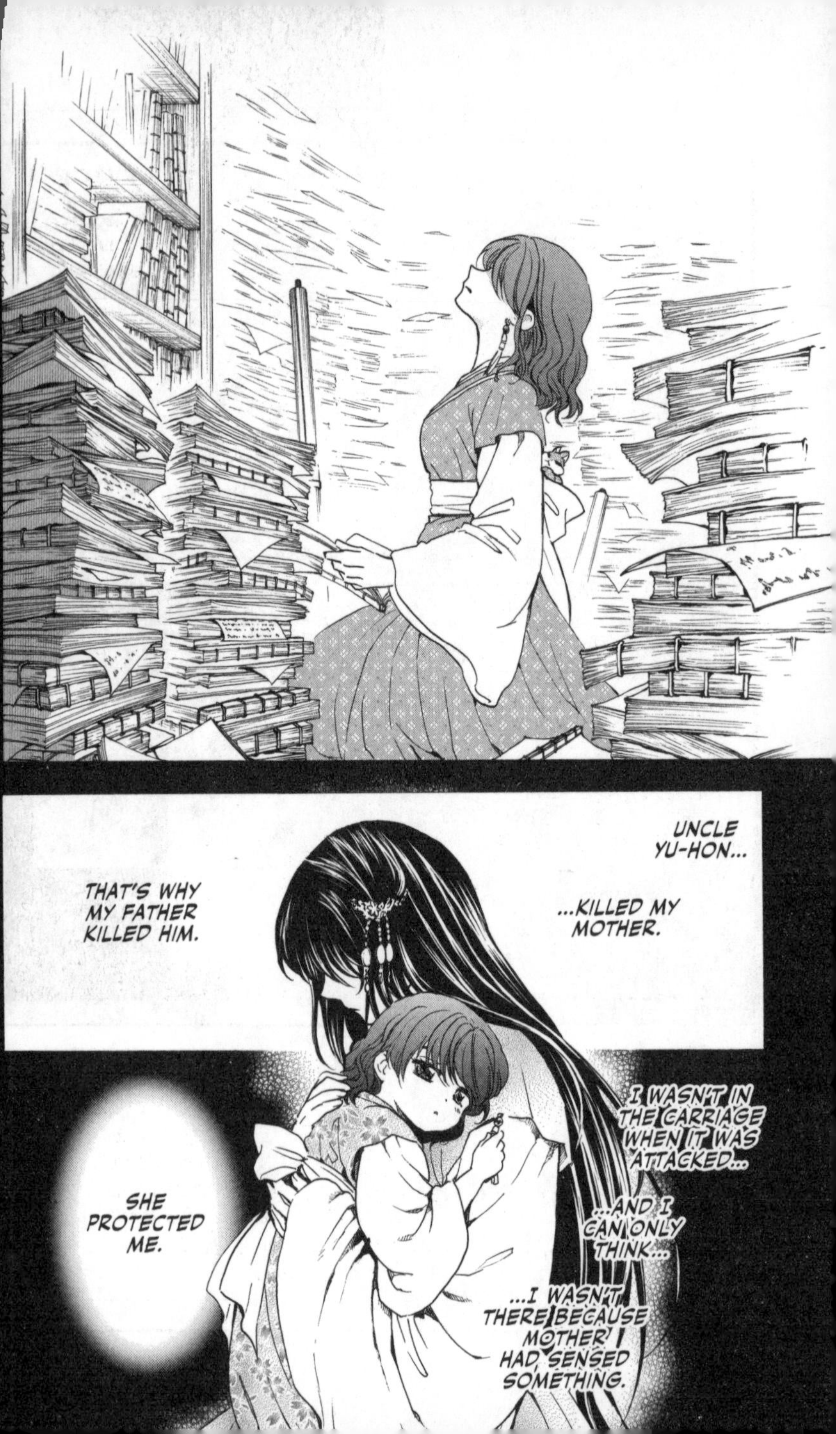
UNCLE YU-HON...
...KILLED MY MOTHER.
THAT'S WHY MY FATHER KILLED HIM.
I WASN'T IN THE CARRIAGE WHEN IT WAS ATTACKED...
...AND I CAN ONLY THINK...
...I WASN'T THERE BECAUSE MOTHER HAD SENSED SOMETHING.
SHE PROTECTED ME.

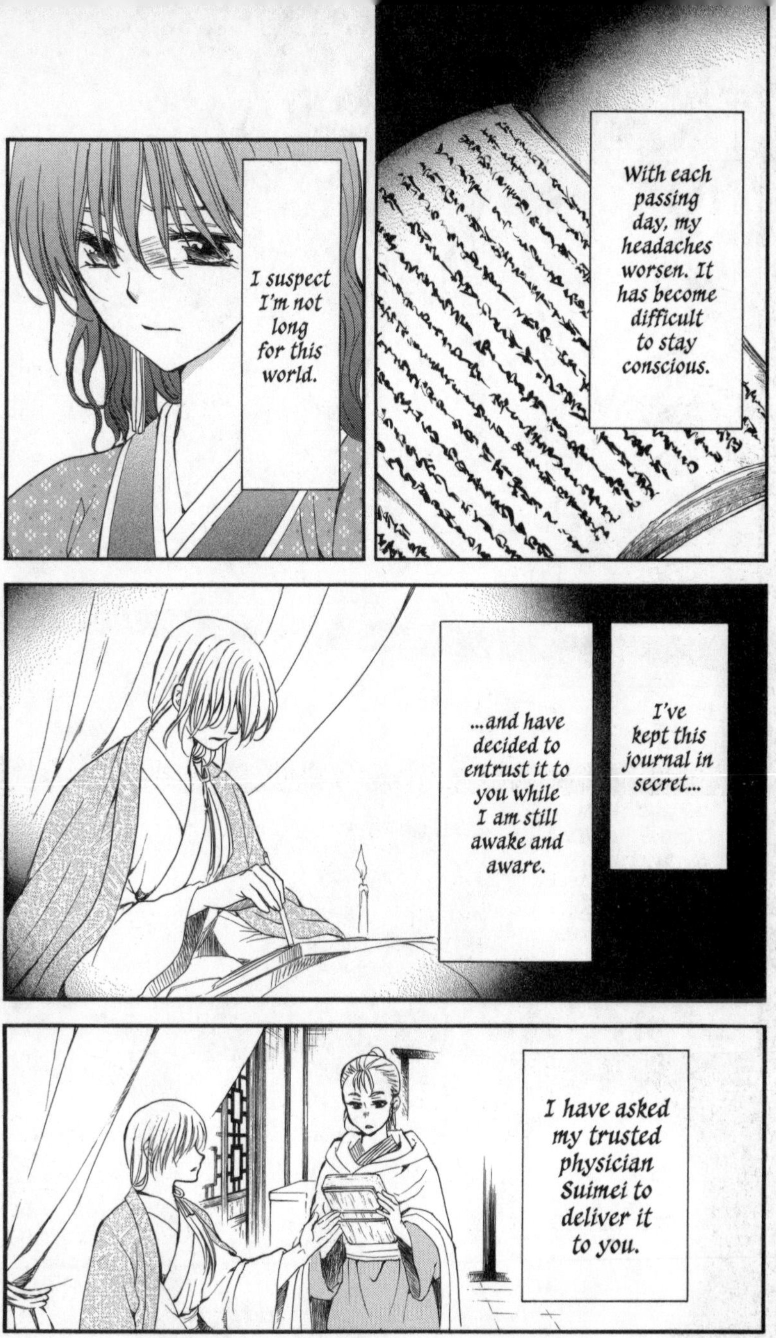
With each passing day, my headaches worsen. It has become difficult to stay conscious.
I suspect I'm not long for this world.
I've kept this journal in secret...
...and have decided to entrust it to you while I am still awake and aware.
I have asked my trusted physician Suimei to deliver it to you.

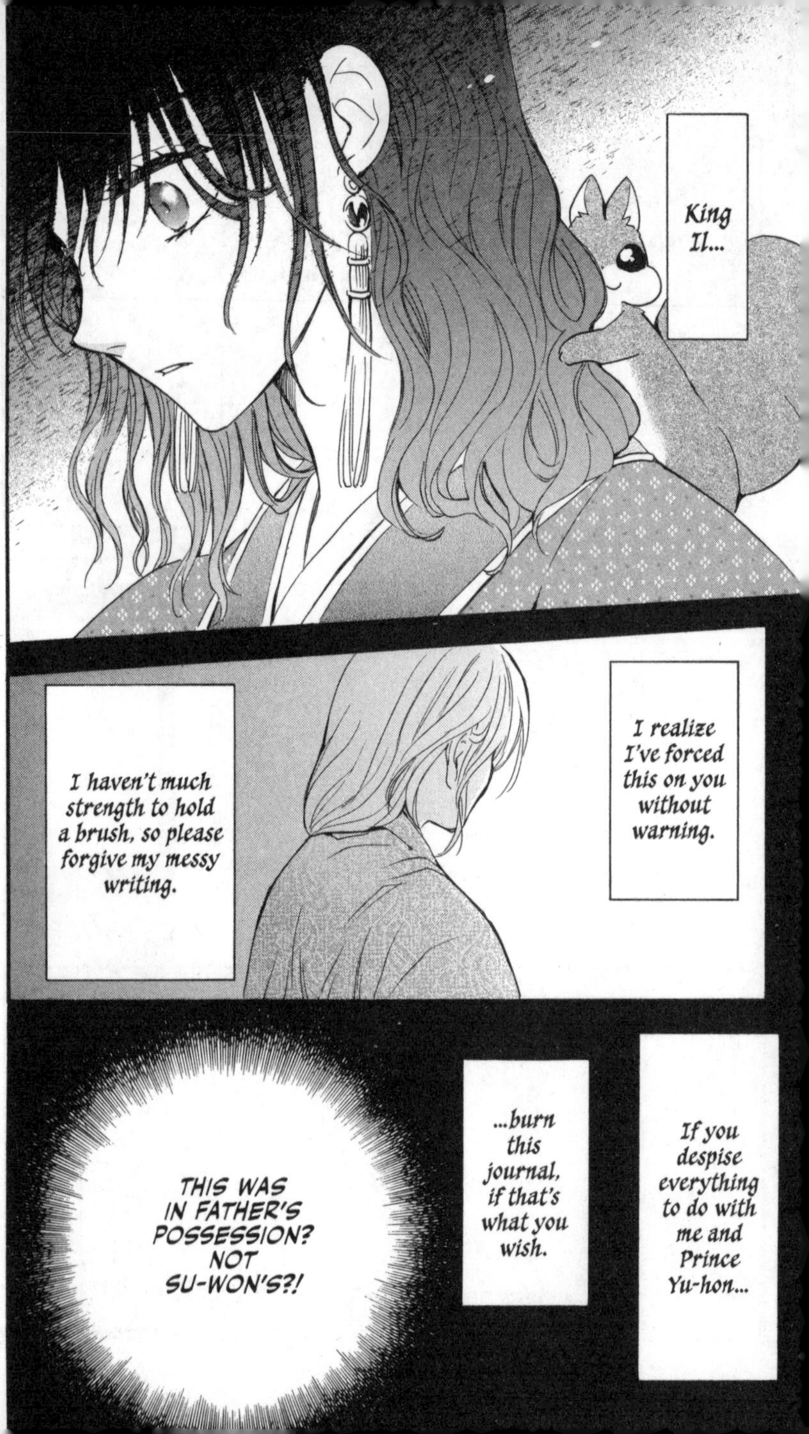
King Il...
I realize I've forced this on you without warning.
I haven't much strength to hold a brush, so please forgive my messy writing.
If you despise everything to do with me and Prince Yu-hon...
...burn this journal, if that's what you wish.
THIS WAS IN FATHER'S POSSESSION? NOT SU-WON'S?!

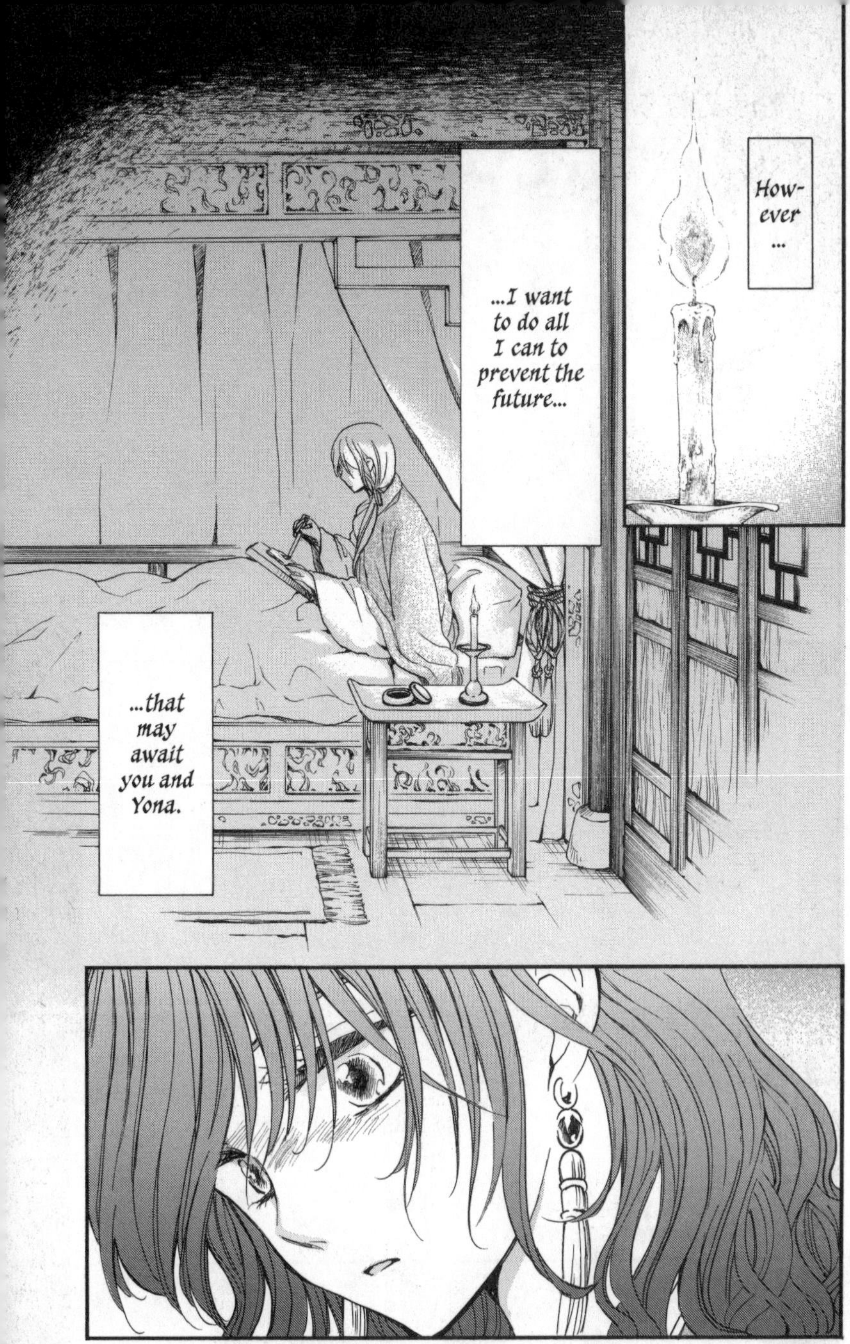
However...
...I want to do all I can to prevent the future...
...that may await you and Yona.

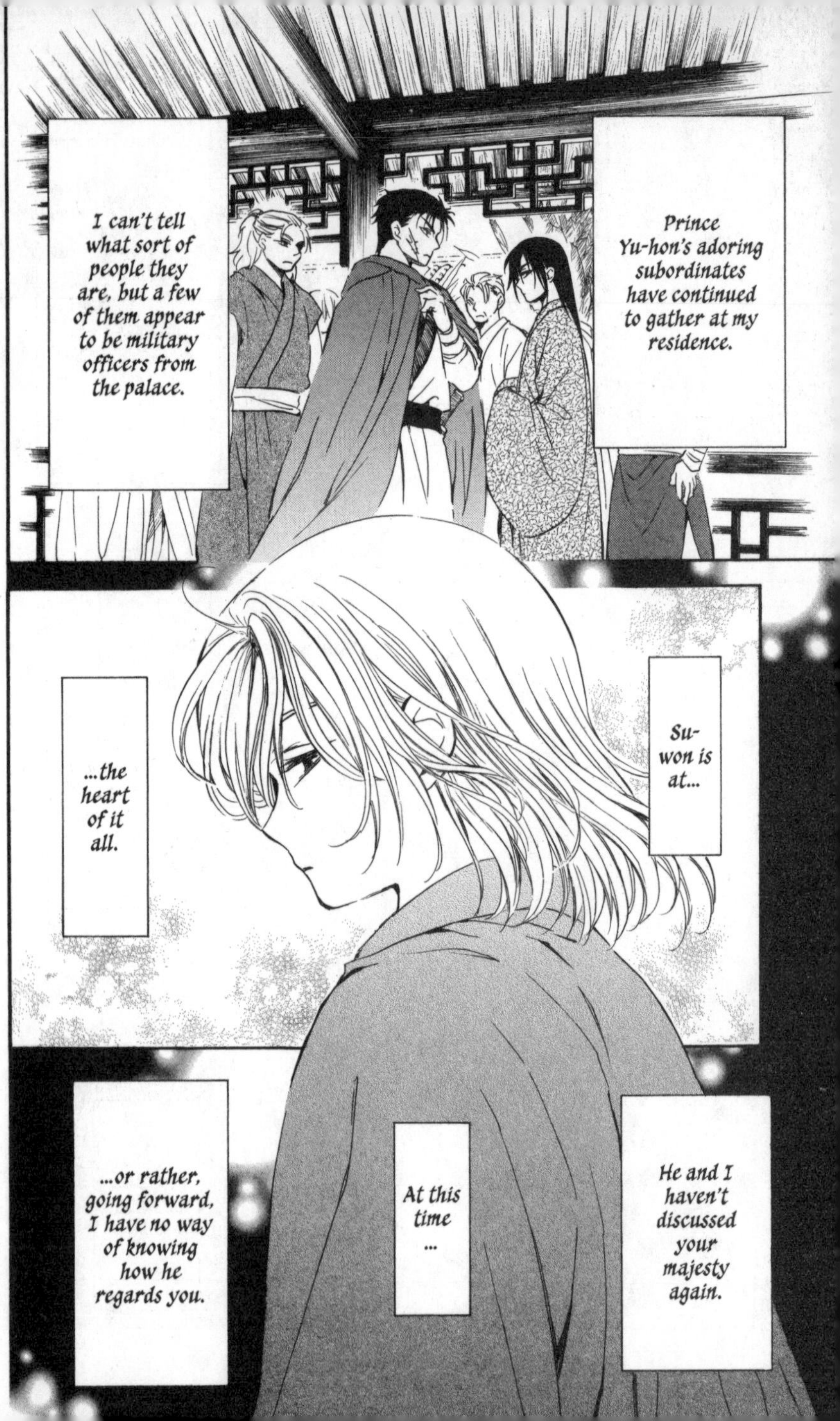
Prince Yu-hon's adoring subordinates have continued to gather at my residence.
I can't tell what sort of people they are, but a few of them appear to be military officers from the palace.
Su-won is at...
...the heart of it all.
He and I haven't discussed your majesty again.
At this time...
...or rather, going forward, I have no way of knowing how he regards you.

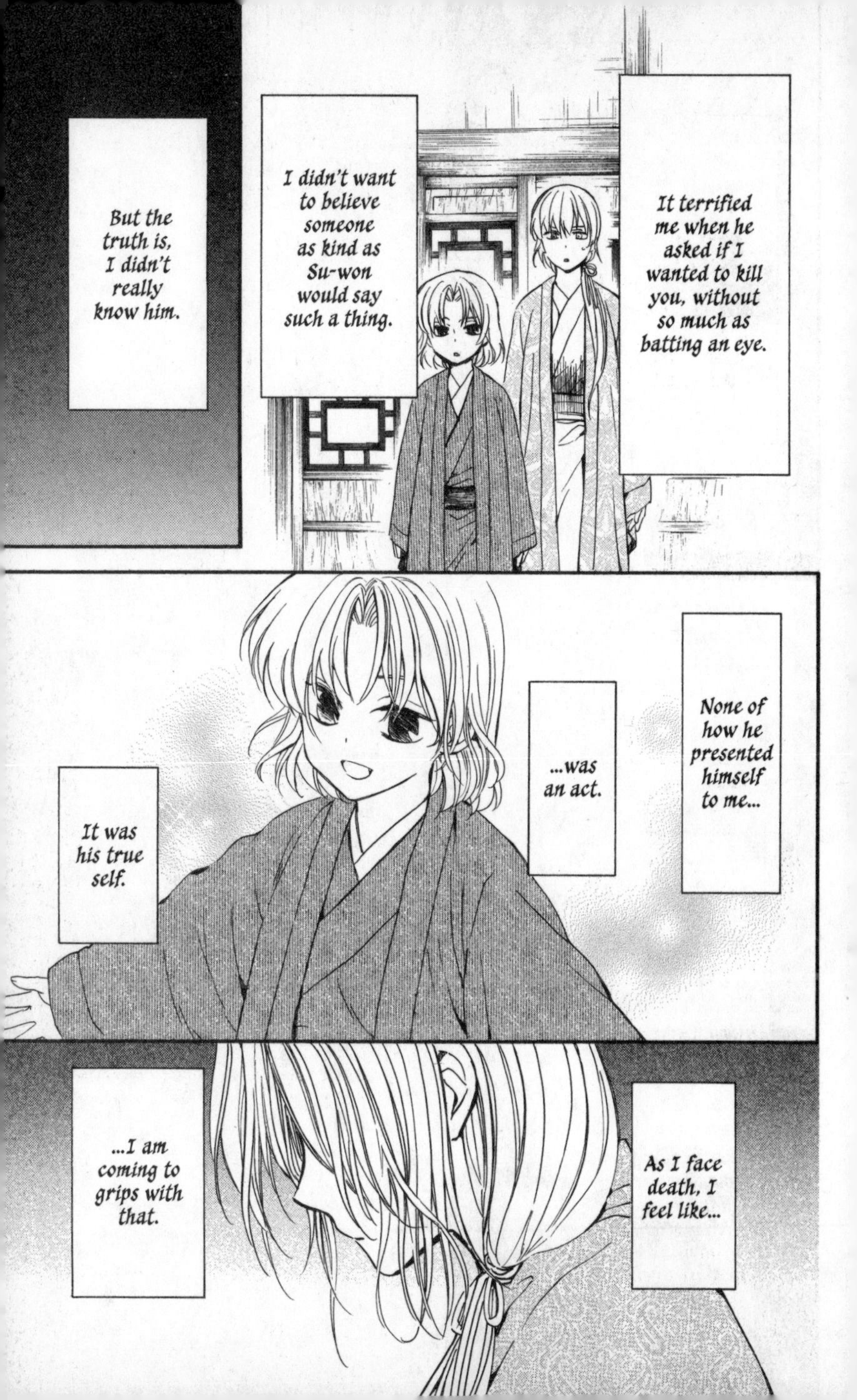
It terrified me when he asked if I wanted to kill you, without so much as batting an eye.
I didn't want to believe someone as kind as Su-won would say such a thing.
But the truth is, I didn't really know him.
None of how he presented himself to me...
...was an act.
It was his true self.
As I face death, I feel like...
...I am coming to grips with that.

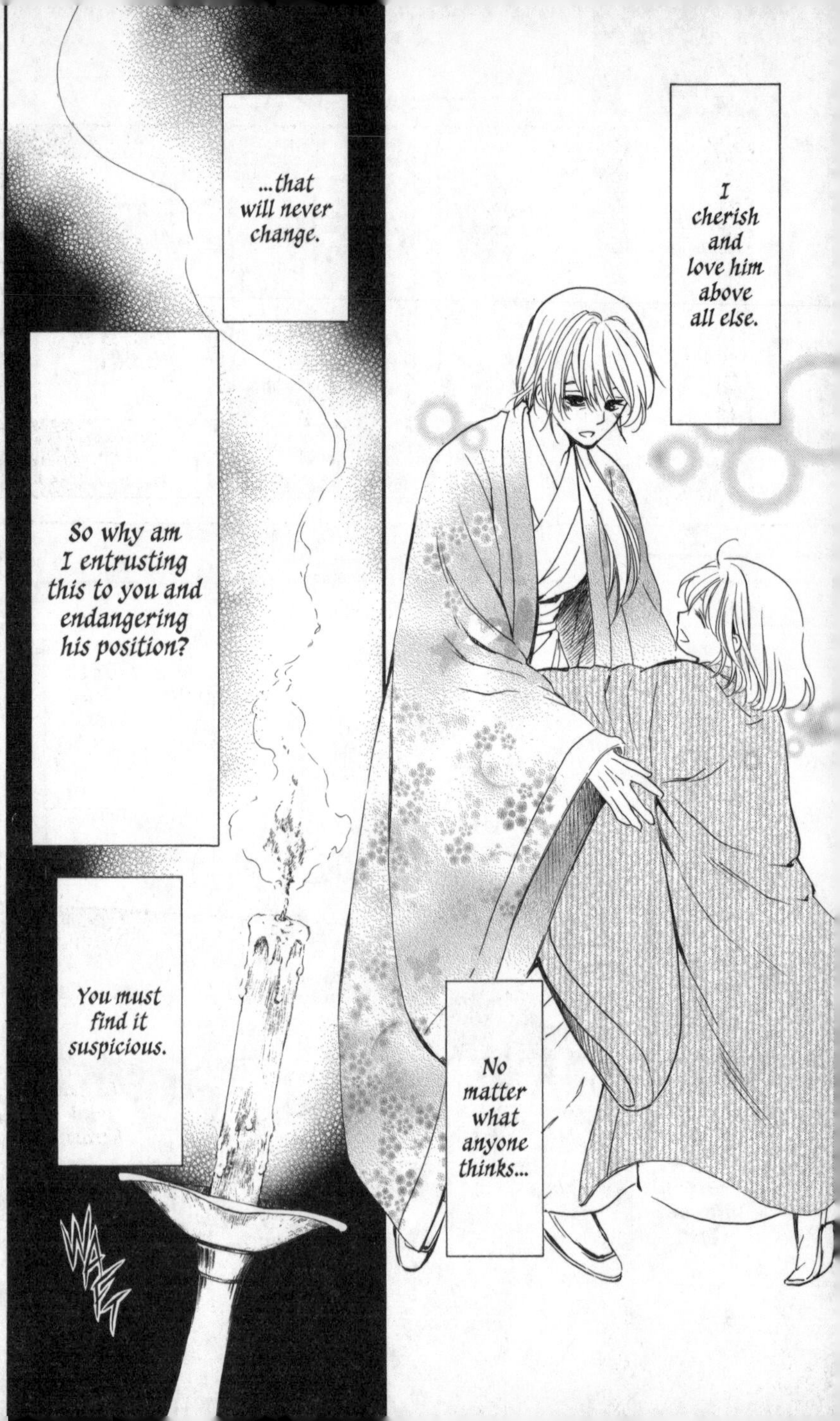
I cherish and love him above all else.
No matter what anyone thinks...
...that will never change.
So why am I entrusting this to you and endangering his position?
You must find it suspicious.

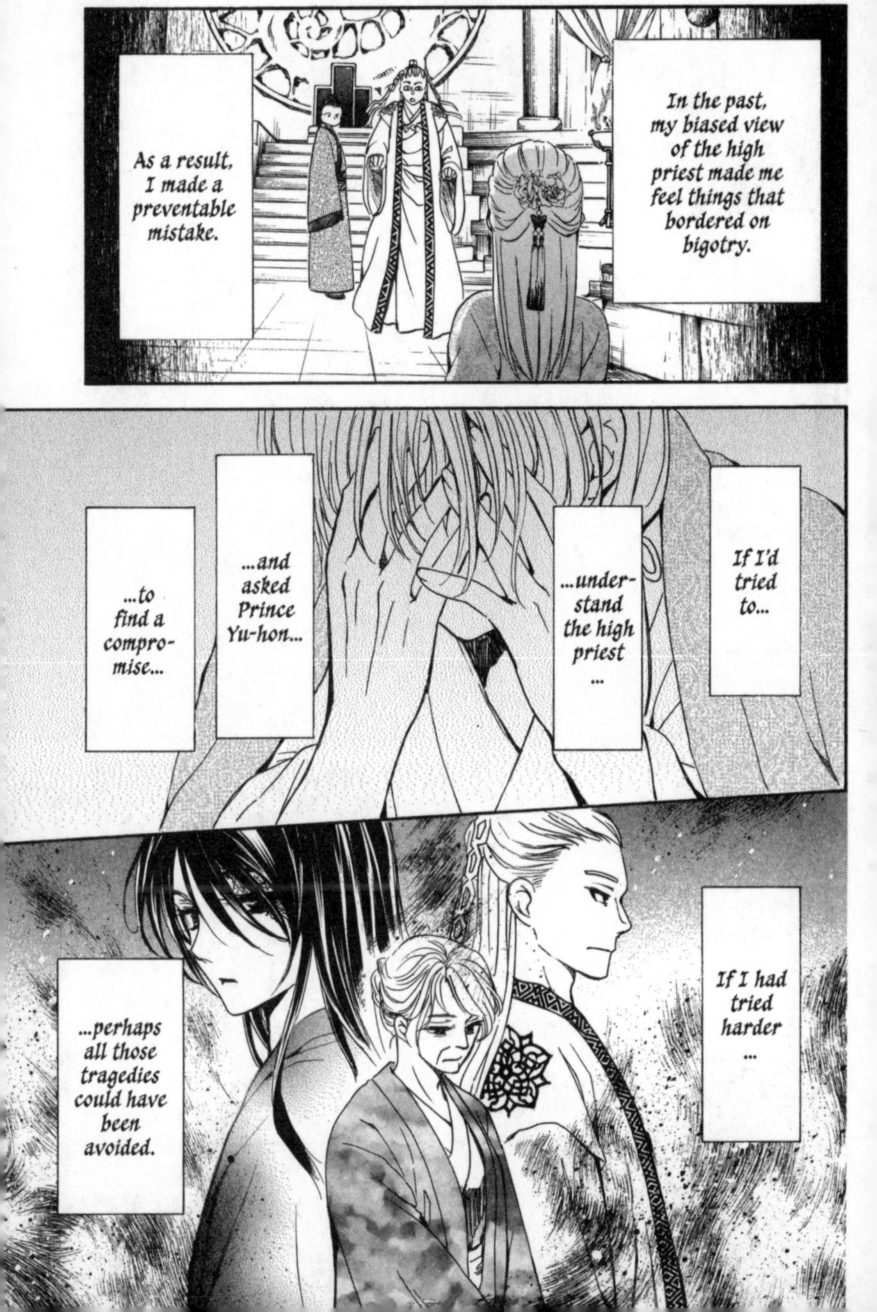
In the past, my biased view of the high priest made me feel things that bordered on bigotry.
As a result, I made a preventable mistake.
If I'd tried to...
...under-stand the high priest ...
...and asked Prince Yu-hon...
...to find a compro-mise...
If I had tried harder ...
...perhaps all those tragedies could have been avoided.

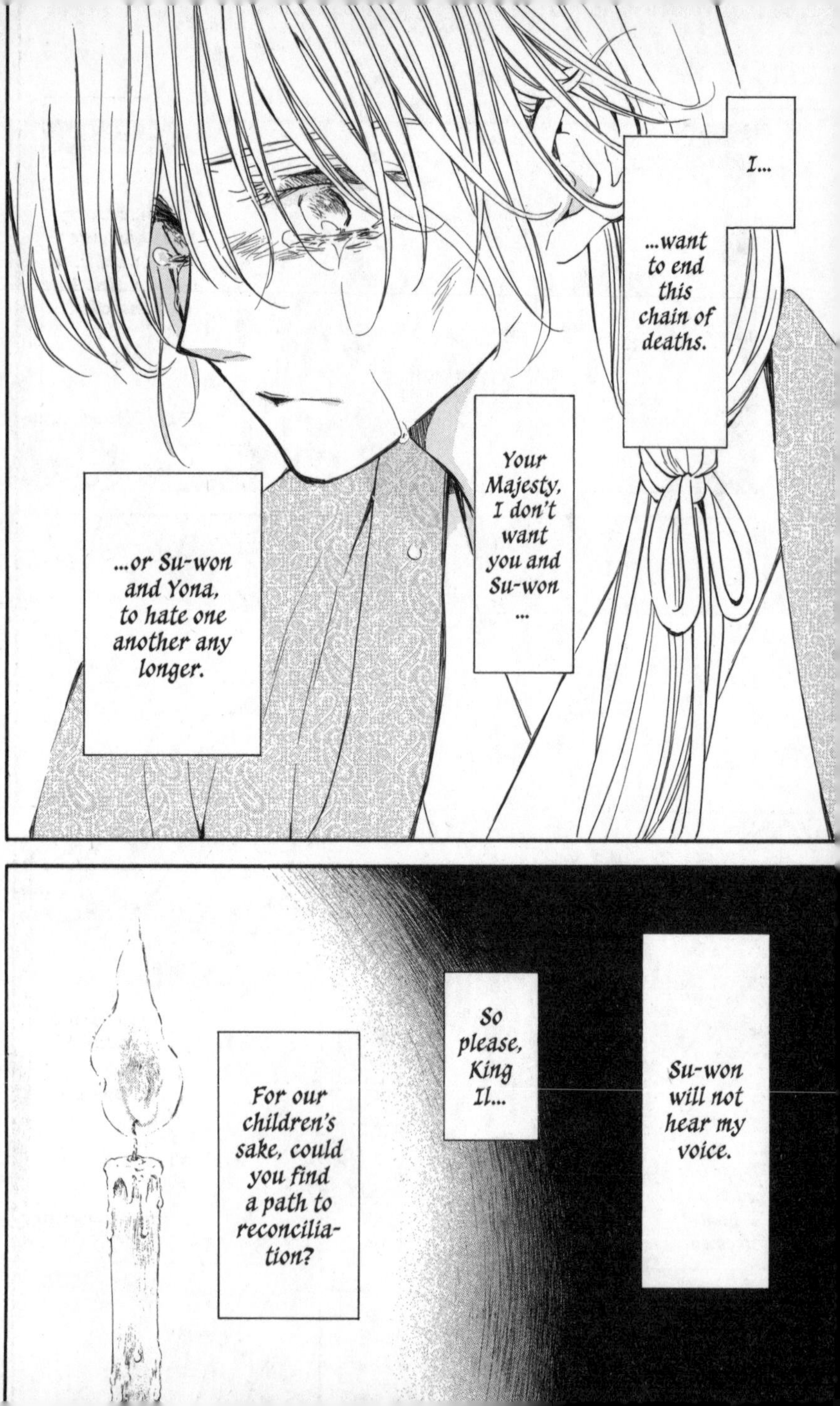
I...
...want to end this chain of deaths.
Your Majesty, I don't want you and Su-won ...
...or Su-won and Yona, to hate one another any longer.
Su-won will not hear my voice.
So please, King Il...
For our children's sake, could you find a path to reconciliation?

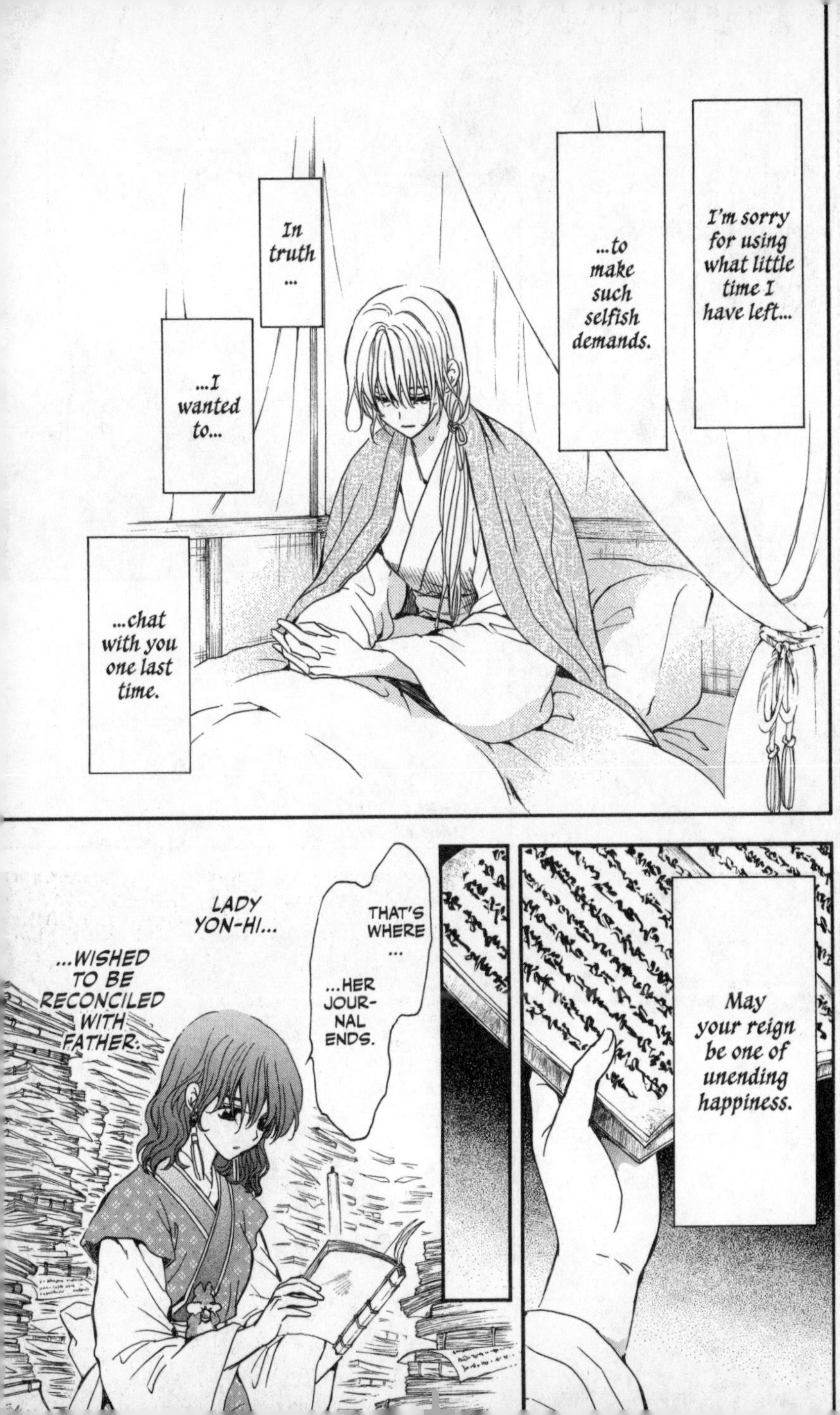
I'm sorry for using what little time I have left...
...to make such selfish demands.
In truth...
...I wanted to...
...chat with you one last time.
May your reign be one of unending happiness.
THAT'S WHERE...
...HER JOURNAL ENDS.
LADY YON-HI...
...WISHED TO BE RECONCILED WITH FATHER.

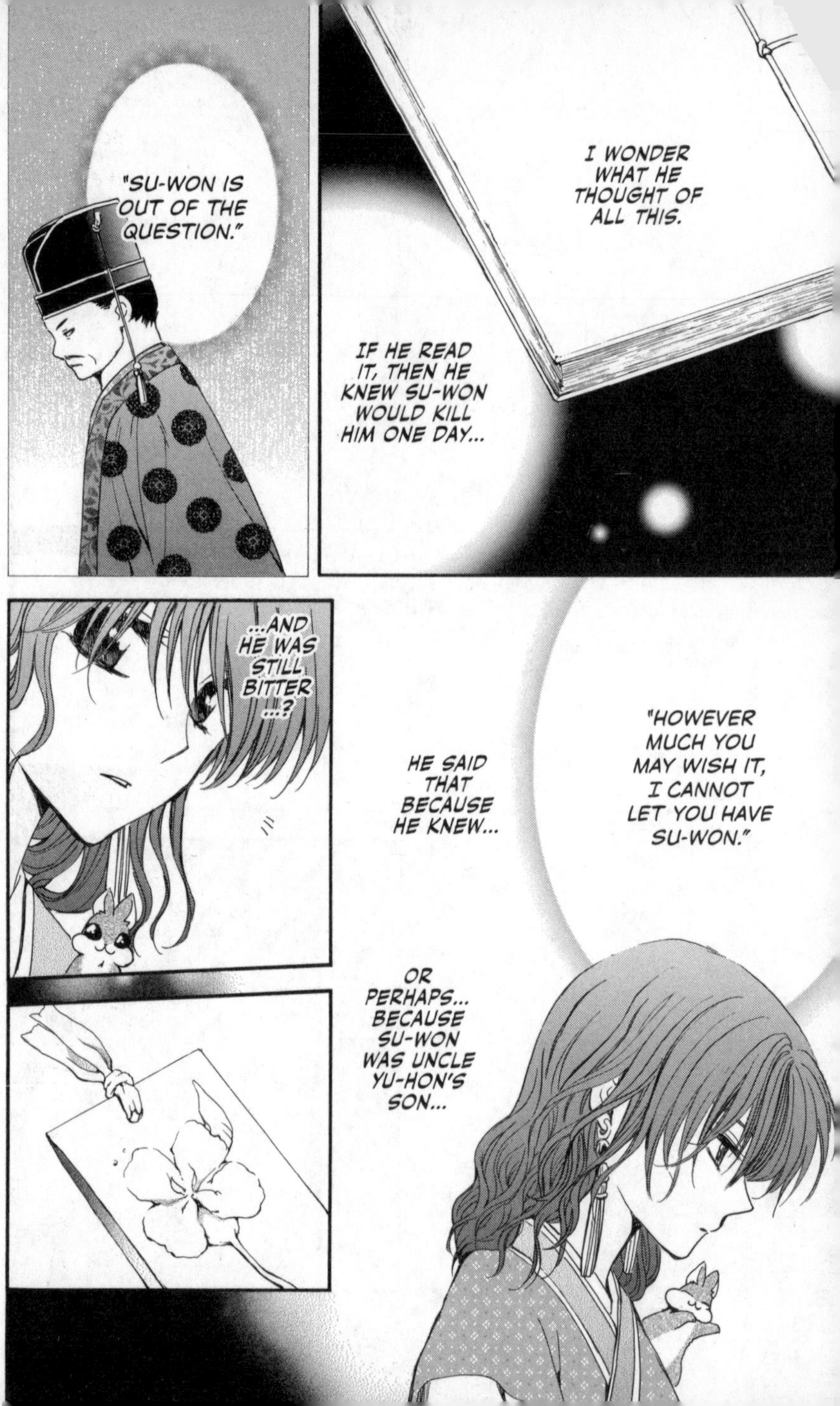
I WONDER WHAT HE THOUGHT OF ALL THIS.
IF HE READ IT, THEN HE KNEW SU-WON WOULD KILL HIM ONE DAY...
"SU-WON IS OUT OF THE QUESTION."
"HOWEVER MUCH YOU MAY WISH IT, I CANNOT LET YOU HAVE SU-WON."
HE SAID THAT BECAUSE HE KNEW...
OR PERHAPS... BECAUSE SU-WON WAS UNCLE YU-HON'S SON...
...AND HE WAS STILL BITTER ...?

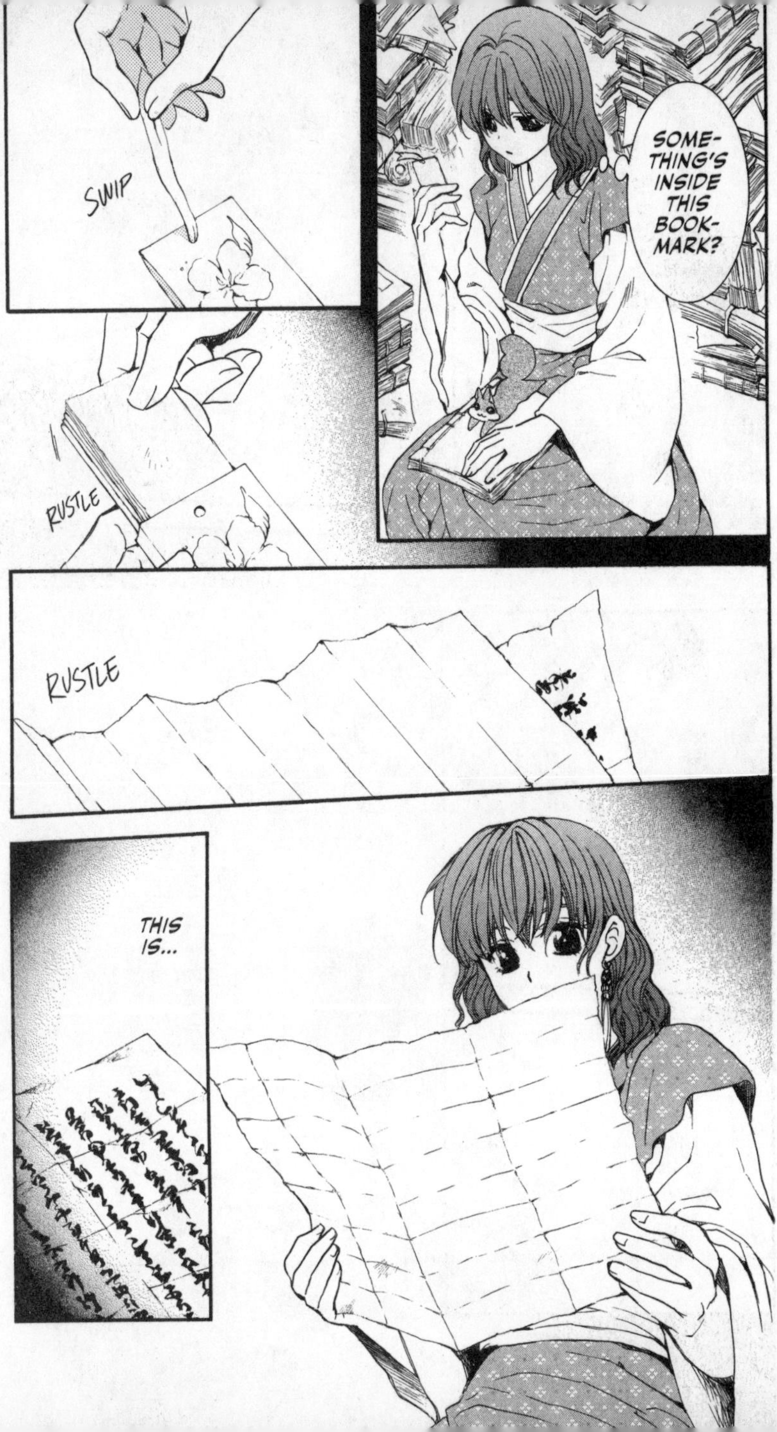
SOME-THING'S INSIDE THIS BOOK-MARK?
SWIP
RUSTLE
RUSTLE
THIS IS...

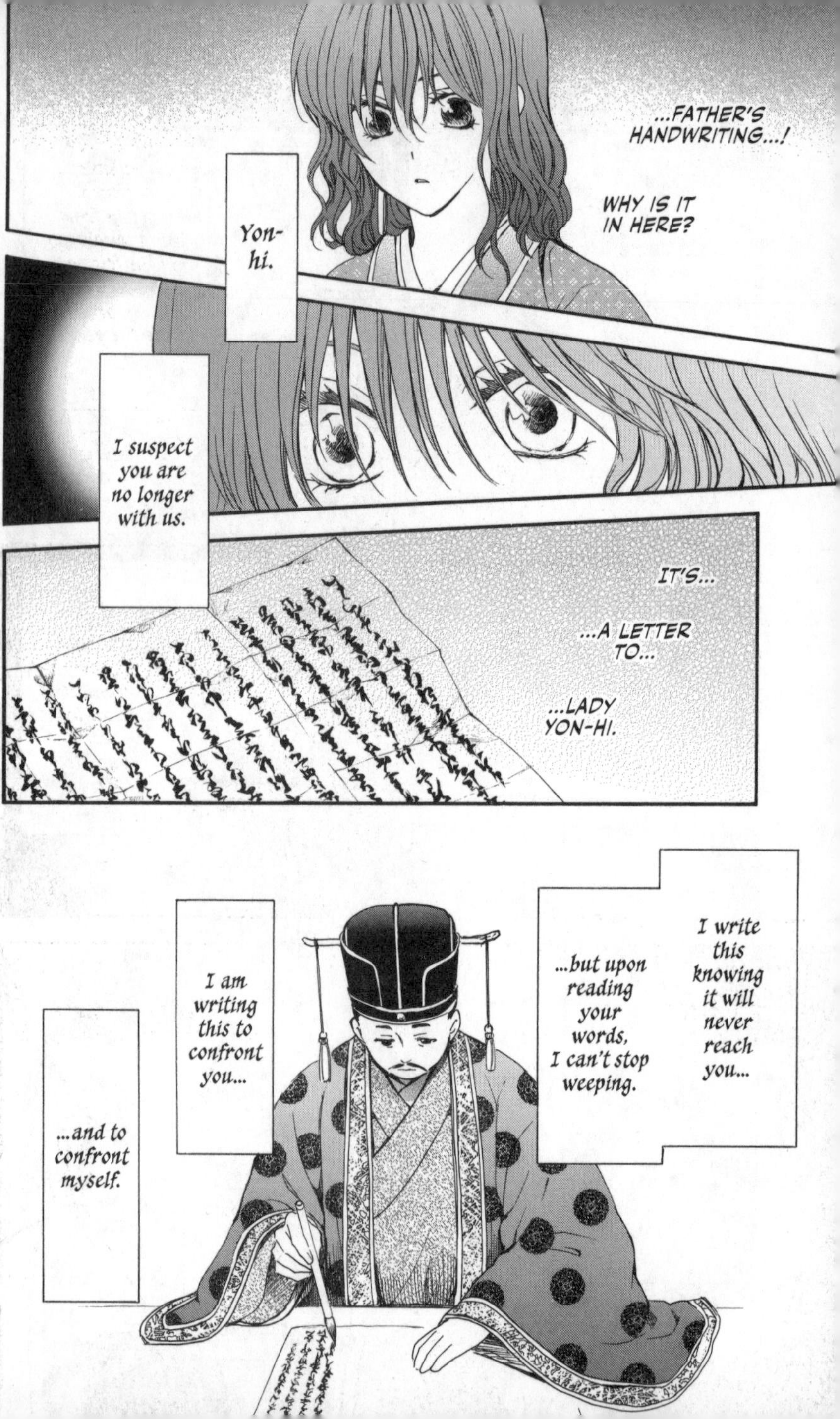
...FATHER'S HANDWRITING...!
WHY IS IT IN HERE?
Yon-hi.
I suspect you are no longer with us.
IT'S...
...A LETTER TO...
...LADY YON-HI.
I write this knowing it will never reach you...
...but upon reading your words, I can't stop weeping.
I am writing this to confront you...
...and to confront myself.

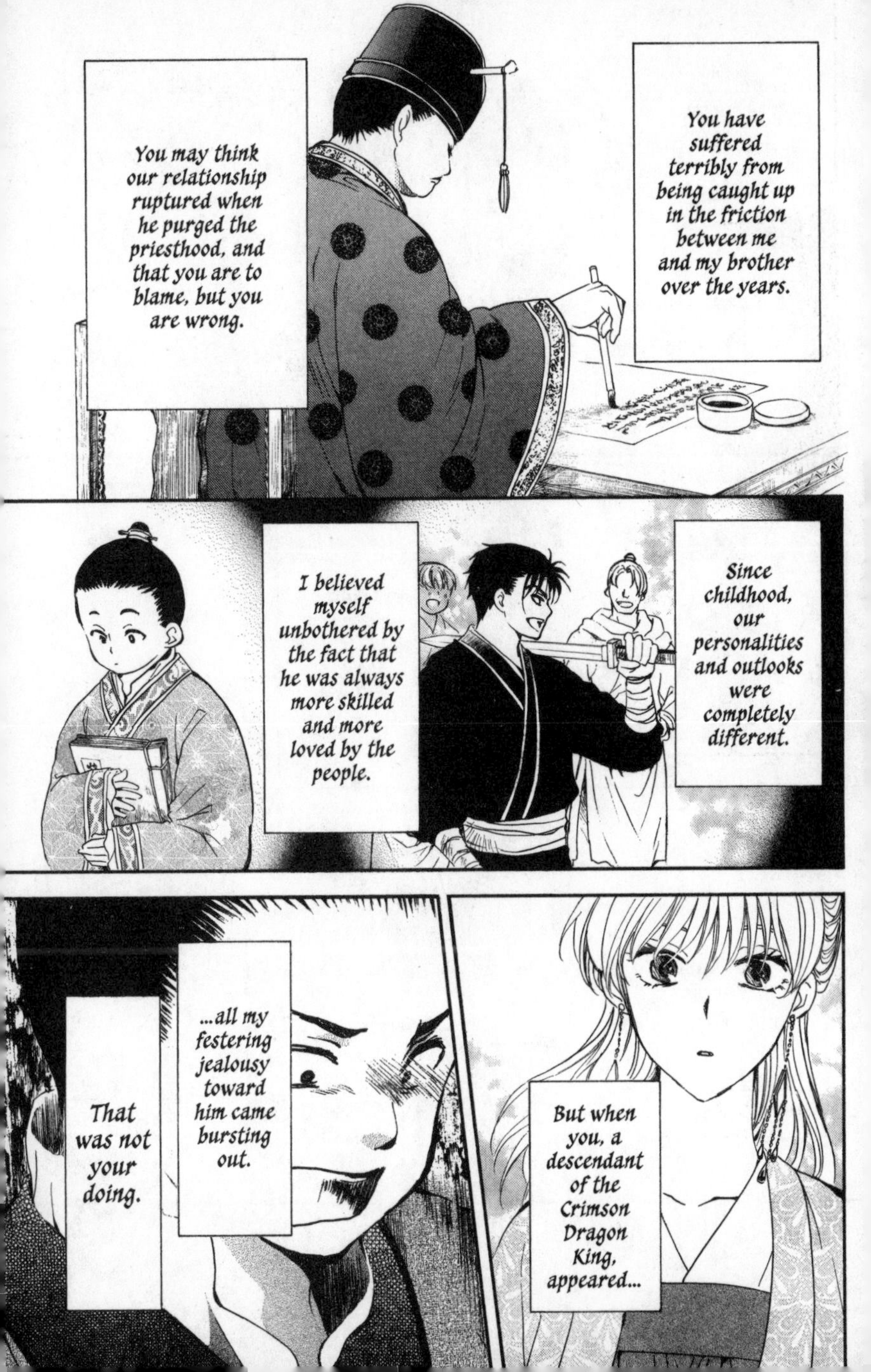
You have suffered terribly from being caught up in the friction between me and my brother over the years.
You may think our relationship ruptured when he purged the priesthood, and that you are to blame, but you are wrong.
Since childhood, our personalities and outlooks were completely different.
I believed myself unbothered by the fact that he was always more skilled and more loved by the people.
But when you, a descendant of the Crimson Dragon King, appeared...
...all my festering jealousy toward him came bursting out.
That was not your doing.

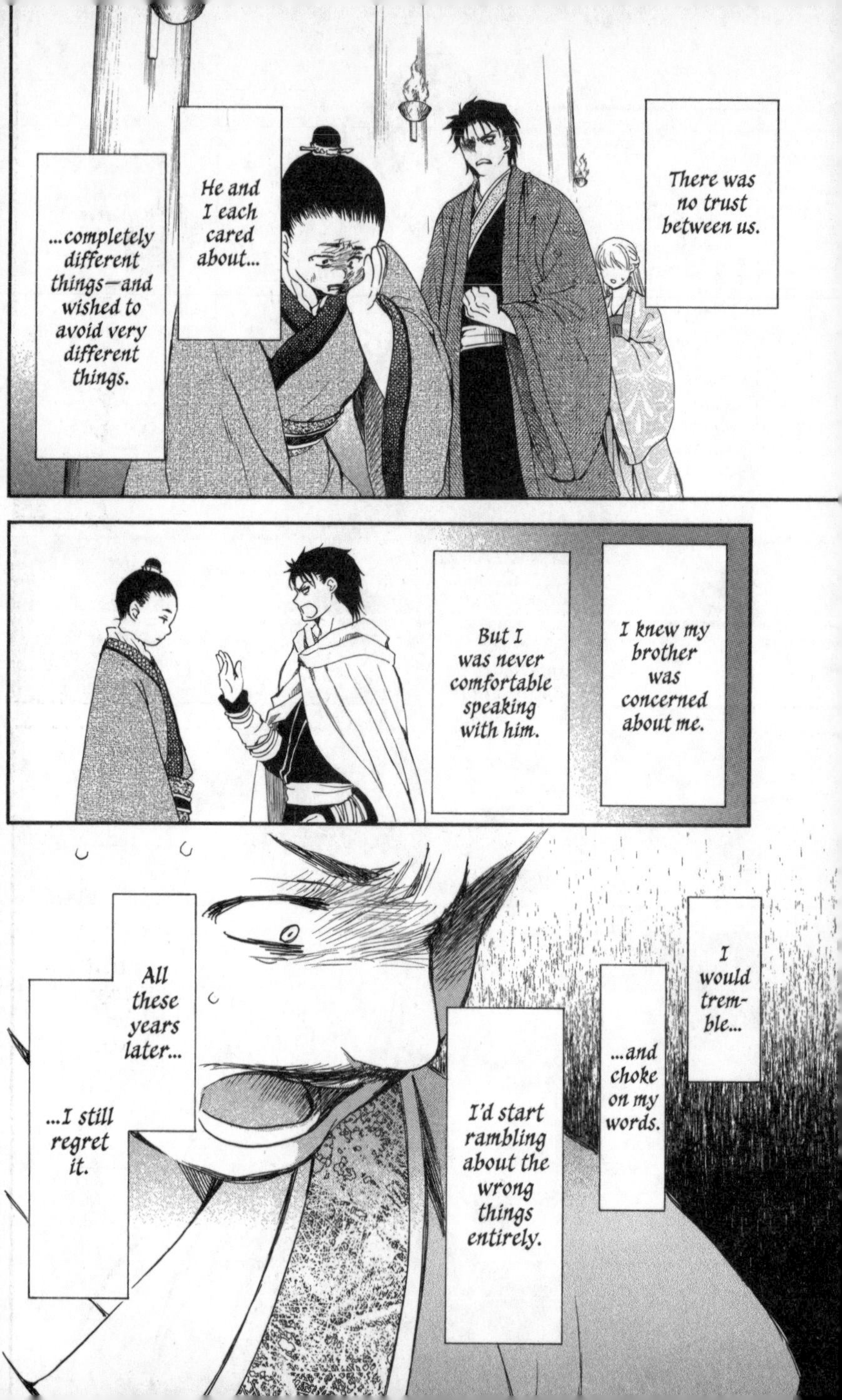
There was no trust between us.
He and I each cared about...
...completely different things—and wished to avoid very different things.
I knew my brother was concerned about me.
But I was never comfortable speaking with him.
I would trem-ble...
...and choke on my words.
I'd start rambling about the wrong things entirely.
All these years later...
...I still regret it.

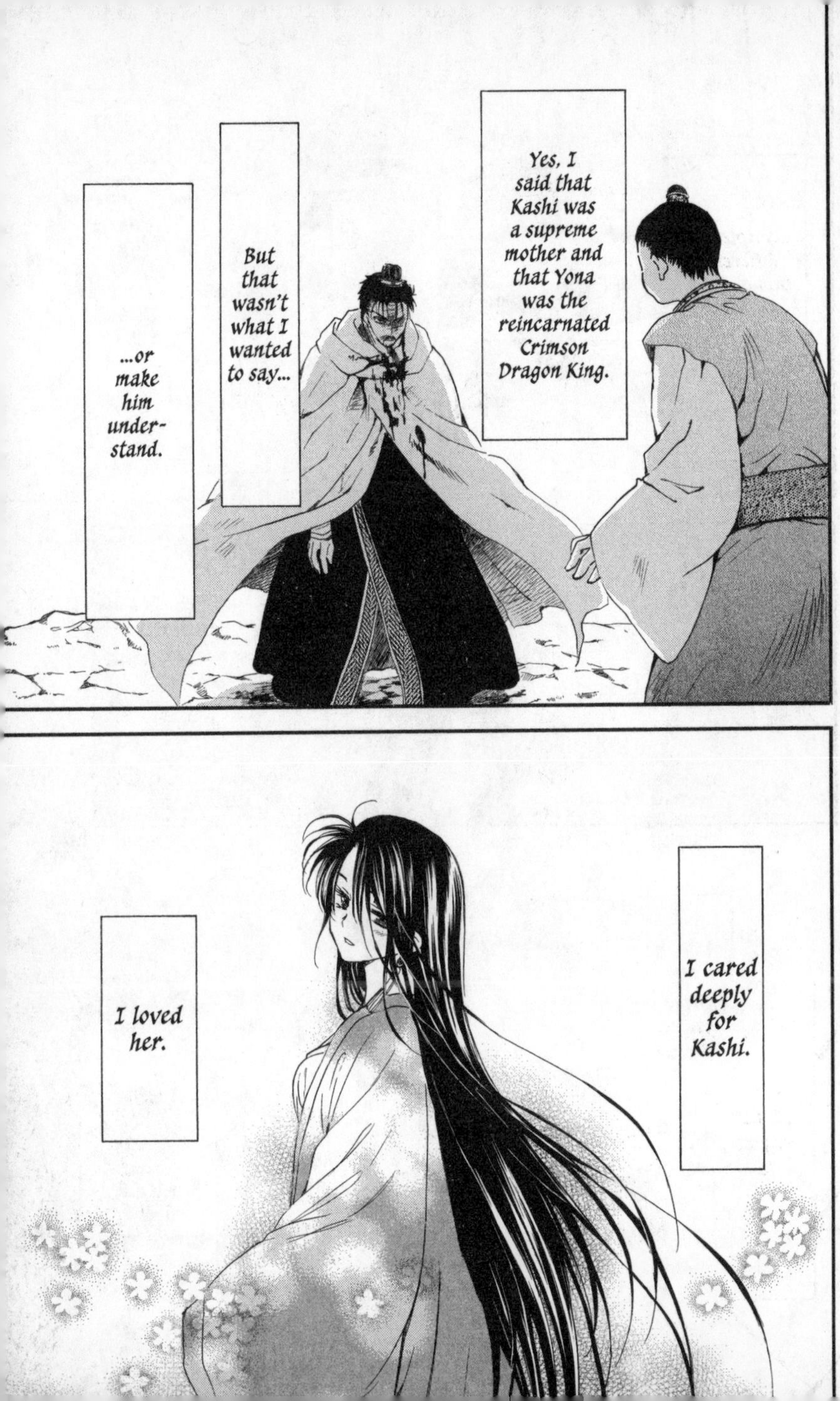
Yes, I said that Kashi was a supreme mother and that Yona was the reincarnated Crimson Dragon King.
But that wasn't what I wanted to say...
...or make him under-stand.
I cared deeply for Kashi.
I loved her.

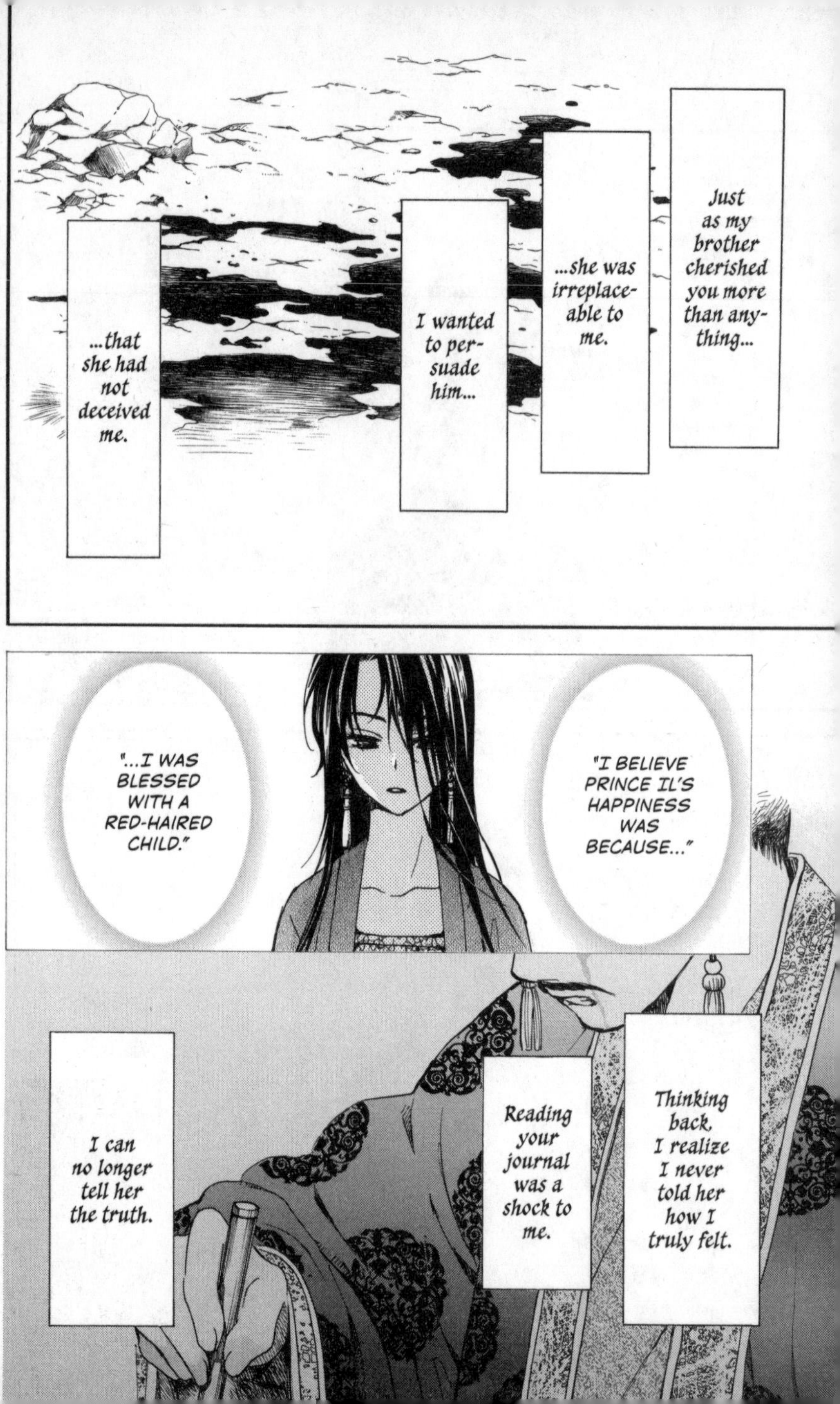
Just as my brother cherished you more than anything...
...she was irreplaceable to me.
I wanted to persuade him...
...that she had not deceived me.
"I BELIEVE PRINCE IL'S HAPPINESS WAS BECAUSE..."
"...I WAS BLESSED WITH A RED-HAIRED CHILD."
Thinking back, I realize I never told her how I truly felt.
Reading your journal was a shock to me.
I can no longer tell her the truth.

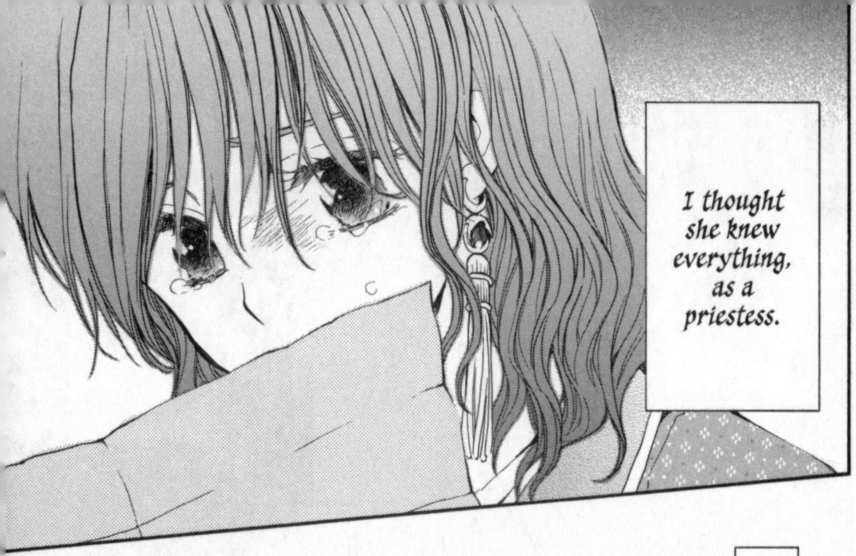
I thought she knew everything, as a priestess.

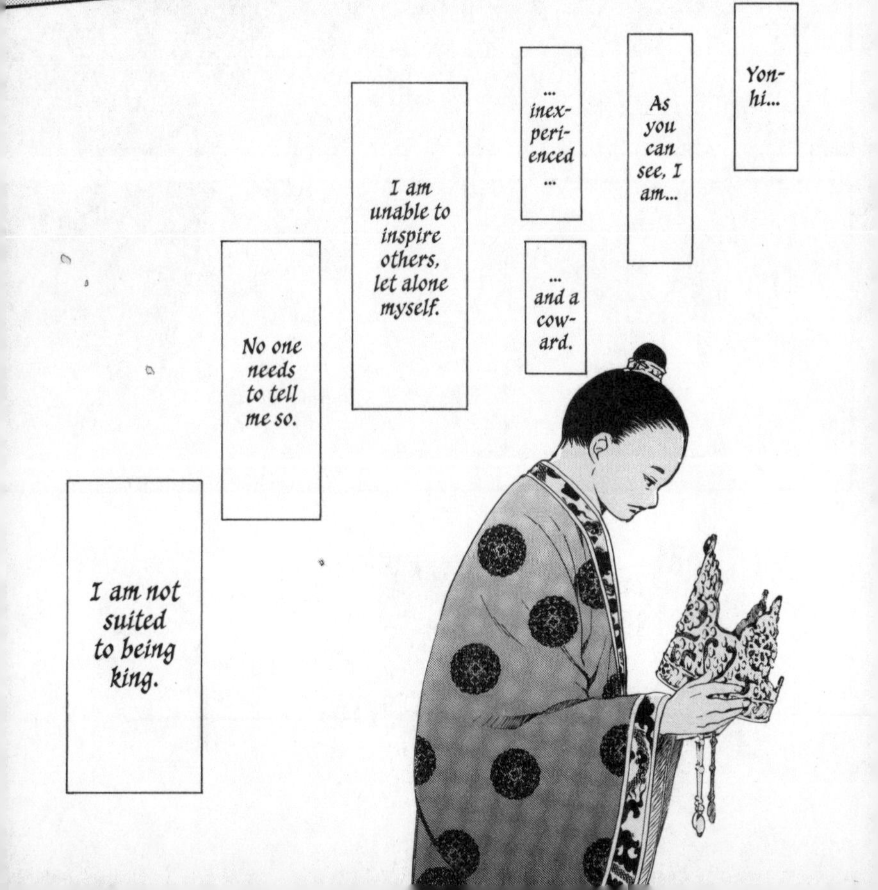
Yon-hi...
As you can see, I am...
... inexperienced ...
... and a coward.
I am unable to inspire others, let alone myself.
No one needs to tell me so.
I am not suited to being king.

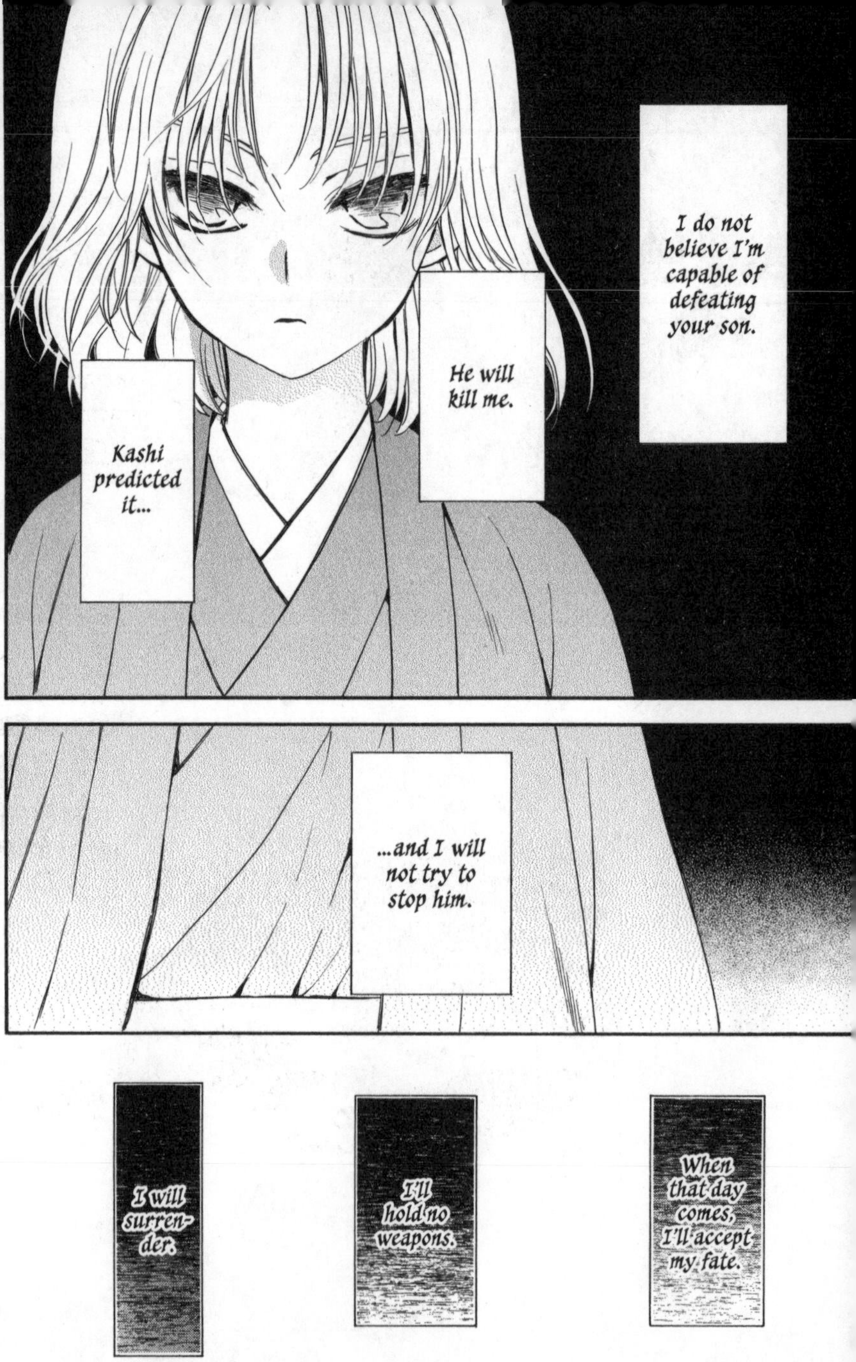
I do not believe I'm capable of defeating your son.
He will kill me.
Kashi predicted it...
...and I will not try to stop him.
When that day comes, I'll accept my fate.
I'll hold no weapons.
I will surrender.

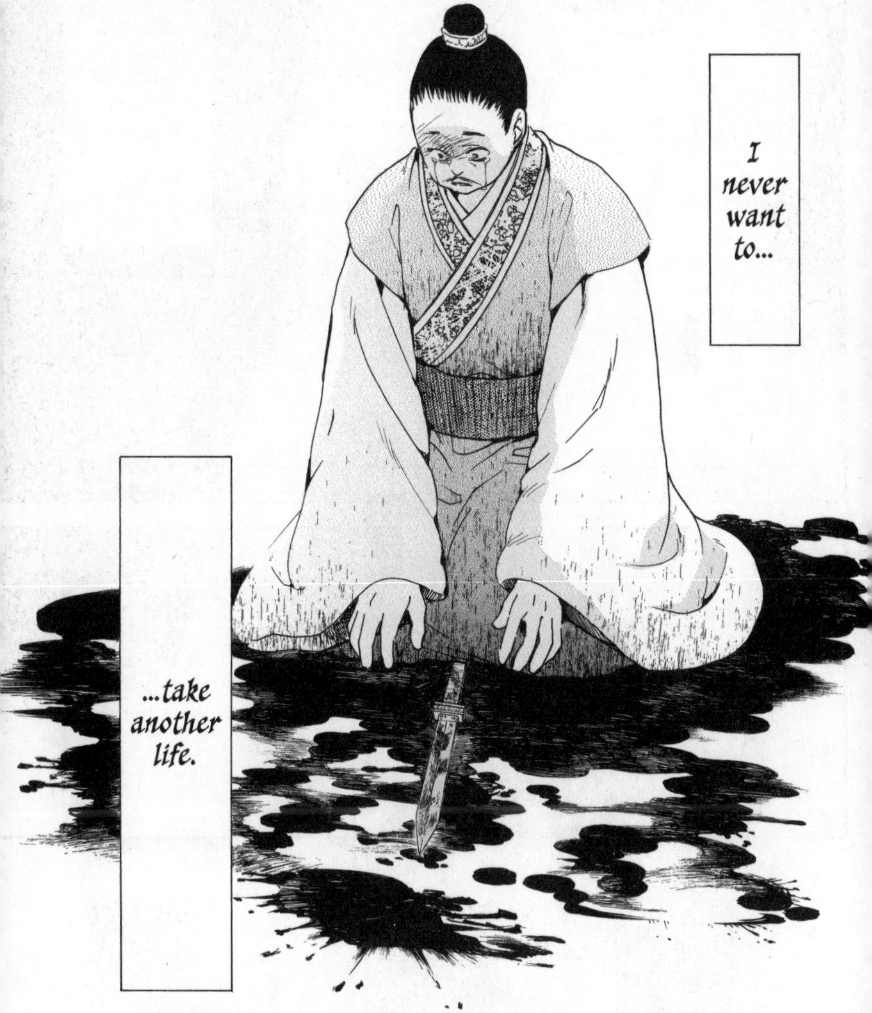
I never want to...
...take another life.

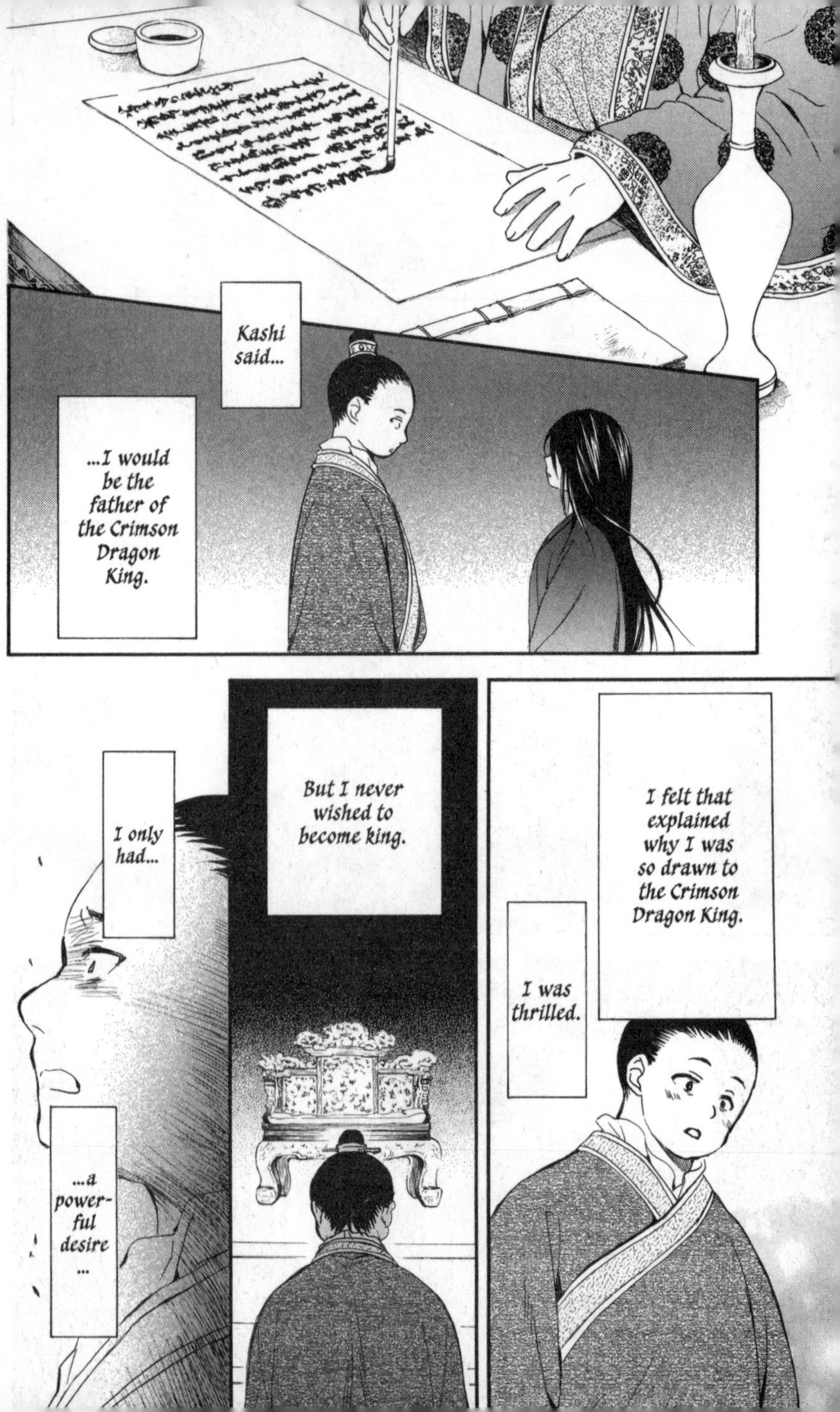
Kashi said...
...I would be the father of the Crimson Dragon King.
I felt that explained why I was so drawn to the Crimson Dragon King.
I was thrilled.
But I never wished to become king.
I only had...
...a powerful-ful desire...

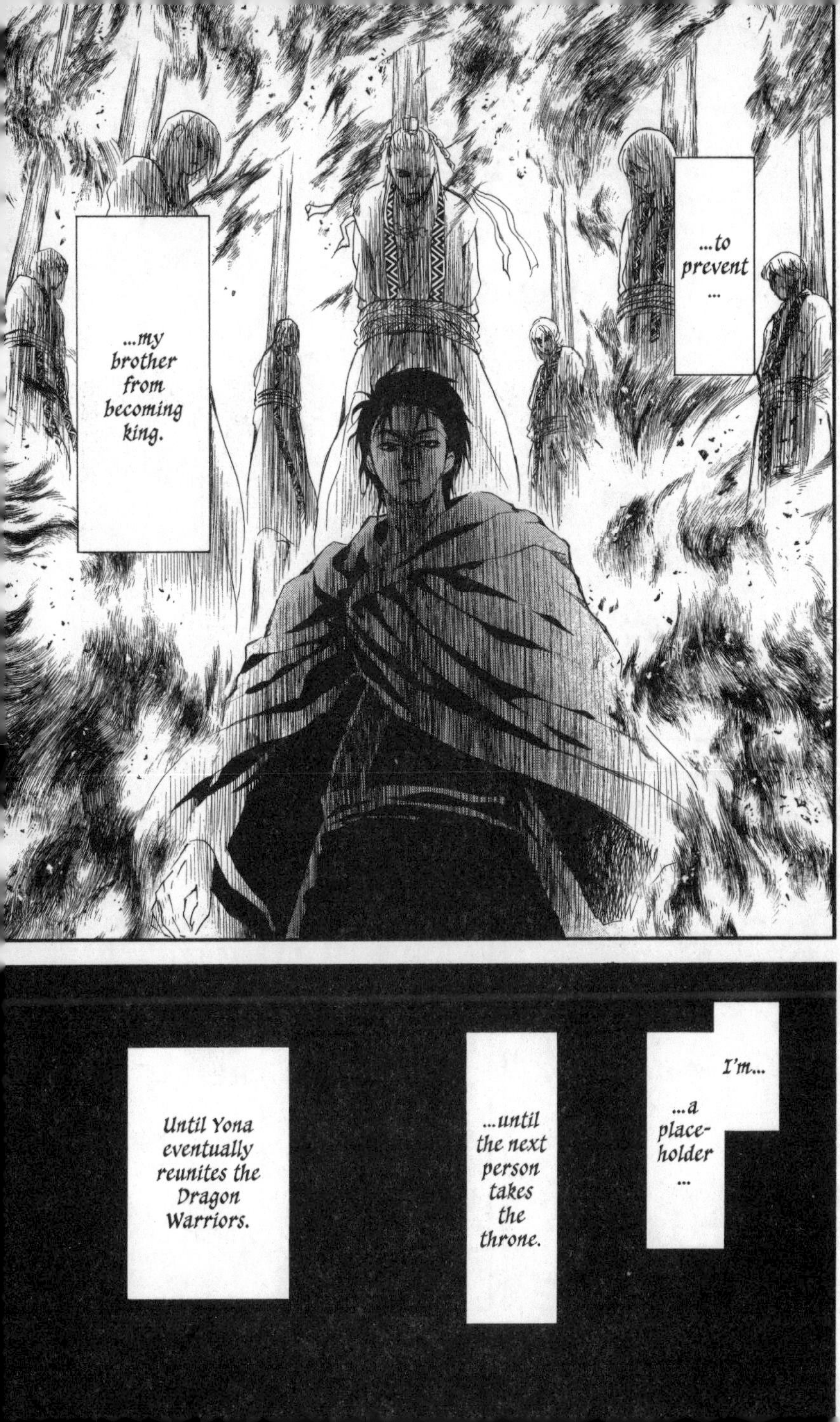
...to prevent ...
...my brother from becoming king.
I'm...
...a place-holder ...
...until the next person takes the throne.
Until Yona eventually reunites the Dragon Warriors.

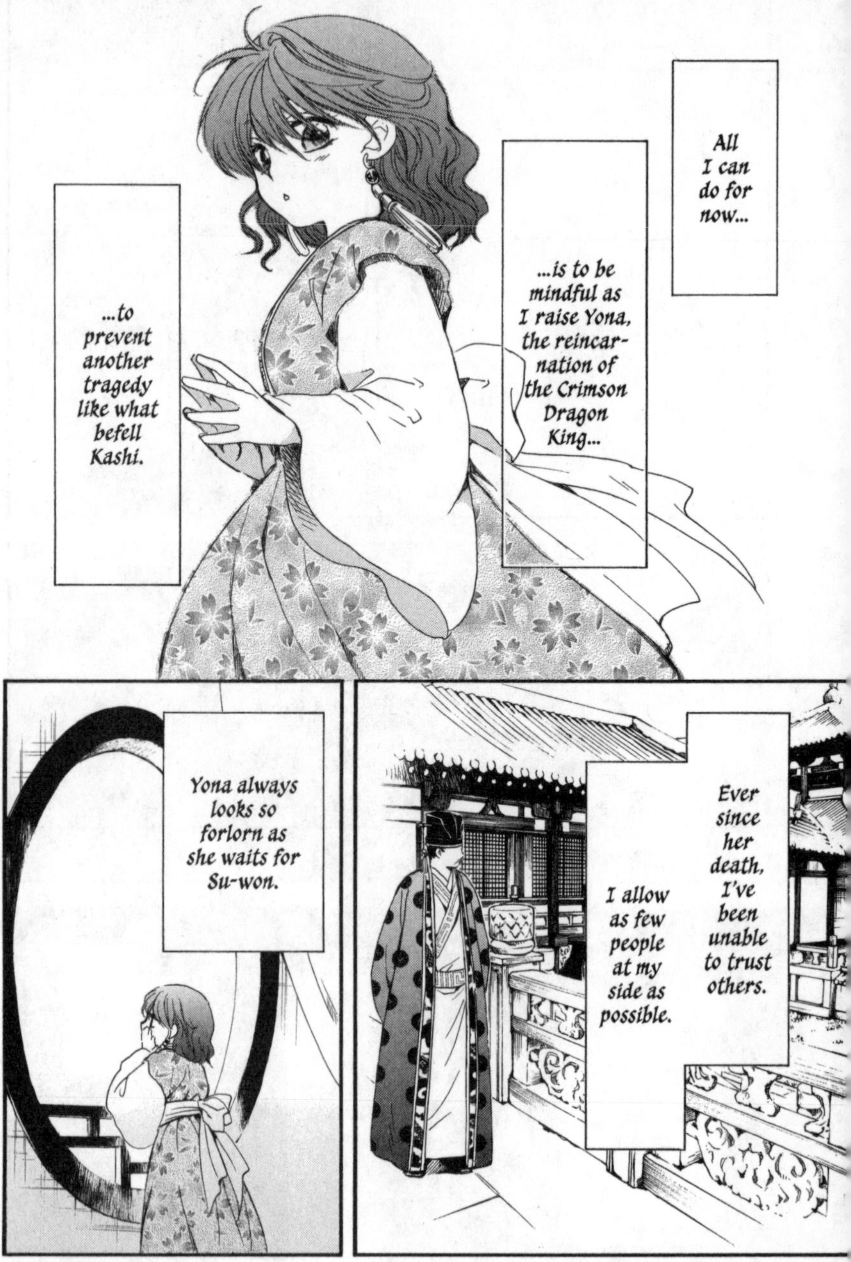
All I can do for now...
...is to be mindful as I raise Yona, the reincarnation of the Crimson Dragon King...
...to prevent another tragedy like what befell Kashi.
Ever since her death, I've been unable to trust others.
I allow as few people at my side as possible.
Yona always looks so forlorn as she waits for Su-won.

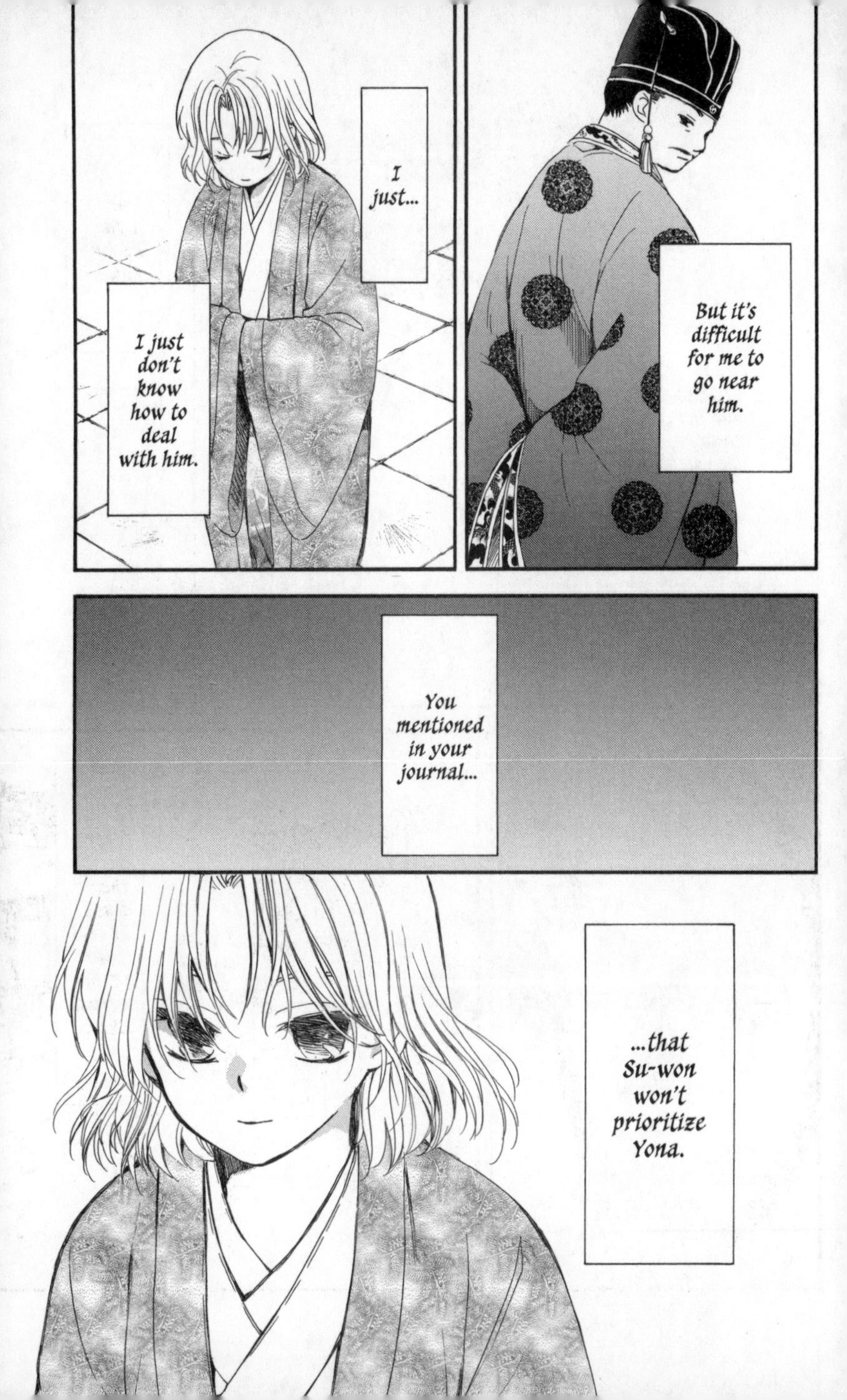
But it's difficult for me to go near him.
I just...
I just don't know how to deal with him.
You mentioned in your journal...
...that Su-won won't prioritize Yona.

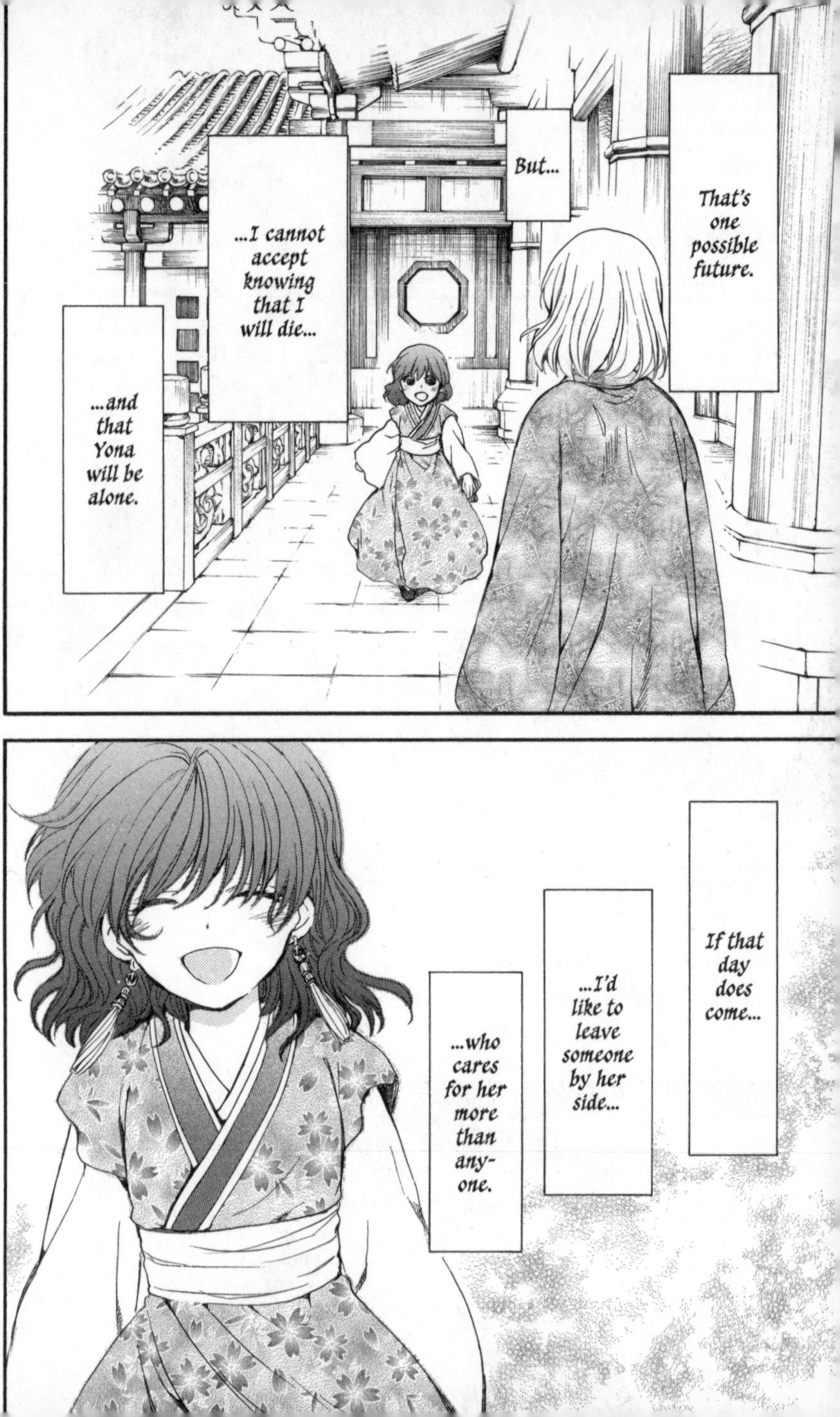
That's one possible future.
But...
...I cannot accept knowing that I will die...
...and that Yona will be alone.
If that day does come...
...I'd like to leave someone by her side...
...who cares for her more than anyone.

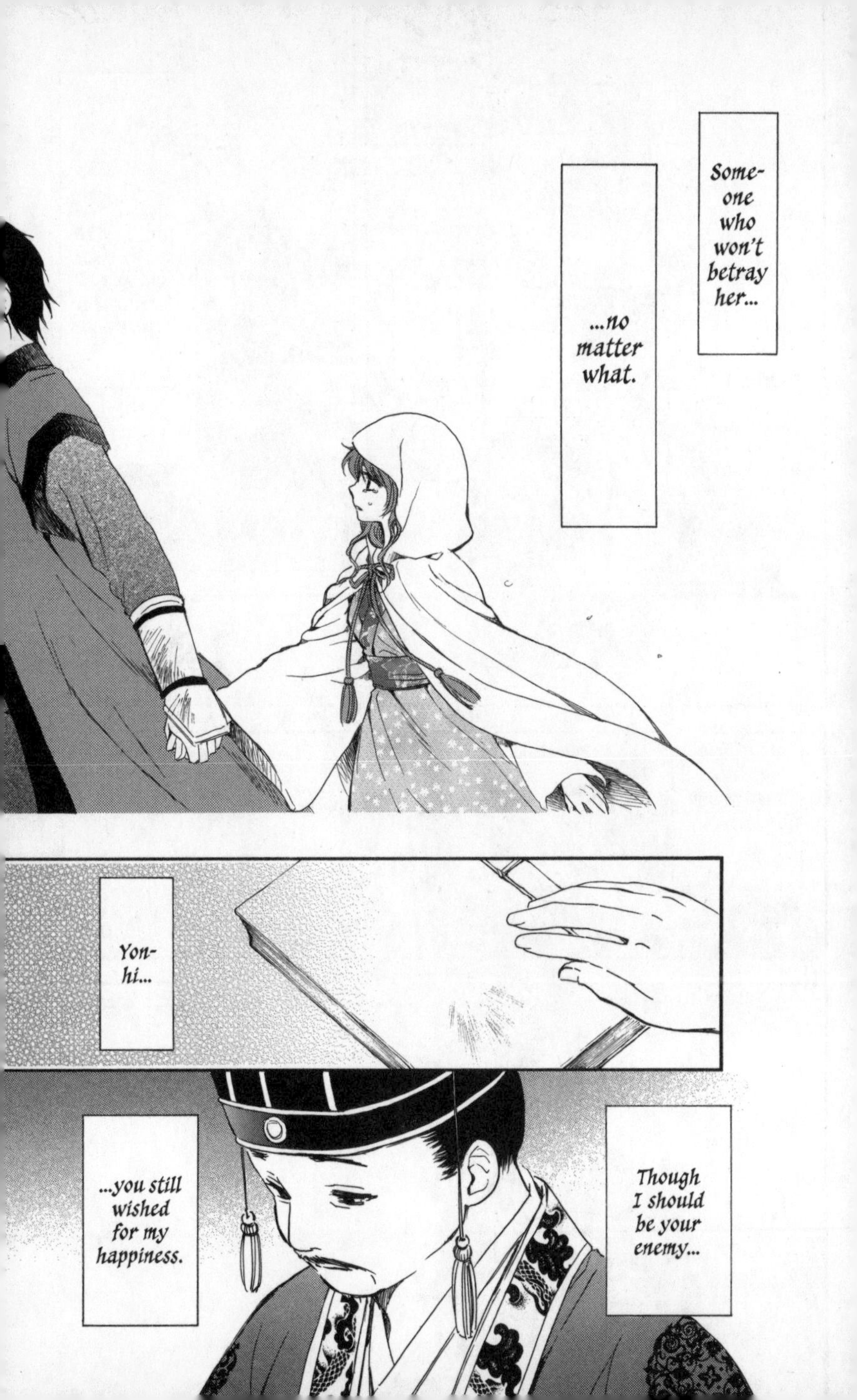
Someone who won't betray her...
...no matter what.
Yon-hi...
Though I should be your enemy...
...you still wished for my happiness.

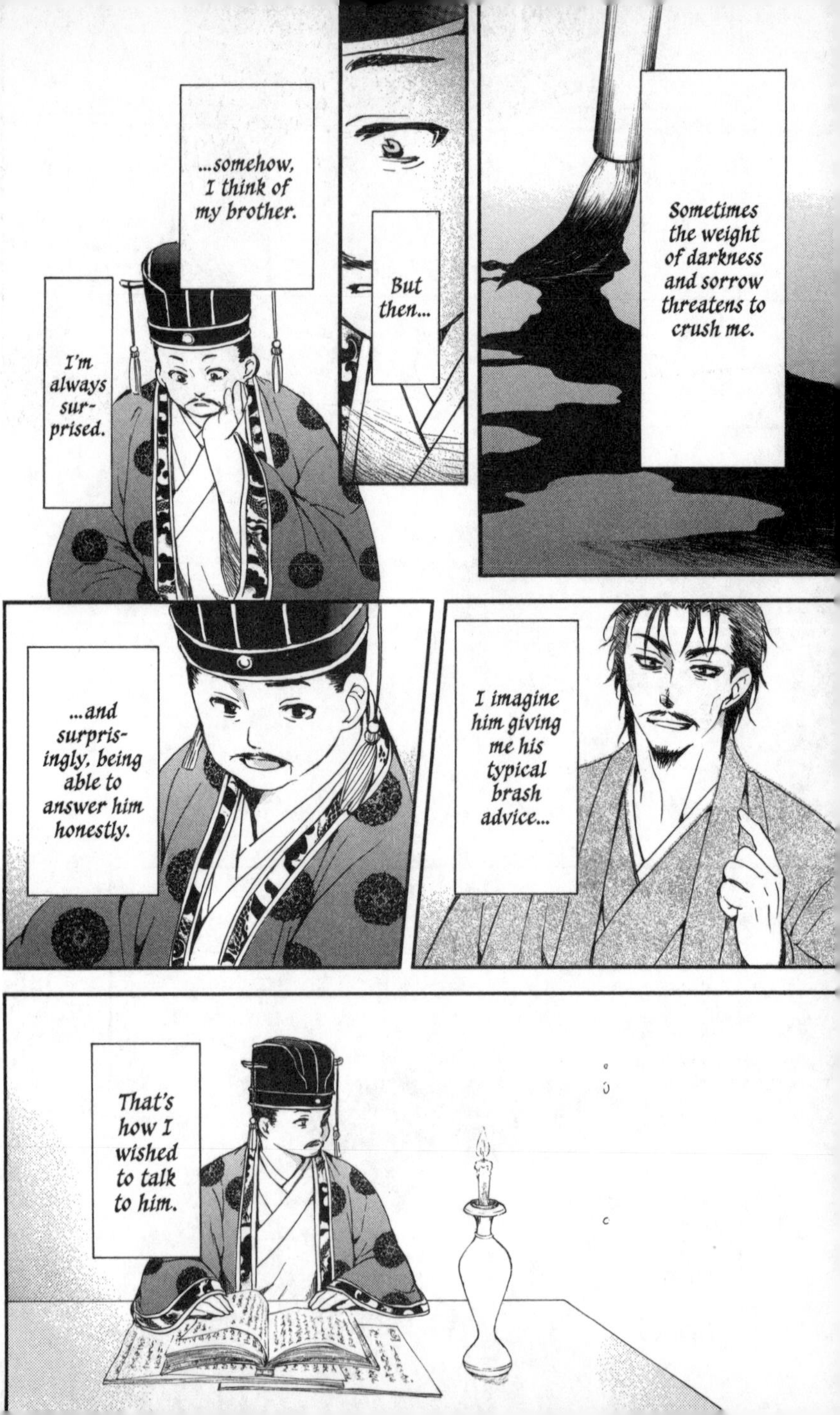
Sometimes the weight of darkness and sorrow threatens to crush me.
But then...
...somehow, I think of my brother.
I'm always sur-prised.
I imagine him giving me his typical brash advice...
...and surpris-ingly, being able to answer him honestly.
That's how I wished to talk to him.

It's so strange.

This journal is full of painful memories...

...and yet, I find myself searching for reminders of those who are no longer here.

I can't bring myself to burn it.

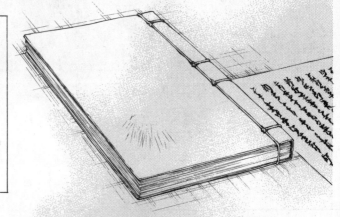

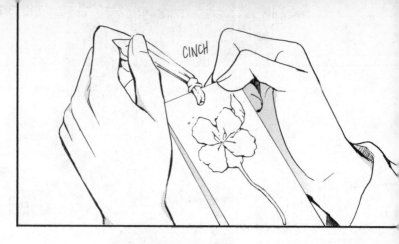

CINCH

CHAPTER 197 / THE END

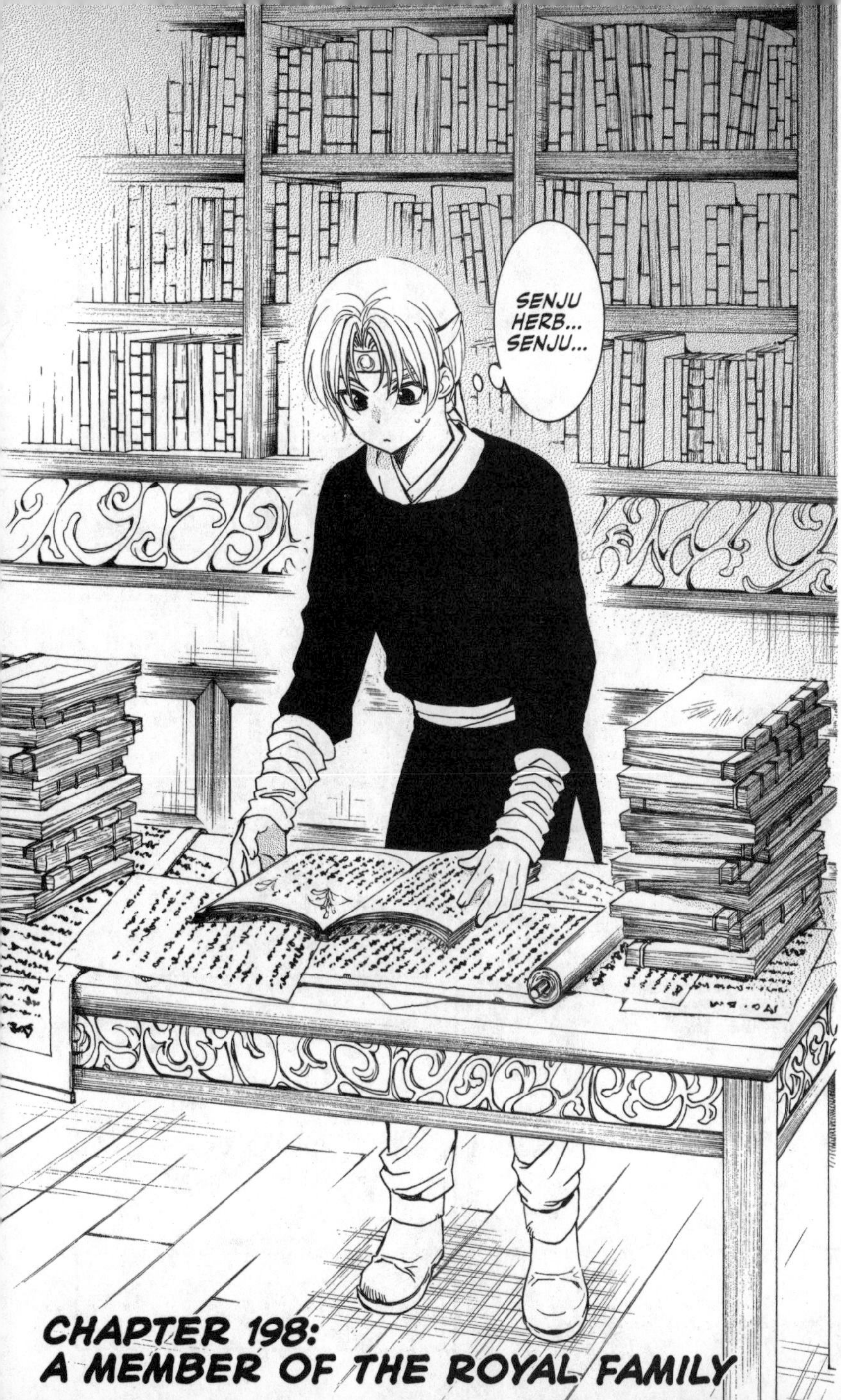
SENJU HERB... SENJU...

CHAPTER 198: A MEMBER OF THE ROYAL FAMILY

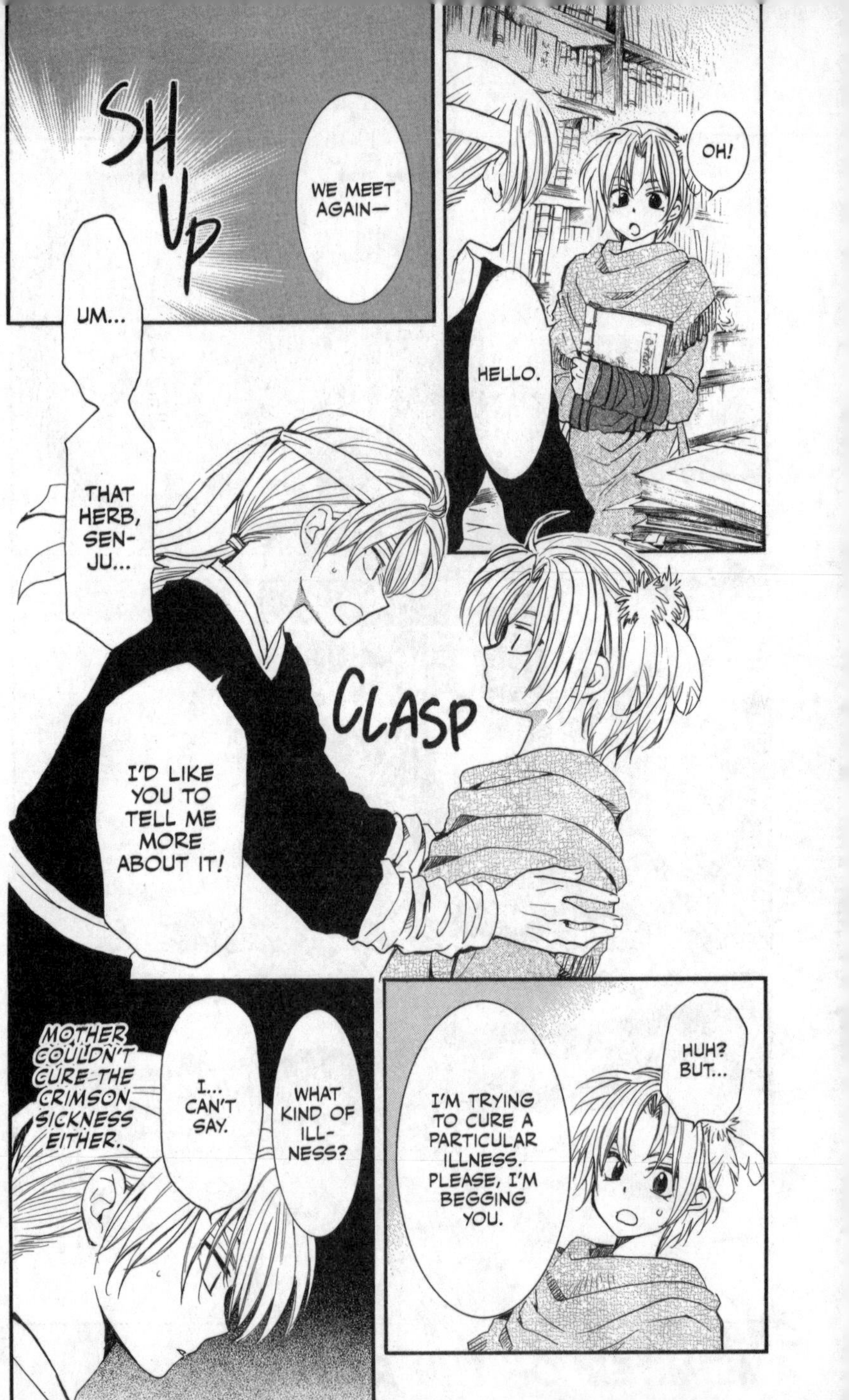
OH!
HELLO.
WE MEET AGAIN—
SHUP
UM...
THAT HERB, SEN-JU...
CLASP
I'D LIKE YOU TO TELL ME MORE ABOUT IT!
HUH? BUT...
I'M TRYING TO CURE A PARTICULAR ILLNESS. PLEASE, I'M BEGGING YOU.
WHAT KIND OF ILL-NESS?
I... CAN'T SAY.
MOTHER COULDN'T CURE THE CRIMSON SICKNESS EITHER.

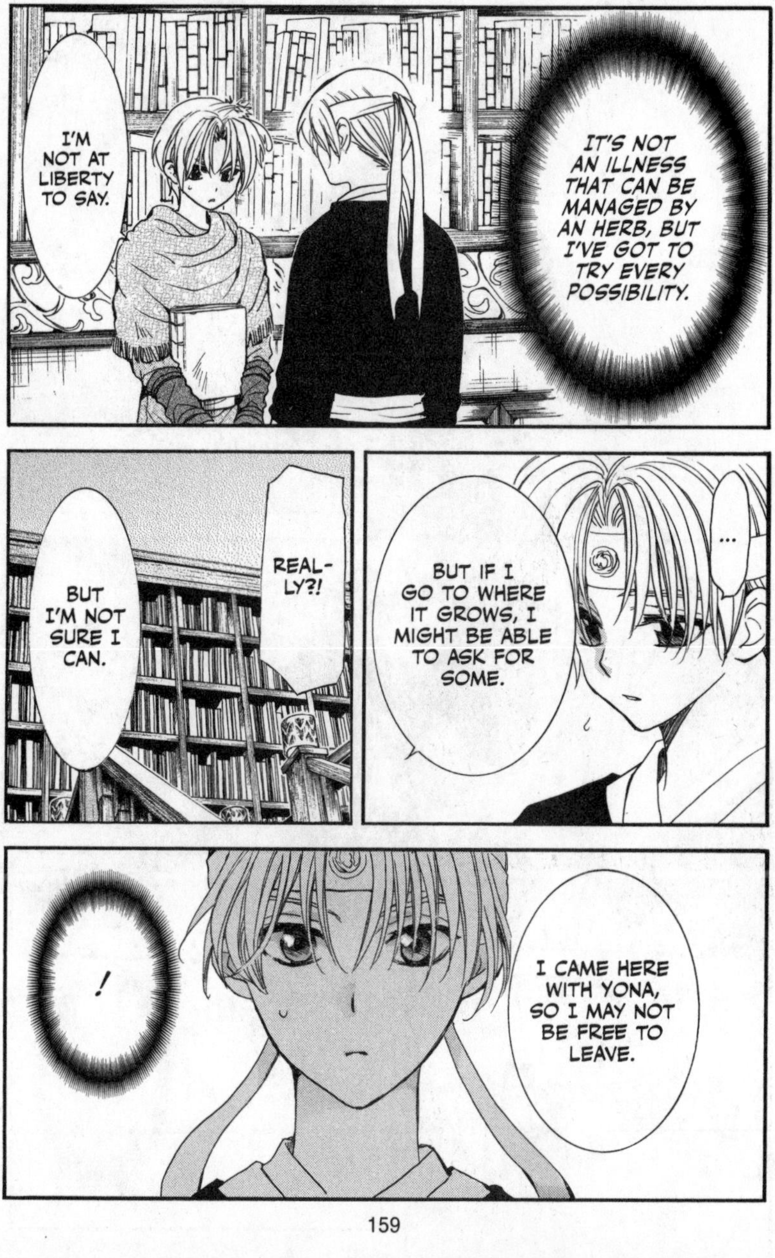
IT'S NOT AN ILLNESS THAT CAN BE MANAGED BY AN HERB, BUT I'VE GOT TO TRY EVERY POSSIBILITY.
I'M NOT AT LIBERTY TO SAY.
...
BUT IF I GO TO WHERE IT GROWS, I MIGHT BE ABLE TO ASK FOR SOME.
REAL-LY?!
BUT I'M NOT SURE I CAN.
I CAME HERE WITH YONA, SO I MAY NOT BE FREE TO LEAVE.
!

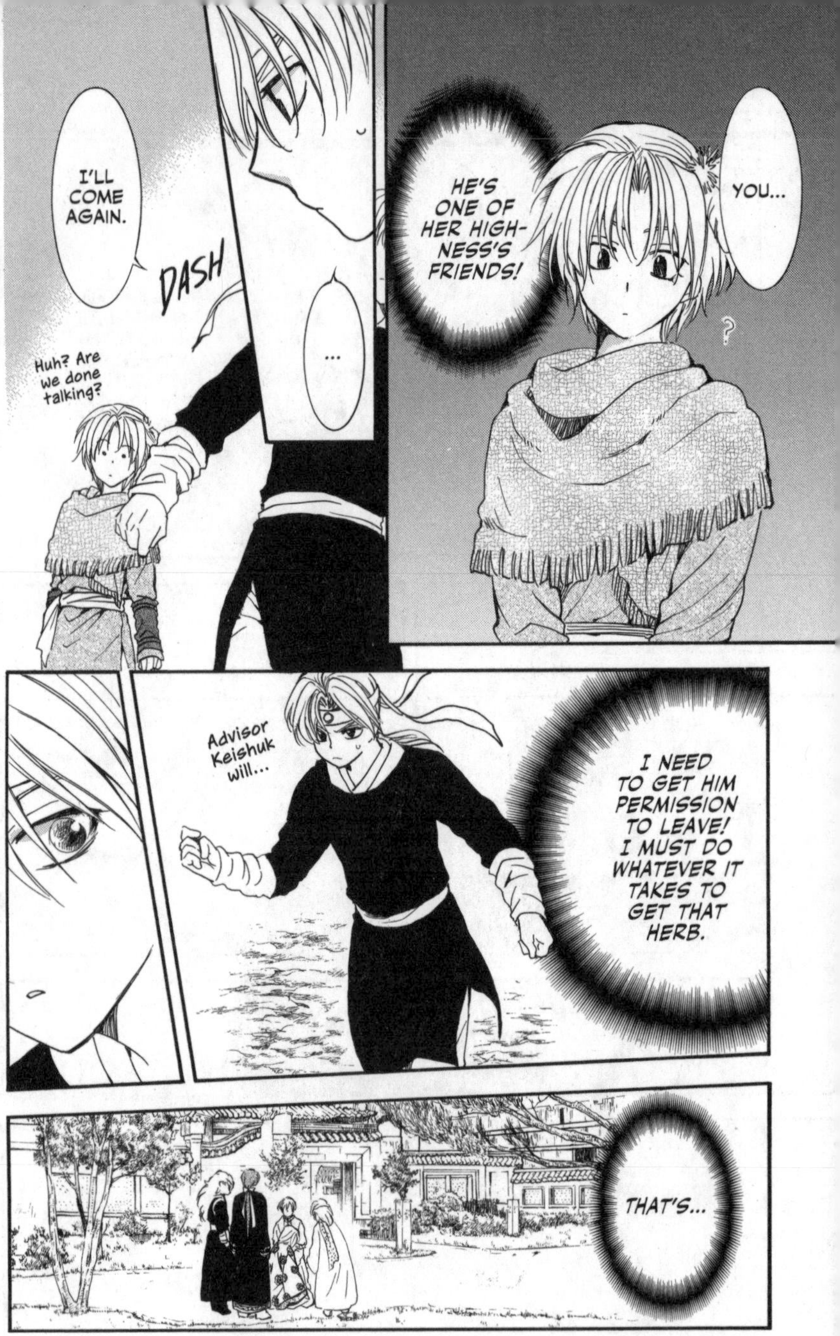
YOU...
HE'S ONE OF HER HIGHNESS'S FRIENDS!
...
DASH
I'LL COME AGAIN.
Huh? Are we done talking?
I NEED TO GET HIM PERMISSION TO LEAVE! I MUST DO WHATEVER IT TAKES TO GET THAT HERB.
Advisor Keishuk will...
THAT'S...

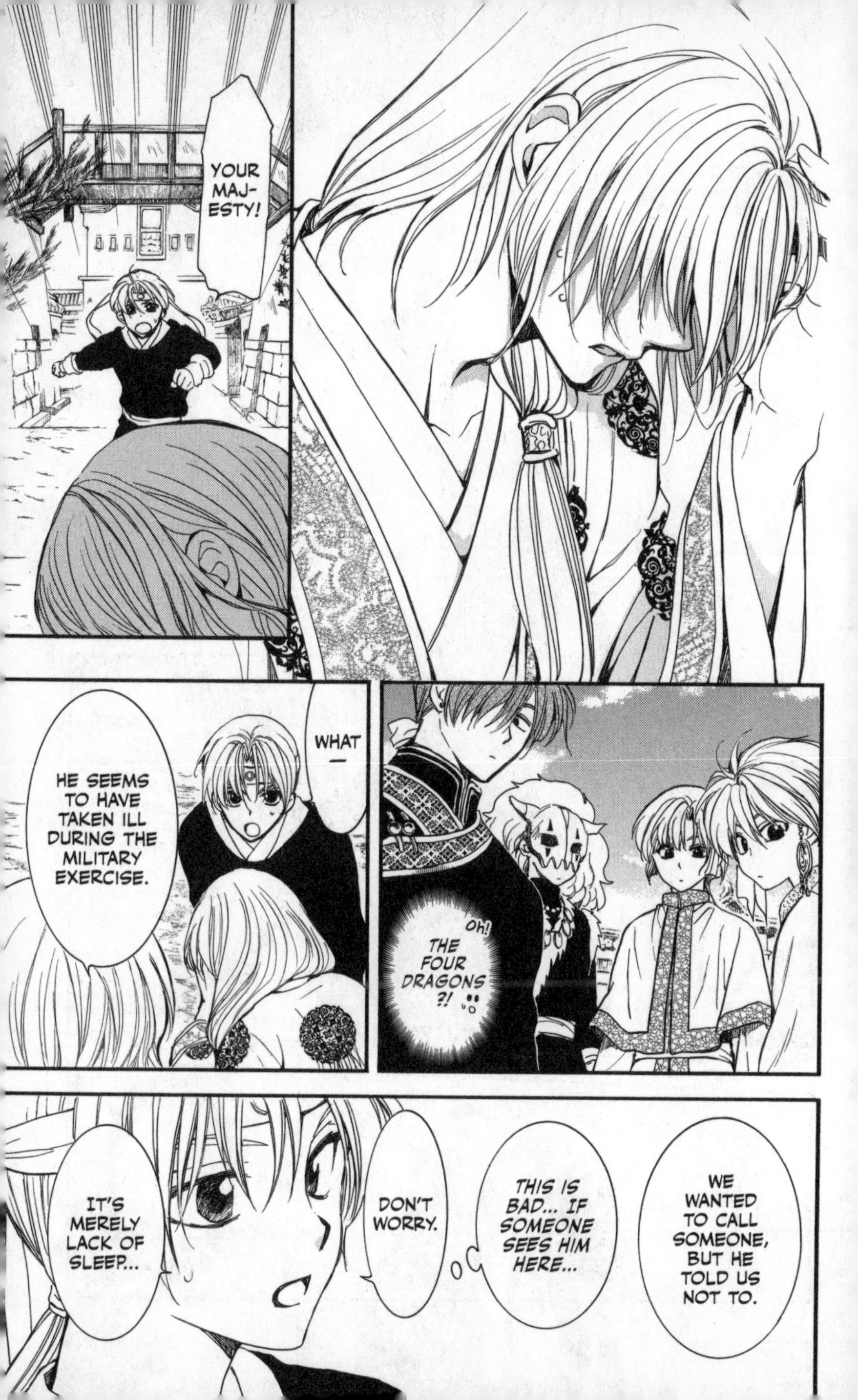
YOUR MAJ-ESTY!
Oh! THE FOUR DRAGONS?!
WHAT —
HE SEEMS TO HAVE TAKEN ILL DURING THE MILITARY EXERCISE.
WE WANTED TO CALL SOMEONE, BUT HE TOLD US NOT TO.
THIS IS BAD... IF SOMEONE SEES HIM HERE...
DON'T WORRY.
IT'S MERELY LACK OF SLEEP...

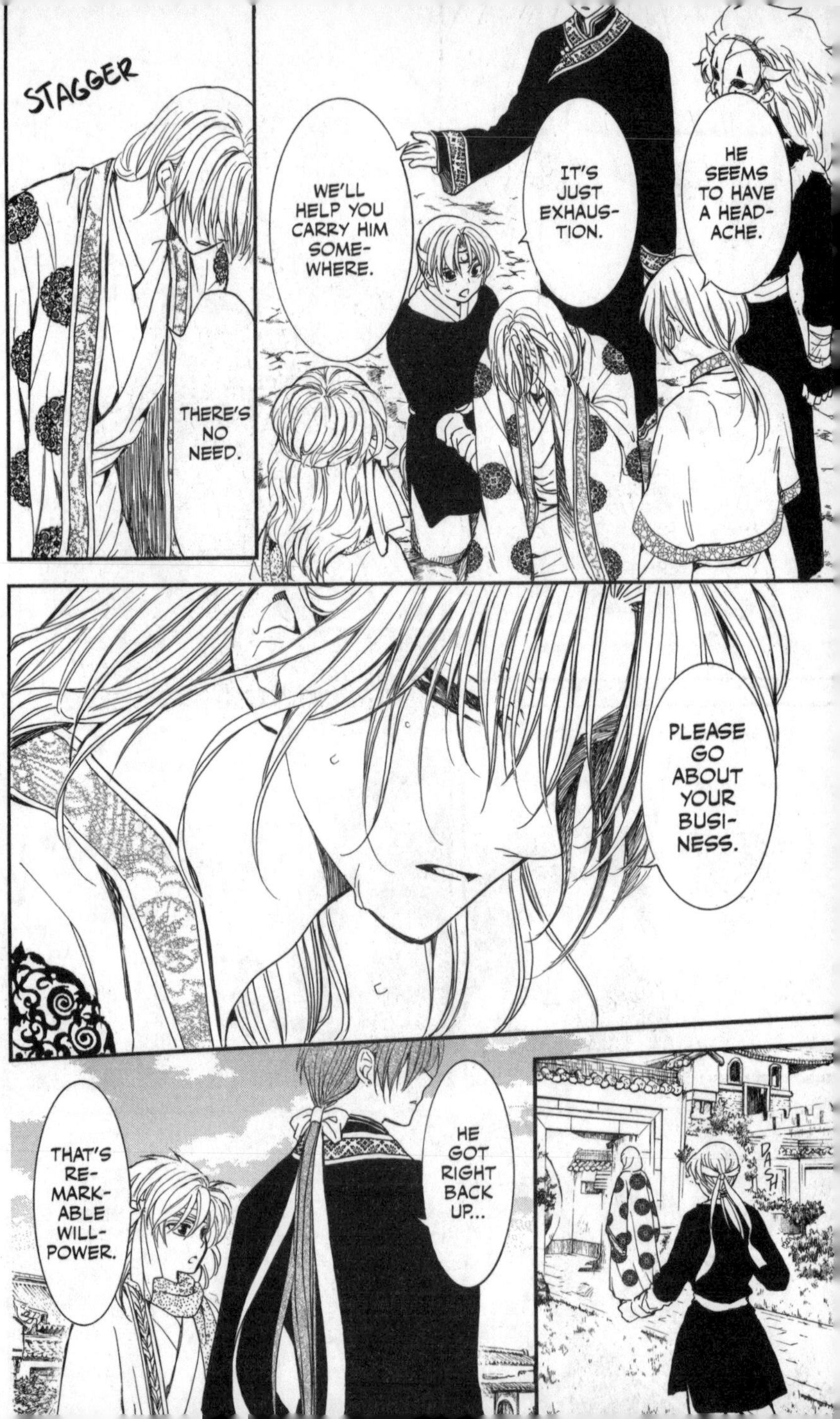
HE SEEMS TO HAVE A HEAD-ACHE.
IT'S JUST EXHAUS-TION.
WE'LL HELP YOU CARRY HIM SOME-WHERE.
STAGGER
THERE'S NO NEED.
PLEASE GO ABOUT YOUR BUSI-NESS.
DASH
HE GOT RIGHT BACK UP...
THAT'S RE-MARK-ABLE WILL-POWER.

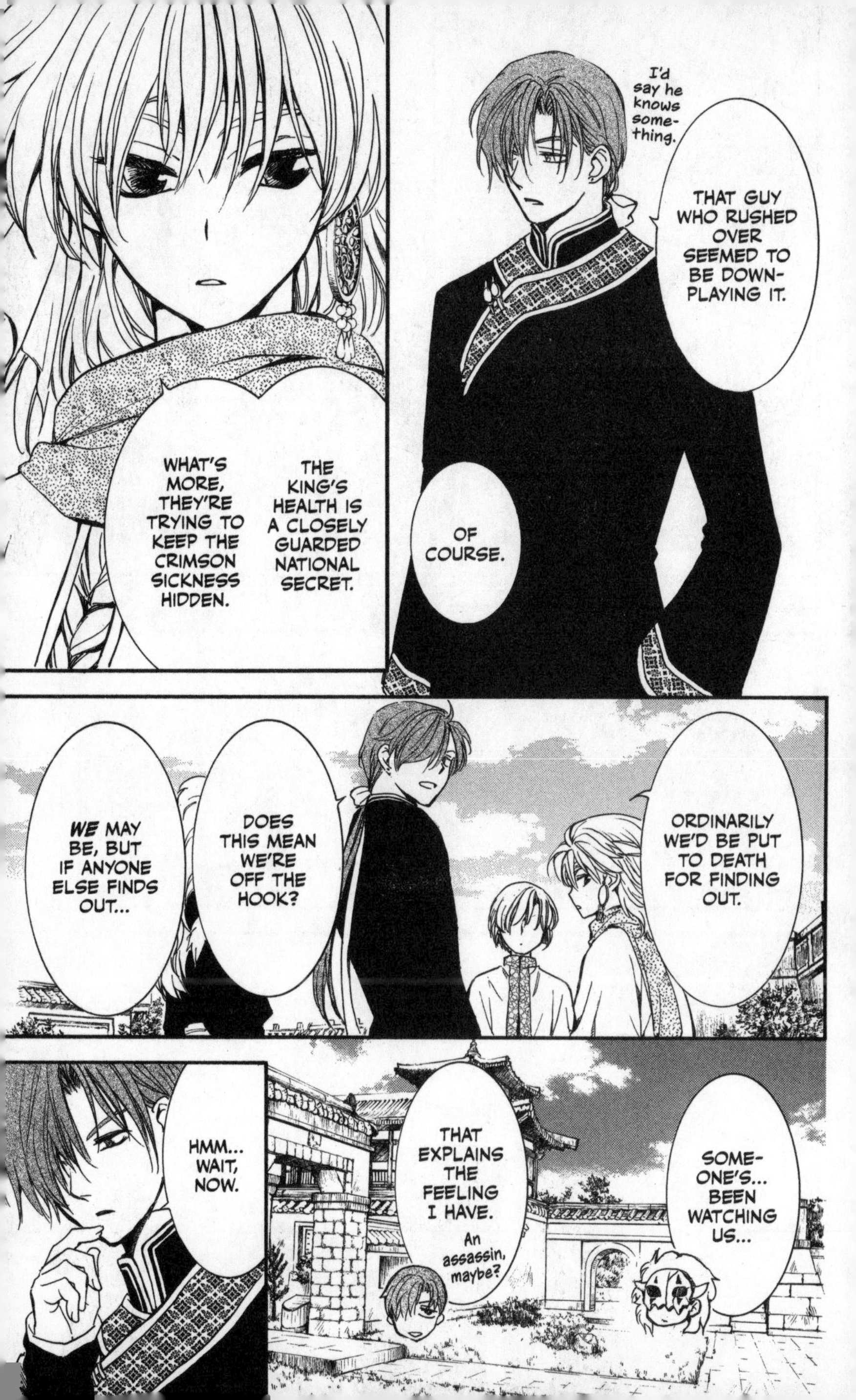
THAT GUY WHO RUSHED OVER SEEMED TO BE DOWN-PLAYING IT.
I'd say he knows some-thing.
OF COURSE.
THE KING'S HEALTH IS A CLOSELY GUARDED NATIONAL SECRET.
WHAT'S MORE, THEY'RE TRYING TO KEEP THE CRIMSON SICKNESS HIDDEN.
ORDINARILY WE'D BE PUT TO DEATH FOR FINDING OUT.
DOES THIS MEAN WE'RE OFF THE HOOK?
WE MAY BE, BUT IF ANYONE ELSE FINDS OUT...
SOME-ONE'S... BEEN WATCHING US...
THAT EXPLAINS THE FEELING I HAVE.
An assassin, maybe?
HMM... WAIT, NOW.

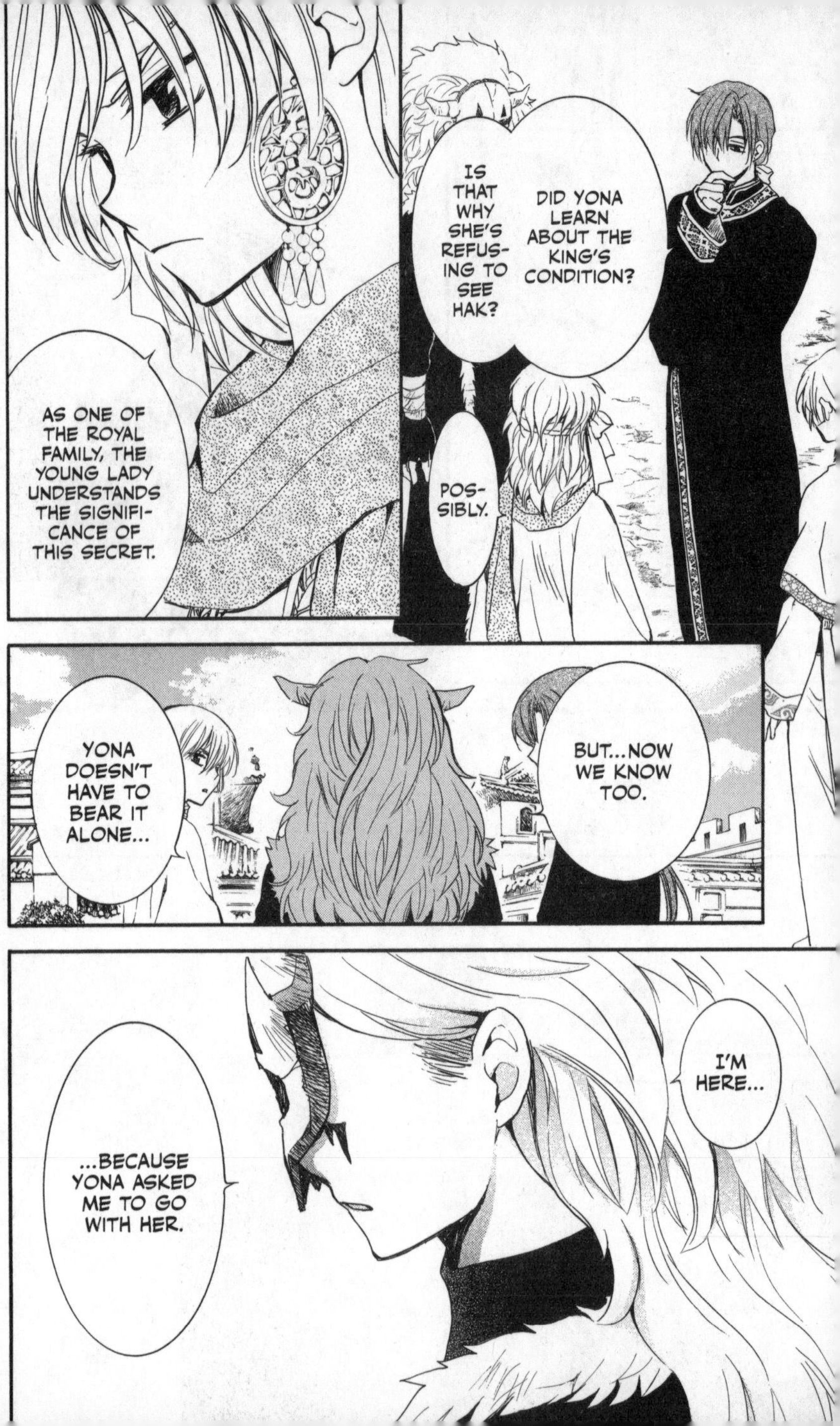
DID YONA LEARN ABOUT THE KING'S CONDITION?
IS THAT WHY SHE'S REFUS-ING TO SEE HAK?
POS-SIBLY.
AS ONE OF THE ROYAL FAMILY, THE YOUNG LADY UNDERSTANDS THE SIGNIFI-CANCE OF THIS SECRET.
BUT...NOW WE KNOW TOO.
YONA DOESN'T HAVE TO BEAR IT ALONE...
I'M HERE...
...BECAUSE YONA ASKED ME TO GO WITH HER.

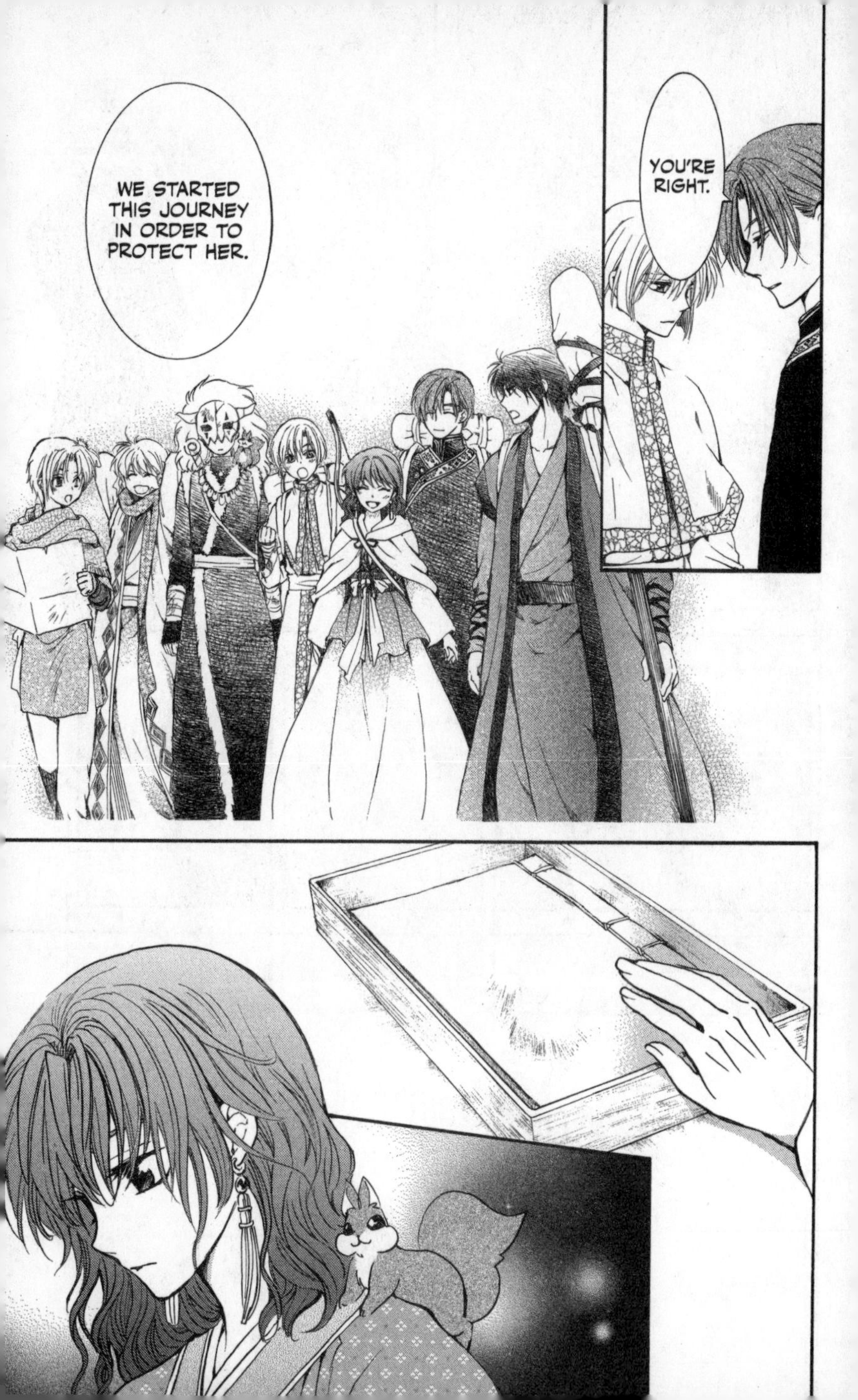
YOU'RE RIGHT.
WE STARTED THIS JOURNEY IN ORDER TO PROTECT HER.

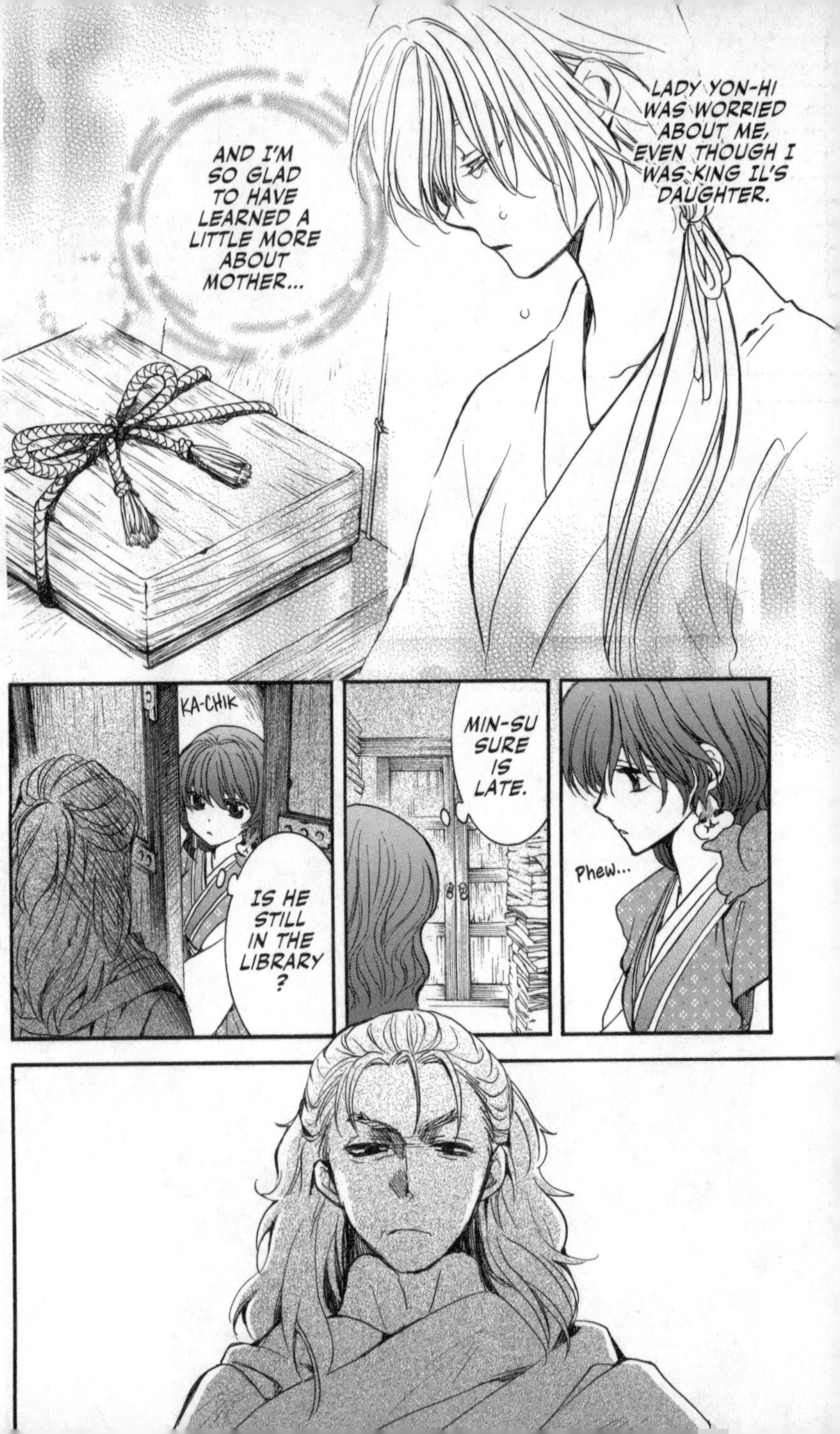
LADY YON-HI WAS WORRIED ABOUT ME, EVEN THOUGH I WAS KING IL'S DAUGHTER.
AND I'M SO GLAD TO HAVE LEARNED A LITTLE MORE ABOUT MOTHER...
Phew...
MIN-SU SURE IS LATE.
KA-CHIK
IS HE STILL IN THE LIBRARY?

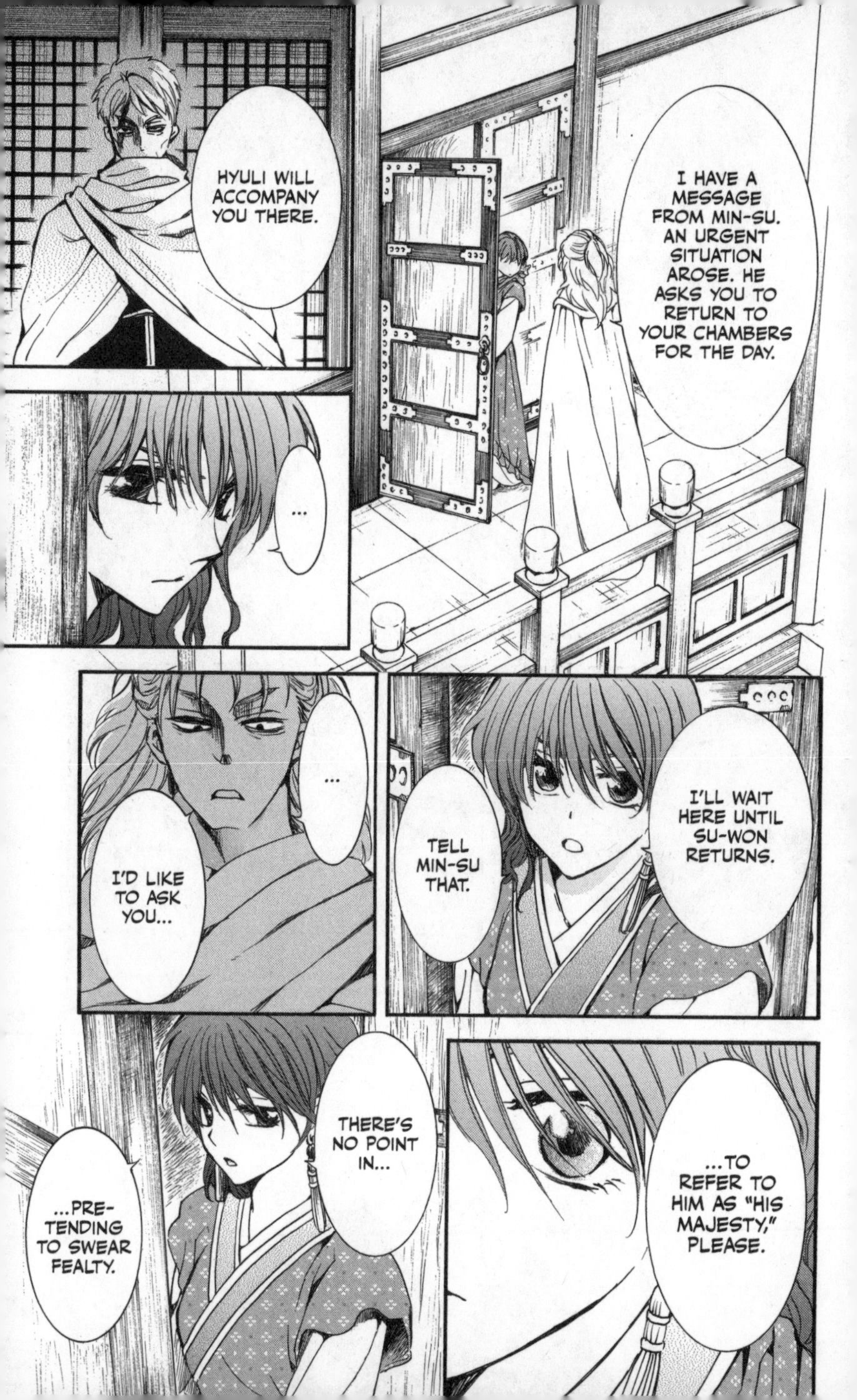
I HAVE A MESSAGE FROM MIN-SU. AN URGENT SITUATION AROSE. HE ASKS YOU TO RETURN TO YOUR CHAMBERS FOR THE DAY.
HYULI WILL ACCOMPANY YOU THERE.
...
I'LL WAIT HERE UNTIL SU-WON RETURNS.
TELL MIN-SU THAT.
...
I'D LIKE TO ASK YOU...
...TO REFER TO HIM AS "HIS MAJESTY," PLEASE.
THERE'S NO POINT IN...
...PRE-TENDING TO SWEAR FEALTY.

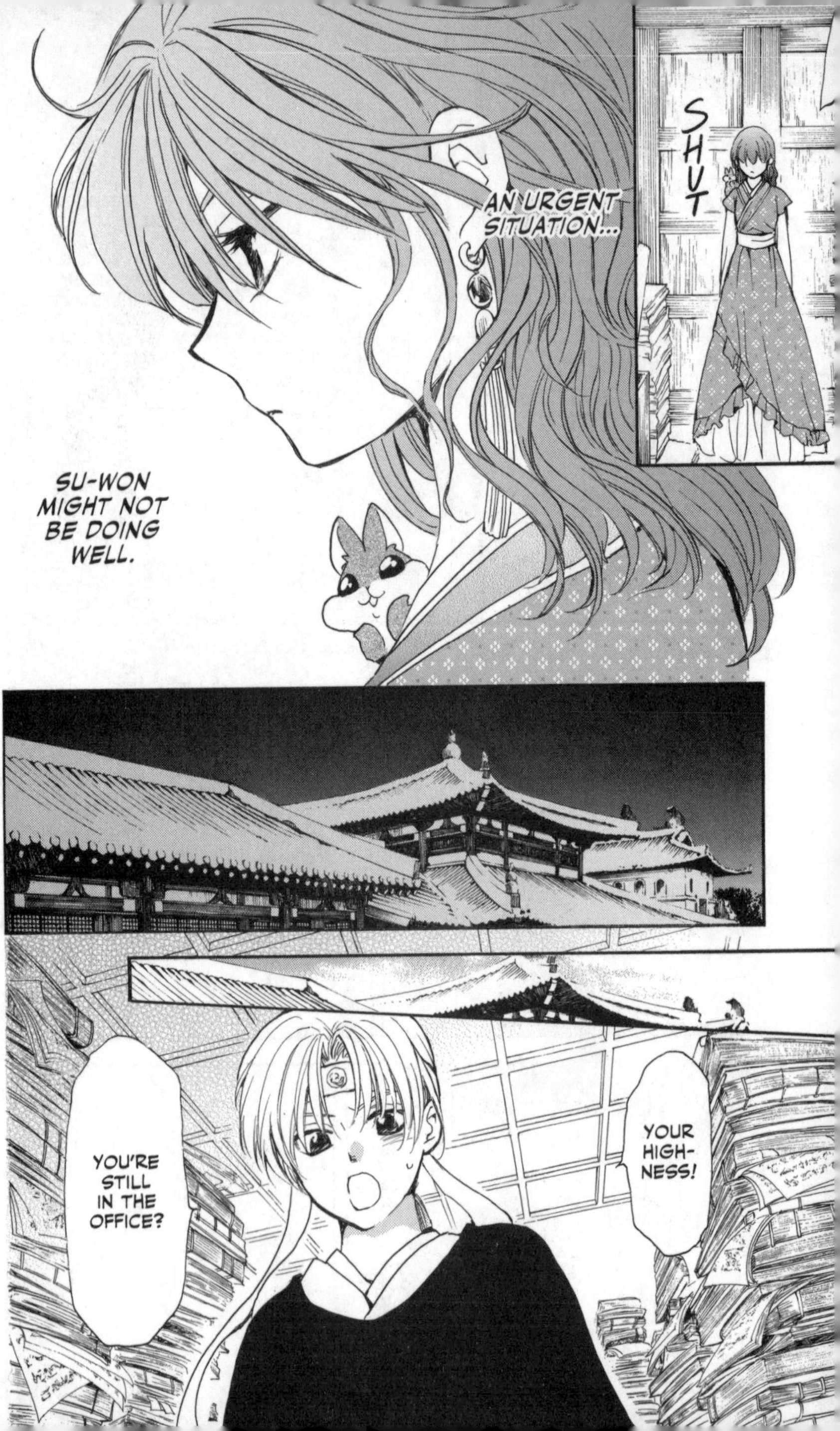
SHUT
AN URGENT SITUATION...
SU-WON MIGHT NOT BE DOING WELL.
YOUR HIGHNESS!
YOU'RE STILL IN THE OFFICE?

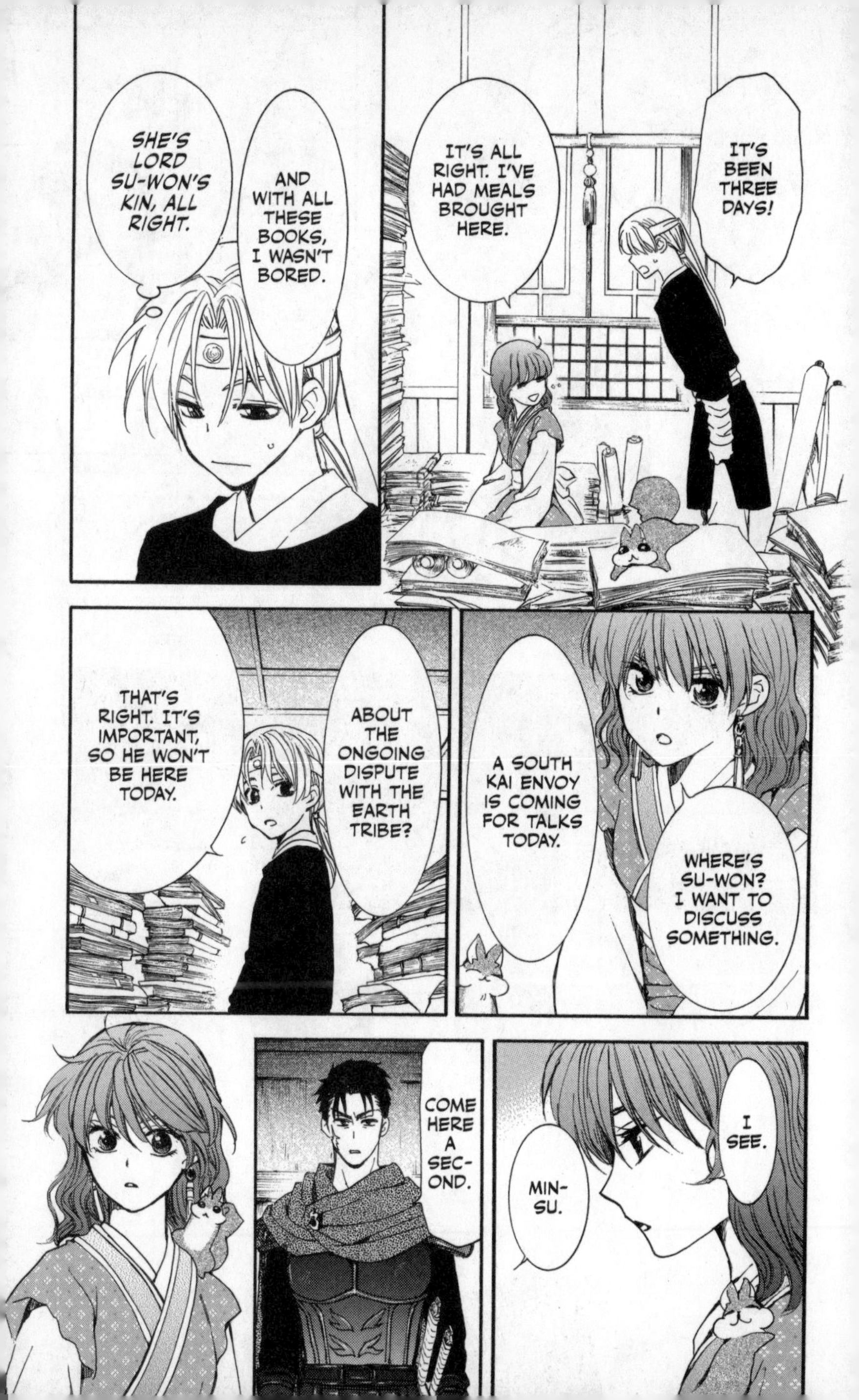
IT'S BEEN THREE DAYS!
IT'S ALL RIGHT. I'VE HAD MEALS BROUGHT HERE.
AND WITH ALL THESE BOOKS, I WASN'T BORED.
SHE'S LORD SU-WON'S KIN, ALL RIGHT.
WHERE'S SU-WON? I WANT TO DISCUSS SOMETHING.
A SOUTH KAI ENVOY IS COMING FOR TALKS TODAY.
ABOUT THE ONGOING DISPUTE WITH THE EARTH TRIBE?
THAT'S RIGHT. IT'S IMPORTANT, SO HE WON'T BE HERE TODAY.
I SEE.
MIN-SU.
COME HERE A SEC-OND.

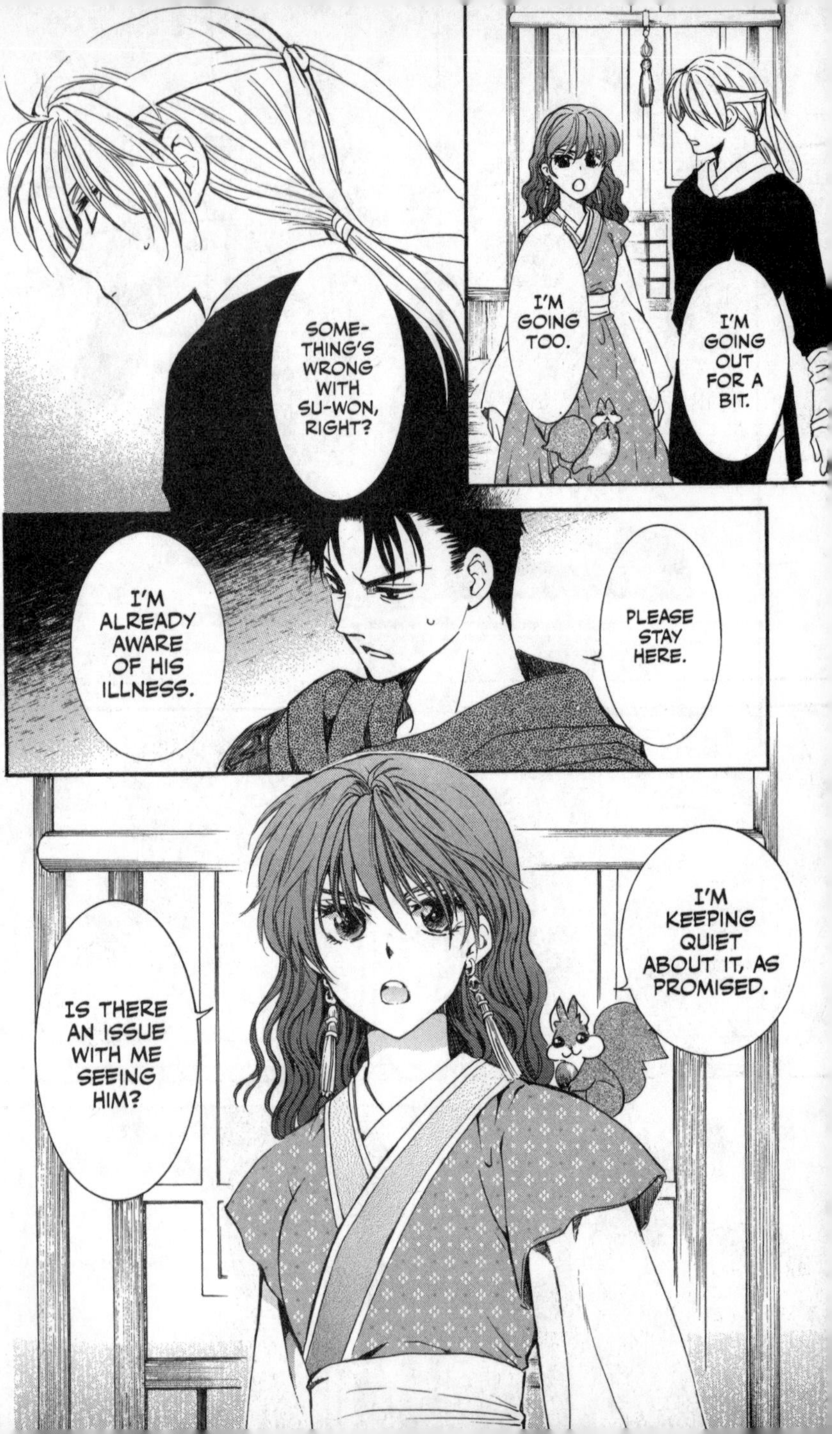
I'M GOING OUT FOR A BIT.
I'M GOING TOO.
SOMETHING'S WRONG WITH SU-WON, RIGHT?
PLEASE STAY HERE.
I'M ALREADY AWARE OF HIS ILLNESS.
I'M KEEPING QUIET ABOUT IT, AS PROMISED.
IS THERE AN ISSUE WITH ME SEEING HIM?

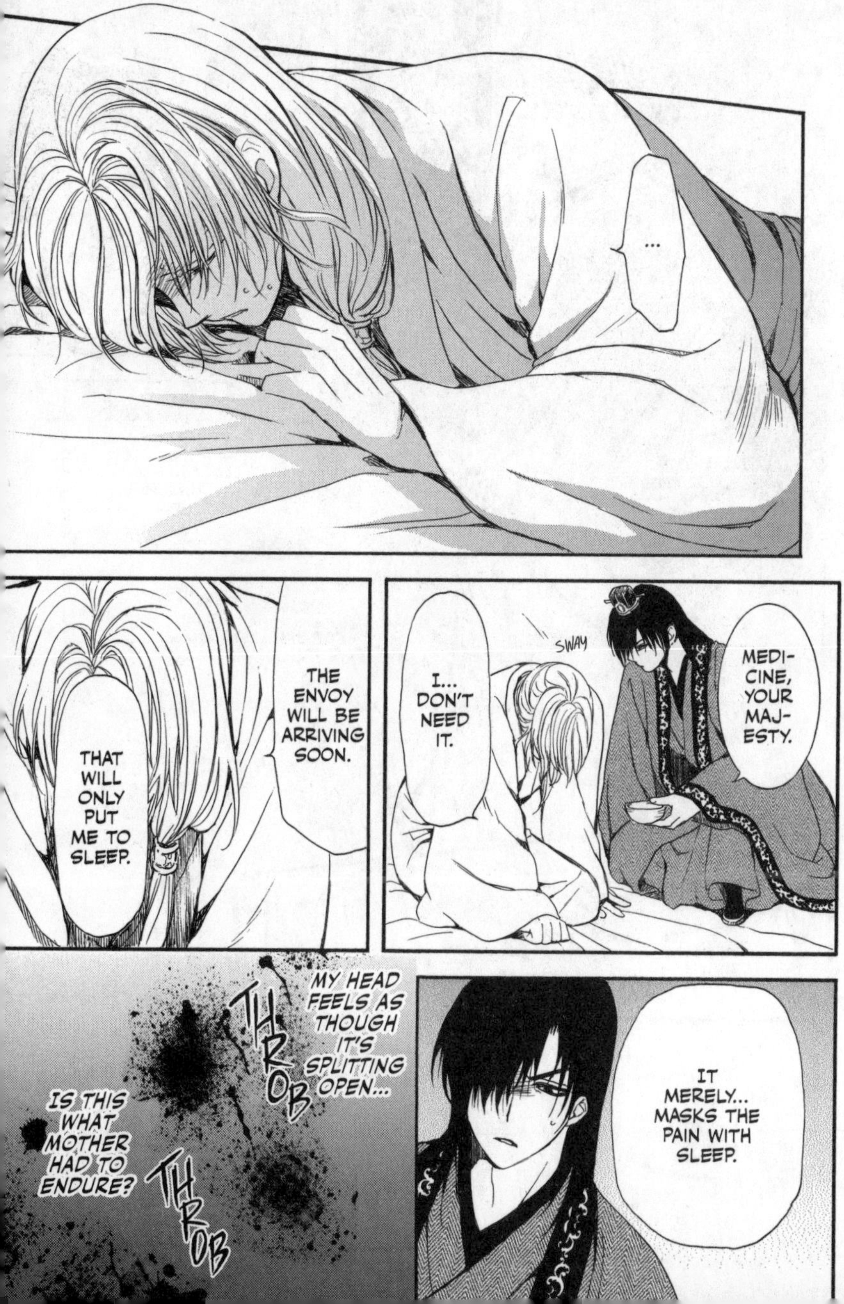
...
MEDICINE, YOUR MAJESTY.
SWAY
I... DON'T NEED IT.
THE ENVOY WILL BE ARRIVING SOON.
THAT WILL ONLY PUT ME TO SLEEP.
IT MERELY... MASKS THE PAIN WITH SLEEP.
MY HEAD FEELS AS THOUGH IT'S SPLITTING OPEN...
THROB
IS THIS WHAT MOTHER HAD TO ENDURE?
THROB

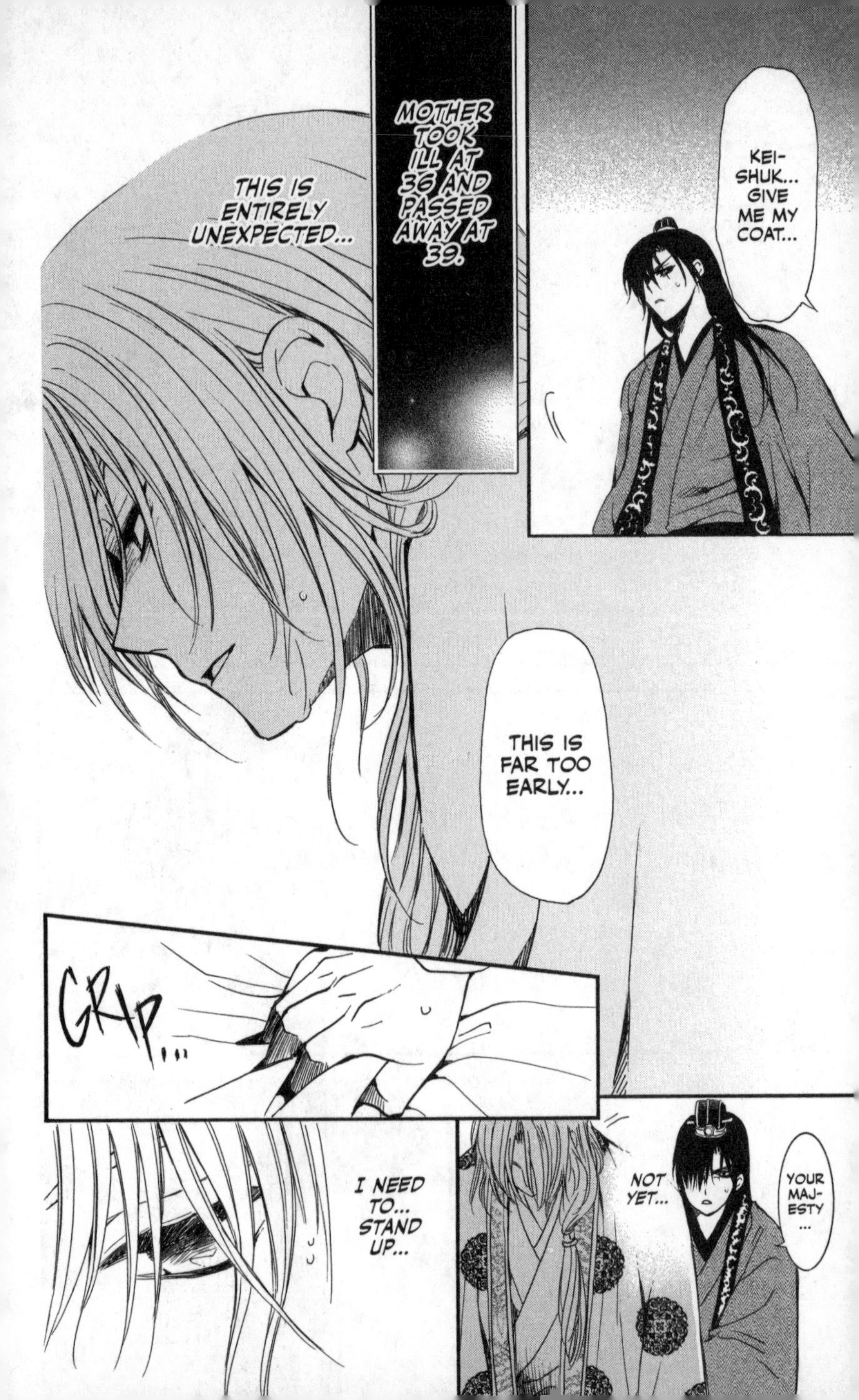
KEI-SHUK... GIVE ME MY COAT...
MOTHER TOOK ILL AT 36 AND PASSED AWAY AT 39.
THIS IS ENTIRELY UNEXPECTED...
THIS IS FAR TOO EARLY...
GRIP...
YOUR MAJ-ESTY...
NOT YET...
I NEED TO... STAND UP...

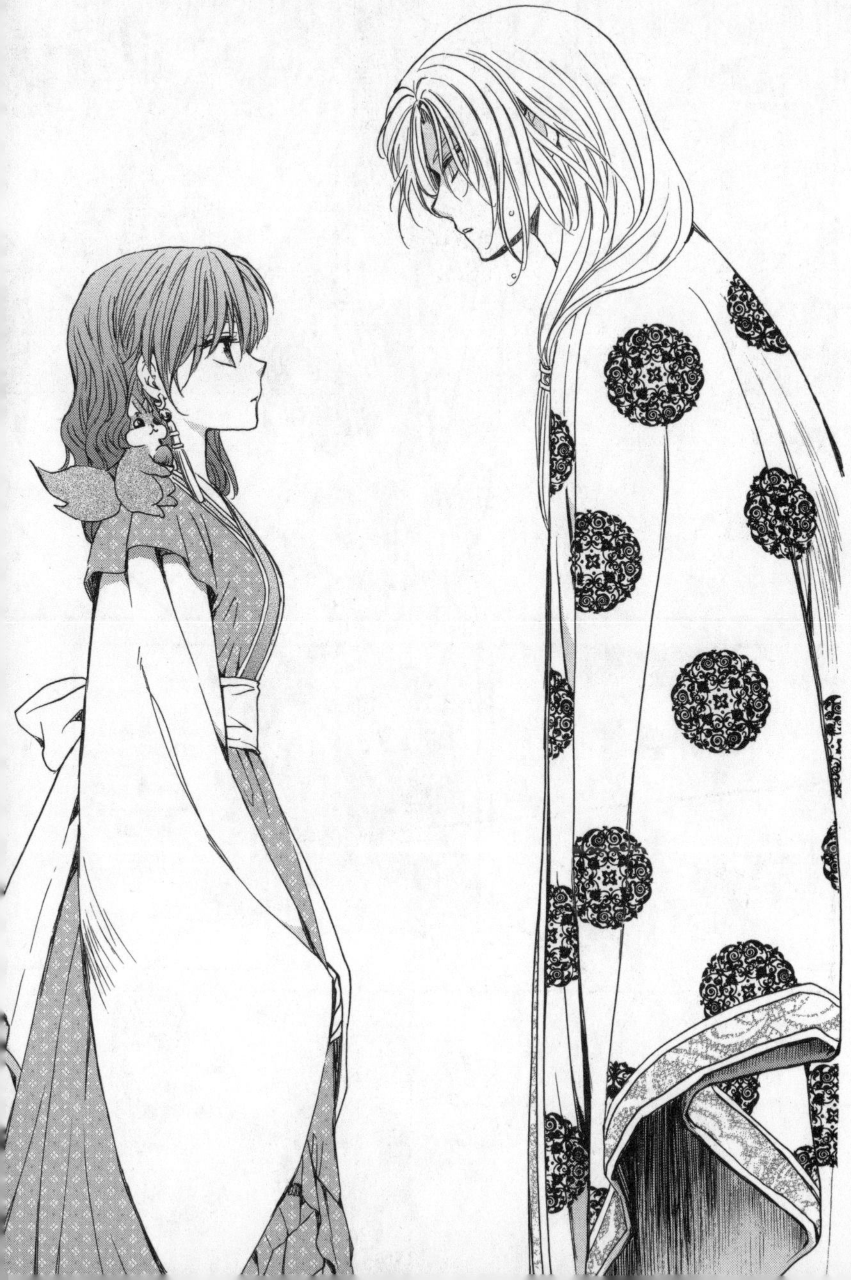

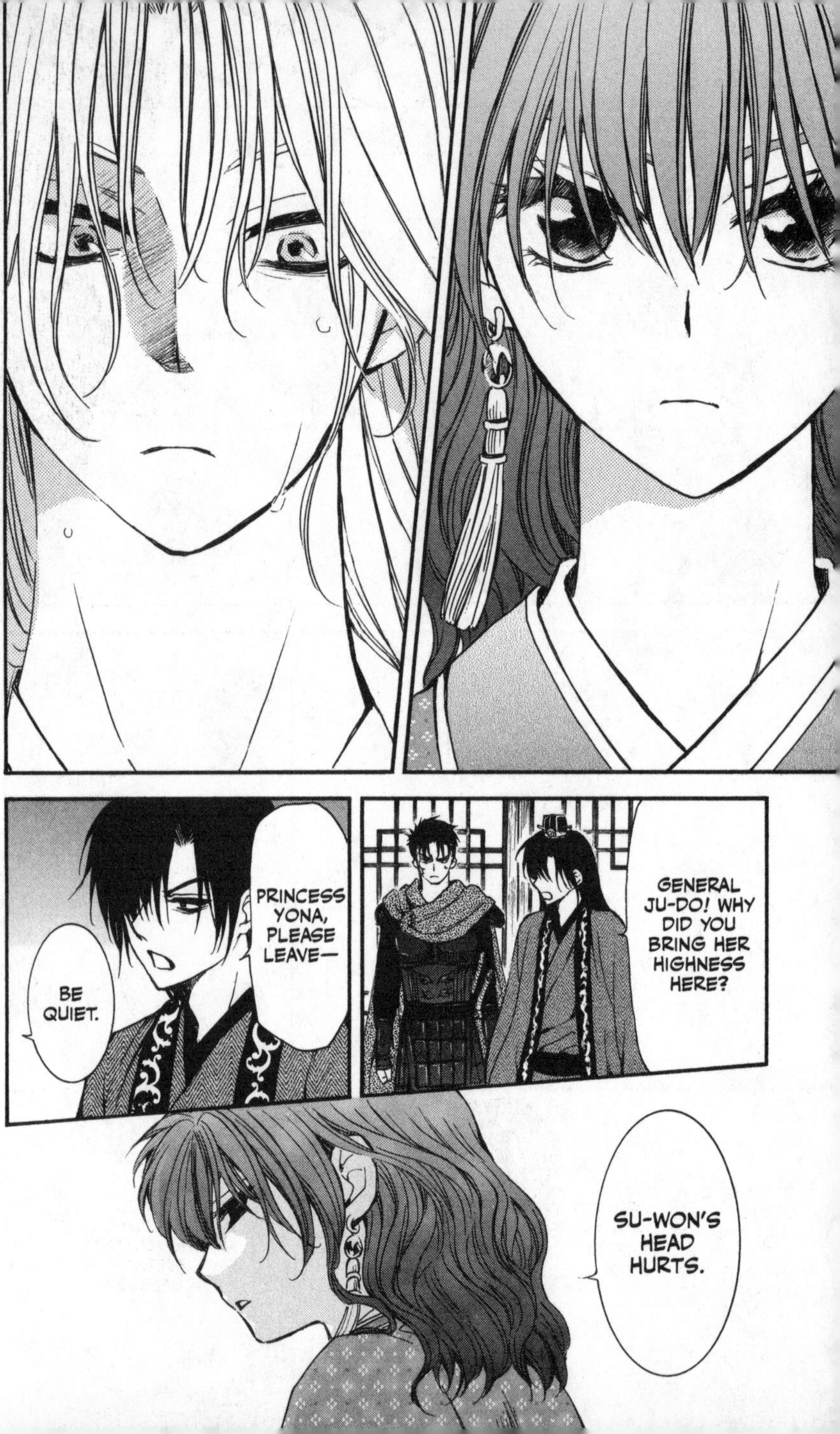
GENERAL JU-DO! WHY DID YOU BRING HER HIGHNESS HERE?
PRINCESS YONA, PLEASE LEAVE—
BE QUIET.
SU-WON'S HEAD HURTS.

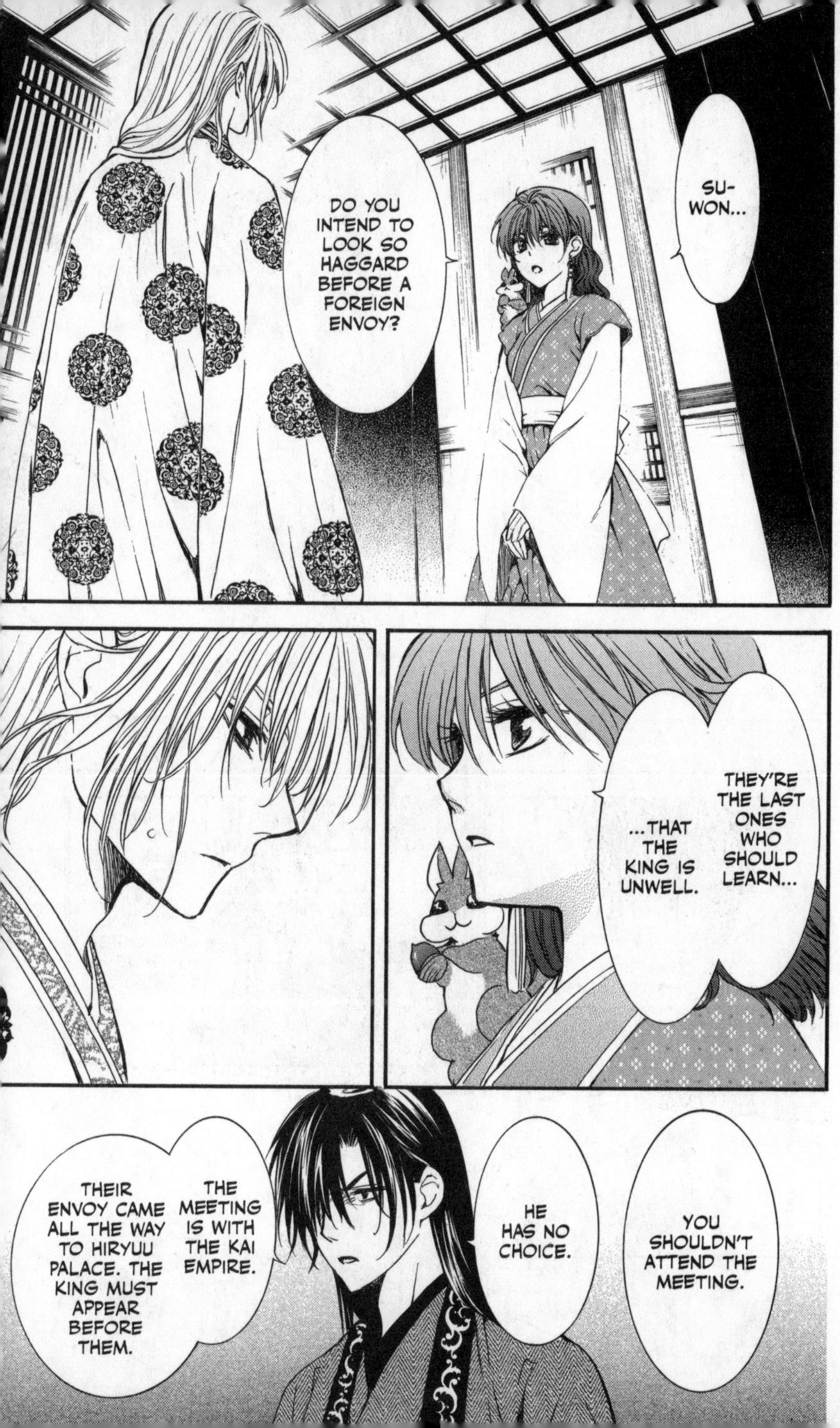
SU-WON...
DO YOU INTEND TO LOOK SO HAGGARD BEFORE A FOREIGN ENVOY?
THEY'RE THE LAST ONES WHO SHOULD LEARN...
...THAT THE KING IS UNWELL.
YOU SHOULDN'T ATTEND THE MEETING.
HE HAS NO CHOICE.
THE MEETING IS WITH THE KAI EMPIRE.
THEIR ENVOY CAME ALL THE WAY TO HIRYUU PALACE. THE KING MUST APPEAR BEFORE THEM.

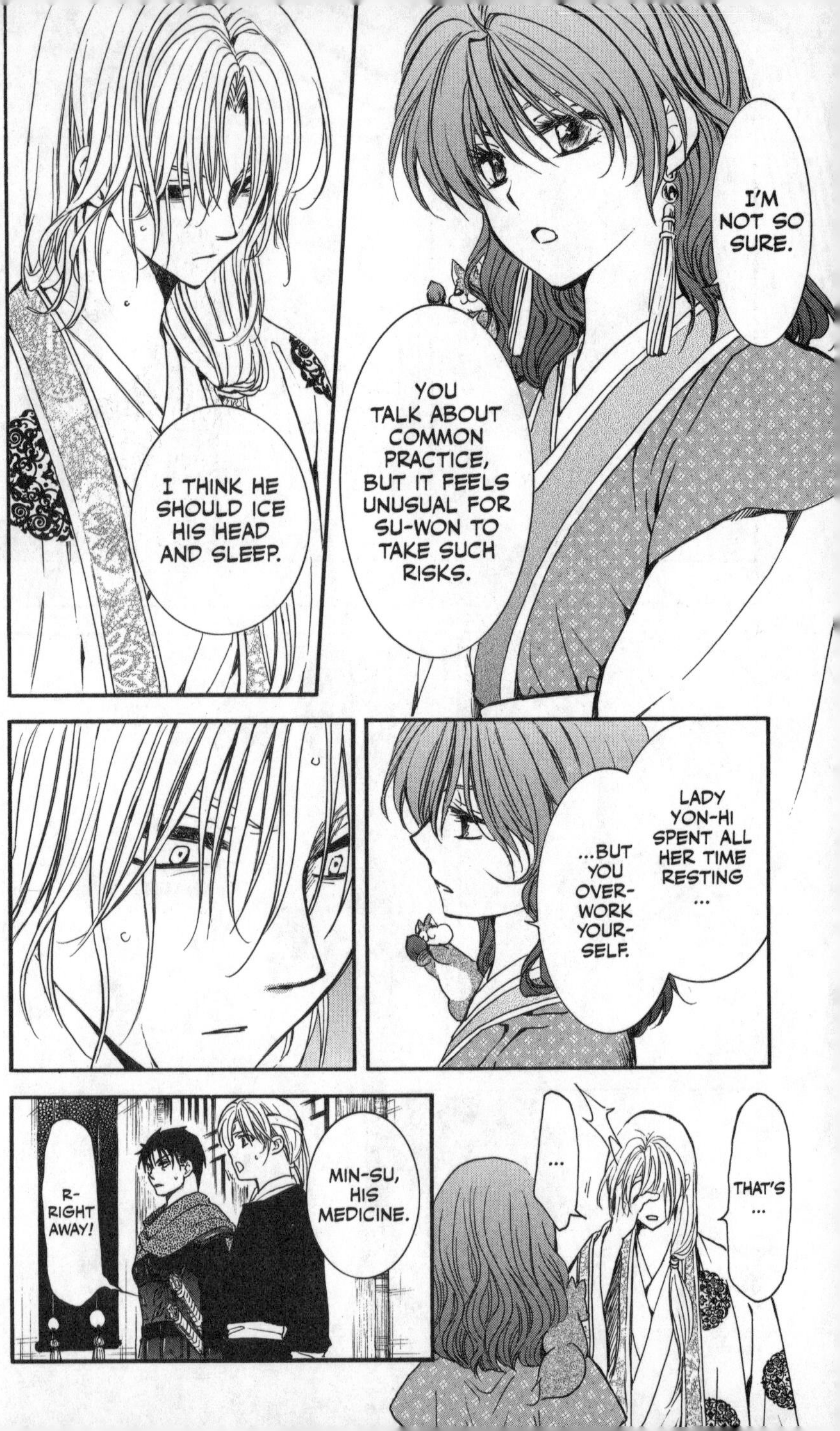
I'M NOT SO SURE.
YOU TALK ABOUT COMMON PRACTICE, BUT IT FEELS UNUSUAL FOR SU-WON TO TAKE SUCH RISKS.
I THINK HE SHOULD ICE HIS HEAD AND SLEEP.
LADY YON-HI SPENT ALL HER TIME RESTING ...
...BUT YOU OVER-WORK YOUR-SELF.
THAT'S ...
...
MIN-SU, HIS MEDICINE.
R-RIGHT AWAY!

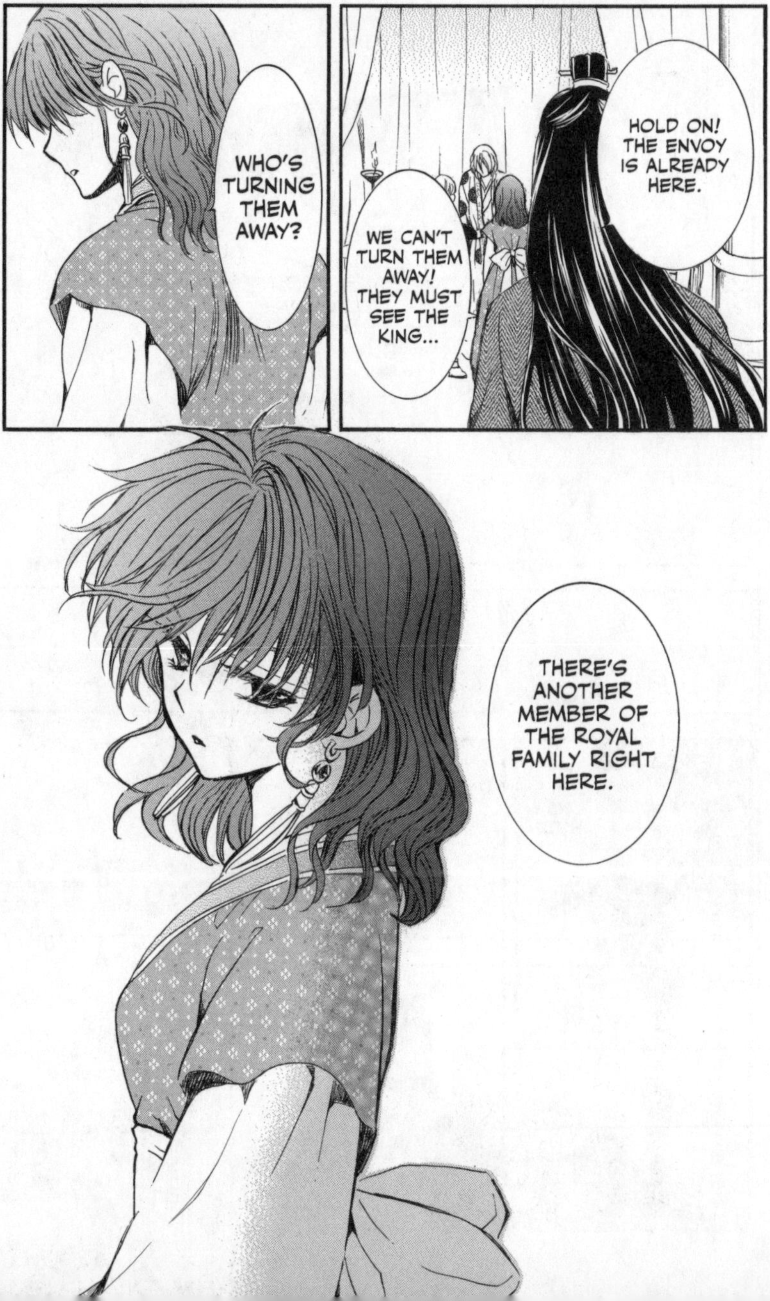
HOLD ON! THE ENVOY IS ALREADY HERE.
WE CAN'T TURN THEM AWAY! THEY MUST SEE THE KING...
WHO'S TURNING THEM AWAY?
THERE'S ANOTHER MEMBER OF THE ROYAL FAMILY RIGHT HERE.

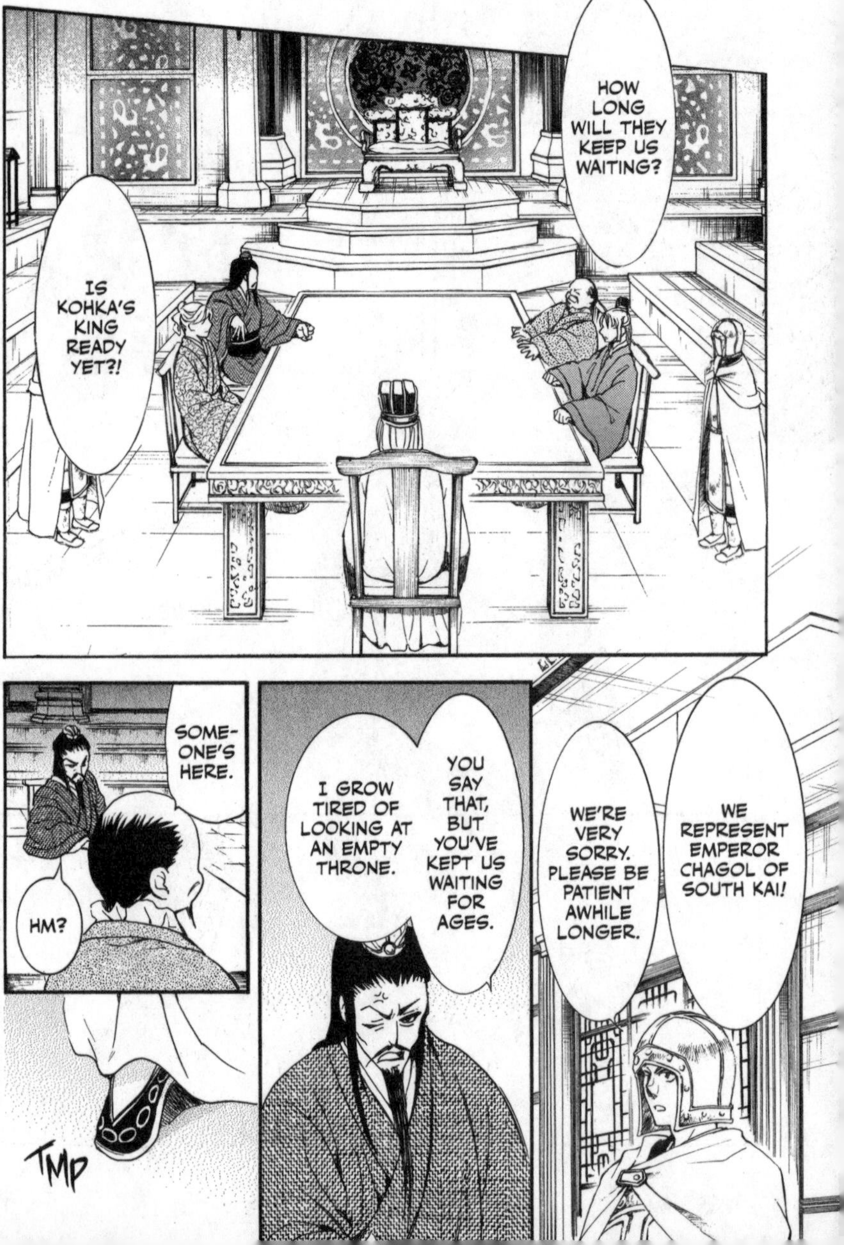
HOW LONG WILL THEY KEEP US WAITING?
IS KOHKA'S KING READY YET?!
WE REPRESENT EMPEROR CHAGOL OF SOUTH KAI!
WE'RE VERY SORRY. PLEASE BE PATIENT AWHILE LONGER.
YOU SAY THAT, BUT YOU'VE KEPT US WAITING FOR AGES.
I GROW TIRED OF LOOKING AT AN EMPTY THRONE.
SOME-ONE'S HERE.
HM?
TMP

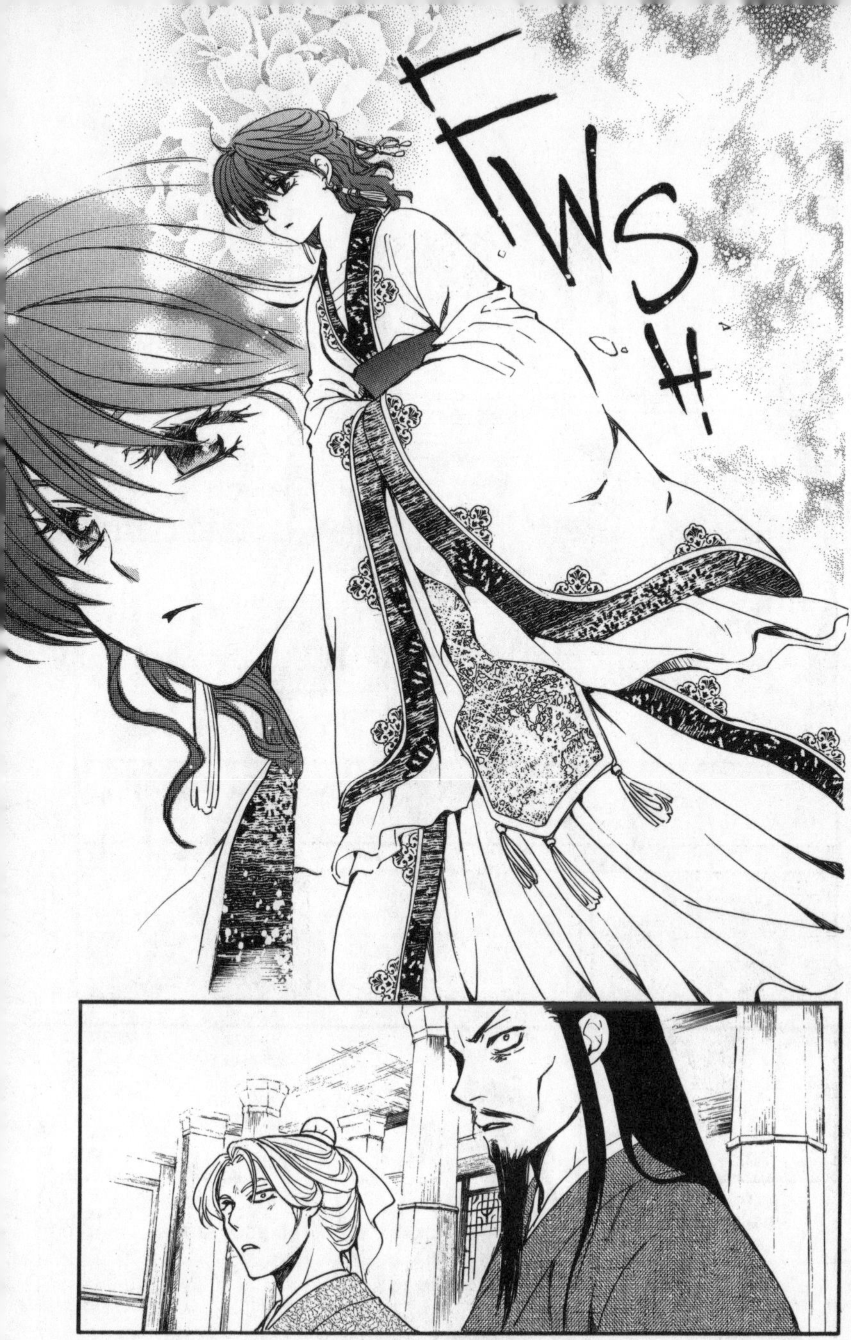
FWSH!

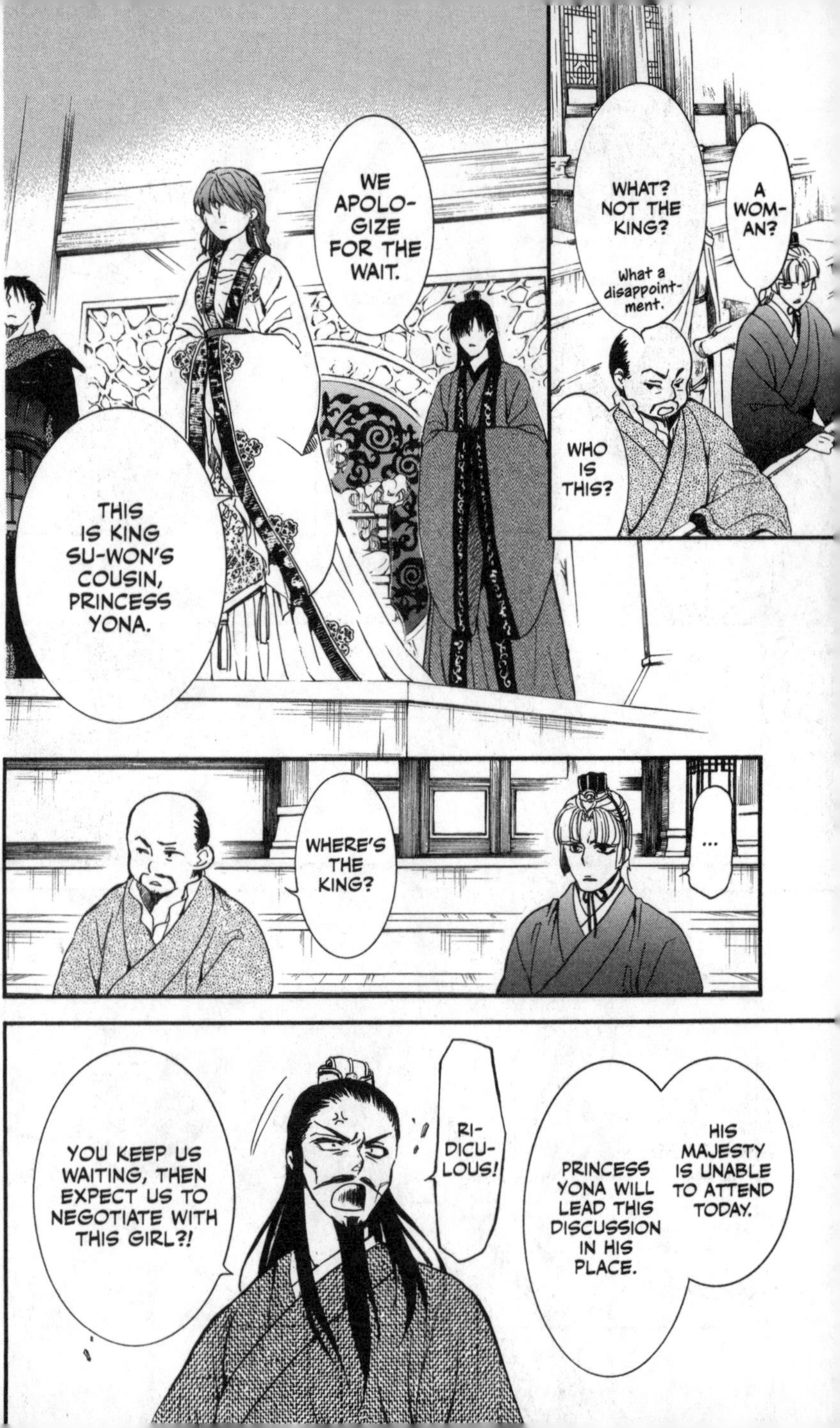
A WOMAN?
WHAT? NOT THE KING?
What a disappointment.
WHO IS THIS?
WE APOLOGIZE FOR THE WAIT.
THIS IS KING SU-WON'S COUSIN, PRINCESS YONA.
...
WHERE'S THE KING?
HIS MAJESTY IS UNABLE TO ATTEND TODAY.
PRINCESS YONA WILL LEAD THIS DISCUSSION IN HIS PLACE.
RIDICULOUS!
YOU KEEP US WAITING, THEN EXPECT US TO NEGOTIATE WITH THIS GIRL?!

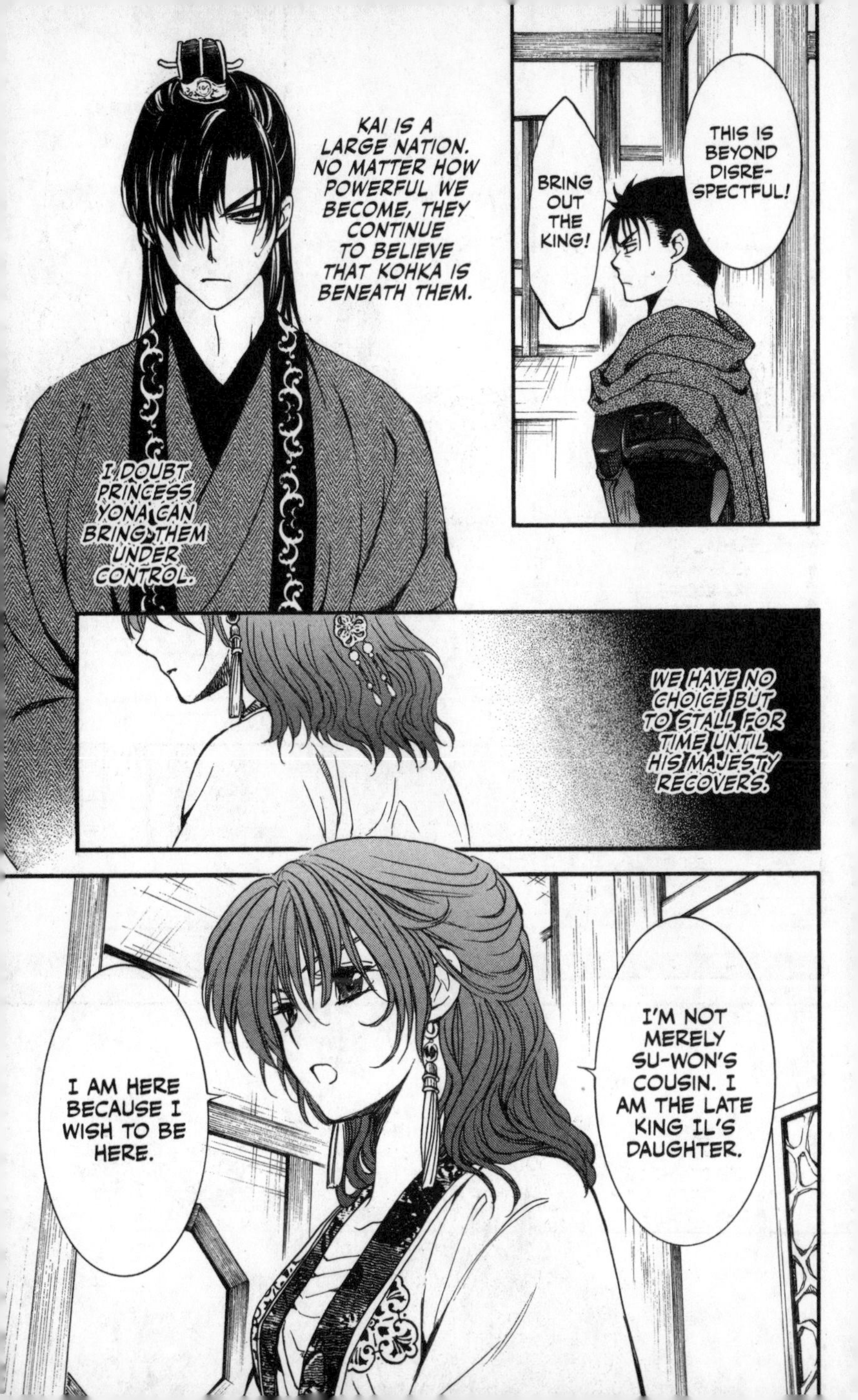
THIS IS BEYOND DISRE-SPECTFUL!
BRING OUT THE KING!
KAI IS A LARGE NATION. NO MATTER HOW POWERFUL WE BECOME, THEY CONTINUE TO BELIEVE THAT KOHKA IS BENEATH THEM.
I DOUBT PRINCESS YONA CAN BRING THEM UNDER CONTROL.
WE HAVE NO CHOICE BUT TO STALL FOR TIME UNTIL HIS MAJESTY RECOVERS.
I'M NOT MERELY SU-WON'S COUSIN. I AM THE LATE KING IL'S DAUGHTER.
I AM HERE BECAUSE I WISH TO BE HERE.

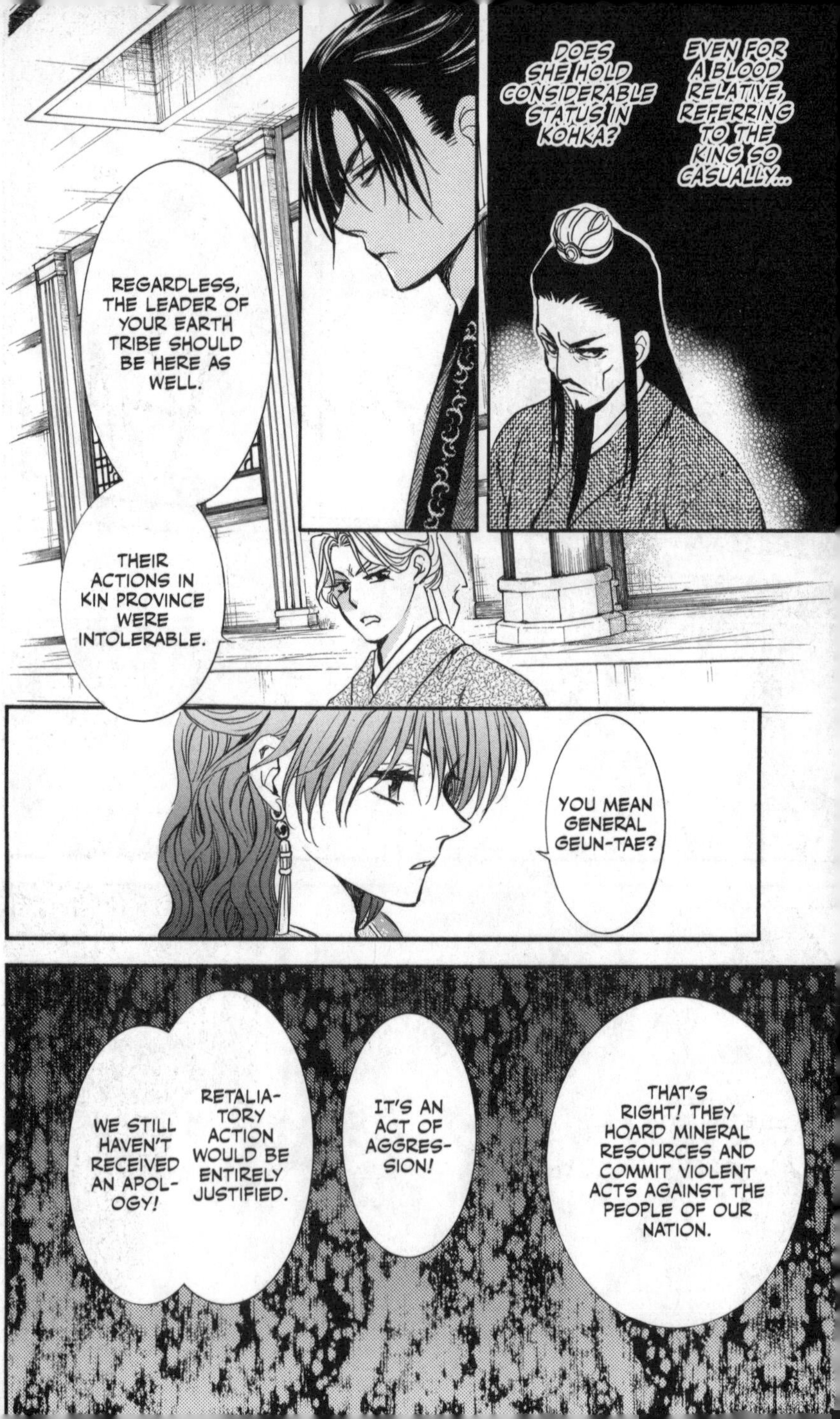
EVEN FOR A BLOOD RELATIVE, REFERRING TO THE KING SO CASUALLY...
DOES SHE HOLD CONSIDERABLE STATUS IN KOHKA?
REGARDLESS, THE LEADER OF YOUR EARTH TRIBE SHOULD BE HERE AS WELL.
THEIR ACTIONS IN KIN PROVINCE WERE INTOLERABLE.
YOU MEAN GENERAL GEUN-TAE?
THAT'S RIGHT! THEY HOARD MINERAL RESOURCES AND COMMIT VIOLENT ACTS AGAINST THE PEOPLE OF OUR NATION.
IT'S AN ACT OF AGGRES-SION!
RETALIA-TORY ACTION WOULD BE ENTIRELY JUSTIFIED.
WE STILL HAVEN'T RECEIVED AN APOLO-OGY!

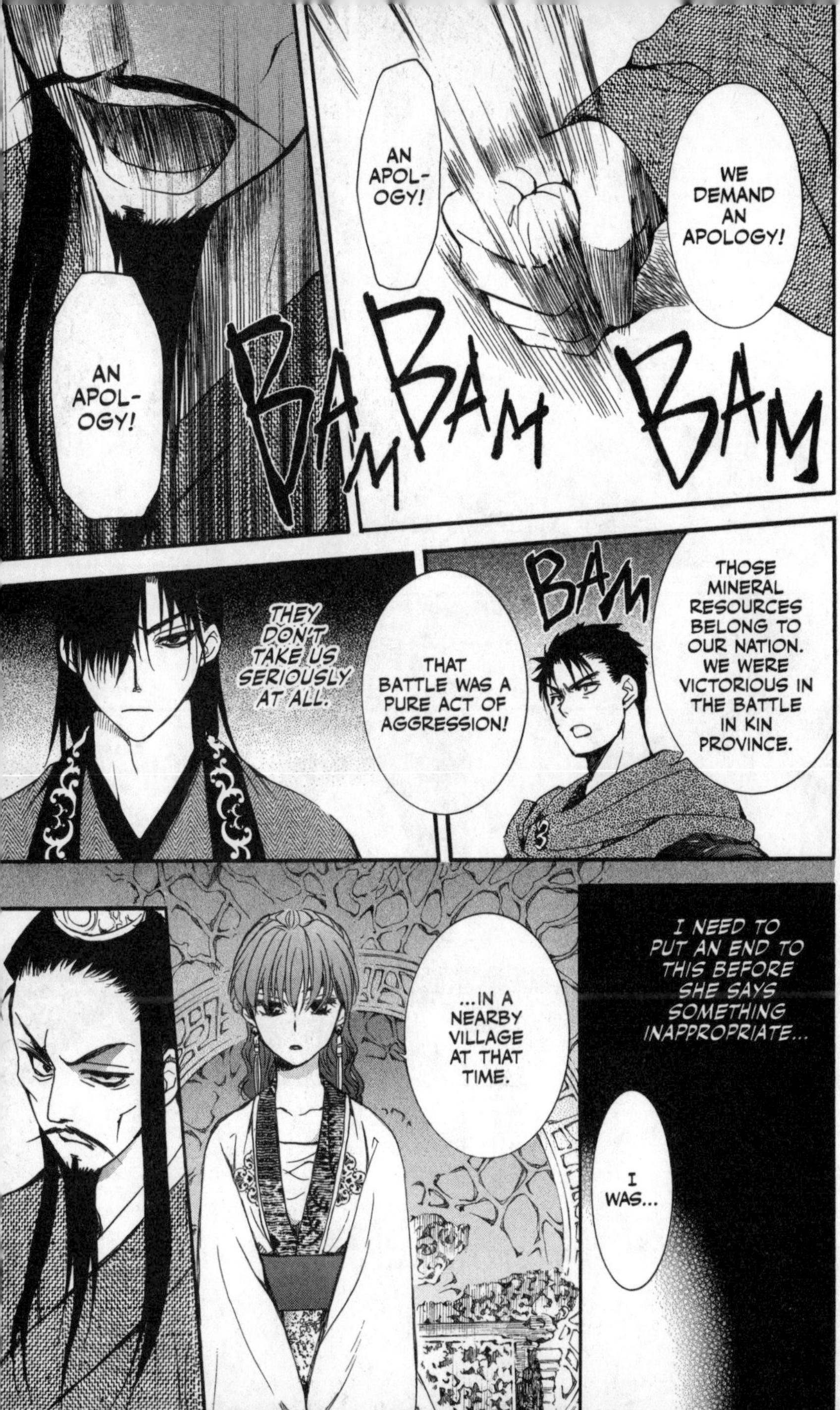
WE DEMAND AN APOLOGY!
AN APOLOGY!
BAM BAM BAM
AN APOLOGY!
THOSE MINERAL RESOURCES BELONG TO OUR NATION. WE WERE VICTORIOUS IN THE BATTLE IN KIN PROVINCE.
BAM
THAT BATTLE WAS A PURE ACT OF AGGRESSION!
THEY DON'T TAKE US SERIOUSLY AT ALL.
I NEED TO PUT AN END TO THIS BEFORE SHE SAYS SOMETHING INAPPROPRIATE...
I WAS...
...IN A NEARBY VILLAGE AT THAT TIME.

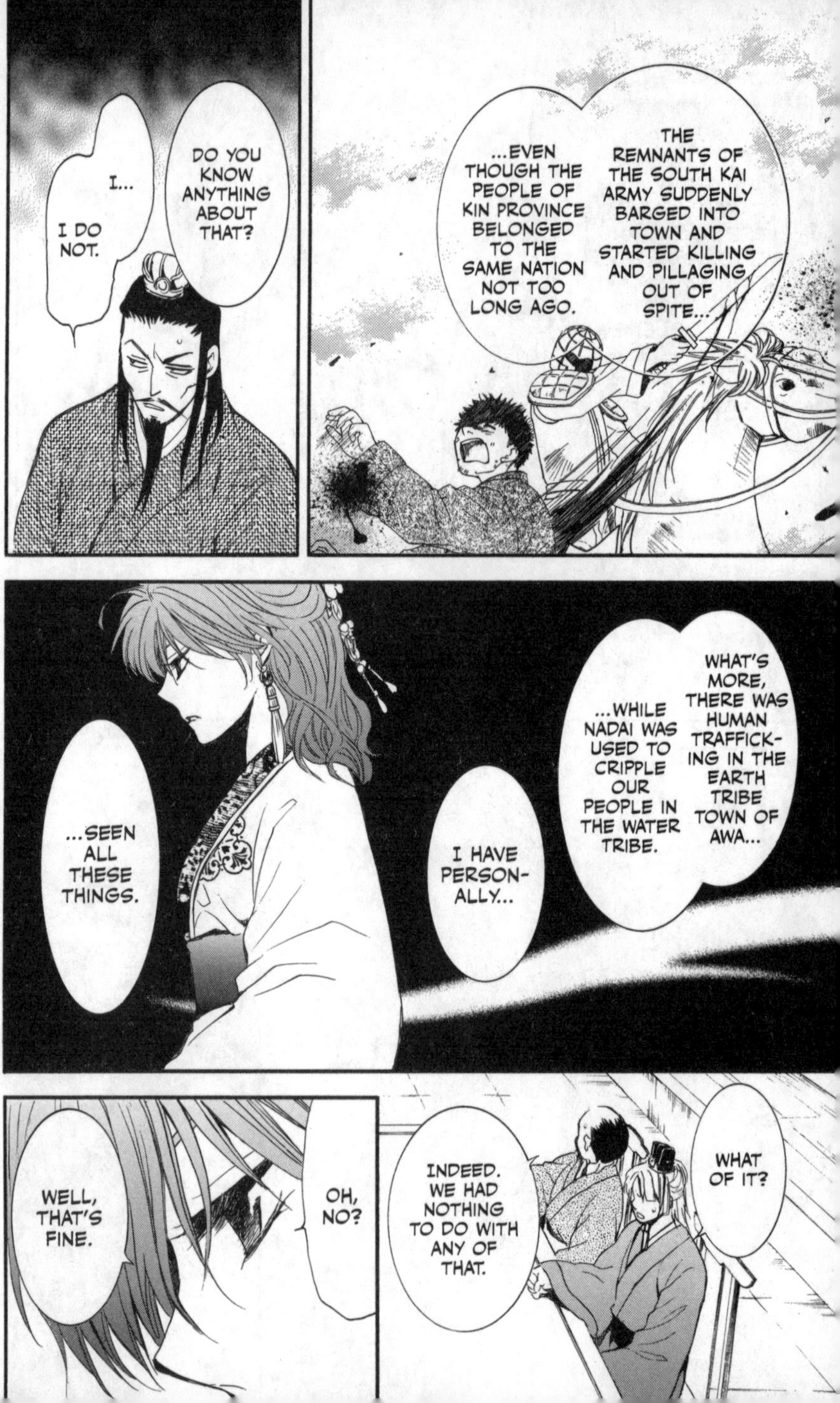
THE REMNANTS OF THE SOUTH KAI ARMY SUDDENLY BARGED INTO TOWN AND STARTED KILLING AND PILLAGING OUT OF SPITE...
...EVEN THOUGH THE PEOPLE OF KIN PROVINCE BELONGED TO THE SAME NATION NOT TOO LONG AGO.
DO YOU KNOW ANYTHING ABOUT THAT?
I... I DO NOT.
WHAT'S MORE, THERE WAS HUMAN TRAFFICK-ING IN THE EARTH TRIBE TOWN OF AWA...
...WHILE NADAI WAS USED TO CRIPPLE OUR PEOPLE IN THE WATER TRIBE.
I HAVE PERSON-ALLY...
...SEEN ALL THESE THINGS.
WHAT OF IT?
INDEED. WE HAD NOTHING TO DO WITH ANY OF THAT.
OH, NO?
WELL, THAT'S FINE.

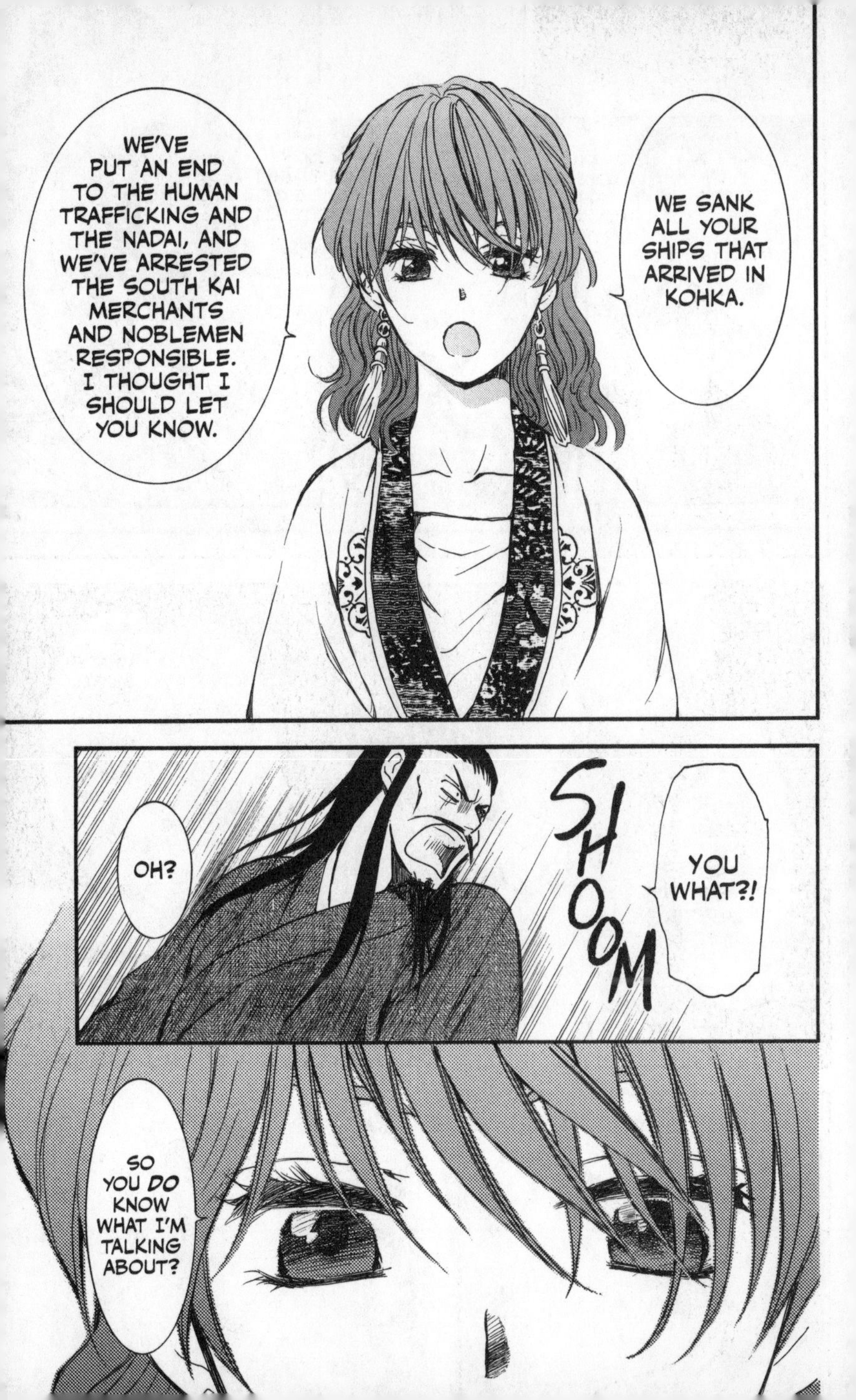
WE SANK ALL YOUR SHIPS THAT ARRIVED IN KOHKA.
WE'VE PUT AN END TO THE HUMAN TRAFFICKING AND THE NADAI, AND WE'VE ARRESTED THE SOUTH KAI MERCHANTS AND NOBLEMEN RESPONSIBLE. I THOUGHT I SHOULD LET YOU KNOW.
YOU WHAT?!
SHOOM
OH?
SO YOU *DO* KNOW WHAT I'M TALKING ABOUT?

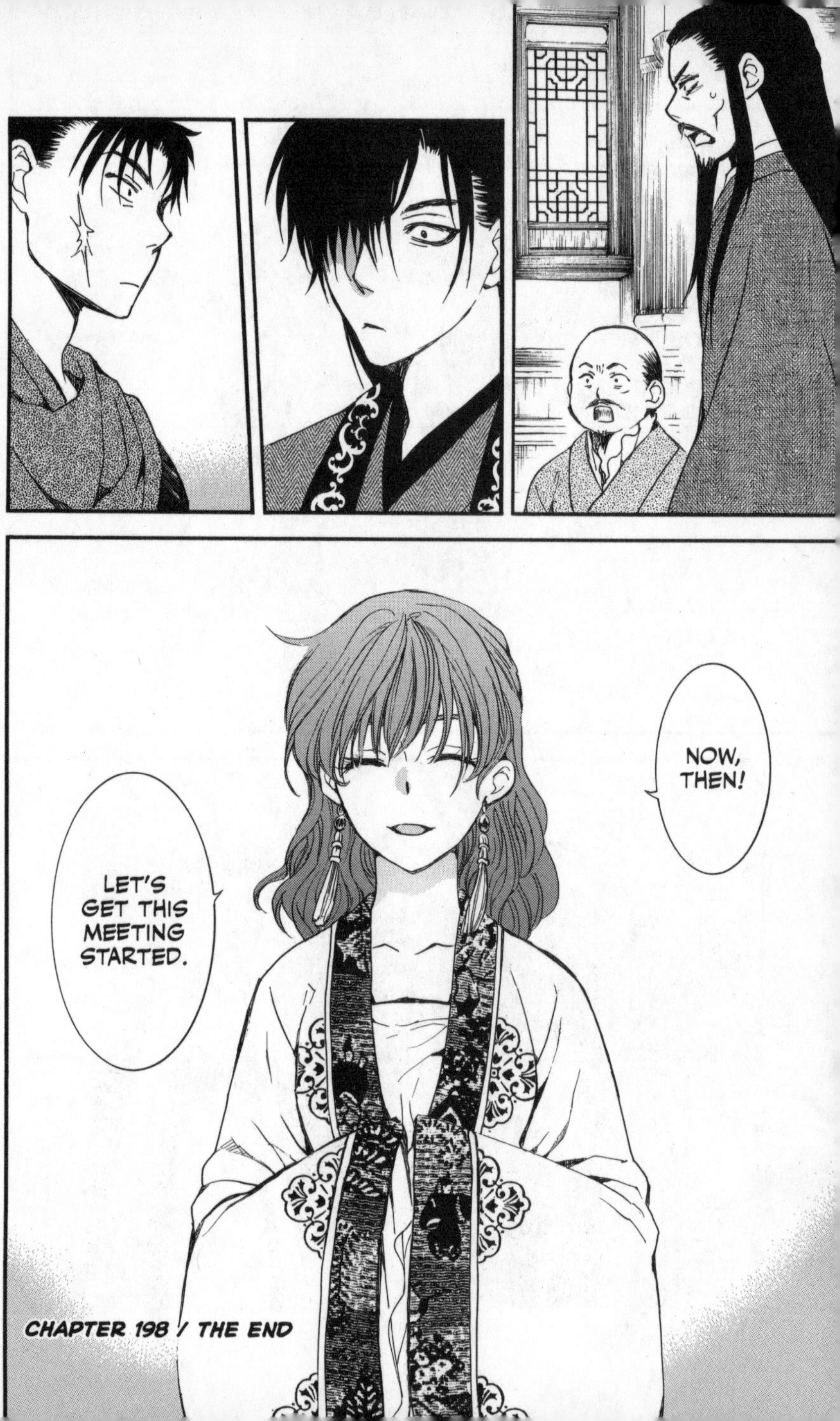
NOW, THEN!
LET'S GET THIS MEETING STARTED.
CHAPTER 198 / THE END

Afterword

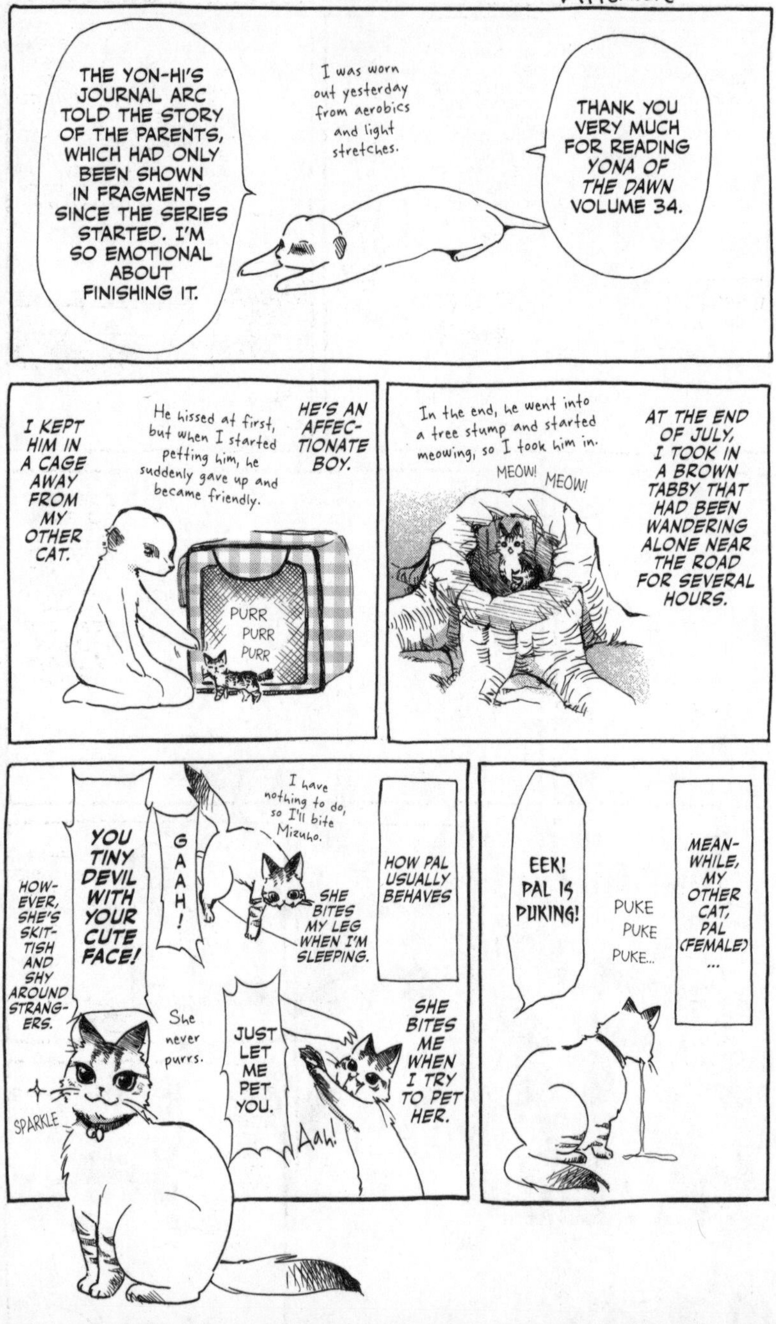
THANK YOU VERY MUCH FOR READING *YONA OF THE DAWN* VOLUME 34.
I was worn out yesterday from aerobics and light stretches.
THE YON-HI'S JOURNAL ARC TOLD THE STORY OF THE PARENTS, WHICH HAD ONLY BEEN SHOWN IN FRAGMENTS SINCE THE SERIES STARTED. I'M SO EMOTIONAL ABOUT FINISHING IT.
AT THE END OF JULY, I TOOK IN A BROWN TABBY THAT HAD BEEN WANDERING ALONE NEAR THE ROAD FOR SEVERAL HOURS.
In the end, he went into a tree stump and started meowing, so I took him in.
MEOW! MEOW!
HE'S AN AFFECTIONATE BOY.
He hissed at first, but when I started petting him, he suddenly gave up and became friendly.
I KEPT HIM IN A CAGE AWAY FROM MY OTHER CAT.
PURR PURR PURR
MEANWHILE, MY OTHER CAT, PAL (FEMALE)...
PUKE PUKE PUKE...
EEK! PAL IS PUKING!
HOW PAL USUALLY BEHAVES
I have nothing to do, so I'll bite Mizuho.
SHE BITES MY LEG WHEN I'M SLEEPING.
GAAH!
YOU TINY DEVIL WITH YOUR CUTE FACE!
SHE BITES ME WHEN I TRY TO PET HER.
JUST LET ME PET YOU.
Aah!
She never purrs.
HOWEVER, SHE'S SKITTISH AND SHY AROUND STRANGERS.
SPARKLE

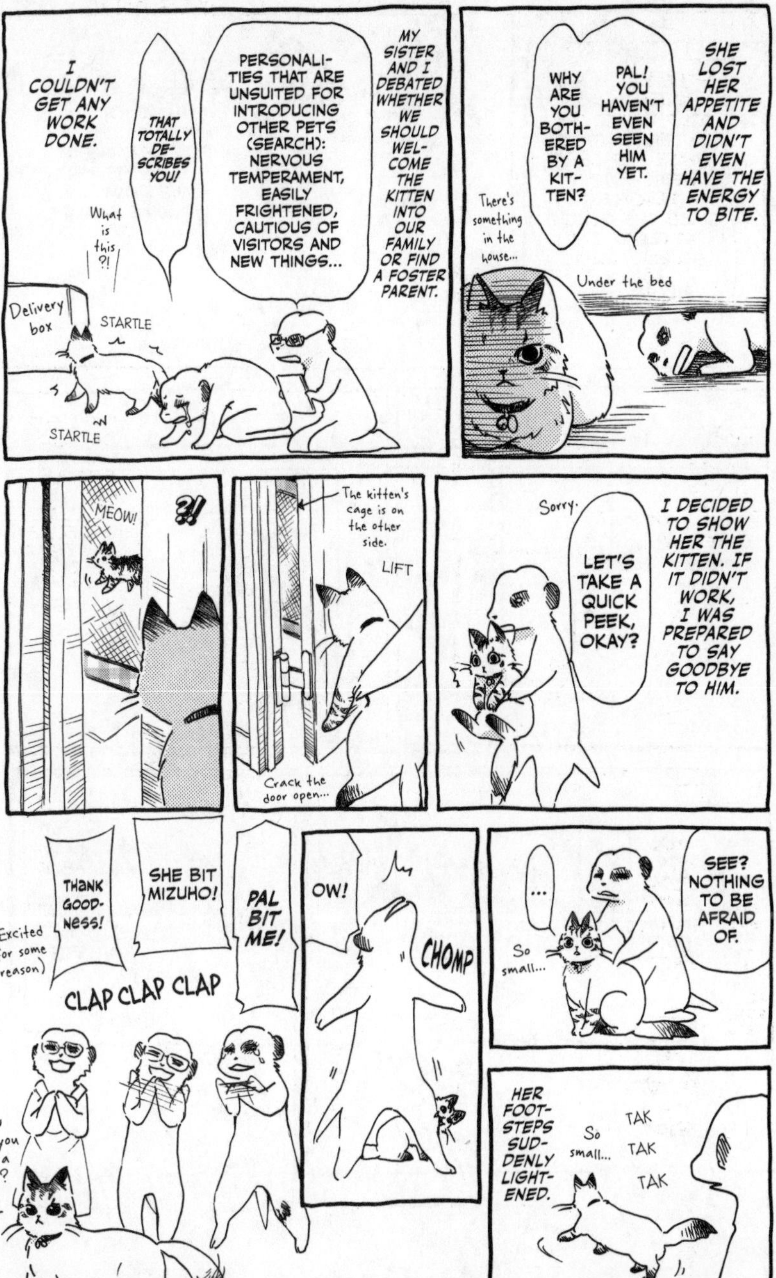
SHE LOST HER APPETITE AND DIDN'T EVEN HAVE THE ENERGY TO BITE.
PAL! YOU HAVEN'T EVEN SEEN HIM YET.
WHY ARE YOU BOTH-ERED BY A KIT-TEN?
There's something in the house...
Under the bed
MY SISTER AND I DEBATED WHETHER WE SHOULD WEL-COME THE KITTEN INTO OUR FAMILY OR FIND A FOSTER PARENT.
PERSONALI-TIES THAT ARE UNSUITED FOR INTRODUCING OTHER PETS (SEARCH): NERVOUS TEMPERAMENT, EASILY FRIGHTENED, CAUTIOUS OF VISITORS AND NEW THINGS...
THAT TOTALLY DE-SCRIBES YOU!
I COULDN'T GET ANY WORK DONE.
What is this?!
Delivery box
STARTLE
STARTLE
I DECIDED TO SHOW HER THE KITTEN. IF IT DIDN'T WORK, I WAS PREPARED TO SAY GOODBYE TO HIM.
LET'S TAKE A QUICK PEEK, OKAY?
Sorry.
The kitten's cage is on the other side.
LIFT
Crack the door open...
?!
MEOW!
SEE? NOTHING TO BE AFRAID OF.
...
So small...
HER FOOT-STEPS SUD-DENLY LIGHT-ENED.
So small...
TAK
TAK
TAK
OW!
CHOMP
PAL BIT ME!
SHE BIT MIZUHO!
THANK GOOD-NESS!
(Excited for some reason)
CLAP CLAP CLAP
How dare you get a pet?

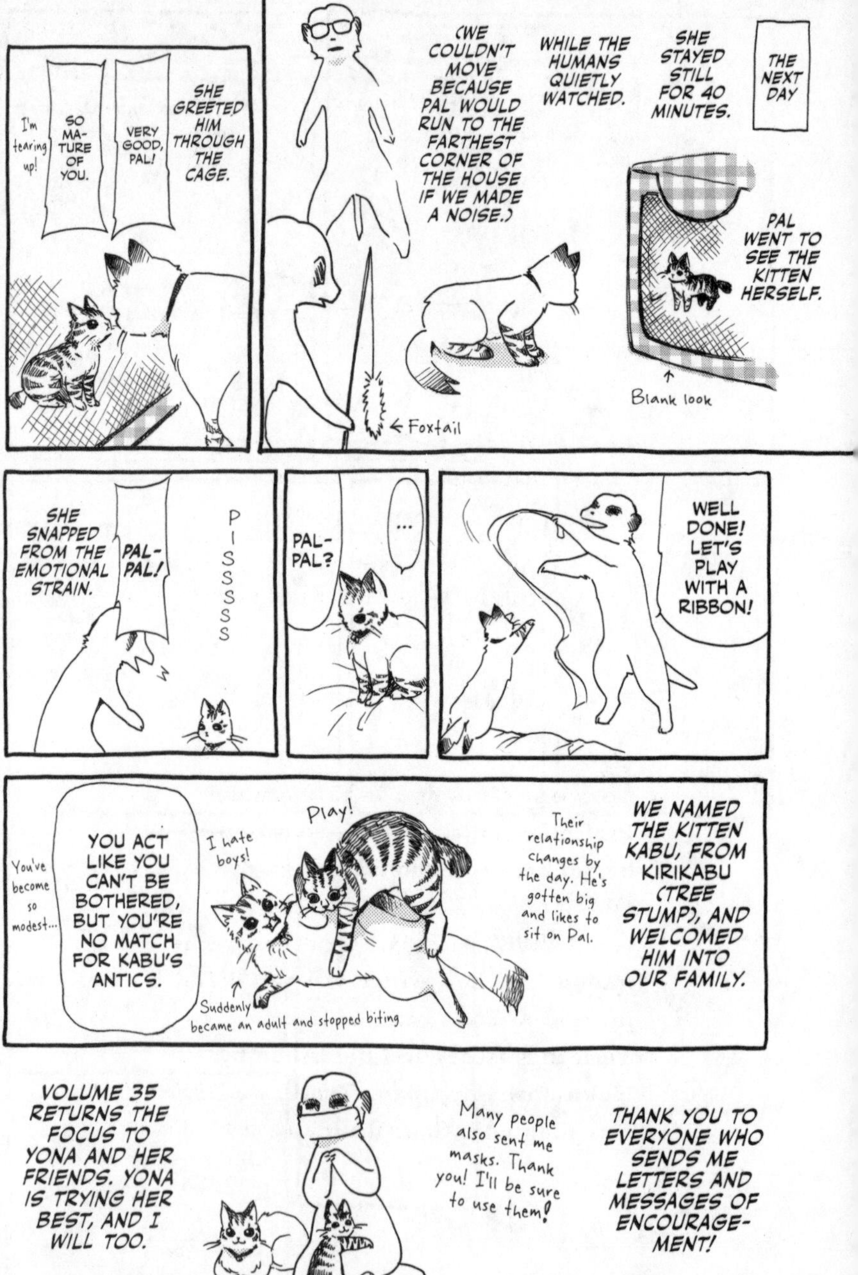
THE NEXT DAY
SHE STAYED STILL FOR 40 MINUTES.
WHILE THE HUMANS QUIETLY WATCHED.
(WE COULDN'T MOVE BECAUSE PAL WOULD RUN TO THE FARTHEST CORNER OF THE HOUSE IF WE MADE A NOISE.)
PAL WENT TO SEE THE KITTEN HERSELF.
Blank look
Foxtail
SHE GREETED HIM THROUGH THE CAGE.
VERY GOOD, PAL!
SO MATURE OF YOU.
I'm tearing up!
WELL DONE! LET'S PLAY WITH A RIBBON!
...
PAL-PAL?
PISSSSS
PAL-PAL!
SHE SNAPPED FROM THE EMOTIONAL STRAIN.
WE NAMED THE KITTEN KABU, FROM KIRIKABU (TREE STUMP), AND WELCOMED HIM INTO OUR FAMILY.
Their relationship changes by the day. He's gotten big and likes to sit on Pal.
Play!
I hate boys!
YOU ACT LIKE YOU CAN'T BE BOTHERED, BUT YOU'RE NO MATCH FOR KABU'S ANTICS.
You've become so modest...
Suddenly became an adult and stopped biting
THANK YOU TO EVERYONE WHO SENDS ME LETTERS AND MESSAGES OF ENCOURAGEMENT!
Many people also sent me masks. Thank you! I'll be sure to use them!
VOLUME 35 RETURNS THE FOCUS TO YONA AND HER FRIENDS. YONA IS TRYING HER BEST, AND I WILL TOO.

AFTERWORD / THE END

The Yon-hi's Journal arc is about Yon-hi, Kashi, Yu-hon, and Il—their respective stories and the relationships between them. Since this arc exists outside the world of Yona and her friends, I found it quite refreshing.

—Mizuho Kusanagi

Born on February 3 in Kumamoto Prefecture in Japan, Mizuho Kusanagi began her professional manga career with *Yoiko no Kokoroe* (The Rules of a Good Child) in 2003. Her other works include *NG Life*, which was serialized in *Hana to Yume* and *The Hana to Yume* magazines and published by Hakusensha in Japan. *Yona of the Dawn* was adapted into an anime in 2014.

YONA OF THE DAWN
VOL.34
Shojo Beat Edition

STORY AND ART BY
MIZUHO KUSANAGI

English Adaptation/Ysabet Reinhardt MacFarlane
Translation/JN Productions
Touch-Up Art & Lettering/Lys Blakeslee
Design/Philana Chen
Editor/Amy Yu

Akatsuki no Yona by Mizuho Kusanagi
© Mizuho Kusanagi 2020
All rights reserved.
First published in Japan in 2020 by HAKUSENSHA, Inc., Tokyo.
English language translation rights arranged with
HAKUSENSHA, Inc., Tokyo.

Printed in Canada

Published by VIZ Media, LLC
P.O. Box 77010
San Francisco, CA 94107

10 9 8 7 6 5 4 3 2 1
First printing, February 2022

viz.com   shojobeat.com